HOPE, HARMONY, AND FOOTBALL

A Novel by Kevin Giffin

Braughler™
Books
braughlerbooks.com

Copyright © 2023 by Kevin Giffin. All rights reserved.

This is a work of fiction. Names, characters, businesses, places, events, locales, and incidents are either the products of the author's imagination or used in a fictitious manner. Any resemblance to actual persons, living or dead, or actual events is purely coincidental.

This book or any portion thereof may not be reproduced or used in any manner whatsoever without the express written permission of the publisher except for the use of brief quotations in a scholarly work or book review. For permissions or further information contact Braughler Books LLC at:

    info@braughlerbooks.com

Front and back cover photos: iStockphoto
Cover design: Paul Curtis

Printed in the United States of America
Published by Braughler Books LLC., Springboro, Ohio

First printing, 2023

ISBN: 978-1-955791-65-6

Library of Congress Control Number: 2023912255

Ordering information: Special discounts are available on quantity purchases by bookstores, corporations, associations, and others. For details, contact the publisher at:

    sales@braughlerbooks.com

    or at 937-58-BOOKS

For questions or comments about this book, please write to:

    info@braughlerbooks.com

Braughler™ Books
braughlerbooks.com

Home is a place you grow up wanting to leave, and grow old wanting to get back to.

—John Ed Pearce

CHAPTER ONE
  Somewhere in Ohio 1

CHAPTER TWO
  Football is Life 17

CHAPTER THREE
  Back to Civilization … Maybe 25

CHAPTER FOUR
  Stuck 29

CHAPTER FIVE
  A Sports Writer, I am Not 37

CHAPTER SIX
  Shrine to High School Football 47

CHAPTER SEVEN
  A Spec on the Map: Ferndale 57

CHAPTER EIGHT
  A Black Coach in South Heaven? 67

CHAPTER NINE
  Fundraiser 81

CHAPTER TEN
  Frontier Week 91

CHAPTER ELEVEN
    The Rifle Game 105

CHAPTER TWELVE
    Just a Bad Snap, That's All 133

CHAPTER THIRTEEN
    A National Tragedy. 157

CHAPTER FOURTEEN
    Home At Last—Or Am I? 179

CHAPTER FIFTEEN
    Hall of Fame, Who Knew? 233

CHAPTER SIXTEEN
    War Hill of Marlboro. 259

CHAPTER SEVENTEEN
    A Regime Change. 273

CHAPTER EIGHTEEN
    No Wait, You're In!. 293

CHAPTER NINETEEN
    Without Any Respect. 319

CHAPTER TWENTY
    Columbus and Ohio Stadium 347

Chapter One
Somewhere in Ohio

Approaching Noon

With a couple of decades under my belt, I thought I was too old to be consumed by the sensation of homesickness. For the educated, such a sensation had to be a weakness of a shallow and uncreative mind. I was hardly that person. Still, as cityscape bled into suburbia, suburbia touched the fringes of small-town America, and small-town America recognized the serenity of the country, I felt a disappointing twinge and tingle in my gut. Beyond the family vacation, I never had a reason to leave Cleveland and home.

This trip was to be different. I could feel it. This trip was an assignment and a chance to advance my career. My destination was known, and so was my purpose. Unknown, however, was the amount of time I would be away from home.

"Ain't from around here, are ya, boy?" The voice was genuine but definitely unwelcomed.

Lost and desperate to assume the voice belonged to a mere Good Samaritan, I was cold with uncertainty as every hair on my body stood erect like a mature oak. Toying with my paranoia, my Rand McNally refused to cooperate and mend itself back into some sort of a fold. I exacted punishment on the paper object, flinging the map back into the driver's seat of my Camaro. By the time I mustered enough courage to glance over my shoulder, the stranger found me.

"Ya know another word for ruse?" A wooden cane, as smooth as and the color of the head of a Titleist driver, was smartly tucked under his arm. He held a gnawed and stubby green pencil in one hand and a folded section of a newspaper in the other. "Seven, no eight letters." He had a tobacco-infested gruff tone, which only served to add to my suspicion of the stranger.

"South Heaven ... Do you know where it is?" South Heaven, according to my boss, held the next saga in my life as a young reporter.

"Never get these here puzzles." He seemed harmless. Less than intimidating in a wedding-cake-icing white shirt and trousers, he had the appearance of a tenured college physics professor, with a patriarchal alabaster full top that lacked organization but sparkled in a full and impressive sun, and a narrow, pointed chin that jutted out as if the result of years of rubbing to discover the answers to difficult questions. A set of bifocals, rimmed with an extremely thin piece of silver, rested on the edge of a thick sparring-partner's nose that was contorted and laced with the veins of age. "Kinda like the missus, ya know? Never figure her out, neither." Inexplicably, the old man exchanged the newspaper and snub pencil for the mangled mess of a map in my car. "S'pose she'd say the same thing about me, though."

The absurdity and audacity of this stranger's act served to relieve a small bit of my anxiety. As he folded the map and spoke nonchalantly about his and Ellen's last vacation to some lake in Canada, I could only muster a cheap laugh. "I'm looking for South Heaven. Can you help me?"

He nodded his head, tossing my folded map on the hood of my Chevy, then secured his eyeglasses and stuffed them into his left breast pocket.

Although I had little more than a saturated shirt and pant shorts to corroborate my belief, the temperature on this early August day in 1980 had to be hovering between a cauldron and a blast furnace—much too uncomfortable for a man from the Lake Erie-side of Ohio. The pristine and cloudless blue sky above me was comforting in poetry and prose only. The sun-faded paved road had enough room on its gravel and dirt shoulder to hold my car. A tread or two of white walls encroached on the perimeter of a cornfield.

He meandered toward his car, a lime-green monster carrying the tag of Cadillac. "Eaten yet?"

"What?" I blurted, annoyingly adjusting my sweat-soaked undergarments.

"Almost one o'clock. We were expectin' ya an hour ago." The old man had a slow gait, no doubt due to a bum right leg. "Don't know 'bout you, but I'm in the mood for a hoagie."

"What? Wait. What do you mean you were expecting?"

The eight barrels under the hood of the Caddy rumbled to a thunderous hum, after a handful of harsh cranks, as if the heat also had a stranglehold on the massive engine. Tucked away in his own saddle, the old man inched his ride forward until the pilot's seat was even with me. Despite the old man's stoutness, his frame was nearly lost in the vastness of the bench seat, like a waste can on a grungy factory floor. "Just follow me."

"Uhh, no offense, but I'd…"

"Ya ain't gonna find South Heaven just sweatin' there in the sun, boy. You best be followin' me."

Two appetizing and appealing all-American cans of Pepsi clung to the tail end of a six-pack plastic holder, devilishly teasing my parched taste buds. With barely enough room to remain pristine and undisturbed, the two cans held ground among scores of what appeared to be carpet swatches in the backseat of the Caddy.

"You follow me down the road here a ways, and you'll find the best fountain drink this side of Columbus." As if sand scratched at his cornea, he squinted harshly with his left eye, gazing down the sun-drenched road.

Surely, if he had known my journey from civilization had begun numerous hours previously, he certainly would have granted me reprieve and been on his way. Besides, I was driving a car without the comforts of air conditioning or FM radio, had not eaten since consuming a fast-food breakfast sandwich outside of Parma, and was drowning in my own perspiration. "I just need to know if I'm heading toward South Heaven."

"Follow me to Frankie's Pizza." With a mammoth talon wrapped around the thick column shift, he moved the car to drive, agitating the mighty Caddy.

"I've taken County Road Twelve to County Road Fourteen to County Road Twenty-One. I'm no closer to finding this South Heaven now than I was five hours ago when I left Parma. You can barely find this place on the map, for crying out loud!"

He snuffed out his thick and richly brown stogie into a dashboard ashtray, already lousy with used stubs, and then smiled, exposing a smidgeon of humor and confidence. He depressed the accelerator and disappeared down County Road Twenty-One.

For twenty minutes, I sat precariously behind the wheel of my '67 racing-blue Camaro, staring at a diner sign of a smiling pizza affixed to the roof of Frankie's. The sign was ailing with more than a few burned-out bulbs. I searched for an explanation on my decision to become a reporter. Four years of study at Oberlin leading to a journalism degree; two summers of an internship refilling coffee mugs and proofreading gibberish; and two years of writing and rewriting a thesis had brought me to the middle of nowhere in search of a story on the economic decline of the Midwest. Of all the nooks, crannies, towns, and hamlets dotting the landscape of Ohio, let alone those surrounding my newspaper's home of Cleveland, my employer was interested in the economic stability of a town on the western hinges of the state. South Heaven, Ohio, despite holding solid ground in the farm belt, had been home to two automobile manufacturing firms. But similar to those various towns and hamlets around the state as well as Cleveland, it had been wrought by an economic plague.

Frankie's was overwhelmed with a tasty tang of garlic. Small table lamps mounted into the wood grain wall panels above the booths provided enough illumination to view faces and shapes. There appeared to be plenty of windows in Frankie's, but someone must have decided it best to conceal them all with dark merlot curtains.

My overt desire was to make a beeline for the only occupied booth and give the old man a rash of my frustration for leaving me high and dry, assuming he was among the throng of people both occupying and standing watch over the upholstered vinyl benches.

Frankie's was devoid of pizza eaters.

"Pepsi you drink of choice, Honey?"

"What?"

She inched closer, departing the sanctity and comfort of the familiar crowd. She wore too much eyeshadow and perfume for my taste. Red hair had never tickled my fancy, either. She was also old enough to be my mother's sister. "It's all we serve here—Pepsi." Stitched into her maroon Frankie's smiling pizza t-shirt, just above the assumed position of a left breast pocket was the name Sweetie. She tucked her hand under my elbow. "So you gotta name, Honey?"

"Where's the old man?" I extricated myself from Sweetie.

"Honey, this here's South Heaven." Sweetie wiped the loose crumbs from an adjacent table into an open palm. "That's all we got is old men."

"You mean this is South Heaven?"

"And speaking of old men." Sweetie ceded the stage.

"Yeah, I guess you wouldn't know it be South Heaven. Our welcome sign blew down last spring in a storm." Grease splotches and red, ripened tomato stained the white apron he wore trimly about his waist. A hairnet matched the color of his bushy dark moustache. "Name's Frankie. I own this here place. Don't think I caught your name, pal." A soiled dish towel covered his right shoulder.

"Melvin. Melvin Wright."

Frankie's hands were coarse and engulfing. "I suppose city council's waitin' on that settlement money from American Genuine Motors to do any roadwork."

As quickly as possible, my hand disengaged from his. Despite the logic behind his reasoning, I could not agree with my grandfather on the correlation between strength of hands and respect for manhood. Adhering to Grandpa's idealism would lead one to believe Frankie and his Herculean grip were next in line for enshrinement into a legend's hall of fame. To me, Frankie appeared to be nothing more than a blue-collar ruffian.

"This here place, it'll light up at football time. B'sides, you dun missed lunch hour." He appeared to be the least experienced of the crowd, no more than a year or two removed from high school. A strappy lad, he gave every indication he was allergic to sleep with a scraggly and lazy beard and midnight blue patches hugging the undercarriages of his eyes.

"Beefy's right, ya know." Frankie pushed the remainder of his potato chips in front of the kid. Four or five hefty ones clung to a dinner plate drizzled with pickle juice. "Lunch is over."

"Your name is Beefy?"

He had no concern for social grace. "That's what they call me."

To my dismay, Sweetie returned. She balanced a circular drink tray like someone who inherited the position of waitress. A lone but tall purple-tainted plastic tumbler assumed the role of passenger on the tray.

Sensing every eye on me, I relieved Sweetie of the tumbler and proceeded to produce watery eyes with the chillness of the drink. The taste was awesome—perfect temperature for an annoying and omnipresent thirst with just a splash of cherry flavoring that made my taste buds stand and cheer. "Not bad."

"You dun drank half in one gulp." Retrieving an opened and gnawed-upon Zero bar from the left front pocket of his blue collared shirt, Beefy reiterated for the third time that my drink contained real cherry flavoring. "Willie Tee, he says it's better than what they got up at the state fair, and all them say state fair's got the best."

Standing behind the booth and underneath a neon red exit sign leading to a miniscule foyer, Willie Tee, as introduced, removed his gold-plated toothpick and stated, without hesitation, "Ain't no likin' to it." Decked out in all red like a freshly painted fire hydrant, capped with a 1975 Cincinnati Reds World Champions t-shirt, Willie Tee was obscure in posture. He wore tube socks to his comically bony knee caps and a pair of Chuck Taylor red canvas high-tops.

Two more savoring gulps finished off my drink.

"You a salesman?" Beefy licked his stubby fingers clean of potato chip grease.

"Would any salesman be dressed in a t-shirt and tennis shoes?" I retorted.

Of course, the big boy was too much the dolt to perceive I was patronizing him.

Sweetie, on the other hand, became taciturn, claiming some of the salesmen from the yogurt plant in Frederick come to Frankie's for lunch.

"You a scout!" exclaimed Beefy. "Shoot! I bet from New Jefferson. No! Frederick."

Suddenly, an awkward fear crept into my being.

With both hands tugging at his uncombed brown locks, Beefy was a man searching for a fix. He appeared lost in the surreal, as if possessed by the bizarre and frightening. As he retreated for the exit door, I could hear him utter, "Those Frederick…"

Willie Tee escaped with the remaining pizza slices from the pie plates on the booth table. "Bless ya."

"So, none of you all have seen an older man, rock salt-colored hair, bifocals?" I asked.

As if he knew the teacher could hear him ask me for the answer to the third question on the chemistry exam, Frankie pulled me aside. "Just think you oughta know, Beefy there ain't been right since his pappy was killed a couple of years ago." He collected the two empty and well-used pizza plates and disappeared into the kitchen area.

When the swinging door separating kitchen from dining room lost its man-induced momentum, I found myself in the same uncomfortable spot I had been absorbed in only several minutes earlier: alone and in a foreign territory without direction.

Bursting into the dining area through a side entrance, Willie Tee begged me for a ride to the high school. He gracefully held a cigarette in one hand and religiously clasped a glass 40-ounce beer bottle in the other. "Dat be yuhr Camaro, right?"

"Yeah. Listen, I'm just looking for the local newspaper."

"Miss Myra, she be runnin' da Sun. Better watch it, she's a looker. Gotter momma's looks and her daddy's guts."

Before I could resist further, Willie Tee had nestled into the passenger's seat of my Camaro. "Paper be right near da school…" Like the family pet thrilled to be on a leash and walking the neighborhood, Willie Tee was childishly giddy, incapable of keeping his smile under control. He was adamant about getting to the practice field before the end of the hour.

"You really need that?" I asked Willie Tee as he laboriously consumed alcohol from a paper bag. The stench of cheap beer only served to further depreciate my olfactory bulb. Based upon the aroma Willie Tee gave off, it appeared as if he had no discipline for personal hygiene.

"Whattaya doin'?" Willie Tee shook his head then proceeded to lecture me on my navigation skills.

My U-turn pushed the Camaro precariously close to the shoulder's edge and an inconsequential ravine littered with rusted beer cans and the refuse of human gluttony. I winced with every pebble and stone that snapped at the bottom of my car.

"You ain't from dese here parts."

I avoided a dingy yellow grocery truck heading out of town, weakly commanded by a driver unfamiliar with a gear shift. The truck had a smaller box to it. The stenciled name on the cab door panel of the passenger's side had faded, with only "LLERS" still obvious in white. The "MI" was faintly visible.

"Dat dere be Jerry. He be headin' out ta Myer's—pick up beans and corn."

My rearview mirror was clogged with a picture of black exhaust from the open-bed truck.

South Heaven, past Frankie's Pizza, was much less congenial than the cornfields leading into the town. With only two islands and four pumps, the service garage held a handful of cars at bay, waiting for petrol. The SOHIO sign swung askew, frailly clinging to its post with but one hook. The downtown business district was quintessential America, on the surface. Two-story brick buildings, connected one by one to each other and on both sides of the street, presented a welcoming and warm sensation of home and glory years previous. Unfortunately, too many of the bottom-level storefronts were shamefully boarded or held vacancy signs in front windows. Those shops that didn't display a foreclosure sign had familiar and generic names like Ron's Barbershop, Alton Drugs, and Miller's Grocery.

"Turn up 'ere," Willie Tee blurted as he fidgeted maniacally in the passenger's seat.

At the corner of Elm and our current passageway was a majestic structure with antebellum pillars connecting a third story to concrete stairs. It was massive in size and glistening in the sun. Red brick led to a dome crest of farm-fence white. In black lettering, just above the red brick facing, was an inscription indicating the building housed the courthouse for Harper County. "The statue in front there. Who is he?"

"Dat be Jeremiah Harper. Done founded dis here place. Alls I knows, teams be named fohr him."

White specks, which I presumed to be bird droppings, covered the shoulders of the man in granite.

"School be up 'ere on da left."

The parking lot behind the school was ravaged with potholes in the black top. After putting the Camaro through an obstacle course, of sorts, frustration pushed me to park it in a reclusive haven next to an outlet door of the school. Words the faithful would never discover in the Good Book had been spray-painted above the double-glass doors. To this point in my assignment, South Heaven had been anything but exuberant or welcoming. The graffiti epitomized a general feeling of malaise quickly overwhelming me.

Willie Tee hopped out of the passenger's seat then tossed his bottle on a heaping load of trash that was pushing the limits of a 55-gallon drum, rust displacing the navy-blue hue. "Gotta few minutes before crossin' Samm's Crik." Willie Tee carried a lustrous silver pocket watch in his sock. Polishing the trinket with an excess piece of his shirt, he proudly clasped the two pieces together. "Bless ya, man. Bless ya."

"Crik?"

"Samm's Crik. First day a practice, da sofmores, they gotta build a bridge to get ovohr Samm's Crik to da practice field."

My concern for what was the actual significance of his story endured long enough for me to interrupt Willie Tee and request directions to the newspaper office. I had no intention of offending Willie Tee. However, I was not interested in high school football—only in finding a feature on the demise of America as quickly as possible.

Willie Tee quickly lost favor with me. "Back on Elm. Make youah left on Main. Miss Myra, she be on da right." He nodded then strutted with a flimsy but important stride toward the front of the school.

My expression of gratitude earned me a mere wave of the hand from Willie Tee. So I retreated and followed his direction out of the school, past the tarnished monument, and into an open parking spot along Main Street. The meter that presided over my car listed to the right and was nearly torn from its broken and crumbled concrete sidewalk base. Still, it demanded my dime, and I had nothing but quarters.

A trio of men, ranging in stature, occupied a high-back park bench that stole a view into the shop-room window of Krisp's Periodicals. The bench was anchored into the sidewalk by two malignant and rusty posts attached to its seat. The color of the wood had long ago relinquished its dark green hue. Occupied with a newspaper or two, all men were oblivious of me and of my quandary of fitting a quarter into a dime slot.

Without a ticket patrol in sight, I opted for the risk and forewent paying the city.

"Officer Fifer be comin' 'round here shortly." The voice came from behind the sports section. "You best be payin' the meetah."

Embarrassment was a condition I had spent my short quarter-century of life avoiding ardently. "Any you fellows have change for a quarter? I have not a dime on me." Into the heat and sun, I flashed a dull and grungy Washington coin with a 1974 date stamp. "Anyone?"

Without concern for me, not one even rustled their paper.

"Tell ya what." I placed the quarter on the arm of the bench. "If this ... Pfeifer comes here, give him this quarter, would ya?"

The sports page vibrated, and a crusty man appeared from behind it. He wore an oil-stained blue cap with a Ford patch sewn to the front. A man who possessed a white frothy beard slammed the paper to the concrete. "Fifer don't care 'bout no quarter."

"No, sir," came a choreographed reply from the man's two partners.

"No money in da meetah, and Fifer be writin' a ticket."

"That's right!" The two friends were a few years the man's junior.

I begged to be forgiven but only roused the trio. "Look, I'm just ... I just wanna see Myra Epstein, at the paper. None of you have any change?" I grabbed the quarter from the bench, produced another one from the shallow wells of my pocket, and then offered them both for any dime.

"I'll take it, sport." The screen door protecting Krisp's closed with the help of a bitter squeal from the overhead spring. "Two quarters for a dime, why not?" She held no more years on the calendar than I did, and promptly inserted a dime into the meter. "Awful hot out here, boys." She had a petite yet authoritative frame. "Isn't your wife expecting you to be down at employment services, Mister Billy?"

Mister Billy owned the Ford cap, the sports page, and a patronizing sneer for the lady. "Ain't gonna help none. Ain't no work down there."

"I'm sure she'd be thrilled with you hanging out with Alfie and Morris."

"Miss Myra, we waitin' on our money from AGM. I be gettin' money from the settlement soon. That'll keep us all okay." The man, a score of years younger than Billy, battled the flint of his lighter to ignite a previously used and half-burnt cigarette.

"I don't suppose you were in line either, eh, Alfie?"

"Myra Epstein?" I asked shyly.

"That's right, sport." Her movements were terse and purposeful, like her taut frame. Her demeanor reminded me of my parents' dachshund and his feistiness toward his larger roommate, Rex, the German Shepherd. "I was told to look for a rebel wannabe with a boy-next-door face." She brushed aside the bangs on my forehead. "The Beatles look disappeared with the onset of disco, sport."

"As opposed to flowers on bell bottoms?" I retorted with a glib grin, earning a few accolades from Billy and the Boys.

She only returned the smile and asked me if I cared to follow her then darted up the street.

"Bettuh go," said Billy. "Miss Myra, she don't like to be waitin' nun."

When Miss Myra disappeared into an adjacent building, I peeled my eyes away, only to catch a glimpse of the trio, once again wielding the newspaper as a shield. "Well, thanks for all the help."

Lugging a bulging backpack, I entered the offices of the South Heaven Sun with an obnoxious announcement from the cowbell attached to the solid-wood door. "Hello?"

The office, about the size of a quaint Paris café and painted in, of all colors, Easter pastel blue, was devoid of human life. Behind a front counter were four desks arranged in a square fashion, all containing the various auspices of a reporter's life. Three clocks hung from a wall, side by side, and all displayed a time from a different area within the United

States. The one on Pacific Time was five minutes to the slow side of the other two.

A hotel desk bell, perched on top of the counter, begged to be utilized. "Hello?"

Miss Myra, as the trio seemed to refer to her, appeared from a backroom, carrying two large black folders in her left arm and a Diet Rite in her right hand. "You know that bell's for aesthetic purposes only?" She dropped the files on the countertop and stretched to reach the handle on the interior door separating the lobby from the office.

The door swung open as if gravity worked horizontally, jerking it away from the frame. The crash was innocent, however, thanks to the bumper along the kick plate of the wall.

"You must be Melvin Wright?" She stared through a jeweler's eyepiece at the black and white photos filling the pages of the folders. "Got a call from The Republic in Cleveland. They told me—did not ask me, of course—to expect you."

My attempt at witty banter yielded only the fact that my social skills required much polishing. I apologized for the short notice by my editor then slumped into the office, with bag in tow.

She was taciturn in requesting the reason for my presence, expressing frustration in an inability to produce an explanation from my editor, Tony Esposito, whom I believe Miss Myra referred to as the offspring of an unwed mother.

Although under strict orders to reveal little about my visit, I was a sucker for a pretty face, and those soft chocolate-brown eyes and perfectly tanned skin had my number. I would have given up nuclear secrets, and to the dismay of my paranoid boss, spilled my guts to the woman with the sexy tomboy look. I told her every detail of my quest for a story on the loss of South Heaven industry.

She appeared apathetic, offering no opinion or glimpse of emotion, as she disappeared through another door. "You can use the desk in the corner next to the coffee urn."

I followed the voice into an adjacent office hiding bundles of newspapers—hundreds, on a guess.

Miss Myra was rummaging through more large binders, as thick as two to three Webster's dictionaries. "Here." She turned the binder 180 degrees for me to read right-side up. "This is the beginning of the announcement that American Genuine Motors was closing the brake plant." Her voice had a sultry masculinity to it, like that of a garage band lead singer after a long set at the microphone.

"Well, my story's more about the people…"

"I'm only second generation in this town, but I am still one of those people. All these articles are about the people."

Again offering another apology, I attempted to change subject matter by asking the whereabouts of her staff.

She led me out of the storage room and into her personal office space. "Let's see, Amy is doing a follow-up with Doctor Brady, the school superintendent. And I believe Megan is down at the practice field covering the crossing of Samm's Creek. Nate is supposed to be delivering an ad contract to Sieler's Leasing, although, I would be willing to bet he's probably over at the bank visiting that new woman of his… Who else? Oh yeah. Phil, our award-winning sports guy, is out on sick leave—chicken pox."

"Sounds like a rough day."

"Banner day in South Heaven, sport." Hers was not a manufactured scent, but rather a naturally appealing one.

The editor's office was the mere size of a transient college instructor's work station. Miss Myra, at least with the office presenting itself as such, lacked even a remote hint of organization. The two guest chairs resting in front of her desk housed folders, loose papers, markers, pens, and even a stapler. Drawers to the double file cabinet could not be secured, crammed full of excess paper. The desk was no source of pride, either, littered with notebooks, a dictionary opened to the Ps, and too many writing utensils to count within reasonable time.

"I bet if you were to walk down to the creek right now…" She tossed her empty soda can into a loaded wastepaper basket. "…you'd find a score of people there, watching those kids collect rocks to build that footpath." She concurred with me on the insanity of such an endeavor. "It's football season."

Staking a corner of the desk, I rested my hindquarters and retrieved one of a handful of travel brochures from atop an empty pencil holder. The brochure was only front and back of a single thin, cardboard-like page, advertising, in full color, the lure of Clearwater, Florida. Knowing a little about the Gulf Coast, I inquired as to her vacation plans.

Subsequently, she relieved me of the brochure and asked me to leave.

"Where do you suggest I start with my story?"

After a snide comment about a big-city reporter requesting advice from a two-bit country editor, she suggested I visit the library.

"Yeah. I don't need any new reading material."

"Ethel Buchanan. She's the librarian and resident historian…"

Early Dinnertime

A couple of miles outside of downtown, near the interstate and standing bruised and battered but still representing the people of South Heaven, was the Triangle Industrial Park. For thirty years, the industrial complex harbored the dreams, livelihood, and future of South Heaven residents. Housing two buildings of American Genuine Motors, including their largest brake-production facility in the U.S. and one brick structure—a truck-cap plant—owned by the Lessee Corporation, Triangle Park once employed six-thousand people. My initial research, prior to the journey west, produced information indicating that the brake plant closed shop first, eliminating a massive three-thousand employees. With sagging sales, American Genuine then broke the back of South Heaven, closing the car-part facility. Within a year, Lessee moved all equipment and inventory on the interstate and out of Harper County to a larger facility in Pittsburgh.

A florid red and royal blue Vordon Real Estate sign hung condescendingly from the oxidized chain-link fence hugging the entire perimeter of the AGM plants. Although chained together and held by a padlock the size of one that secured the entrance to a medieval castle, the two gates could be pulled apart without much effort. A single-man guard shack, with shattered windows and a gaping hole that once held an air conditioning unit, impotently warned against trespassing.

I stood between two weeds arching up through the faded and broken asphalt while my memory reverted back several months earlier to when I had reported on an inner-city Cleveland high school near collapse. I was unsure what would be found from an empty factory. A reporter always hopes for the immaculate story. Ultimately, I hoped for a quick end to this trip to Western Ohio, immaculate story or not. Although I had been guaranteed quality print in a Sunday issue, The Cleveland Republic had fallen a few steps behind in covering the plight of the auto worker. Thus, any story, no matter on which page it appeared, was not about to merit me any prestige or award.

"Boy, exactly whattaya plannin' on findin' here?"

Startled, I swung around and saw the man from the Cadillac who had ditched me on the side of the road.

"Thought you'd checked into the Holiday Inn by now."

"And, I thought you were going to be at that restaurant. Thanks for leaving me back there on the road."

"That hotel reservation's only good 'til six." He held a full cigar between his fingers, unlit though it was. "It's just down here a ways, next to the highway. I dun called Sue Ellen. She'll see to it that you get an upgrade to one of them suites." He limped toward a crumpled pack of Marlboros stuffed into a crack in the asphalt. He seemed to bellow his age as he groaned to bend and retrieve the trash. "Darn kids think they own this place." With a twist, turn, and tug, he snatched open the plastic round tub top from a grungy aluminum trash can receptacle. "See this here?" He shuffled his hand though a stash of depleted beer cans. "This place's become their hangout." Curtly, he asked why I was taking photos of nothing. "It's a parkin' lot, and a shabby one at that."

I aimed my camera lens on a few choice words spray-painted on the brick façade of the front office area. "Mister, my paper sells gloom. That's America."

"For who?" He had alertness and dedication to his prestigious battleship-gray eyes.

"The era of happiness has long expired, mister … I don't even know your name."

"Schmidt," he replied. "Ira Schmidt."

"Well, Mister Schmidt, America loves the underdog and the downtrodden."

"Downtrodden?" He snipped the end of his cigar, and about the length of a knuckle fell into an open palm. His lighter was polished chrome with engravings of some sort on both sides. "Been in this here town for a long time, boy. Never seen downtrodden."

"Look around you." I gloated without paying any respect. "This is downtrodden. No jobs. No life. No future."

"Them are your assumptions, boy."

"Sometimes assumptions are a reporter's best friend."

"Shoulda asked me. I knew Ethel was outta town. She gotta nephew bein' married in Chicago." He gave me a crusty smile before limping away. "Better be gettin' to the hotel now, boy."

CHAPTER TWO
Football is Life

Opening Time for the Library

Another miserably hot morning on the left coast of Ohio found me hungry and waiting outside of the Harper County Library, nursing a clear plastic Holiday Inn tumbler of ice water. An awning from the neoclassical antebellum structure shaded the majority of a concrete wrap-around porch from an enemy-less sun. A smattering of empty food wrappers gave the otherwise pristine porch a shiner of a black eye.

Having off-loaded their hardcover Dr. Seuss books, three children raced up and down the stairs and back and forth from one end of the porch to the other. The trio's mom or otherwise guardian massaged her left temple. Cloaked in a yellow polka dot sundress, complemented by dark glasses and a broad-rim hat, Mom stood a mere few inches from the entrance to the library, as if she were praying to an altar. All commotion came to an abusive halt with the opening of the front door. After a single round-up call, Mom quickly disappeared into the lobby of the library. Two of the kids nearly trampled me as I attempted to beat them to the entrance.

Waiting just inside to welcome the day's customers was a blue-haired matriarch with an irascible grin and no height on her feeble frame.

"Miss Buchanan?" I guessed, repositioning my book bag from the sore and tired right shoulder to the left.

She wore a dark gray dress suit, like a schoolmaster. From the newspaper rack to the returns table to the front desk, she shuffled without lifting a foot from the worn beige carpet.

Still, I had difficulty keeping pace. "I was hoping you could help me find some information?"

Shooting a glance at her fellow librarian, another blue-haired lady tucked smartly behind the front desk, Ethel laughed, "Well, if I can't get you information, I'm definitely in the wrong business."

I told her Miss Myra had sent me.

"What are you looking for exactly?"

"Background on South Heaven's industry." I offered her some assistance in moving the book cart, but she refused.

"You could push the button for the elevator, though."

The second floor of the library was similar to the first—vast and open. I inquired about the portraits.

"Those?" She sighed, catching her breath as she pushed the loaded cart to the edge of the government-listings shelves. "Heroes of South Heaven."

The majority of the paintings dominating the second-floor walls were of men from eras long past. A few wore white powder wigs, while two staged Civil War-style sideburns. Two, however, featured the faces of younger men. Both wore maroon football jerseys.

I stood underneath the two portraits. "Football players?"

Another presumed employee, much Miss Buchanan's junior, watched her older and fellow librarian heave a husky volume onto a third-level shelf without offering any bit of assistance.

Miss Buchanan steadfastly shuffled toward me. Along the way, she pulled the spectacles that hung via a necklace to the bridge of her nose. "Rocky Roark and Jerry Sanderson. Only in South Heaven would folks hold two Ohio State All-Americans in such high esteem with the founder of the city and two Union Army officers. Rocky lives in Green Bay." She allowed her bifocals to swing from her chain-like lanyard. "Jerry calls Baltimore home. Both of them played for Paul Brown at Ohio State, and neither lost a game in high school."

"And they deserve a spot next to a congressman?"

Three portraits down from number sixty-six, Rocky Roark, was one of George Thomas Delaney, the only Ohio state senator from South Heaven.

"I'm just the town historian, my dear. I offer no opinion—just deal in fact. It's much easier on me that way." Her smile was still vibrant, even if the outward appearance of age on her face suggested differently.

I followed her into an office filled with stacks of chairs.

A single overhead bulb, initiated by a pull string, illuminated the windowless space. A couple of book carts welcomed the one Ethel left behind.

"Which century do you need?" She exuded a laugh of confidence and intellect. Ethel carried an inherent respect. "We'll be entering our fourth in a decade or two. This has always been a town of pride and honor."

"I know I'm late, but I had no one to watch Mikey," a young lady chirped unapologetically. She was out of breath and a few years younger than even I. Her face and long blonde mane were only in view at the threshold, as if she were trying to hide something from us.

"This is your third day in a row, Tammy." Ethel appeared none too pleased. The moment the teenager disappeared, Ethel conveyed her dissatisfaction with the younger female. Apparently, Tammy was perpetually tardy and indolent. "Never in my day would you see someone at seventeen with a two-year-old child." Her ashen face had turned to a muted red, leading me out of the office and into the archive section. "Here. This is the history of South Heaven on paper. Now, if you will pardon me, I must go calm my frustrations with a cup of coffee and a cigarette."

The temptation to spill my guts to Ethel was not nearly as prevalent. I harbored some pride for concealing the truth, at least with one person.

Union Hall

Two-plus hours encased within a surprisingly extensive archive section produced several interesting delicacies for me to digest about the town of South Heaven. There were recent stories on a proposed monetary settlement with the city that had been in perpetual development for over a year. The auto company actually appeared to be a closet contributor to the town of South Heaven, both economically and socially. Throughout their history in the Triangle Park, American Genuine donated money to various churches, the school system, etc. And as if one could not get enough of football, for a handful of years, beginning in the fall of 1952, American Genuine sponsored a trophy for a football game played during the week of AGM's founding. The Harper-Valence Trophy, named for a short-lived coupe, was given to the winner of the contest between the local high school and their opponent.

A predominate family name from my library research was Van Wert. Since the latter part of the 18th century, several generations of Van Werts had held positions of influence, including the head of the local auto workers union for three decades. Mike Van Wert held the latest spot of power, and I decided to pay him a visit.

"He's inside."

Offering gratitude to the surly gentleman, who climbed into the cab of a rusted green pickup truck, for his directions on the location of Van Wert, I waffled through the viscous cloud of cigarette smoke hovering like a Pacific fog within the confines of the union hall.

Serenity was non-existent. Hundreds of voices, vibrating at once, generated a cacophony of anger and incoherence. A score of tables faced an elevated stage that harbored a voluminous wood podium and a handful of folding chairs. Two of the chairs were empty, while three of them held the larger frames of men with stoic grimaces. A taller man in a maroon t-shirt and white ball cap stepped to the podium, mashed his cigarette into an ashtray, coughed, and then informed the crowd, in a dark and resonating voice, that the union reps from Cleveland would not arrive until lunch.

I walked along the opposite wall of the stage, passing the bathrooms, an office, and an omnipresent trophy case, until opting to rest my book bag on the marble top of the bar.

Commotion resumed when the tall man stepped down from the stage and walked in my direction. "You registered with unemployment?"

"I'm not ... I'm looking for Mike Van Wert."

"Who are you?" He disappeared behind the bar and poured himself a cup of coffee from a stainless steel urn. The mug he carried was not a generic one. Although the union crest embellished the white ceramic piece with solidarity, there were too many stains and various other marks of wear to suggest it was not personal.

The bar fed into a small kitchenette with an olive-drab fridge and brick-red stove. The urn held space next to a soda fountain.

The man drank the coffee as if immune to pain or as if the liquid were only lukewarm. "I'm Van Wert." Although not overtly large, he would have had little trouble defending himself in any backyard brawl. A jaw outlined by a beard without sideburns and styled into a point at the chin anchored a pencil-thin moustache. His dark and jaded eyes only added to his intimidating appearance.

"Well, I'm a reporter, and I'd like to ask you a few questions on the closings of the auto plants."

Tapping out the last remaining cigarette from a pack of Marlboros, Van Wert fell into a diatribe about the lack of solidarity within the union. "Yeah. Only about two-hundred of us left, ya know?"

Once the plants closed, Van Wert believed the townspeople abandoned the union cause. He shared an unflattering opinion of American Genuine. "We were a thousand strong workforce, with great pay and a hand in how things were done in this town. Now, too many have taken the cowardly route and left South Heaven. The country folk, they've stayed out of the city and gone back to the farm."

Van Wert reminded me of a Little League coach no parent or opposing coach enjoyed playing against: loud, lacking empathy, and opinionated.

"Of course, they're workin' for eight to ten bucks less an hour than what they were makin' at Genuine. Some of us in here now have done dried up our pension. Just countin' on welfare." Van Wert poured a couple of tablespoons of sugar into a refill of coffee and secured the lid to a Styrofoam cup. With the cigarette lodged between his right forefinger and ring finger, he pointed at me. "Mark my word. This here union built up South Heaven, and we aren't goin' anywhere. We'll be back on top."

I inquired as to the willingness of the other attendees to be interviewed.

"I just gave you their stories."

"Can you tell me anything on this settlement from the company?"

He took a long hit from his smoke, as if trying to develop and formulate a response. "We been hearin' about a settlement for a while now." Another drag prompted a flick of the exposed ash into a glass-block ashtray. "I gotta go. I'm goin' over to the field to check out practice before the Cleveland reps arrive."

Leaderless without Van Wert, most of the cadre had risen and were milling about the hall. Several boxes of assorted donuts had been picked through and scattered atop two separate banquet tables, which were shoved against the wood paneling of the wall where a larger blue banner read UAW 212.

Not sure what possessed me to do so, but I introduced myself to a trio of men as a reporter from a paper in Toledo then asked the holder of a half-eaten glazed about his tenure with American Genuine.

"Six years." He had not the height of the other two, standing at least six inches below his nearest competitor. "My uncle got me the job."

"And you guys?"

"What paper you say you with?"

"The Toledo Star. We're doing a story on American Genuine."

"AGM stole everything from us." He was several years older than the kid who continued to choke down donuts. To match a St. Patrick's-green satin jacket, he wore a darker green pair of nylon sweatpants. A bushy moustache compensated for a receding front hairline and high forehead. "Been here twenty-two years, and now I got nothing."

"Never heard of no Toledo Star." Mr. Skepticism had a dark complexion with a pitted, almost scar-ridden face.

I had not heard of such a periodical, either. "We're a small paper."

"I got two kids in high school and five acres to pay for," Mr. Skepticism commented. "You wanna do a story on American Genuine? Heck, the only hope we got now is with Mike's cousin running for Congress, ya know. He'll bring work back to South Heaven…"

I remained long enough to hear the Cleveland union representatives inform the crowd that the coffers were close to running dry.

Ruth's Diner; Close to the day ending

Turning a booth at Ruth's Diner into a makeshift desk, I had everything but a typewriter sprawled on top of the checkerboard tablecloth, including a plate of french fries.

Although the diner had its fair share of the traditional—counter, grill, and menu—Ruth's lacked quaintness. I suppose it was only a mere microcosm of the Interstate 72 Truck Stop. Sitting proudly just off exit 24, the stop offered little to indicate one was near the "metropolis" of South Heaven.

The dinner crowd had all but evaporated, leaving me with a few truck drivers trying to make time with the waitress at the counter. My fries were churned to a greasy mush and my cherry-flavored cola had devoured all its ice companions. However, I had developed a selling pitch for my article: Create a fictitious family and develop their day-to-day life with and without the income from American Genuine. Of course, it would be stretching the letter of my assignment, but The Republic, I assumed, would give me some leeway. Plus, I actually thought the paper could portray the family as authentic. Although only one of my six spiral notebooks contained notes and quotes, I gave serious consideration to returning home to further develop my story. With a handful of literature and creative writing courses on my college transcripts, I held enough confidence to begin a story. The feigned family would be my protagonists, while American Genuine and their desire to save a buck would fill the role of villain—a perfect concept that would quickly end my trip to "Corn Country," Ohio.

"Wow. You must be some sort of college person, with all them books." Excessive makeup accentuated the mesmerizing effect of her green eyes. Apparently, the amount of cleavage she displayed appealed to the truck driver clientele. Brazenly, my waitress slid into the bench seat opposite me. "I'm goin' to college, ya know?" She did possess a seductive voice that appealed to the very fiber of one's manhood. "Just haven't decided which one yet." She pulled out the gold bow-shaped clasp that held her black hair in a ball. Her locks fell to a stop just below the shoulders. "I do like the colleges in Tennessee—Volunteer State, ya know?"

"Uhh. I don't need anything else," I responded. "Thank you."

She lit her cigarette with the help of a matchbook from Kelleys Island. "Not even a little company?"

Lured by the voice of a heyday-era Hollywood starlet, I commented that my parents had a small lakefront cabin there.

"Wow. Smart and rich." She weakly fanned at her face with an open palm. Ruth's only offered a single overhead fan to combat the heat of summer. "You ain't a typical truck driver. Most of them boys are either in uniform or fat and old." She lavished in the enjoyment of her smoke, as if someone had been denying her that pleasure for some time. "Everybody just comes and goes at Ruth's. They're the lucky ones, ya know? They ain't from South Heaven. They can leave."

I asked for my check, hoping she would return to her duties.

"You ever been to Hilton Head Island? I heard it never gets below sixty degrees there. Ain't that sumthin'? It's always summer there." Slyly, she dropped her smoke into my stale drink. "It's on the house. Just don't tell."

"Can I at least leave a tip?" My stomach turned slightly at the sight of the stub floating atop the residual liquid in my soda glass.

"Tell me where you're going. It's the only pleasure I get anymore—ya know, asking people where they be going."

"I'm not a truck driver." I stashed all my writing utensils into the front pocket of my book bag.

"Makes no difference to me who you are. You're goin' somewhere other than here."

"Rhonda!" The man at the cash register called. "Your break's over!"

She blew the man an insubordinate kiss and inched herself out of the booth. "Football and depression is all we get here in South Heaven. Shoot, anymore, we ain't even got football. Team stinks, ya know?"

"Rhonda!"

"Jeez, Will. I'm coming!"

"Thanks for dinner ... Rhonda."

"Hope you get to where you goin' fast. South Heaven's no place for people livin' life."

CHAPTER THREE
Back to Civilization ... Maybe

Minutes Before Mass

"Off to church, boy?" Old Man Schmidt offered me one of the all-white soft mints from his handful. "Mass starts in a few minutes."

Catholicism was not listed on my personal data sheet, and I conveyed that to him.

"Well, Reverend Clement offers one fine sermon down at the First Baptist, if that's your preference."

I thought my packed suitcase would offer a hint to Old Man Schmidt. "I'm in no need of a sermon today. Advice on the stock market? Sure. But ethics from the self-ordained? No thanks. No, I'm leaving."

"The Lord, boy, whatever your choice, will never do ya wrong," Old Man Schmidt said with a laugh. "I certainly hope we didn't upset ya here in South Heaven?"

"No." I heaved my suitcase off the hotel carpet. "I have what I need."

"Do you? Sure hope a coupla days will only show us in the right text."

I offered him an extended palm and bid gratitude and farewell.

"Have ya eaten yet?" The ivory suit Old Man Schmidt wore glistened in the sunlight that snuck in through the hotel's skylight windows. Every button was secured, and the patent-leather shoes he wore matched the suit in color. "Ranger Boosters gotuh pancake breakfast goin' on at the VFW." He refused to relinquish my hand. "Congressman-wannabe Chuck Van Wert is scheduled to make a stop there."

"You're just not going to leave me be, are you?"

"Can't." He reached inside his left inner breast pocket to retrieve a fresh stogie and the chrome lighter. "Gotta make sure you show South Heaven in a good light."

With a nod of sarcasm and innocent disrespect, I inquired as to his political post in South Heaven.

He needed the cane for only an occasional collapse of balance. "Never had much use for political office. Save that for other folk." He followed closely behind and most of the way into the front parking lot. "Whattaya have back there in Cleveland that we couldn't find for ya here?"

"Are you kidding?"

My Camaro was sandwiched between a corroded hull of a Pinto and a British racing-green Triumph with its soft shell folded down.

With an impressive flame from the chrome lighter, he puffed three times to ignite the cigar. "You sure you're happy with what you got now?"

"I get it. You're a preacher."

"You needta be here for a few more days, boy."

Despite the plea from Old Man Schmidt, I was twenty minutes into my return trip, eastbound on the interstate, when fate struck or dumb luck hit. Never trust a friend of your brother-in-law to fine tune your one and only mode of transportation. The friend, who was also the owner of Bronk's Garage in Westlake, had guaranteed me that my Camaro had another twenty-thousand miles in her. A mere six days later, the hood was spewing a fog of steam, and I was forced to pull the car to the shoulder of the interstate. A Sunday morning offered little assistance in terms of vehicular traffic and subsequent help. The few trucks that did pass provided a few condescending and gloating blares from air horns. Standing beside my means to life, liberty, and happiness, downwind from the acrid stench of rusty water, I had only myself to blame.

Across the eastbound two lanes, a grassy median the size of a suburban front lawn, and two other westbound lanes stood a green Department of Transportation sign, informing travelers they were five miles from South Heaven.

Thirty minutes into my excruciatingly reluctant trek back to the land of a certain and slow death, I was without a shirt, encased in perspiration, and limping on my right ankle. I was certain state engineers had underestimated the distance from the sign to the South Heaven exit, and then a black and white Ford of the highway patrol, lights flashing, pulled to a stop a few yards in front of me.

"You gotta problem?" he barked through an exposed passenger's window.

With a shirt wrapped around my crown and a book bag over my shoulder, I made a delectable target for law enforcement. "No," I mumbled as a cream-white church bus rumbled by us, hauling a full load. Quickly yet subtly, I shuffled away from trouble. Then I heard the car door close and the drill instructor hat being pulled snug with a crisp snap.

"Hey, pal!"

My head flagged as I froze in flight.

"Hey, pal! I asked you a question!"

When I turned around, the tall man in the academy-gray uniform stood with both feet firmly on the gravel shoulder. From a few feet below the road surface, in deep field grass, I looked up into dark sunglasses then obliged his request to join him at the stern of his cruiser.

He held one hand on his holster and one on the receptacle end of a Thermos mug.

I didn't sustain eye contact, my stomach churning as I explained my predicament. Since my undergraduate days, I never held composure well around any figment of law enforcement.

"Don't you know it ain't too smart to be walkin' on the highway?" He tossed out a few drops from his mug.

"Apparently, I'm destined to die in South Heaven."

"Say what?" He had to be well over six feet tall but lacked any mass. Yet society still granted him the power. "What's in the bag?"

"Just notebooks."

He wanted to know the reason I was in his area.

Climbing the small hill embankment, I handed over my possessions to the trooper, dropping the bag on the ground and every item in my pockets on the trunk of the vehicle.

Hidden behind the non-transparent sunglasses, he rifled through my wallet like an experienced petty thief. Amid a handful of receipts, he found press identification. "Reporter?" He glanced from the picture to me, then back to the laminated identification card. "Where's this Parma?"

"Near Cleveland."

"See many Browns games?" He removed his glasses. "Browns always been my favorite team." His black name tag read like a typo: Wyzchek. His narrow and gangly face was as decrepit as his harrowing set of ebony eyes.

Offering no comment, I simply but steadfastly asked for my possessions.

"Once got up to Mansfield for a convention," he chimed, handing over my articles one at a time, nearly fumbling my wallet to the asphalt. "Yeah, I think they should be okay this year. Browns'll probably make the playoffs." A scowl consumed his gawky face as a midget sports car zoomed by us without remorse. He reached for the radio that clung to his belt. The walkie-talkie had two knobs on top of its rectangular frame. He tuned one before pressing the speaker inches from his mouth. "Mikey, ya there?"

"That you, Robert?" the radio squawked.

"Yeah. Say, Mikey, you guys runnin' today?"

I was certain Trooper Wyzchek was radioing ahead to nab the midnight blue midget.

"Whadn't plannin' on it."

He hesitated as if to contemplate a response. "Got one on the highway."

"How bad?"

"How bad is it?" the trooper asked me.

"What?" I responded, tucking away my wallet into the backpack instead of my pockets. "The midget?"

"Huh? No," he barked, removing his cover to wipe away the sweat. "Your car. You're broke down, right?"

"What?"

"A tow truck." He pointed to the radio. "You do wanna tow, right?"

CHAPTER FOUR
Stuck

Jake's Garage

"This engine here's tore up real good."

"You've had my car for three days!"

Beefy wore an oil- and grease-stained lousy set of blue overalls that had to be stretching the safety limits of the clothing manufacturer's inventory. Only the right strap attached the front side to the rear. Despite his occupation and propensity for wearing the scars of the trade, Beefy apparently had an aversion to hygiene and grooming.

"Beefy, d'ya take care of them tires like I askdya to?" My rant had nabbed the attention of Beefy's boss, a squat and caustic man with a coffee mug glued to his hand. "Go on now."

Beefy sulked into the two-car bay that included my one and only mode of transport.

"Gonna need to excuse Beefy." The boss sipped his coffee. "He ain't right upstairs." The antithesis of his employee, he could barely see the dust lining the top of his NCR-model register. "My old partner's boy, ya know?" Stretching the breast pocket of his long-sleeved shirt, he retrieved a wad of rolled bills, bonded together with a thick rubber band. His shirt contained a few of the same stains that had pestered Beefy's garb, but the boss had only "Jake's Garage" stenciled on his.

The lobby of the garage was far from comfortable, with more room allotted for the soda machine and racks of candy bars than seats for customers. Amid the posters of tire advertisements and pictures of John Deere equipment decorating the walls and windows were several framed yearly photos of former South Heaven football teams. Stenciled on the glass of each picture frame, in black, were the year and records of each particular team. Queerly, the frames, together, formed an "S" and an "H."

Intently, I studied the faces of the 1963 team. The smiles were numerous in the black and white photo, as were the victories. According to the black stencil, the team was unbeaten through ten games. "Look, Jake, at least I am assuming you're Jake?" I asked.

From a coffee pot behind the counter and next to the cigarette rack, he filled his mug with steaming hot liquid. "Nah, I'm not Jake. He's out front."

Peeking out the window of the door leading to the single gas island, I saw nothing more than a late-60s GTO primed for a new paint job, a vintage-model tow truck, and an unconscious tan bloodhound. I felt the boss nudge me, and a life of naiveté laugh at me.

"That's Jake," he said.

"Look, I just want my car!" With both talons wrapped around the upright gumball machine, ready to toss it through the door, I was quite certain my temper was the epitome of ridiculousness.

He had the demeanor of an overweight and spoiled housecat. "Camaro, right?"

"Yeah! The one that's been here for three days."

"Ya know, Beefy played on this here '72 team?"

"Can you point me to someone who has some idea of what's going on around here?"

He savored another swill. "'72 team—terrible. That coach we had, Figgins was his name. Terrible. You know, he took a league championship team, and…" He shook his head in displeasure, clasping the framed photo with both hands. "Let's just say, there ain't no one in these here parts that was sad to see him leave. Two years of only seven wins."

I charged into the vehicle bay and demanded the keys to my Camaro. I ordered him to close the hood and pull my car out of the bay.

"We could do that," the boss said. "But you ain't gettin' too far." He groaned and bent over to retrieve a fallen can of oil. "Camaro won't make it out of the bay."

Although the use of steel in tires had decreased over time, the amount in the one at the bottom of a stack of four was just enough to jolt shards of pain through my Converse shoe. More irate than embarrassed, I hopped around the bay like a toddler enthralled in a meaningless game. My rant was passionate, appropriate, and laced with an uneducated vocabulary straight from the smoking area of a U.S. Navy destroyer. It also drew a laugh from Beefy. "Look here!" I winced. "I need my car. This place is killing me!"

Post-Lunch at the Truck Stop

The late afternoon found me wishing for inebriation and slouched in a corner booth at Ruth's.

"The stranger returns," snickered Rhonda. "Come here to see me?"

I offered little in the way of coherent speech.

Rhonda untied her apron to reveal an unflattering earth-brown uniform skirt. With the sigh of a woman who had known nothing but despair in her couple of decades of life, she assumed her usual spot across from me. "You didn't leave."

"I'm enjoying South Heaven's only registered hotel too much."

"Be careful." She yawned and retrieved a few dollar bills and several dimes from her purse. Rhonda dropped stacks of coins on the far ends of the dollar bills, in an attempt to flatten the paper currency. "Stick around here long enough, South Heaven'll latch hold of ya and never let go."

I caught a glimpse of her boss, who was in an all-white uniform, then inquired as to when he would be calling her back to work.

Snapping a bubble from a wad of green gum, she stared out the front bay window. Rhonda may have been young in calendar years, but her complexion possessed too many wrinkles of stress. Several coats of some sort of lip gloss illuminated her thin lips in a glistening red. "Where do you suppose they're all going?" She tapped the glass portal with her forefinger.

"Who?"

"Them, out there on the road. Bet you some are goin' to Virginia."

I offered some geographical order to the situation. Interstate 72 ran east and west, not south.

"Know anything 'bout Virginia? I do. I'd be there, too, if it wasn't for this place."

I straightened within the booth, then rolled my neck counterclockwise. The motion generated a couple of innocuous cracks and pops.

Without shame, Rhonda wrapped her hands around the meat of my shoulders and began to message. "Virginia's for lovers, ya now?"

"Okay."

"I know a lot about Virginia, and other places, too. That's where Washington and Jefferson came from. Most people 'round here don't even know that. If I could just get there. Rick, he thinks South Heaven has all he needs."

It was not one of the current patrons who desired the attention of Rhonda, but rather an irate younger gentleman, without concern of embarrassment, apparently. "Thought I told you to meet me in the car!"

Fortunately, Rhonda had relaxed the grip on my shoulders prior to the entrance of the impressively bulky figure.

"Oww, Rick!" Rhonda cried out in response to the hand wrapped around her bicep.

"I told you to meet me in the car!" It was not possible for Rick to claim more years in life than she. He had the impeccable skin of a child, with an unblemished but slightly chubby face. Rick wore a tattered red tank top t-shirt that exposed a notable set of biceps. His maroon ball cap with the letters "S-H" silkscreened on the white soft front gave him the appearance of a junior high bully.

"Let go!" Rhonda peeled off his ever-relenting hand and scooted away from him.

"Who the heck's this guy?" He pushed his fist into an open palm.

"Someone to talk to." She pulled two bobby pins from her hair. "He's been places, unlike you."

With clumsy but rather large paws, Rick gathered her tip money, fending off her repeated slaps.

"Dang you, Rick! That's mine!"

"It's ours! You don't need any more fingernail jobs."

"Look, why don't I leave you be?" Six inches shy of Rick's height, I stood with check in hand.

He latched onto a finger full of my shirt and began to twist. "Stay away from my girl." The stench of cigarettes was plentiful in the words he shoved into my face. "You hear me?"

"Jeez, Rick." Rhonda gathered her purse and other personals then grabbed the bill from my hand. "He's just a customer."

"I need my…"

She refused to return the green slip of paper worth two dollars. "Just walk out with us. They'll think you paid me earlier."

"What? No way is he getting a free meal."

"Shut up, Rick. I think you're up to thirty-eight free tabs with the number of cheeseburgers I've given you."

"You seein' him or something?" His boisterous baritone was attracting the attention of the other patrons.

The crimson around his ears and the size of his forearms had my attention. My heart slowed to the pace of a broken weathervane. Why was I being punished? I paid my taxes and had yet to fault on a student loan payment. Why me?

Rhonda refused to oblige him with an answer but did exacerbate his rage by tucking her hand under my right forearm and insisting I escort her to the car.

Befuddled, Rick could only watch the two of us exit the diner.

"That's Rick's car over there." She pointed to a red Dodge Charger with a set of menacing black racing stripes running parallel down the center of the hood. A spoiler rested on the platforms, several inches above the trunk. "We can give ya a ride, if ya want?"

Like a dog being led back to the scene of a bladder accident, I resisted her.

"No way," retorted Rick. "Wait a dang minute. You are seein' him!"

"And whatya gonna do about it if I am?"

"Whoa … Whoa!" I pleaded.

"Just like the guy at the roller disco, and the guy at the bowling alley. Now, get in the car and take us down to my Aunt Jenny's place."

"Wh—Why?"

"Because I said so." She pulled up the bench seat to expose the back, insisting I climb inside.

"No way am I takin' this guy anywhere."

"Rick, if you don't get in the car, I'll make sure your softball team knows you passed out when Christy was born."

"Listen, maybe I should just call Beefy…"

Fifteen minutes later, I was dropped in front of a saloon in the downtown area. The Ranger Roost was the bottom occupant of one of those two-story brick structures. Hanging from the corners of the large shop window were two neon blue beer signs, similar to the one clobbering the much smaller glass portion of the door.

Cigarette smoke battled darkness for domination in the bar. The music from the omnipresent jukebox was subtle but too much country and western. Both men were digging elbows into the bar top, and refused to relinquish their stare.

"Three beers!" Rhonda found an open table. She fell into an empty yet cushioned metal chair as if the day had sapped her energy.

Drawn to the jukebox like a horse to a sugar cube, Rick hugged its chrome edges like a toddler longing for the gumball machine to dispense the green one.

"How 'bout three sodas, and y'all get back home to that baby?" She had little joy to her disposition and labored to the table with three bottles of red soda pop. "Who's your friend?"

"Man, you still ain't got no Van Halen in here." Rick thumped his fist on the glass frontage of the jukebox before falling into an open chair. Boorishly, he stretched across the table for the bottle opener.

Rolling her eyes, ignoring both Rick and Rhonda, the barkeep/waitress introduced herself as Jenny. "I'm this one's aunt," she said through an unfeminine voice, pointing at Rhonda.

"Melvin. Melvin Wright." I was reluctant to accompany the couple at the table.

"Well, Mister Wright, I don't know ya from Adam, but keeping company with these two sure don't win ya no points in my book."

Rick suggested that Rhonda fry up something on the grill.

"My sister's oldest, and that one's the father of her kid." Jenny was neither tall nor short, and she snaked in between the half-dozen round tables. Her hair was not overtly gray but was highlighted in a frosted unnatural hue.

"Sit down, College Boy." With her foot, Rhonda shoved a chair in my direction. "He's from Cleveland, Aunt Jenny. Ain't you been there before?"

Aunt Jenny implied it was her husband who had Marine buddies on the west side of the city.

"Which side are you from, College Boy?" Rhonda reached into a purse for a file to tend to a pristine manicure of lustrous red nails.

"Come a long way just to have a drink at my bar, ain't ya?" asked Jenny.

"Well, actually…"

"Say," interrupted Rhonda. "Ain't that room upstairs empty?"

Jenny gathered the unraveled newspaper from an adjacent table. "The two of you are already leanin' on the rest of the family. You don't need no one-bedroom apartment."

"Ain't gonna be for us."

Before I could convince anyone my presence in South Heaven could only be described as temporary, Aunt Jenny was explaining rent terms to me.

With the correct key exposed at the top of the ring, she asked that I follow her into a back room. She wobbled when shuffling, as if pain were very much prevalent in her legs. "That boy's bad news." There must have been three dozen keys on her ring. She was searching them one by one. "Treats Rhonda like a dog."

Near the upper façade of the door that led to a set of wooden and precariously rickety stairs, a sign asked one to watch his or her step.

"Thinks this town owes him something, being a Redding boy." She moaned with each step. Aunt Jenny must have aged harder inward than appearance-wise. Only a few wrinkles had accosted a deep-seeded tan face that displayed an inkling of twilight. "Him and that dad of his thought Rick should've gotten a scholarship." She paused at the top step to massage the base of her back. "Football scholarship." Her key opened the door to an efficiency apartment. "Two of 'em blame my niece for havin' a baby. Don't get me wrong, though, she ain't no angel."

"Uhmm, I appreciate the tour, but I should only be here a couple more nights. God willing."

The apartment rivaled a backwoods roadside motel room in space and comfort but did offer a few other amenities: an icebox and stove. But a solid wood floor gave it some character.

"I just wish my sister's husband was still alive. He'd put both Rick and his dad in their place." There was an honest sense of retribution to her tone.

"Look, I think I'll be fine over at the hotel."

The icebox was operating but empty.

"Stove works too. Cabinets have a few dishes in 'em, and the bathroom's right here."

I stood at the stoop of the lone porthole and gazed across the main street at a gentleman locking the door on his shop. The cobbler shop owner wore a brown tie against his short-sleeved white shirt. "But thanks for the tour."

"Only on game nights does the noise creep up in here."

I placed my book bag on the avocado vinyl cushion of a metal-framed kitchen chair, one of a mere trio.

"We'll getuh crowd after a home game. Most'll come over to listen to the radio on away nights, too." As if presenting a diamond to a potential buyer, she laid the key on the table. Immediately adjacent to an unlaundered and naked daybed was a nightstand with a small lamp as a partner. She opened the miniscule door that covered the bottom cavity of the stand and removed a black phone that probably saw a production date prior to Ike's administration.

"Is yours the only radio in town?" I asked.

"Twenty-dollars a week, includes a meal downstairs."

"Meals?"

An inquiry of the menu earned me advise to opt for the B.L.T. from the bar.

"I'd say you have a deal, but…" I heard the door close behind me.

CHAPTER FIVE
A Sports Writer, I am Not

Friday, the Local Paper

"I don't know. These people can't seem to get the part needed to fix it." The week's end found me with a call in to my editor. "Story's done," I told him.

Passion had long ago replaced blood in Tony Esposito's veins. He was demanding to the point of being overbearing. Tony owned The Republic and was a man who accepted little in the way of excuses. As a result, turnover plagued the paper, unless you too were pushy, annoying, and a genuine pain in the butt. Tony was also ardently loyal to the Browns—a zealot, some would say.

"You think Sipe will have a good year at quarterback?" I plugged him, avoiding the subject of my car. In typical Tony fashion, he blamed me for the malfunction, lambasting my decision to go with the Camaro instead of his mother's used Buick.

Another annoying habit of Tony's was an utter and sudden conclusion to phone conversations. Although professing an inclusion to the left-side of politics, Tony, a traditionalist at heart, disparaged any communication not face-to-face.

Arms folded, Miss Myra stood in front of me, tapping her right foot. Again, she was dressed in a familiar pair of tattered jeans and a collegiate t-shirt—Temple. Her shoulder-length hair had been knotted into a taut ponytail.

Shielding myself from complete embarrassment, I carried a one-way conversation to its proper conclusion, then confidently secured the phone receiver to its base. "My boss."

"This is my office." She pushed me out from behind the desk.

My attempt to assure Miss Myra that one of her reporters had given me access fell on deaf ears.

"You know, I think I was more than accommodating to offer you a desk, sport. But I draw the line at my office, uninvited." Her rhetoric was neither vile nor indignant. Her attention was undivided, focusing on the hunt for a note rather than my transgression.

"Perhaps I can help?"

With both hands buried in a cardboard box loaded with loose sheets and composition books, Miss Myra offered little more than a grunt and a couple of masked four-letter words.

Before I escaped, however, the luck of South Heaven struck again.

"I too spoke with your boss this morning, sport." She had a slight hint of elitism to her tone. "I question how you understand him at times."

"It's a talent."

"I asked for a favor, sport. You know, in exchange for the use of the office?" She offered a hard-fought grin at the discovery of a legal-sized single piece of yellow notebook paper. Creasing the paper horizontally across the middle, she wrote a phone number, including a 215 area code, on the outside in red ink then crammed it in the mid-pages of a Joyce novel.

I had never been at the receiving end of a favor. So I knew Tony failed to take me into consideration before agreeing to any deal. Without haste, I followed her back to the main reporter office area.

"I hear you know a little about football?" With magic fingers that glided over the keys like a high school instructor, she tapped at the typewriter fluidly. "Darn. I before E, simpleton." Rifling through the lap drawer of the desk she occupied, frustration radiated in her futile attempt to locate an eraser.

"I also like listening to Steely Dan." I offered.

She ripped the page from the typewriter's grip then wadded it into a ball. "Anyway, my sportswriter is going to be laid up for a little while longer."

"So?"

"It isn't that hard of a job, sport. Just cover the football season."

"No," I huffed, now adamantly trailing her squirrel-quick pace from desk to desk. "I'm not going to be here very long. As soon as my car is up and running, so am I."

"Mister Esposito tells me you're talented and versatile…"

"Wait a minute! He said talented?"

"And versatile. Your desk is over there, sport, underneath all the South Heaven pennants."

Saturday

Two pleading calls to Tony, including one to his home; an offer to volunteer for the next destination assignment; and an assurance to never complain when a story of mine was moved from the front page failed to provide me an excuse to miss the Saturday afternoon scrimmage. Without a time frame for the return of my car, despite offering Beefy a bribe of two tickets to an Indians game and a few complimentary lessons in grooming and language skills, I arrived purposefully and resentfully late for South Heaven's initial scrimmage of the season. I had no intention of debasing myself in employing effort to report on a game. Had I known that too many years of college were to earn me a spot covering the South Heaven Rangers, my studies would have finished a distant second to beer consumption.

Willie Tee hugged a post section of the chain-link fence that surrounded the sidelines. He stood dead-even with the goal line, still in the same Reds t-shirt and red shorts.

"Quite a crowd," I uttered in between bites of a lukewarm wiener smothered by a soggy bun.

"Everybody's gotta see da Rangers." With the lone instance I had seen Willie Tee, I could not get beyond the omnipresent grin that encased his soul. I felt a sense of pity for him.

The bleacher section of Gottmann Field, the home of the Rangers, was an eclectic gathering of concrete and wood, trimmed in well-groomed maroon and white. Bordering the entire home-team side of the field and one end zone was a half a U-shaped concrete bleacher structure standing no more than twenty rows high. Along the upper reaches of the home bleachers, a two-tiered press box stretched the length of a railroad car. An impressive display of wood and metal bleachers, mainly confined between the thirty-yard lines, welcomed the visiting fans. A steep knoll buttressed against the outer reaches of the open end zone, offering the field a natural barrier. Most of the occupants on the hill were either children employing gravity to roll from top to bottom or townsfolk resting on blankets and enjoying the contents of picnic baskets.

Despite my knowledge for the game, Willie Tee provided an unsolicited explanation for the pretense of a scrimmage. "See, we get only eight plays. Dey done scored on us once."

"Who's they?"

"Daggumit!" Willie Tee exploded, turning his back to the field.

A few moans from the crowd followed an opposing ball carrier some fifty-plus yards to the goal line.

Willie Tee whipped his hat twice against the rail of the fence. "Win games whif defense."

Four opposing players celebrated the long run of number thirty-two with shoulder pad thumps and helmet slaps.

As he stared intently at the remainder of the hot dog in my hand, Willie Tee composed himself. "Don't s'pose you gotta another quarter you'd spare. Get me one of dem dere."

Over his left shoulder, I tossed the remainder of the bun, wrapped in a napkin, toward an open trash drum. "You don't have twenty-five cents?"

Willie Tee patted at his pockets. "Kinda strapped."

I didn't have a quarter but did possess the coinage to add up to the allotment, including five copper pieces.

"Dere we go. Bless ya, man. Bless ya." Willie Tee didn't bother to count the coins, preferring to cram the handful into his right rear pocket. "See dat big ol' boy dere? Numbah fiftah-two?" Although peculiarly in possession of a lighter, Willie Tee was without a cigarette. The cheap plastic device seemed to exacerbate the involuntary neurotic compulsion to ignite the flint.

"Who? The kid in red?"

"No! Fohr Catholic."

"Catholic?"

"Yeah. Limah Central Catholic. Dey da triple A champs from a few years ago. Numbah fiftah-two be goin' on a full ride tah Michigan State next year."

The team in blue and gold, with their obvious size advantage, pushed the home team up and down the field. Despite that, the crowd refused to leap from the bandwagon.

I, on the other hand, left half my soda with Willie Tee and migrated away from the playing field toward the front entrance of the stadium. Amid the myriad of screeching children's voices, I caught a snippet of a warning call before being struck in the back of the head with a flying object. Although neither heavy nor hard, the object knocked me off-balance. The culprit, a grungy yellow Nerf football striped personally with a green marker, wobbled to a condescending stop at my feet. One solid kick with my right foot would have sent the ball at least several yards. The instant before my anger pulled my cocked foot through the strike zone, a towheaded small boy in a knee-length Roger Staubach Cowboys home jersey fell on the ball in a fumble-recovery position.

"What's your problem, mister?" The kid heaved a lofted but taut spiral to his cadre of grass-stained buddies.

"You hit me in the head!"

Without hesitation or fear of repercussion, for that matter, the little brat pushed out an indignant tongue.

I reached for him, but the illusive blond juked left then right, leaving me prone, humiliated, and further aggravated. Their laughter permeated the very depths of my being.

Beyond the brats, a throng of people had gathered outside the stadium in a crude circle, three to four deep throughout the diameter. A full head above the members of the crowd, a man occupied the middle. The tall one who garnered all the attention wore a black Stetson and a heavy five-o'clock shadow.

Those fortunate to possess paper and ink begged the man for autographs. Others simply appeared to be thrilled to have an opportunity to touch or speak with him.

"What's going on?" I asked a teenage boy on the perimeter of the circle

The acne-laden kid jumped on the balls of his feet to reach visually above the crowd. "That there's Johnny Sarian."

"Go Dallas!" the crowd roared in unison as Johnny broke the circle and headed toward the stadium.

Responding to a flick in the ear from his buddy, the kid punched him in the arm then offered an adolescent but harmless epithet. "My dad said they called him 'Blue Laces.'"

"Yeah," piped in the friend. "My dad said he was all-Big Ten at Indiana."

"Plays for Dallas now. Ya know Johnny Sarian?'

Unfamiliar as I was with either the name Blue Laces or Sarian, intrigue led the way, a few steps behind the assumed former Ranger and his entourage of fans. Scrimmage aside, he had become my story for the upcoming edition.

Johnny's strut spilled over the threshold of class, foreign to the concept of humility and hardly analogous with the struggles of his former fellow citizens. Although the black jeans and cowboy boots seemed too much for the summer heat, the attire screamed big paycheck and big city. He had a manufactured drawl to his boisterous cackle. Johnny was posing for the cameras, directly underneath a placard in the shape of a football. Maroon in color, the placard possessed a white number forty-one. I could only assume the seven other numbers etched into football-shaped signs attached to the outer facing of the stadium and adjacent to the "Forty-One" had been worn by former players. Sarian was a natural for any camera lens—in confidence, posture, and looks.

With the last of the initial throng of amateur photographers snapping his last memento, I found a chance to invade. "Mister Sarian?"

"Who do I make it out to, partnah?" Instinctively, Blue Laces snatched my pad and pen. He offered a disingenuous movie-star smile in return.

"What? No."

"Hey Johnny, why don't we grab a seat up in the press box?" The man hogging Johnny's personal space was tyrannical and pompously verbose, as if he assumed all needed to hear him speak. Dressed to match Sarian in boots and black, he was all about arrogance.

Johnny used the man's back to scribble on my notepad. "I'll just leave the 'To' line blank. Here ya go."

In blue ink spilled from my pen, plastered on the front page of my pad, the genuine autograph of one Johnny "Blue Laces" Sarian smiled at me. Dumbfounded, I moved eyes from the manufactured signature to Johnny and his shadow as they climbed the ladder of stairs to the first level of the press box.

"You can get autographed photos of the greatest Ranger at the Redding Agency," the arrogant one gloated.

The stench of an inferior cigar preceded Old Man Schmidt. Two disturbing coughs vibrated his upper frame. Once calm again, he sucked happily on his stogie, before stepping with me to the edge of the concession stand. "Only Ranger ever to make All-Pro; means a lot to these people."

"What about the other one with him?" With my head turned away from Old Man Schmidt, I failed to notice his departure, and suddenly, the only one available to answer my question was the would-be bratwurst connoisseur standing at an adjacent counter. "How ya doing?" I asked, handing him a mustard container.

"Ya sure ya want no popcorn with that?" asked the concessionaire.

"Nah," I replied, catching sight of Old Man Schmidt behind me. "Just looking for my ordained guide."

"Well, we'll have fresh popcorn, here in about 5 minutes."

I found Old Man Schmidt but a few score of yards from the concession area. "You one of them who believes God and a football player are one in the same?"

"God's in the conscience. A great ballplayer's in the heart," Old Man Schmidt replied.

Helpless, I could not resist the tempting aroma of fresh popcorn and returned to the concession stand to drop a quarter on the counter. "How old is this?" The corn had a bright-yellow tint.

"When a boy can bring every townsperson to the stadium every Friday night simply 'cause he can run the ball like the wind, then maybe he is a god." Old Man Schmidt stood precariously, straddling the first and second stair of the ladder well to the press box. "Ya know, adoration of a football player ain't no transgression."

"No. It does seem to be a huge waste of time, though." With only a handful of popped kernels missing, I discarded the checkerboard box of popcorn into an adjacent trash bin. "Retired numbers?"

Although mocked, he smiled. "We been playin' ball since 1920. That there wall's a shrine to these folks 'round here." As he struggled from stair to stair, Old Man Schmidt spoke of the legacy of Johnny Blue Laces. "We had only to beat Chestertown to win the league." His voice increased a couple of pitches, holding ground on the middle landing. "Drizzle—off and on all day long—lifted by game time. Fog slowly began to fill the valley where Chestertown Field stood. By the end of the game, the field was covered with it." Old Man Schmidt sidestepped an oblivious man covered in green, both sweatpants and shirt, carrying two clipboards in each hand.

Against better logic, I began to climb the steps to the press box.

Old Man Schmidt's raised voice was uncomfortable. "Chestertown had scored with about five minutes to go. They had themselves a four-point lead when we forced them to punt with just thirty seconds to go." A couple of puffs from his cigar invigorated him. "Fog suddenly became soup, so thick no one in the stands could see the field. There was so much silence you could hear the boot of the ball from their punter. Seconds later, the fog lifted. Next thing we all seen was blue laces glowing in the lights of Chestertown Field—Johnny was alone in the end zone."

I spent the remainder of the scrimmage loitering at the aft end of an ebony-black Chevy Blazer, windows tinted the color of a starless night sky. An Ohio tag hung from the rear of the Blazer, inscribed with INSMAN. I wanted to subtly ambush Johnny Sarian. Fending off snide comments and odd stares from passers-by, I waited anxiously for my story. The petty and trivial Sun was destined to change its M.O. with me in charge of the sports page. I had always been a writer first. Any soul could simply observe and report.

"Johnny Sarian?" I caught him and his associate as they broke from a small crowd of admirers and headed for the Blazer.

The arrogant one stepped in front of me. He was an impressive man in size, with a jutting barrel chest and thick forearms. "Johnny's given all the autographs he's going to give today."

Without deference, I asked him not to push me then interjected my purpose. "I was wondering if he simply had a few minutes for the local paper."

He laughed. "Johnny don't do local papers no more."

"I'm sorry, you are?"

He dug into his pocket for a set of keys. "Name's Bo Redding."

CHAPTER SIX
Shrine to High School Football

Frankie's

The sun engulfed the inside of Frankie's. Every curtain was drawn away from the dozen windows decorating the dining room.

Curiously, with cherry-flavored Pepsi in hand, I held ground in front of what could only be considered a shrine.

From ceiling to floor and one end to the other of the wall that separated the kitchen from the dining room, thick wooden shelves blended well into the wood grain of the bulkhead. Spaced symmetrically and gapped enough to highlight each object were scores of football helmets, each authentic and distinct from the next. A brass plaque in front of every helmet displayed the name of a team a particular headgear represented. To an outsider, the helmets appeared to be in no specific order.

"What's this?" Miss Myra's question was more a demand than an inquiry. Her appearance suggested she had either completed a mile on the track or was ready to spar. Despite the lack of cosmetic assistance, Miss Myra maintained a flawless complexion.

"There must be forty helmets here." I drained the few sips of my soda. "Are they all real?"

She shoved familiar pages of transcripts into my face. "This is your story?" With hands hugging narrow hips, Miss Myra bit at her lower lip.

With the meddling of an undisciplined juvenile, I removed a royal blue helmet from its foundation. "Bisum Blue Devils," I read from the brass plate. "All this is either amazing or sad. I can't really decide." I rubbed at the red paint marks on the white "B" stickered to the side of the helmet. My dull fingernail was a weak weapon at peeling off the blunt red mark.

Miss Myra dropped my story on a neighboring table. "You are supposed to report the games. That's it, sport." Grabbing the headgear by the facemask with both hands, she replaced it on the mantel. "These are prized possessions. Just like Johnny Sarian."

From the wall of helmets, I migrated toward an oversized trophy case, offering Miss Myra no mind.

Encased in glass, the trophy case held a half-dozen bronze footballs mounted on a solid block of dark-stained wood. Sharing space with the footballs was a much larger trophy, one with a wide base and a tower shape. It appeared to be simply a collector's showcase.

"Heck, are there any autographs in this place?" I asked. "We have everything else."

"We send the paper to print at three today, sport." Miss Myra grabbed my wrist to expose the steel-gray Timex. For someone with such small hands, she had a convincing grip. "You've got two hours to recap the scrimmage."

Despite its obvious age, the bronze football trophy in the upper left-hand corner of the case proudly displayed a charming sense of care and discipline. The ball, nearly the size of a regulation one, gleamed with layers of polish. Its tarnished faceplate was dated 1942. "I gave you a real story. You should thank me."

"Yes. What was I thinking? Thank you, sport."

The omnipresent trophy in the case represented the Ohio State title.

One by one, she shredded each page of the story I submitted to her on the famous Johnny Blue Laces. "Two hours. I want a report on the scrimmage."

I retrieved a handful of shreds. "I don't know what your problem is, but it seems my paper is doing yours a favor. I'd be grateful for anything you got from me." With a passing waitress, I inputted my request for a refill of soda with a passing waitress.

"Listen, sport, save the 'light the world on fire' story for the big city. This is South Heaven. One, there is no audience for story writing, trust me. Two, it's taboo, sport, to disparage a hero. Johnny Sarian may be an immature jerk with the brain matter of a corn cob, but these people around here see him in a totally different light. Oh, and another thing, sport, Frankie was honored when the school offered him these trophies. You want a story, sport? You want to prove you're better than any of us … country folk? Write a story about Frankie."

A hardtack breadstick made me appreciate my cherry-flavored Pepsi. Despite the dryness, I retrieved a second one from the basket in the center of the table. "Johnny Sarian's the bully that made good." The breadsticks were thin but possessed a sharp garlic taste. "All he knows is how to carry a football. This is a hero for this town?"

With the quickness of a snake, Miss Myra ripped half of a breadstick from my hand. "Since it appears you failed to watch the scrimmage, I want an article on your introduction to the community. You have an hour."

"Seriously?"

Jake's Garage

To spite Miss Myra and the nobility she tried to convey as the educated heroin of her hometown, I submitted my initial story to the Sun—two paragraphs detailing my family's summer vacations to the Gulf coast of Florida.

"Ain't got good news for ya tonight." A thick and obtrusive finger punched two keys on the cash register, forcing open the till. He emptied the drawer of a thin stack of bills that included at least one fifty. "Still ain't got the part." With a set of innocent brown eyes peering at the back of his oil-splotched hand, Beefy read aloud the combination to the safe, which he'd scribbled there. His first attempt at engaging the tumbler lock failed, however.

"You guys don't have a phone here? Where is this parts place? For crying out loud, you can't call them?"

As if he were studying each bill to memorize the serial number, Beefy counted the money before wrapping a rubber band twice around the wad. Without solicitation, he offered up a profit and loss statement, casually informing me that sixty-one dollars was the most he ever put in the safe. The amount of root beer in his bottle was most certainly not enough to sustain Beefy's foot-long meatball sub. Holding the sandwich with a single claw served only to exacerbate the mess of onion and tomato sauce on the wax wrap. "Toby says he just ain't got the part." He lumbered to the soda machine. "Say, I hear you're the new sports guy for the paper?"

I spared little in rejecting Beefy's offer of a bottle of root beer, opting instead to berate him and his co-workers again.

Unraveled and reserved, Beefy popped the cap of the soda bottle with a utensil from his utility knife then wiped a blob of sauce from his bulbous chin. "That there," he mumbled with a full wad of food, pointing to the expensive red and foreign sports car in the distant bay. "That's Butch Boyd's car; problem with a starter."

"And by chance, do you have the part to fix it?"

"Oh yeah," he declared, licking at his fingertips. "We always make sure Mistah Boyd got the part he needs."

"Beefy, do you guys just not like me?"

Beefy offered an innocent laugh at my attempt to twist off the cap. "Says it's made in New York." He tossed the bottle cap into an adjacent metal trash can. "I like to read where things are made." Beefy washed down a bite with a chug that extinguished half the bottle. "All the parts we get in, they be made all over. Nuthin' ever made here in South Heaven, though. Least nuthin' I read."

With my stomach churning in disgust, my face crinkled as I watched Beefy retrieve a fallen meatball from the bare and less-than-hygienic counter and consume it in one bite.

"You should talk to Mistah Boyd 'bout your paper. His boys have all been quarterbacks…"

Ranger Roost, Wednesday Breakfast

The tea had a manufactured simplicity, but at least it was not coffee. Aunt Jenny was definitely no gourmand in boiling my favorite addiction. I shared the morning menu special, bacon and eggs, with two men from the street-sweeping crew who were looking for breakfast advice.

"Getya more toast?" Rarely was Aunt Jenny without a cigarette resting between two thin lips.

"I'll take another belt of coffee, Jenny," burped the fat man on the bar stool.

She grounded her cigarette into the ashtray on my table. "Russell, you needta be on your way. You know Georgia has to be gettin' to work by noon."

"Just one more."

"Ghit!" Aunt Jenny scooped up the empty saucer plate that had been home to my wheat toast. "Boys don't know when to quit." She shooed them with both hands. "Got wives at home that needta work also … Ah Lord, look what the cat drug in."

Rick and Rhonda preceded the nudging of the door closed.

With a magician's touch, Aunt Jenny slipped away, leaving me exposed to the combination of agitation and voracious jealousy.

"Well, well, well. If it ain't the big-city reporter." Ensuring the viewing public had an opportunity to take in his muscular frame, Rick was decked out in his best green mesh tank top and pro-wrestling tight white shorts. His John Deere cap nearly compared kindly to the color of his shirt.

Rhonda laid a path for the bar, securing a spot behind the counter. "Thought you were gonna have an article in the paper?" She poured from a fifth bottle of clear alcohol, catching the flow with a plastic juice tumbler. "Just says we needta look for your report next week."

My complimentary copy of the South Heaven Sun was still resting undisturbed at the corner of my table. I had caught a glimpse of the feature story—gibberish about a poor yield of sweet corn.

"Right there in black and white." Without solicitation, Rick dropped his tobacco spit cup next to my finished plate and his rear on an adjacent chair. His lip bulged with the assistance of a wad of snuff.

The smell of saliva and wet tobacco was nauseating. I swallowed a last bite of bacon and opened the paper to Section Two.

Shimmying herself from the bar to my side, Rhonda rubbed against my back, leaning over my shoulder. "See?"

Snuggled in the bottom right corner of the front page of Sports was an insignificant article introducing me as the substitute sports reporter? No bio. No mention of credentials. Just a name and my new function with the paper. "Well, that…"

"Witch," Rhonda added. "No one likes Miss Myra much."

Otherwise occupied, flexing his short supply of brain cells to read a hot rod magazine, Rick failed to notice his flirtatious girlfriend.

"Jeez, Rhonda!" Aunt Jenny saved me from my sudden realm of discomfort. "Man's probably got enough problems as it is. Leave him be. Can I get you anything else? Besides a pass to avoid these two?" She scolded Rick for propping his feet on the table.

"No, I think I have an impromptu date with Miss Myra."

"Whatya want with her?" Rhonda pouted when Aunt Jenny confiscated her cocktail. "Thinks she knows it all just 'cause she's been to an important college in Pennsylvania." Rhonda's was a personality of impertinence and honesty, a combination that would typically land a male on the losing end of a bar brawl. On the other hand, she possessed a manufactured beauty of excess makeup and seductive perfume that simply landed her an overgrown child of a man with a handful of excuses and little in the tank of future resources. "Bet she don't know nothing 'bout Pittsburgh, though. It's a steel town, ya know? And I would want…"

"Hey babe, this here's the car I want."

"Maybe you could afford it if you'd get yourself a job with your dad."

"I'm not selling insurance, ol' woman."

"What about the bicycle plant in Frederick?"

"Maybe if you'd just give Rhonda a job here, we could afford more!"

"You ain't even registered for classes yet at the junior college, have you? Heck, that dad of yours is flippin' the bill for that…"

"Okay. I think it's time for me to go." I thanked Jenny and found the door.

"See ya soon, I hope," Rhonda called.

Sticking Rick with another shot of verbal abuse, Aunt Jenny followed me out the exit. She lit another smoke and moaned a sigh of satiation, as if the nicotine were a more powerful narcotic for pain.

"Your sister's kid, eh?"

"Rhonda's momma's been gone for years now, ever since her husband died. She's been drunk since planting him in the ground. I try…" she exhaled through three successive coughs. "I try to look out for Rhonda, ya know? She's just got no respect for herself or any care in the world. I'd give her a job here, ya know. I'm just not sure I wouldn't wind up firin' her the very next day."

"So what's the special for dinner tonight?"

"You'll probably find Miss Myra across the street at the courthouse." She waved at an elderly woman struggling to exit her robin's-egg-blue Buick. "Actually, there she is now."

Across Main Street, Miss Myra was walking, hand-in-arm with an older gentleman.

With northbound traffic halted at the stoplight, I darted across Main Street, unintentionally preventing the sputtering progress of a city maintenance truck hauling several small but dead maple trees. Over the belching and angry horn of the truck, I could decipher the tobacco-infested voice of Aunt Jenny calling out the evening's special: meatloaf. I caught up to the duo, approaching them from behind, before they could enter Wendy's Cakes and Donuts.

Her authentic laughter soured suddenly. "Wow, sport." She tapped at the glass of her wristwatch. "Not bad. Two hours and fifteen minutes late for work. Is that how you big-city writers go about doing your job?"

With a charcoal tint to his full top, the man escorting Miss Myra was hardly of our generation or the one previous, for that matter. Taller than average, with auspices of age surrounding his waist and face, he had a dapper and impressive masculinity about him. He was attired in plaid trousers and a red casual shirt—country club and anachronistic for South Heaven, in my opinion.

"I saw the paper this morning." I peeked at the wrecked shop window display of wedding cake paraphernalia, an unorganized mess of bride and groom figures. Of the half-dozen cake plates, only one contained an actual wedding cake. The aroma of sugar glaze and flour was tempting an already-full stomach. "Didn't notice my article, though."

"New sports writer?" the gentleman asked. "Where are ya from?"

"Sport here's an important reporter from Cleveland." Miss Myra grinned in triumph.

Myra's companion climbed the two concrete steps to the door of the shop, opening it for a youngster and his mother. Mom carried two pastry boxes wrapped in string. "I knew a pilot on the Hornet who was from Cleveland."

"Really? Maybe I know him. After all, Cleveland is such a small place."

"You will forgive him, Mister Boyd," Miss Myra insisted. "Sport's probably used to getting his way." She slapped me on the shoulder, never allowing her smile to subside. Miss Myra obliged his extended hand, gently and gracefully placing her fingers in his palm.

"Boyd, eh?"

She held the door ajar then acknowledged my pettiness, "Mister Boyd, this is Melvin Wright. Sport, this is Butch Boyd."

"Say, I got a glimpse of your car at the garage."

Once again, Miss Myra tapped at her watch glass. "Clock is ticking."

"I'd like a chance to talk to you, Mister Boyd. Or, can I call you Butch?"

The left edge of his lip cropped as he smiled. He had a sharply shaved-clean face, as if a spokesman for a razor company. "For a sports article. Tomorrow's the passing scrimmage up at Ferndale."

"Maybe a good idea to cover it for next week's paper," Miss Myra added.

"Speaking of passing, I hear your family has owned the position of quarterback in this town?"

Miss Myra disappeared into the shop, begging Butch to follow.

The Apartment

The second set of knocks on the door pulled me away from my magazine and out of an uncomfortable worn-blue recliner. "Yeah, hang on."

Miss Myra had two white boxes of takeout cradled in her left forearm and balanced two soda cans in the other. "Hope ya like Chinese." She shuffled inside as if the apartment were hers, dropping the boxes on the dining table. "This great little couple opened up shop last year." She savored the initial bite of a perfectly fried brown egg roll. "They make the best sesame chicken."

"You're about an hour late. I had my fill of the meatloaf special."

With cynics' gumption, deceptive beauty, and, for that matter, possession of knowledge of my Achilles' heel, late-evening snacking, Miss Myra opened every container of the takeout. From wonton soup to the sesame chicken, the pungent yet delectable aroma of garlic was omnipresent. "I haven't eaten since breakfast." The manner in which she began to devour her chicken attested to hunger but did dampen her appeal slightly.

Despite an occasional stomach grumbling and salivating glands, I resisted a seat at the table and her insistence to eat while the food was still hot. Instead, I offered Miss Myra either a beer or diet soda—members of two separate six-packs and the lone occupants in an empty refrigerator.

"I have something, sport. In fact, there's a second soda here for you."

Although not my particular taste, the first sip of Stroh's was enough to quench the thirst of uneasiness around me. Aunt Jenny insisted I take the six-pack for assisting her with stocking the bar's cooler. "So, you have no place to call home to eat dinner? I'm sure Mister Butch has a mansion on the hill, or at least a throne."

With the presence of that coy yet engaging grin, Miss Myra swallowed a nimble bite and dusted her hands free of crumbs and grease on a plain white paper napkin. "South Heaven owes much to Butch Boyd, sport."

"And you?"

Dipping a wad of rice into a tiny vat of soy sauce, Miss Myra, with every ounce of sarcasm and petty needling she could muster, suggested I was jealous of a man twice my age.

To that accusation and assumption, I interjected a laugh. The can of Stroh's tasted better with each and every swill.

"Are you going to eat or not?"

I dug into the carton of egg rolls.

Miss Myra pushed aside the Styrofoam cup of soda in favor of the beer. With my fridge door open, she critiqued my diet then asked if I had any wine on hand.

"And where would the best wine cellar in Corn Country be?"

"In all of Corn Country?" She chucked the pull tab at me, bouncing it off my chest. Beer appeared to be an unwelcomed taste for her. With every feeble sip, her face contorted slightly. "Jenny has a couple of California merlot bottles downstairs."

"Wouldn't think the patrons of the Roost could spell merlot, let alone have ever tasted red wine."

Miss Myra walked toward the dense sun that dominated the open window with carton in hand. Balancing the food in one hand, she was apt and athletic and still able to use chopsticks. "Mister Boyd has offered to give you a lift to Ferndale tomorrow."

"Ferndale?" With a mouthful of eggroll, I felt soy sauce dribble from the corner of my mouth.

She parked herself on the extended window sill, withstanding the heat and glare. A teasing breeze, entering through a slightly abused and misaligned mesh screen, ruffled the napkin in her hand. "You know, I was once in your shoes, sport—the world by the throat. It was not so long ago that I had carte blanche to disparage the undeservingly wealthy and ordained powerbrokers of Pennsylvania politics."

"Are you looking for employment or therapy?"

"Scrimmage starts at ten in the morning."

"Listen, haven't we experienced enough of this charade? I mean, you've had your practical joke. Why don't we just call it quits, or even, or whatever, eh? You don't actually need me on this staff, and I certainly have no interest in being on your staff."

She called through the mesh screen of the open window at a group of three outside the building, inquiring about the well-being of the mother of a man named Paul. With every word she spoke, it seemed like Miss Myra was on the verge of losing all vocal function. Another couple bites of rice and soy generated a swill from the brown and bronze-colored can of Stroh's. "You want the story of South Heaven?"

"The story?"

She shuffled by me, setting the beer can on the table. "You know, the story on the settlement, the real reason you came here. The American Genuine story?"

I heard the door handle but did not wait for it to open. "What … is this story?"

"Butch will pick you up in front of the bar at nine. Help yourself to the rest of the takeout," she said before disappearing down the stairs.

CHAPTER SEVEN
A Spec on the Map: Ferndale

Ferndale

Hardly would I refer to it as devotion to job. Given that fact, though, I was comfortable in the plush leather surroundings of Butch Boyd's sports car, the same red Alfa that took precedence over my car at Jake's. A passing scrimmage was insipid, yet I was on my way to Ferndale. "So, where does one find such a foreign vehicle out here in nowhere?"

Fifteen minutes along yet another country road, and Butch offered only one-word, affirmative or negative responses to my barrage of questions.

"In a town owned by an American automaker, I'm sure you're a popular guy."

"Yep." With a sudden shift into fourth gear, Butch nosed the front edge of the Alfa into the opposing lane then thumped on the accelerator and blew by a blue tractor hauling a long wagon of hay.

The operator of the tractor was hardly the idea of a quintessential farmer. Without shirt or concern for surroundings, the young boy seemed to be swaying to his own tune, bobbing his head and jigging with his hands.

I gave the kid a wave of the victory sign, thrilled not to be in his circumstance but envious of his innocence. "So…" I yawned, opening my book bag to retrieve a pen and notepad. "Your sons, all quarterbacks for the hometown team? Gotta be proud of those genes."

"Yep."

As the Alfa slowed, stalks of corn relented to an oasis of a small campus. Ferndale High was a building of yesteryear and far removed from the town. A dilapidated marquee in the middle of a treeless yet spacious front lawn gave visitors an unfettered but less than congenial welcome to "Falcon Territory." Behind the crumbling brick and broken glass marquee was a square three-story building that matched the color of the brick welcoming sign. The school was more of a relic than an active learning house.

Butch snuggled the Alfa close to the chauffer-side of a South Heaven school bus, leaving just enough room for me to exit the car without fear of scratching the paint from a bump against the yellow monster.

It was obvious that progress had surpassed space requirements for a school built pre-Depression. In the rear of the building were a half a dozen unattached but enclosed trailers.

"Have they given thought to a new school?"

Butch, even if he were in a mood to reply instead of utter, could not hear me. On a direct line for the football field, he was several scores of yards ahead of me.

With backpack in tow, I weaved through parked cars, en route to the opening in a chain-link fence feeding fans to a doghouse-sized ticket booth. Everything visual about Ferndale was completely primitive, with the exception of the stenciling and artwork adorning the ticket booth. I was amazed and awestruck at the intensity of the mural etched on the side of the one-person structure: a falcon, pristine in detail, with wings and talons sprawled. Brushing my fingers across the artwork, I was dumbfounded at how the end of civilization could generate such talent and beauty.

"Welcome to Ferndale," Old Man Schmidt piped. "You ain't gotta pay to get into a scrimmage, don't ya know?"

"Just admiring the work."

Old Man Schmidt offered me one of the two seat cushions he carried then insisted I follow him to the press box.

The problem in Western Ohio, at least during a hot summer, was a lack of a horizon. On the very edge of the playing fields, baseball diamond, etc. was … well, corn. The land was flat. A man could see nothing but green stalks. The flatness was only amplified when I climbed into the press box and gazed out upon a landscape of no hills, no rolls, and no indentation.

Not a soul greeted Old Man Schmidt or me in the precariously rickety wooden box. Except for the stagnant breeze blowing uninhibited through glassless portals, the press box was empty. A contiguous wooden bench ran the length of the structure, like a lunch counter, in front of the windows.

Old Man Schmidt gently laid his cigar on the edge of the windowsill, with the burnt end hanging over the side. "Always the best seat in the house—up above all." He rested on his Ranger-red cushion.

"I've seen better construction in tree houses." With a light foot, more like a big toe, I pressed on a squeaky board that already allowed sunlight to pass through from a gaping hole. "We gonna be safe up here? I mean, why don't we just join the crowd in the stands?"

"You know ol' Butch there, he was the guy in charge of American Genuine?"

Dust and several rusty nails covered the floor. I had collected a handful of the metal pins before realizing there was no trash bin. "Guy in charge?"

"Twenty-eight years the plant manager." He moaned as the cane assisted him to his feet. Leaning his head out an open window, he bellowed out an angry sentiment toward the heat of summer. "Came here outta the Navy." The rubber bottom of the cane nearly found another hole in the floor as he waddled back to the cushion.

A team in black and white was sprawled out in callisthenic formation near the end zone that harbored a flag pole—one without a banner. With the aid of height, I counted off exactly thirty players for the home team. "Man in charge of the plant that closed? And he hasn't been run out of town?"

From the caverns of the inside of his sport coat, Old Man Schmidt retrieved a flask. "Butchie begged that company to stay in town. Town, they respected him. Besides, at the time, his third boy was playin' quarterback. He wasn't about to leave, nor would South Heaven let him."

Without any sense of haste, a pre-adolescent labored into the press box, hauling a set of binoculars by the strap. "Here, Grandpa."

"Did you get lost?" Old Man Schmidt asked the boy, before directing me to retrieve the field glasses.

"Thought this was the best seat in the house?"

Old Man Schmidt focused the lenses on the gaggle of Rangers encircling their coaching staff. "To be avoiding the fans, yes."

Slyly, I made use of the seat cushion, hoping he would not further elaborate.

"Some of 'em, like that Bo Redding, all he does is talk great about his kid and bad about every other player. He hates losin' more so than he loves to win."

"Redding? I've had a few but unpleasant encounters with a Rick Redding…"

"That's Daddy Redding down there on the sidelines. Big shot insurance salesman, don't ya know?" He pointed to a burly man who seemed to be commanding the attention of the sparse crowd around him.

"Yeah. The man with that Sarian character."

"Bo Redding owns himself an insurance business in town. He and the missus think they're royalty in South Heaven. She's with Vordon Realty."

"Vordon? Same company that has its sign on the auto plant?"

"Vordon done got their name on every house for sale in town. Papa Redding's other boy's our startin' quarterback."

Three referees wandered toward the center of the field, which precipitated the movement of both teams toward respective sidelines.

"Of course, Waddell's got no choice. Gary Redding's all he's got."

From the goal line of the end zone to my left, the larger combatants of the scrimmage, the linemen, gathered. Numbers-wise, the Rangers in maroon jerseys counted more in their posse than did those wearing black.

Old Man Schmidt caustically commented, "Papa Redding probably done complained about how his kid looks in all-white pants instead of the red striped ones."

A player wearing a jersey numbered eleven, holding his helmet and adjusting the chin strap, stood next to a black fellow, the only minority in Ranger coaching attire. "So who's Waddell?"

Gary Redding's first pass against the skeleton defense of the Falcons resulted in a bad incompletion.

"Can't miss him. First ever black coach here at South Heaven." Old Man Schmidt had a hard grimace appear when Gary missed an open receiver on the post pattern. "Surprised?"

"Should I be?"

Old Man Schmidt asked me if I had a thirst then, without waiting for a response, verbally retrieved his grandson again.

Ferndale Field possessed a small section of wooden bleachers underneath the press box. Despite the shade covering most of the bleachers, fans were more interested in hugging the open sidelines to watch Gary Redding complete his first pass—a slant to a split end.

"Freddy Waddell don't need to be back here. Should've just stayed down south—no job or not. Came back home when his Uncle Gibby died. Our school board then goes and offers him the job here when they fired that other clown, Figgins." Old Man Schmidt was slightly festered, losing the taste of his cigar. He dampened the light then tossed it out the open door, nearly catching his grandson in the shoulder. "I'll tell ya, he ain't had nothin' but trouble since. Can't seem to win."

"Yes, Grandpa?"

The leather creaked and moaned as he pulled apart the sides of his wallet. "The faithful ain't gonna put up with any more four- or five-win seasons." He retrieved two single dollar bills. "Junior, go down and get me a Pepsi-Cola. You can keep the rest for yourself."

Junior slid one of the bills into his tube sock and departed the press box with much more energy than he had upon arrival.

Old Man Schmidt returned to his binocular viewing and griping about South Heaven's inability to throw a pass. "Freddy Waddell was the first black ball player to be all-county from South Heaven."

Out of South Heaven's twelve or so consecutive plays, they completed only three passes before turning the game over to their skeleton defense.

Ferndale's offensive game was no more adept at throwing the football than South Heaven. Unlike the remainder of his teammates, the quarterback for the Falcons wore a gray jersey. He had a truncated three-quarter delivery that forced the ball to flutter high.

"He had him a coachin' job somewhere in Tennessee."

"And you don't like this guy because…"

"Uh-oh," Old Man Schmidt mumbled in response to a deep Ferndale pass completion.

Junior slinked into the press box. He sucked the life out of a giant purple Pixistick.

"Freddy shouldn't be back here 'cause he done left once." Old Man Schmidt climbed to his feet and relieved Junior of the soda. "Once you got the ticket out of town, don't give it back. Ya gotta cash it in." He pushed the kid out of the press box then pulled the door closed.

"I didn't take you for the metaphor type."

"Don't get me wrong, boy. I've given my heart to South Heaven and will always love it. And because of that, I can't leave. But if someone gets the chance, though…"

Thunderstorm in August

It was my turn to gather the meal. Four dollars and change bought a large cheese pie. Frankie gave me a deal: the price of a medium for a large and two cherry-flavored Pepsis.

Mid-evening brought relief from the heat of summer in the form of dark cumulous. The storm barreling in from the west had an ominous hue, a dangerous wind, and a frightening roar. Balancing the sodas atop the checkerboard pizza box, I braced my rear against the wind, walking backwards and fending off the storm from wreaking havoc upon dinner. An ear-splitting clap of thunder trumpeted an aerial assault of pebble-sized hail.

Withstanding only minor blows from the crystallized rain, I darted for the awning of the paper's entrance, only to find the front door locked. I spoke the ripened language of a gym locker room, kicking at the door.

The menacing storm patronized me, momentarily halting the hail before unleashing a deluge of water. Suddenly, the gusts shifted direction and blew the rain toward me, and with every drop that drenched my clothing, the harder I kicked at the door.

A barrage of expletives engendered an appearance by Miss Myra. Her smile and lack of urgency only served to agitate me further.

"Open the door!"

Haste was absent, but spite was not, and as soon as she opened the door, I shot inside.

"Do I get the pizza for free, sport? You know I called over thirty minutes ago?"

My entire back side was completely sodden. "I hope your pieces are cold." Dropping the saturated pizza box on the lobby counter, I pulled the water from my hair then whipped it from my fingers.

Miss Myra helped herself to a hefty slice. The piece was cut perfectly without strings of cheese clinging to the remainder of the pie.

Wind threw rain against the glass of the office front window. The shrill sound was wicked, like a string of beads being rattled across the bones of a skeleton. The day had muted to black.

"So how was the scrimmage?"

Boom! The one-two combination of lightning and thunder quickly stole the power from downtown.

She handed me a durable metal flashlight. "Lead the way."

"What?"

"To my office. You know, candles?" She sidestepped me to get to her desk. "I could use some light over here." Miss Myra retrieved two long white candles but only a single holder. "Here." She pushed a booklet of matches into my sternum.

Another clap of thunder reiterated the fact that power had been stripped from South Heaven.

I inquired about the possibility of a tornado, knowing the plains' propensity to attract the worst of the severe weather.

"The last one to roll through here was the April '74 storm. So as long as we are not on a six-year cycle, you should be fine."

Two failed matches, and I was no further in lighting any candle. A third attempt engendered a hint of embarrassment.

"Pizza's only getting colder."

"Ha!"

"Well, congratulations, sport." Miss Myra steadied the candle, guiding the small wick into the ever-weakening match flame. She made a petite kitchen table out of the Metro writer's desk. Hers was a tidy workspace with loose papers squarely stacked and marking utensils stowed in a cup holder. "Megan would have a fit if she knew I was eating on her desk." She wiped a glob of sauce from the outer edge of the pizza box. "It's been a while since I had a candlelight dinner." Miss Myra suggested I head out into the storm to retrieve Aunt Jenny's famous bottle of Merlot. Apparently, the watered-down cherry-flavored Pepsi was not to her liking. "So, tell me, sport," she said, opening one of Megan's desk drawers to find two small packets of wet hand towels. "Is there a lucky lady back home?"

Although not in the same league as a Louie Ray pie back in Oberlin, Frankie's tangy sauce could quickly garner fans. Despite a spell in the rain and several minutes removed from the oven, it had a good taste.

Even while relishing in the moment, I inquired as to the primitiveness of the power grid in Western Ohio. I caught myself instinctively, without decorum, licking the garlic and butter residue from my fingers.

The news blotter, tucked away in the corner of the room and powered by a major battery, began to chatter furiously. With pizza in hand, Miss Myra answered the blotter's calling, tearing the sheet from its spigot.

"Well, Daddy was right, I suppose. The machine is money wisely invested," she chimed, handing me the tear sheet.

Careful to avoid the transfer of grease, I held the sheet precariously between my small and ring fingers. "National Weather Service in Lima has issued a severe thunderstorm warning for Harper County." I cast the sheet aside. "Better late than never."

"The epitome of South Heaven."

"Dissention?"

"Please. You don't actually believe that my ultimate goal in life is to run this paper, do you, sport?"

A surge into the darkness toyed with the lights and power of the office. The blotter fluttered again, forcing Miss Myra to her feet, like a Pavlov subject.

"I should be in the front of the line for overseas reporter with the AP."

"So why aren't you?" I snatched the wadded ball of paper she had thrown to the floor.

"You answer my question, first," she retorted.

"About what? Do I have someone at home, waiting for me to return? Nah, just the job."

The print on the teletype indicated that the storm was to spread into counties east and north of us.

I told her that besides my parents there was no one significant in my life.

"This is Daddy's paper, and someone needs to run it."

With curiosity, I watched as she snooped in her reporter's desk, rifling through drawers and stacks of papers.

"Someone could be found, well, anywhere," I commented.

"Most of these guys in here don't have the education I do. They have two-year journalism degrees from some obscure community college." She lamented and rearranged the pieces of Megan's desk, as if to play a practical joke on the unsuspecting. "Most of 'em have no idea of true journalism."

"So, you're some sort of savior?"

"Sure, I guess."

With the terseness of a finger snap, power returned to the office.

I suggested that she allow me to submit a story for the next week's edition about Coach Waddell and being black in a hick town.

"You're not going to win the Pulitzer here in South Heaven, sport. Trust me."

"Okay. Then let me in on the story."

"In due time, sport."

CHAPTER EIGHT
A Black Coach in South Heaven?

First Practice of the Day

A monstrous sycamore tree provided relief from a late-morning sun. The big wood with the bi-colored bark stood as either a survivor or the sole king of its own domain on the eastern side of Samm's Creek.

With my back pressed against the sycamore, I was grabbing a piece of the soft, sand-like creek bank, enjoying a hefty helping of Aunt Jenny's menu item number five: deli ham on rye.

The sun was nearly at its peak, and there were but a handful of weak clouds to ruin a perfect day. For the first time since my arrival, Mother Nature had relented and granted South Heaven a palatable day of comfortable temperatures and desert-like humidity. However, mosquitoes and other flying creatures also appeared to be enjoying the paragon of an oasis, hovering around me like vultures.

Three bites and a couple of sips into my sweetened iced tea, I heard the racy language of adolescence in the distance.

A score of yards south of my picnic spot, at the makeshift footbridge, a stream of Rangers began to cross the creek. Players could only access the bridge one at a time, with the causeway no wider than a regulation home plate. All were uncovered, and most carried their shoulder pads in hand. Few saw me, and those who did ignored the "kook" by the creek.

I swatted at the mosquito on my arm before grinding the loathsome creature into the sandy earth. Wrapping the remainder of my sandwich in its original wax paper, I lumbered to my feet.

Players became more numerous, with many of them bunched on the bank and awaiting their turn to cross the manmade bridge.

I found a kid with a serious case of adolescent acne and asked the whereabouts of his coach.

His coal-black hair glistened with perspiration, as if practice had concluded only minutes earlier. He asked a fellow player but received only a shoulder shrug. "Guess he's still on the field." Sweat dripped from the edge of his nose.

One after another passed, but none in excess of high-school age.

I had no interest in waiting for Coach Waddell, at least on the lee side of Samm's Creek. So, impatience and annoyance by the bugs pushed me past the oncoming rush of players and onto a wide rock that could hold both my feet. I decided to make my own bridge to cross the water. Drawing an audience of small laughter, I picked out jutting rocks and hopped from one to the other. Half-way across, still dry and gloating with pride for my accomplishment, I heard a voice shout the coach's name.

A black man with a swollen chest towered above a smaller player, lecturing the boy. It appeared that right underneath my nose, Coach Waddell had crossed Samm's Creek. He clutched at the strings of the rope that carried a whistle.

After a terse tirade, I started to reverse course … until my right foot opted not to cooperate. Samm's Creek, at its deepest, could only register a sounding of a dozen-plus inches. Despite the summer, the water was chilled and breathtaking. Embarrassment yanked me to my feet.

A cacophony of laughter infested the air.

"You know we got us a bridge right over there?" For such an athletically powerful man, Coach Waddell offered a higher-pitched voice than most male adults. "Most of my boys've managed to stay dry over the past two weeks." His lumberjack biceps yanked me from the water.

"Coach Waddell?" I asked in as dignified a manner as possible. Water dripped from my extended palm.

With tree trunks for thighs and a thick neck barely visible above a set of defined shoulders, Coach Waddell had the physique to punish rather than receive a beating on the field of play. Impervious to my sodden person, he possessed a coarse but not large hand that denigrated my grip of less than ardent masculinity. Huffing into his whistle, he chastised two players engaged in horseplay on the footbridge. "Daggone kids." He waved toward another adult in like attire: maroon coaching shorts and white t-shirt. Despite the respite from extreme and exhausting temperatures, Coach Waddell's white shirt was laced with sweat stains.

I introduced myself, without tremendous pride, as the new sports reporter for the paper.

"Usetabe guy, called himself the Pigskin Prognosticator, worked for the paper." Coach Waddell, bumming a smoke from an assistant coach, instructed the crusty old bear of a man to ensure the jerseys got collected and washed. "Be smellin' here real soon."

"Let's just soak them in the creek here," the assistant coach bellowed, examining my person with a patronizing eye.

"Big Pete Purkey, this here's a sports writer," Coach Waddell added. "He may make ya famous."

Big Pete claimed every bit of his nickname: circus height with shoulders wider than a city block. "Already famous in another one-horse town. Got no need to be famous in two. Too old."

"You coach here?"

"Nope. Just like the get-up." He tugged at his shorts.

"Big Pete runs the defense for us," said Coach Waddell.

"Your specialty?"

"Thirty-six years." Big Pete had the facial features of a hockey defenseman: square head, distorted nose, and missing teeth.

Coach Waddell quickly drained any residual supply of patience, picking and pulling at his sodden shirt and spitefully dragging a plain white cotton hankie across a high and obscure forehead. "Don't think we got any clothes up dere at da school for ya, do we Pete?"

"I'll stay out in the sun, thanks."

"Suit yourself."

Both Waddell and Big Pete turned around before ascending the hill leading to the school.

"I'd liketa get a few words from you about how you came to South Heaven." Soaked clothing or dry attire, the mosquitoes refused to seek pity upon me.

"I'm guessin' it'd be County Road Four via Tennessee." Coach Waddell retrieved a laugh from Big Pete.

I swatted at the creature that had just made a landing hard enough to engender an immediate red welt on my forearm.

"If you can write and walk at da same time, Newspapuh Man, you can follow me up to school."

Swatting the creatures clear of my face, I studied the sharply inclined hill with a reluctant gleam.

Unkempt, thick and tall grass covered the face of the hill, along with industrial-sized rocks, overgrown weeds, and numerous bushes. A piercingly narrow and well-worn foot path snaked from bottom to top.

A short but steep climb pulled at my quadriceps. I caught up to my story subject, as he was gracious enough to await my presence at the top of the hill.

"Useta make us run dat dere hill," Coach Waddell said. "That is till we lost Junuh Belpre. Dumb fool stepped on a rock, broke his ankle."

Big Pete had a much slower gait than his head coach. He fell behind as we made our way to the school.

Coach Waddell exhausted every inch of his smoke, depleting the cigarette down to an obscure blunt before flicking it into the landscape of gravel and stone. "I ain't never seen you in South Heaven. What brings ya here?"

Without answering, I asked the same question of him.

"Well, s'pose it's home."

I wrung a few quarts of creek water from my shirt. "High school football in Corn Country?"

"Agggh," Big Pete exclaimed, catching up to us. He struggled to keep pace due to a set of bum knees encircled with worm-like surgical scars. "Should've quit this sport years ago." Big Pete continued his laggard movement through the school's parking lot, swerving around vehicles randomly dotted across the broken asphalt.

On the sloped hood of a brown Nova, Coach Waddell found a brief respite, his thick arms barely able to reach a fold over the massive bulge in his chest. "Wise man once told me high school be the last good in the game." He asked for a smoke then uttered some chastisement for my negative response.

"I heard you have college experience?"

"Yup." He smiled, lifting his ball cap to scratch his noggin.

I suggested a move from college to high school might be perceived by some as a downgrade.

"You here to be critickin' my career, Newspapuh Man?" He scolded two of his players who were loitering outside the school.

"Heard from a good source that you were a star player among white players, in the heyday of South Heaven?" Although the newly formed breeze had little masculinity or anger to it, any strength it did posses provided me, given my wet clothing, with just enough misery to cause a constant shiver.

As I followed in slow step behind him, my introduction as a true reporter for a major Cleveland paper seemed to fall on deaf ears.

Coach Waddell rifled through the glove box of a Ford Bronco, leaning into an open passenger window. "I wasn't the only black player on the team." Climbing down from the side runner, he had an unlit smoke between his lips and a pack of many in his hand. "Me, Junuh, Bip Jones, we all played here. We all part of a championship team. Wadn't for us, this town would be with one less trophy."

"I'd like to do a story about your time here at South Heaven."

He laughed, as if the activity were not a favorite of his. "Dis here town, they don't wanna hear anymore 'bout me. They already know enough. Don't be wastin' your time, Newspapuh Man."

Again, I reiterated my South Heaven gig was only temporary.

"Where'd ya say you from?" Coach Waddell interrupted. "Cleveland?"

"We have readers beyond Cleveland. Others pick up on this, and you could get beyond the high school ranks."

"You could do that?" He pulled the hat from his head and wiped his scalp clear of perspiration. His smoke was only half-extinguished before he discarded it. "Ah heck, probably ain't no matter. Just another hot summer in South Heaven, story or not." He looked up into the sun, shielding his eyes. "I'm the coach of the Rangers, nuthin more."

Sunday, a Day to Relax

LeSaint Park belonged to the people of South Heaven, and it served as the division between the haves and have-nots on the town's west side. Every season and sport was confined within the dilapidated fence surrounding the park. It seemed each backyard buttressing the fence had its own private entrance. In the distance, nearest the park's main gate, a pickup game of three-on-three, shirts versus skins, occupied one side of the basketball court. The late-morning hour found the caged tennis courts without patrons, a rarity for a Sunday in Cleveland, mind you. A stenciled and fabricated football field, with a goalpost at one end, bordered both the tennis and basketball courts. Unlike its neighbor, the gridiron drew a crowd of multi-colored uniforms.

Several hundred yards from the future football event, I became attracted to the omnipresent aroma of an open-pit barbeque mass-producing a variety of charred meat. With Aunt Jenny out of town, I had missed breakfast.

"Hey, Melvin!" Beefy, adorned proudly in a Jake's Garage softball jersey and his omnipresent but doltish grin, closed his game of catch on Field Three. And like a mouse caught in a maze, he lumbered to find the gap in the raised fence separating fans from the field of play. "We're up in ten minutes."

All three home plates of the softball diamonds on one end of the park backed up to and surrounded a bulky concrete structure painted a peeling and flaking blue tint and lined with cracks.. An overbearingly prodigious banner draped the structure's side Vote Charlie Van Wert for Congress. A grill was but a few feet from the structure, and I held second position in line to drop seventy-five cents on a brat and a burger.

"Here's your jersey." Beefy handed me an Oakland A's green-colored t-shirt with a gold silkscreened logo above the left breast that informed all I would be playing for his employer.

Number thirteen had been assigned to me, a man with two years' experience as a reserve infielder on the cellar-dweller of the Yankee Conference. "I still have no glove," I said, dropping three quarters into the concession attendant's hand. She was a weak amateur at both making change and efficiently filling orders. Of course, given the fact that she projected more masculinity than most men, enhanced by a black Harley t-shirt and red bandana, I was not about to suggest she find another line of work.

Beefy munched methodically, like a bull on cud, on an ultra-size wad of tobacco. His blue Ford ball cap barely covered the circumference of his ogre-like noggin. He insisted I don the jersey and get on the field, exaltedly telling me that our opponent, Redding Insurance, had been seeded first in the lower bracket.

"I just need a bite to eat." I had allowed Beefy to convince me the previous day that playing third base for the garage team would not only be enjoyable, but also beneficial to the team's chances of netting a trophy in the tenth annual UAW tournament. Borrowing an archaic but durable set of black leather spikes from Aunt Jenny's attic and a baggy set of unwieldy cotton baseball trousers, striped once in red along the seam and hanging loose like a burlap sack in a two-legged race, I was prepared to offer just enough effort so as not to embarrass myself—fielding groundballs either hit directly at me or on my glove side. Once I entered the first-base dugout, Beefy stuttered through an introduction of my other teammates. Of course, I failed to log any name into the memory bank. I grabbed a seat on the splinter-ridden bench between two coolers. Upon opening the aluminum cooler, decorated with vacation destination stickers, my assumption was validated. The cooler was loaded with beer—and bad beer at that.

"Hey pal, you don't contribute, you don't drink." He had a premature gray and full beard and a bony set of knees wrapped in bandages. The man tended to his antique and corroded first baseman's mitt, tying knots in wayward strings.

I mumbled an apology before gingerly closing the cooler lid.

"All right, we're home. Let's take the field." Beefy's boss tossed me a glove—a Rawling's dark hide that had not been well maintained, with rot marks in the leather. "Hope you field as well as you complain."

My vintage cleats, heavy and cumbersome, sank into the soft dirt infield.

"Nice get-up, College Boy!" In the on-deck circle, the mighty Rick Redding swung not one, but three bats while warming up for his turn at the plate. He represented his dad's business as well as any directionless son could. Apparently, though, Daddy Redding, or at least the agency, had deep pockets because Rick and his teammates were enriched in pristine white uniforms with a royal blue pinstripe from cap to stirrup sock. In blue silkscreen, across the front of each jersey, was a gaudy but scripted "Redding."

My glove opened like a farmhouse cellar door as I cleanly fielded a practice grounder from our beer-guarding first baseman. However, the few years of absence from active play were vividly displayed as I uncorked a rocket ten feet over my intended target. The ball ricocheted with a humiliating and echoing clatter off the metal scoreboard behind the first-base dugout, earning me a thunderously patronizing round of applause from our opponents, particularly from Papa Redding himself, occupying the third-base coaching box.

"Look out, boys, this one here's a wild one," Papa Redding cackled. His uniform either rode an extra cycle in the dryer drum or the extra-large size was unavailable. In the snug outfit, he looked more corpulent than athletic and stout. He hardly noticed, however, and stood like a sculpture of a WWII general, with an overtly wide stance and both hands locked on his hips.

Desperate to slink my head between my shoulder blades, I conducted a quick scan of the dugout used by my naysayers—or rather, opponents.

"When I asked you to get more involved in the job, I didn't imagine this, sport."

"That's why I gave you that glove," Beefy's boss clamored. Apparently, Rick advanced to second when the ball exploded off my forehead and rolled out of play.

Wwith an egregious pain radiating throughout my skull and at least half a dozen gawkers standing over me, I remembered two events before my sleep: Miss Myra's sudden appearance along the third-base side of the fence and the smacking sound of aluminum compressing yarn and cowhide.

Beefy and the cooler-guard helped me to my feet, patting me on the back and urging me to continue. However, I was in no condition to play a couch potato, let alone third base in a game of softball. Grayish blue had encased my vision, and queasiness filled my inner space.

Disappointed in my decision not to continue, my teammates quickly abandoned me. Beefy's boss tore the ragged mitt from my hand, nearly fingers and all. I received yet more ribbing from Papa Redding and his team, including Blue Laces. The only hint of sympathy received was from Miss Myra. She made her way through the gate to lend me assistance in walking a steady line.

"Go home, College Boy!" Rick barked from his hardly earned perch at second base.

"Ah yes, sport, nothing like humiliation to soften the soul."

I could feel the welt on my forehead, tender and enlarging.

A Good Samaritan or some jerk who just felt pity for me delivered a bag of ice.

Myra extended an appreciative "thanks." She pressed the bag against my knot. "I suppose you'll be needing a ride back to town?"

A Tour of Town in an Ambulance of Sorts

Instead of a direct path toward town, though, Miss Myra opted for the scenic route, before convincing me to accompany her to the Epstein home for lunch.

"This is Hollywood." She made a left onto Jackson Street. She pulled the steering wheel to the right, stopping along a curb of shambled concrete. Rifling through her purse, she found a small pillbox.

I begged of her to simply drop me off at the apartment.

Hollywood did, though, remind me of the less-adorable spots of Cleveland. In the infancy of my career, I covered the city for the Metro section. Houses of elongated rectangular shape, twice as long as high; decay; abandoned vehicles; and neglect were all part of my coverage area.

"Here." She insisted I take two aspirin.

We had yet to draw the attention of those lounging on porch swings, due to the fact that Miss Myra's car was not much of an improvement to the street scenery.

Conditions failed to improve as we turned onto Jefferson Street. The tour of the neighborhood also failed to alleviate the pain from the the softball. I remained buried in my seat, slumped as low as possible.

"Folks here were the unfortunate few who didn't get into American Genuine." Miss Myra abused the gears in bringing the car to a stop. "If you can find your way through that bit of irony."

Presidential Avenue led the path out of Hollywood.

"Here is where the lower class of American Genuine call home. These are the lucky ones."

Conditions improved on Washington Avenue, but color remained constant.

"Park separates white from black in South Heaven. People along Washington and Kennedy have roots that go across generations, including veterans of both wars, proud owners of South Heaven football players, and Coach Waddell." She pointed to a white traditional with a detached one-car garage, shaded flagrantly by a monumental oak tree.

Kennedy transitioned from have-not to have as houses grew larger and amenities multiplied. She did not dwell on this neighborhood. She had no reason to. We interrupted a game of two-hand touch football and received several glares of contention from the dozen or so kids adorned in their mock Ohio State jerseys. The street was just wide enough so vehicles parked on either side of it would not disturb the progress of the game.

As street names began to assume those of famous golf courses, houses and lots doubled in size, trees became more magnanimous, expensive vehicles assumed places on elongated driveways rather than the street, and the surreal took control.

"Welcome to Legendary Country Club, sport."

Through the backyards of the homes on Oakmont Drive, I could plainly see a twosome navigating a golf cart along a plush green fairway.

"Totally private, even though the city forked over a large chunk of money to build it." She adjusted the tuner on her car radio to replace static with a Zeppelin tune from In Through the Out Door. "That idiot Mayor Marquis gave total ownership to American Genuine, on the cheap. Of course, he was run out of town."

Murfield Court was a putridly small cul-de-sac, secluded with only three homes penciled in among towering pine and maple trees. Miss Myra pulled onto a winding and cobblestone driveway that fed into the garage of a colonial. She continued with her rant, which, thanks to her soothing tone, placated my pain. "Supposedly, the settlement is to include the course."

With ice pack nearly melted but still pressed against my forehead, I followed Miss Myra in the back entrance of the home, through the marble-tiled kitchen and to a formal dining room where a group of four were strangely pushed onto one side of a twelve-person table.

A glorious spread of fruits, breads, and cereals covered the wide table, along with fresh flowers and clear glass pitchers of red and orange juices.

"Mother." Miss Myra hugged and kissed the senior of three ladies. She assumed the seat next to her mom, instructing me to find an open chair.

All attention had been directed toward me and my wound. A maid, who presented the table with a platter of finger sandwiches, relieved me, with feigned courtesy, of my ice bag. However, that act of grace failed to relieve me of an audience.

"Daddy, this is my new sports writer." Miss Myra reached for the container of cereal. "My father, Reed Epstein."

"Pleasure," I said.

"Bullcrap." He remained seated with legs crossed and the front section of The Columbus Post at half-mast. What hair still surrounded the base of his head had long since lost the color of youth. His face was ashen and dotted with age spots. The hands holding the edges of the paper shook ever so slightly.

"Sarah, our guest could use a little of Daddy's vodka in his orange juice." Miss Myra smiled as she applied heaping amounts of sugar to her cereal flakes.

"For heaven's sake, what happened?" My seat was next to an attractive girl of Myra's age. She felt a desire to tend to my wound with her silky touch.

"Take it easy, Rebecca. He's only on loan to me."

Rebecca had to be a sibling. Her features matched those of Myra, including a small, almost stuffed-animal-like nose. "Unfortunately," she responded to my question regarding twins.

"I'd avoid her, sport. Divorced twice."

Senior Epstein snapped the paper closed to tend to his Eggs Benedict. He had a troubling cough that developed from deep within the chest.

I declined the offer of food, explaining to Mother Epstein that lunch had been served at the ballpark.

Mother Epstein had a proud appearance to her. Although crow's feet were unwelcomed guests at the corners of her eyes, she had handled any effects of age aptly.

Senior Epstein, on the other hand, had a malignancy about him. A brown pipe clung to his shirt pocket. A small flask hugged the starboard side of his place setting, next to his glass of tomato juice. Salt was added to his egg concoction, implying a rude jab at the chef. "People," Epstein coughed harshly. "People of this town know a fraud when it comes to football, Myra." Epstein chased two horse pills with a swill of tomato juice. "If your new reporter here doesn't know what he's talking about, both you and he will be strung up from the nearest yard arm." He cursed Sarah for serving weak coffee, a rant that appeared from nowhere.

"Daddy, you would have everyone believe the paper would be nothing without the sports section."

"I … with all due respect, Mister Epstein, know enough about the game to present an honest effort." Even though I was no fan of my current assignment, I refused to roll over and accept yet another punch to a weakening gut. I swiped two finger sandwiches from the silver platter—roast beef and horseradish.

"Really?" Rebecca reached her hand under my bicep. "Do tell."

I choked down the spicy sauce, which was not one of my favorite condiments, so as not to draw anymore unwanted attention. "Let's just leave it that I know enough about the game." Quickly, my iced tea disappeared, with a small amount dribbling from the left corner of my mouth.

"No, please, do tell." Senior Epstein straightened in his chair, albeit with a struggle.

I tried to shelter behind Miss Myra, but her allegiance appeared to be with Daddy. Before relenting to my audience, I thanked Sarah for the refill. "I, um, played the game for a couple of years in high school."

"Wow," said Rebecca.

Miss Myra laughed. "Never guessed you as any sort of an athlete given that from your half-inning performance today."

Senior Epstein asked my position before revealing that he saw action for the 1938 Ohio Conference Champion Otterbein College Cardinals, as a guard and linebacker.

"Quarterback."

"And now, I'm supposed to trust you'll cover South Heaven football with passion and honesty?"

"Sir," I retorted, vigorously stirring the sugar into my drink, "I've been asked to merely report the game, not give my heart to it."

"And what college did you attend?"

"Oberlin."

He was deliberate and careful in lighting his pipe. The flavor had a delectable berry scent to it. "Good school. I'm quite certain that basic journalism at Oberlin required any reporter to give heart to each and every story?" Rather than polish off his tomato juice with a couple more swigs, he sipped at the tumbler, savoring the vodka. "Football is passion. It's like food and oxygen to this town. It's dreadful, at times."

"You know, Myra dated herself a football player here." Rebecca was impervious to all but her being. Her smile was more seductive than that of her twin.

"Shut up, Becca."

"He wound up playing in the pros, don't ya know?"

"Shut up, Becca!"

Seemingly caught in his own world, Senior Epstein had become indulged in the TV Guide, muttering unpleasant comments about the airing of the upcoming Republican Convention.

Rebecca gleamed at her twin. "He's back in town, I hear."

"Dallas released him," Senior Epstein added.

"Wait a minute," I chimed.

"I hope you choke on your alimony." Miss Myra bared her teeth at her sister.

"Johnny Sarian?"

With one more jab, Rebecca insisted that Miss Myra and the football star were quite an item at one time. She worshipped an elongated cigarette that was housed in a black holder.

"Democrat or Republican?" Senior Epstein glared toward me, as if looking for a particular answer to the question. His bifocals rested at the very edge of his nose. "Got an important election upcoming. I hope the righteous side can count on your vote?"

I heard the man but comprehended nothing. Focus was with Miss Myra. "Wow. A real football star?"

"Only Myra decided it would be best for her to go to Penn…"

"As opposed to chasing any man over the age of forty who has a Mercedes, Becca?"

"Now, Myra." Senior Epstein pulled himself from the chair. "Your sister just has a vice, like us all." He coughed heavily again and then patted her on the shoulder. "Johnny's back in town for a while. I heard his knees are bad…"

CHAPTER NINE
Fundraiser

A Volleyball Match

Despite every door to the gymnasium being open, the breeze from the outdoors was not enough to stifle the heat. The gym was small and past its prime, with noticeable chunks missing from a handful of parquet blocks that constituted the floor. Red and white banners in the shape of pennants dotted the wall in uniform fashion, opposite the Longiness scoreboard. Few, if any, of the banners recognized the female athlete. Instead, most highlighted men's league titles.

Sitting on the top row of bleachers, I was one of a handful of fans in attendance for the Ranger match with Dillard. In fact, the entire fan base could have been counted in less than ten seconds. No matter, though. I was the sports writer, and it was my job to cover South Heaven events. I knew what it meant to set a player for a kill, but beyond that, I cared little to learn more. Besides, there was no other place to hide. My initial story for The Republic on Coach Waddell required a little editing and attention to detail. With every other reporter, including Miss Myra, sucking up oxygen at Epstein's paper, Aunt Jenny's establishment undergoing fumigation, and Rhonda serving tables, I needed a cover to clandestinely finish my introduction piece.

Despite a lack of consent from everyone involved, my story took precedence over all negatives. Coach Waddell and South Heaven were worth an explanation to a Cleveland audience who would appreciate a struggle to achieve in a white world. A more liberal base would perceive Coach Waddell as a genuine martyr who deserved adulation. These brutes who referred to the Sun as their weekly news had not the depth of thought to see anything else but black and white or wins and losses. Coach Waddell would be my story, a feel-good story of accomplishment and overcoming odds.

"You watch much volleyball?"

He startled me such that my pen flew from a shaken hand, striking two bleacher benches before the floor below.

"I say, boy, you watch much volleyball?" Old Man Schmidt lugged up two more steps before sighing and resting on the bench below me, both hands on the ball-top of his cane. He fingered the notepads located at my side. "So, what's goin' on?"

Nonchalantly, I glanced at the scoreboard then to the Dillard player serving. "Well, it's thirteen serving six."

"What game?"

Again, another glance. "Second."

"Actually, it's the third. Daggum bulb up there's been burnt out since last winter." Why did Old Man Schmidt always appear at the most inopportune or precariously embarrassing moments?

I neglected to acknowledge his coy laugh at my expense. Instead, I offered a huff through my nose then dug into a paper bag filled with red licorice.

"They ain't too good," Old Man Schmidt moaned, watching the Dillard team congratulate one another following match point. He insisted South Heaven never had fielded a quality girl's team, with the exception of the '74 cross country team. "The Marian sisters finished third and fourth in the state."

Red licorice was a vice of mine, and I had a mouthful upon asking why Old Man Schmidt was at an event for which he obviously had little passion.

"Well." He leaned back to stretch out his bum leg. "We gotta dinner here shortly."

"Dinner? It's at least ninety degrees in here."

"It's the annual spaghetti dinner."

Both teams collected their gear and belongings, with the home Rangers disappearing into the locker room and the visitors leaving through an outside exit. The commotion quickly subsided, leaving the gym virtually vacant.

"Football Mothers put this shindig on. Also got us an auction in the cafeteria."

"Wait," I stammered, with a thin rope hanging from the corner of my mouth. "You have the auction in the cafeteria and the dinner in the gym?"

"Just the dinner alone makes 'em some seven-eight hundred bucks." He made certain the gym was clear of players and fans before striking the flint of his chrome lighter. "You should stick around." He flashed me his watch. "Starts in an hour or so. Besides, you can help us out."

Helping meant setting up chairs and managing the roll of entry tickets. By the time the last ticket was sold, every table in the gymnasium was filled with the patrons of all-you-can-eat spaghetti. At two dollars and fifty cents per person, the event was clogging the till with revenue. Inquiring of the controlling and unremorseful president of the Football Mothers, Valerie Redding, about the ultimate destination of the profit, I discovered that most of the money supported pregame meals during the regular season, while a tiny percentage was diverted to the cheerleading squad. An hour into the dinner, the only hitch that had developed was a sudden depletion of garlic bread, a lapse in judgment from the supply manager and brow-beaten vice president. However, that fire was extinguished when Cam Brewster, husband to Wendy Brewster of the bakery and patron of the dinner, appeared with a couple dozen loaves and a friend of the family: Johnny Sarian.

Once again, the famed and former Ranger star wowed the faithful. Many a fan stood to applaud as Blue Laces weaved among the cafeteria tables and toward the serving line to grab a plate. He appeared to relish in every ounce of appreciation, with his politician's smile and tip of the Stetson.

Deep into the meal, I had been moved from table set-up duty to ticket seller to bid collector at the auction, a dubious honor and task shared with Big Pete.

The coach was not far removed from his normal daily working attire. Having removed his whistle and cap, Big Pete wore a cleaner white t-shirt, maroon shorts, and a sour attitude.

Items for bid touched the very fabric of life in and the lore of South Heaven, ranging from autographed footballs to an oil change from Jake's. I was amazed at the amount of cash collected for offers. People without hope of employment and whose livelihoods had been stolen by corporate greed forked over lumps of cash for a framed photo of the 1956 unbeaten South Heaven team, an opportunity to be a ball boy at a home game, and, of all things, a binder collection from the anonymous cartoonist, the Pigskin Prognosticator.

With his preteen son two steps behind him, an overtly proud man approached the table I occupied to claim his piece of trivia: a pair of cleats worn by Jim Westerman. He exposed one ten and one five-dollar bill.

"Interesting." I handed the squat man, who was more in need of a monitor for his waistline than a piece of so-called nostalgia, a shoebox without a lid. "Don't think you'll be wearing these, do you?"

"Wear? Man, these here belong to Jim Westerman."

Big Pete examined one of the shoes, ensuring that all the cleats were securely fastened.

"Thanks." The father beamed with pride. His son loafed behind, trading punches with another freckled kid, both oblivious to the proud man with someone else's shoes.

"That guy probably has no job, yet he's dropping fifteen bucks on a used pair of thirty-year-old cleats?"

Big Pete employed three quick shakes to extinguish the light of his match. At an expeditious but probably normal rationing rate, he was depleting his pack of Raleigh's. Tobacco was either a religion for him or a simple means to an end. "What are ya, his preacher?"

I tallied the till: two-hundred and fifty, excluding the base fifty for change. "This is sad." Without a bid made to claim every prize, there were several auction items that appeared to have no destination. The oil change, a cord of firewood, bags of animal feed, and free groceries were but a few items left without bids.

Big Pete dropped his smoke, only half-extinguished, into a Styrofoam cup holding a residual amount of coffee. The helpless ashtray next to the cup was stuffed beyond capacity. As one of his players passed by, Big Pete barked at him to retrieve him another cup of coffee. "Large!"

A few members of the football team did their adolescent best to serve as quasi-waiters, attending to those participating in the auction.

"Whattaya care anyway, 'bout what these people spend their money on?"

The player was quick to return with Big Pete's demand.

"Come 'ere, boy," Big Pete ordered. He handed the kid two packs of sugar and the lid to his cup. "You like football, boy?"

"Yeah, Coach." He did not have much football mass to him.

"Buckeyes your favorite?"

The gawky kid wore a maroon practice jersey with a number eighty-eight peeling off the front of it. He appeared comfortable and not fearful of the coach. "Yeah. I love the Buckeyes, Coach."

"What's your daddy do for a livin'?" Big Pete powered through the steaming hot coffee like a lost soul in the desert with a ravenous desire for water.

His smile abated, and he became a little uneasy, wiping sweat from underneath his ball cap. "Nothin' now, Coach. Not since last year."

"Well, let me ask ya this. If you had a choice between bringin' home money for your family or spendin' the same amount on tickets to a Buckeyes' game..." Big Pete unraveled the wrapper of another pack of Raleigh's. "...what would you do?"

The kid took a few seconds of biting at the corner of his lip before uttering, "I s'pose I'd have to bring money home for my momma. But I don't think I'd get there if my dad found out I turned down Buckeyes tickets."

Big Pete pinched his left eye closed with an exaggerated wink then dismissed the boy with a gruff salutation.

Encroaching on the small line of winning bidders at the foot of our table was a pair of what appeared to be college-aged men adorned in like maroon short-sleeved dress shirts and patriotic multi-colored campaign buttons. "Charlie Van Wert, he's running to be your representative in Congress," one of the young men said, distributing the same metal button to those in line.

With some trepidation, Big Pete extended his hand to meet that of one of the duo, while I met the other with a handshake.

"Charlie Van Wert will bring jobs to South Heaven." Although he carried few if any credentials in physical stature, the young man with the burnt-orange hair did possess a confident, almost combative tone. "He cares about the people of South Heaven."

His partner reminded Big Pete that the candidate would be speaking at the Frontier Week celebration. "Come on out. Listen to what Charlie Van Wert can do for you."

"Where's he at today?" Like the final trump on a hand of pinochle, Big Pete tossed aside the campaign button that read "Van Wert in '80." "Team could use his support today."

"Well ... um..."

"Candidate Van Wert," blurted the confident one, rescuing his partner, "is campaigning elsewhere today but really wishes he could be here."

"Well, you tell Mister Van Wert thanks for the button."

Friday and Another Scrimmage

Fortunately, before leaving civilization, I paid my landlord two months' worth of rent, instead of the typical current-month payment. My first paycheck from Miss Myra was not quite humiliating. There were enough figures on the check from the First Bank of Western Ohio to pay Aunt Jenny, stow a feeble wad of cash in a rolled-up pair of underwear, and patron the lasagna buffet lunch at Frankie's. The maestro of the South Heaven pizza pie made acceptable lasagna, but it was the garlic bread that compensated for the taste of processed ricotta.

Between a salad topped with restaurant-quality Thousand Island and another helping of mouthwatering bread, I apathetically pieced together my weekly sports submission. With the upcoming edition set to contain the annual football introduction, I was being pushed by Miss Myra to produce something—not just anything. Fortunately, I was able to recall, thoroughly enough, the preseason special edition from the Parma Free Press, the same paper that covered my Parma South High Titans.

The table adjacent to mine hosted three maroon practice jerseys. Just a few days before the start of school, two until Labor Day, and several hours before the final scrimmage of the year, the three boys, all of a larger frame, enjoyed the fruits of Frankie's labor free of charge. With the jukebox muted, the trio's conversation was very much evident. The overwhelming theme appeared to be uncertainty, at least for a high school kid. The vocal leader of the group was number fifty-five, a stumpy kid with a razor-close buzzed haircut and a boisterous, probably incorrect or fabricated opinion on every topic of discussion.

I plotted an emphatic period on my last sentence then decided to join the trio at their table. My introduction was welcomed by each kid stealing a glance at one another, as if to ask whether one of them knew me. I eased their queasiness and uncertainty by telling them of my current profession.

The mouthpiece of the group, number fifty-five, suddenly blossomed, and I learned that he was the starting center and a senior.

"What about you two?"

"Aren't ya gonna write all this down?" The mouthpiece searched me for a reporter's notepad.

I reached behind me to retrieve my cherry-flavored Pepsi, all the while convincing the trio that mine was a photographic memory. "So you guys linemen, too?"

"He is." The mouthpiece punched the kid next to him. "Only he don't start."

"What about you?" I asked the third member.

"JV," chimed the mouthpiece. "He's only a sophomore."

Two burnt pie plates contained loose pieces of seasoned bacon and savory sausage, a few chunks of crust, and a plethora of crumbs.

"You covering our scrimmage tonight?" asked the mouthpiece. "You know we don't stand much of a chance against Saint Edward. Big School, ya know? They won eight games last year."

I asked the trio their thoughts on Coach Waddell.

"My dad says he better start winnin' soon or won't be coach no more." Mouthpiece either had not attended any social grace classes or was simply comfortable talking with a sizeable portion of food in his mouth. "I say, if he don't let us throw the ball, we ain't gonna win, and he ain't gonna be coach no more."

"I dunno, Tim," the backup lineman interjected softly, almost apologetically. "Lamont's a good runner."

"Ain't gonna matter none. If Gary ain't passing, we ain't scoring. And if we don't score, we ain't winnin, doofus." He thumped the backup lineman on the meat of his left bicep.

"So you don't think he's a good coach?" I licked the ink end of my pen in an attempt to get five more minutes of usage from the durable disposable.

"Listen, mister," Tim smiled. "I ain't no fool to answer that question." Tim's sudden departure from the table was led by another thunderous jab to the arm of the backup lineman.

I turned just far enough to see him approach another duo of players with the adolescent greeting of faint punches and pro-wrestling-style headlocks.

"Don't worry 'bout him none," chimed the sophomore. "Tim's always in the camp of the winner, if ya know what I mean? Been that way since I known him."

Stirring the ice in my soda, I inquired of the duration of that relationship.

"Cousins. Our mamas are kin."

"You always called South Heaven home?"

"Pretty much. Tim's always been here. Me, my dad got on at AGM with the help from my uncle, Tim's dad."

"What about you?"

After choking down a bite of food, the backup lineman replied, "Whole time." Rubbing his hands together, he dusted them clean of crumbs. "Been stuck here forever."

Tim returned and demanded that his cousin leave with him. Apparently, he wanted to get to school early to prepare for the scrimmage.

"You're not going with them, Stu?" I had heard the kid's name from the salutation from the other two.

With a teenage yawn of apathy, Stu confessed that he had to check in on his mom before reporting to school. As he stood, he removed three bills from a red wallet that was secured by Velcro.

"I got it." I pushed a five and two ones toward him. "It's on me."

He begrudgingly thanked me, as if my generosity would somehow get him into trouble. "Coach Waddell, I like him, ya know. Some think he should leave, though."

"Why?"

With a slap of open hands, Stu greeted the busboy, a kid no more Stu's senior but with awkward basketball-center height. "Heard you saw one of them recruiters?"

"Yeah," the busboy replied, clearing the plates and pie pan from our table. "Thinkin' of joinin' the Army." Randy was the kid's name, and he appeared to be genuinely excited about enlisting. "Gotta get outta this place, man."

"So why do some people want Coach Waddell to leave?" I asked as Randy moved onto his next assignment.

Stu shook his head as he visually followed Randy. "Man, Randy's parents are never gonna let him join up."

CHAPTER TEN
Frontier Week

Labor Day

For every other town in America, life and the ordinary, not the least of which is football, always revolved and was planned around traditions and annual rites of passage. Calendars were chiseled with a set date or time period. Festivals, fairs, and ceremonies represented American heritage and were therefore cherished. Frontier Week, a celebration of South Heaven's eighteenth-century founding, had always been planned for the second stanza of any given August, until, of course, the love of football devoured logic.

During the apparent heyday of Ranger football in the early '60s, it was the idea of one South Heaven councilman, heavily influenced by his older brother, the elementary school principal, to move the festival to the opening week of football. So instead of the town, which was supposedly proud of its heritage, honoring the life of one Jeremiah Harper, a brave frontiersman and revolutionary war hero, it allowed Frontier Week to play second fiddle to the first game of the Rangers' regular season.

The streets of downtown were blistered with generic yet obligatory red, white, and blue flags draped from every light post and fixture. Two large banners, each at separate ends of the main thoroughfare, were hung above the street and welcomed visitors, the naysayers, and the like.

Along with hundreds of the interested that lined the street, I was drowning in perspiration impatiently awaiting the start of the Frontier Parade, which coincidentally served as a Labor Day gala.

Krisp's Periodicals capitalized on the day's heat. His cooler was adjusted slightly to ensure that all bottles of soda pop were satisfyingly cold.

As the sound of emergency vehicle sirens initiated the parade's beginning, I held two sixteen-ounce bottles, next to Willie Tee, on the park bench outside of Krisp's.

The bench appeared to have been the victim of a precision air strike by pigeons or some other larger birds. A generous section of the seat was pestered with grayish-white droppings.

Dogs confined to leashes howled in agony with the passing of eight different ambulances, fire trucks, and police vehicles, each one carrying a different and excruciating pitch of siren.

"No, suh." Willie Tee enjoyed his bottled soda at my expense. "Saint Edward be a team in da playoffs come Novembuh." He hollered above the whaling of the newer-model sparkling red engine of the South Heaven volunteers. Remnants of soda clung to the edges of his pencil-thin moustache.

I counted five members of the volunteers, not including those in the cab, riding in view and waving vigorously at the crowd. Each man had apparently not bothered to read the day's forecast and was in full combat gear, from fire retardant yellow jacket to black hard hat.

Willie Tee continued to clamor about the scrimmage just past as sirens gave way to a monster contingent of United Auto Workers. "We gotta be doin' somethin' 'bout our line."

The union sponsored a float that led several dozen who participated in the parade on foot. In large, white block letters, pressed against the maroon that dominated the lower portion of the square float, UAW 212 told the crowd that they had been proudly serving America for thirty-five years. The slogan "Van Wert in '80" accompanied a placekicker, in pose, booting a ball through the uprights, with a scoreboard game clock striking zero.

"Ain't got much of a quarterback either," added Willie Tee's friend, who also enjoyed a soda pop at my expense. "Best we got gonna be Dickies."

Lamont Dickies was indeed impressive against St. Edward over the weekend. A power type of runner, Dickies ran effectively against a much larger JohnniesJohnny's team. The last scrimmage of the season lacked any impressionable indicators, however, for the upcoming ten games. In only three quarters of regulation, the Rangers scored once, on a long run by Dickies, but surrendered four scores to the St. Ed. Johnny's. It was a mere four days from the start of the regular season, and all signs were pointing towards another lackluster one for Coach Waddell and Big Pete.

"Ya gotta believe," responded Willie Tee to my comments regarding the impending disappointing season.

Once the throng of unemployed auto workers meandered past us, we were entertained by the Football Mothers Association and the slogan "Take It in '80." Accompanying a few mothers who were walking and tossing miniature footballs into the crowd was a float of a Ranger player standing on a platform holding a trophy.

I interrupted Willie Tee's expressive concern about South Heaven's lack of a pass defense to ask the meaning behind the Football Mothers' slogan.

"What?" he demanded, appearing incensed that I disturbed him. "Zugellder Trophy."

"The what?" Dead center in the chest, I was struck by a small flying object. The soft plastic football was nearly all harmless cushion, though. It did, however, appear to be taunting me as it fell into my lap. Stenciled on the red ball was a "Go Rangers" logo with a picture of a Revolutionary soldier.

"League championship trophy." Willie Tee admired my new possession, like a begging dog awaiting his master's attention.

"Here."

Willie Tee cupped it in his hands as if it were an open book of psalms.

"What?" exclaimed Willie Tee's friend. "He don't deserve that. He just let it collect dust in the rest of that good-for-nuthin' collection he's got."

"Shut up, Reggie."

"Ya getta free pizza at Frankie's widdat," Reggie insisted.

Willie Tee rebuffed my attempts to reclaim my former prize.

"I dun gotta place for this at home. Got me one of these for all parades."

The festival's blue-ribbon winner of floats paraded by, after the color guard and contingent from the U.S. Marine Corps League. The prize-winning float was a recollection of South Heaven's past—football past, that is. Dressed in carnations, maroon and white, were football figures in representative uniforms from three different eras. At the feet of each player was a banner displaying a year for every championship in a given era. A combined total of sixteen championships were represented by the three flowered figures. The South Heaven Jaycees claimed ownership.

"Good-size band."

The large group presented pageantry well, with the band in full and complete regalia and uniform, despite near-record warm temperatures. In appropriate formation, two majorettes were in the lead, and a score of girls waving generic flags assumed the rear. With a hiccup in the procession, the sixty-plus-member band halted in front of us and then broke into a solid and rhythmic version of "Hang On Sloopy."

"Best band in da area." Willie Tee nodded.

Against better judgment, I gave Reggie three quarters and sent him on a mission into Krisp's for three more sodas. Normally employing a sluggish demeanor, Reggie wasted no energy in disappearing, as if he had just been given the key to a treasure map.

"Will he be back?" I asked Willie Tee as the high school student council float drove by us.

Willie Tee flipped a toothpick, end to end, with his tongue, before retrieving it to use as a pointer. "Lookie there, dat ain't no float."

The council float was nothing more than a white Cadillac decorated in maroon streamers, with a panel board on the side recognizing the two passengers in the rear bench seat: Heidi Fossitt, student council president, and Seth Goldman, vice president.

A glistening green John Deere pulled a flatbed trailer of Cub Scouts, who were actually representing the original mission of the festival.

"They all outta red pop." Reggie returned with much less hurry to him. The vast majority of his root beer had vanished. "Gotya orange."

The scouts were decked out in frontiersmen and Revolutionary War attire. With their Scout leaders standing, gazing at the horizon with eye pieces, the Scouts were perched on the perimeter of the trailer. Each young boy carried a musket. Sadly, though, a placard hung on the outside of the trailer wishing the Rangers luck against Frederick.

My ears burned with a hit from the warm soda pop, teasing an empty stomach. "So, Willie Tee, whattaya think of Coach Waddell?"

"Ain't no matter what I think."

"You seem to be knowledgeable about South Heaven."

A drum and flute corps passed by us.

It appeared as if Willie Tee could hardly control the slight but obvious twitch on the left side of his face. The imperfection transgression only added to his feebleness. "I knows everything dere is 'bout dis here game of football."

After the varsity and reserve cheerleaders drove by on a float christened in white streamers and carnations, throwing candy and waving pompons, Coach Waddell and Big Pete were escorted in the bed of a black '49 Ford pickup. Both of them stood in the bed, leaning against the cab and casting an occasional and obviously uncomfortable nonchalant wave.

Picking at the caramel between his teeth, Reggie shook his head then uttered, "Dat man shoulda never come back here. Ain't nuthin' here."

My soda had gone beyond acceptable. I opted to drain the remainder of my warm drink into the street.

"Whatcha doin'?" Reggie lurched forward to save what he could from the soda bottle. "This here's good drink."

Two floats passed one after the other, and each represented a different church—one St. Margaret and the other First Baptist.

"Round here, you be white, you Catholic. Colored, you Baptist. Nothin' more, nothin' less. Everybody goes to church 'round here." With a proper moustache, one tucked neatly before the corners of the mouth, Reggie had an astute look to him. Whether it was a genuine outlook on life or simply that he enjoyed the moment, Reggie wore a simple grin, leaning his head on the bench's backrest. "Not me, though," Reggie said with a laugh. "Just coffee and football speak every Sunday."

Following the set of six mounted horsemen from the local 4-H club, Mayor Montgomery and his wife drove by in a 1956 AGM Classic; cherry-red glaze glistened like factory-new.

In a throng of ladies dressed in eighteenth-century attire, I recognized two familiar faces, one of which approached us with an embarrassing grin.

"Miss Myra, lookin' good," said Reggie.

Miss Myra was in garb that had to be extremely uncomfortable. The heavy skirt and bonnet she wore engendered a face doused in sweat and not conducive to accepting sarcasm. "Had I known, sport, that you enjoyed parades…"

"I know. You would've ridden in the mayor's car?"

The flock, although at a laggard pace, was distancing themselves from an agitated Miss Myra. Approaching their six position was the grand finale of the Frontier Day Parade: the senior Ranger football players.

"I suppose that's my cue," she said, responding to calls from the flock. "After all, the star of the show is here."

"Stay cool," I called as the flatbed hauling the team concluded the parade.

"Ya know, Reggie, he be right." Willie Tee was often abrasive in his delivery. "Waddell should've never come back here." He began to clap intently at the appearance of the Ranger players.

Meet-the-Team Night

Progression and yet digression capitalized the celebratory week of the Frontier Festival. With the presence of visiting historians and professors from state universities, speeches and lectures were the major highlights of honoring the past. Late Tuesday afternoon, I happened upon one presented by the Daughters of the American Revolution in the VFW hall. Given by a Doctor Donovan from the local satellite branch of Ohio State University, the lecture, possessing the advertised title of "General St. Clair and the Indian Wars," attempted to draw upon the patriotism of the townspeople. Patriotism, however, was not enough to attract an audience. Attendance was shameful at best, with the only patrons being a handful of veterans. It seemed heavy attendance was more prominent at the Van Wert rally. The South Heaven contingent had packed the union hall to hear the candidate assure them that prosperity would return to the town.

Despite daily visits to Jake's, I had yet to see my car leave the garage bay. I was certain it was spite for my performance on the softball field. Surely, they had to have located the lone part needed to get my car back on the road. Spite prevented those employed by Jake's from applying a wrench to my wreck. That spite also prevented me from leaving and forced me into a third-row seat at Gottmann Field on "Meet-the-Team Night."

It was, after all, Frederick week. Every first game for each of the past eighteen seasons, South Heaven contested the Frederick Pirates for the right to claim some sort of Lion's Club Trophy. According to Willie Tee, Frederick was returning 15 starters from a team that won eight of ten the previous year. The majority of those in attendance shared Willie Tee's thoughts—excited about a new season but reticent to go up against Frederick.

"I can't wait for the season," Billy Hainesworth's mother said. She was plain, the antithesis of the other ladies in the crowd of fans and without a hint of enhancements through cosmetics or Ranger mascot colors. Yet Mrs. Hainesworth was genuinely excited about potential and the chance to see her senior son play. "Frederick's real good, though. Their quarterback already has a scholarship."

Meet-the-Team Night appeared to be some sort of eccentric gala-like event for the people of South Heaven. But it contained neither the formality of dress and pomp and circumstance nor the impromptu energy of a pep rally. The stands were congested with people who just felt the need to be seen. It was bizarre. Yet self-indulgence acquiesced to the activity on the field when, in silent cadence, the marching band they called the "Pride of South Heaven" glided onto the turf in full attire. All chatter in the stands gradually dissipated as the lead squads of the band reached the thirty-yard line. My focus and respect were on and paid to the kids at center stage, until Old Man Schmidt spoke.

"Hey, boy! Up here!"

I glanced about me to find the voice. Fortunately, by the time I turned around to look up, "Across the Field" piped from the horns, and the crowd lurched to its feet to cheer as the band marched in formation toward the midfield.

From his perch in the press box, Old Man Schmidt was waving at me. The fight song and alma mater masked my escape from the crowd.

"Come in here, boy."

Although the stands were seemingly filled to capacity, Old Man Schmidt made room on the bench seat. It was a small convention of veterans, and not one of the dozen men in the press box had a birth date after the Harding inauguration. Each man, cloaked in white, smoked some form of tobacco, such that the entire box was one large gray cloud.

"Felluhs, this here's our sports writer."

"Isaac Wessell." The eldest-looking man of the bunch stood. Wessell possessed a crisp and clear voice, like that of a bygone radio commercial announcer. His full moustache was the color of undisturbed snow. "Lucas, speaking of newspapers, where's the Prognosticator been?"

A larger man, Lucas tested the durability and strength of the wood bench, prompting the question of exactly how he made it up the stairs. "Said we'd beat Union by two touchdowns."

"Twenty-eight to eight, they beat us. Worse prediction he could've made." Wessell held up the sports section from an older copy of the Sun, pointing to a cartoon below the headshot photos of the Ranger senior players.

Under the title of "Pigskin Prognosticator," a cartoon Ranger was trampling a cartoon General, running over the defender to score a touchdown. Below the cartoon, in bold print, the author suggested a South Heaven victory by at least three touchdowns.

"I didn't notice a prediction from you, boy."

With "The Stars and Stripes Forever" filling the stadium, the band split and marched into a huge H-formation that covered the entire field between the 30-yard lines. From the locker room tunnel, just outside the north end zone, the South Heaven Rangers gathered in a mob formation. In their white road jerseys with maroon numbers, the Rangers began to holler before storming the field through the "H."

A cheering crowd jumped, welcoming their Rangers.

I squeezed into the seat next to Old Man Schmidt. "So what is this? A pinochle tournament?"

Old Man Schmidt adjusted his seated position to retrieve his deep-brown leather wallet, one that had long since conformed to his backside. From beneath a folded two-dollar bill, he pulled out a laminated card that resembled some sort of license or registration. He passed it to me like a proud grandfather displaying a photo of the grandkids. "We all belong to the Foxxman Society."

Sure enough, the card confirmed that he was an honorary member of the Foxxman Society, class of 1978.

"And this card gets you in here without a cover charge?"

"I believe Wally's a member from '67," he replied as a tall man with diesel-exhaust black hair and an impressive Fu Manchu stepped to the microphone stand that was secured to the home sideline.

The tall man welcomed all to Meet-the-Team Night for the 1980 season. He expressed an overbearing and unyielding grin, neat blue jeans, and the obligatory maroon coaching shirt.

"That there's Teddy Foxx," Old Man Schmidt said of the tall man, who had welcomed Coach Waddell to the microphone "Our athletic director, the greatest round ball player cager to ever play here, and the nephew of Coach Curly Foxx."

"As in Foxxman?"

With a plethora of disturbances and miscues in his undisciplined repertoire, it was very much evident that Coach Waddell either lacked basic skills or required confidence. He fidgeted and was inordinately uncomfortable behind the microphone, stammering through even the most basic and certain words.

"Curly Foxx died on Peleliu ... right on the beach." Old Man Schmidt puffed on his smoke. "He coached only nine years, before the war."

Meanwhile, through the abridged and unsophisticated speech of Coach Waddell, we learned of his staff beyond Big Pete. Coach Ramsey, the offensive coordinator, was a minute and "unfootball-like" man, whose resume pedigree included stints as receivers and backs coach with Pederson High School, another Podunk town in Western Ohio.

Not including Ramsey and Big Pete, Coach Waddell had a staff of four. Each had their own credentials, more subtle than overtly impressive.

"This here club honors Coach Foxx and what he stands for The Old Man gestured. Without any hint of a scripted transition, Coach Waddell, no doubt having his fill of the public stage, suddenly relented control of the microphone to the AD. Foxx definitely had little to no experience at clearing dead air, despite that omnipresent smile.

"So are there monthly dues?" I asked flippantly as Foxx began to introduce the junior varsity team.

"More to the point of lifetime dues, boy."

The applause for each JV player gradually dissipated as Foxx worked his way through the roster, missing the pronunciation of a few consonants.

"Impressive crowd for a roll call."

Foxx's last introduction—Jimmy Winfield—allowed him to cue the band for a crescendo to the varsity squad.

"People been waitin' since November," Isaac said.

With peculiar admiration, I returned the Foxxman Society card to Schmidt and then, more so out of obligation, inquired the group's opinion of the upcoming opponent.

Before introducing Bobby Wiggins, starting defensive end and number forty-one in the program, Foxx, with an apparent irritation in the throat, excused himself to rehydrate with an ephemeral shot from a squirt bottle.

"Playin' Frederick…" Lucas's double chin vibrated with each shake of his head. He was showered with a few head nods and hallelujahs from the flock. "Gotta get The Rifle back."

The crowd stood and cheered with the playing of the fight song, which followed the introduction of Lamont Dickies and Gary Redding. My recent "Football Special" edition included a bio on Redding, who returned as quarterback from the '79 team. According to Coach Waddell, Redding would be capable of handling the offense. I, of course, used poetic license and opted to replace "capable" with exceptional. Dickies and Redding stood in front of the microphone, both as co-captains and the mouthpieces for the 1980 team. Probably several inches taller , Redding owned the height advantage. Although, to give some credit to Dickies, the quarterback was well above average size.

"Rifle's been in their trophy case for too long," Lucas huffed.

"Waddell's yet to win The Rifle." Isaac was resolute.

With the vocabulary of a C student, Redding had public speaking skills that rivaled those of his coach. Nonetheless, his juvenile enthusiasm was energizing the fan base.

"I can only offer a guess at this … rifle?"

Old Man Schmidt replied, "Lion's Club owns The Rifle. A vet over in Frederick offered up to his brother-in-law here in South Heaven his M1 if the Rangers beat the Pirates."

Redding challenged every fan to make the trip to Frederick to support the Rangers, then relinquished the stage to Coach Waddell.

Through puffs from and chomps on his cigar, Old Man Schmidt proudly told me the Rangers won the first "Rifle Game," upsetting the heavily favored Pirates by two touchdowns. "But Isaac's right. Coach Waddell ain't won it since he's been back here. Folks 'round here don't take too kindly to that fact."

A few minutes of absence from the microphone failed to boost Coach Waddell's confidence. He was eloquent enough to offer an appreciation to the fans and a guarantee that the upcoming season would be different than that of years past.

"Lord, I hope so," retorted Isaac. "I sure hope so."

Game Day Minus One

Tucked behind the editor's desk, with a box of opened donuts beside her, Miss Myra held a coffee mug in one hand and a thesaurus in the other. Without a clue of my presence, she flipped through pages toward the aft of the soft-bound book.

"My grandpa used one of those for the daily crossword."

Miss Myra didn't flinch, marking a page in the thesaurus then scribbling a few lines with a mechanical pencil. "Knock, knock. You know, come in?"

Three empty cans of soda dotted a cluttered desk.

"I heard from a little birdie that AGM was about to settle with the city?" I helped myself to the chair next to the desk. Of course, I had to clean the seat of files and loose papers.

"Is that your typical resource, a little birdie?" Miss Myra apparently had rejected the thought of professional attire for the day, cloaked donned in a gray Penn University t-shirt and blue jeans ratted with holes. "You are my sports reporter, not the beat reporter. Besides, you should be out capturing the excitement of the new season."

"Ah yes, football. How about you just humor me on this settlement?"

Rolling her eyes, Miss Myra labored to answer the coal-black rotary-dial phone on the third ring. Her greeting was transient and quickly lapsed into a verbal confrontation with a man by the name of Al. She apparently was ally to the dissenting side, with most of her comments relating to the words "no, never, and absolutely not.'

With her occupied, I browsed the plaques and photos clinging to the cement walls of her office. Bunkered between two Freeman Awards for best stories of 1976 and 1977 was a Master's degree in journalism from Temple University. The printed sheepskin was tucked discreetly in a bruised and demeaning gold-plated photo frame. In a confused arrangement, photos randomly spotted the walls. Above the degree hung a picture of Miss Myra shaking hands in a staged operation with the long-time publicity junkie and senator from the Keystone State, Wallace Burroughs. "I'm sorry, sport. Am I paying you to explore my past?"

"Is that what you call those checks I get?"

Another Kodak moment featured Miss Myra receiving an award from the governor of Pennsylvania, Harold Imes.

"I can always pay you nothing."

"I'll just take a little info on this settlement I keep hearing about." With the pad of a forefinger, I peeled the dust from the horizontal edges of the black frame that held the Imes picture. "When was the last time you cleaned in here?"

"What month is it?"

A tenuous stack of loose-leaf type sheets could not hold the thesaurus and collapsed to the floor with a simple crash. Miss Myra, stepping over the strewn mess, was oblivious to the collapse. She uncovered a pencil sharpener that was mounted on top of a file cabinet.

The phone ring was disturbing to the ear, with a mechanically sickening whimper.

Fortunately, Miss Myra relieved me, answering the call within two rings. "I'm gonna need to take this, sport." She waved at me to vacate the office.

"The settlement?"

She tossed me a legal pad of paper canvassed with handwritten notes on the front page. It appeared as if Miss Myra was some sort of a doodler. The sheet was peppered with various figures and shapes, from flower petals to stars. Fortunately for my lack of taste in elementary art, there were also two dollar amounts circled several times: one million and five million.

CHAPTER ELEVEN
The Rifle Game

Caravan Time

Miss Myra was positioned in the rear of the pack of cars forming a caravan. All vehicular traffic fell in line behind three school buses filled with students, cheerleaders, and the entire contingent of the band.

"There must be twenty-five cars here." I was fanning my chest with the excess of my shirt. "You sure we won't clog up the entire county road system."

With grace and yet aptitude, Miss Myra dug a potato chip scrap from the crevices at the rear of her mouth. "It's usually forty to fifty cars in the caravan."

My small bottle of soda pop did not hold its temperature well in the heat of the evening. My first drink was tepid, the consistency of the seasonal September evening South Heaven was experiencing. Two gulps into the bottle and I could no longer stomach the warm liquid. Excusing myself and convincing Miss Myra we would not be late for the caravan departure, I darted for the gym entrance of the school. A juice machine held a position just inside the door. Without fortune, I yanked on the lead contraption of the first set of double doors. With horns honking, I pulled on the second set of doors. "Holy…"

"Whattaya doin'?" Big Pete had been pushing on the door at the same time I was pulling.

Around the tall man, I caught a glimpse of the neon glowing from the drink machine. "Didn't the team bus leave an hour ago?"

In a complete travesty of my initial perception of Big Pete, an hour and forty minutes from game time found the man lacking any resemblance of composure. His coaching uniform shirt was doused in sweat or some sort of liquid, in the shape of a bib.

I asked the large man if he were feeling well but didn't wait for a response, quickly disappearing inside to inject the machine with a quarter and dime. Within a minute, I was back outside but had lost Big Pete.

A quick scan netted nothing of the coach. Then I heard Miss Myra let loose an epithet, denigrating my Cleveland heritage.

The caravan must have been impressive to the casual and innocent observer as we rolled into the town of Frederick. Casual observer aside, however, the welcoming committee was unimpressed. Dozens lined the sidewalks of the main drag, flashing middle fingers and holding poster boards with various derogatory terms for a Ranger.

Unfortunately, Miss Myra opted to display her juvenile side and apparent disdain for the citizenry of Frederick, rolling down her window to trade insults. "Yeah? You too, buddy!"

Quickly, I adjusted myself in the seat to see behind me. "You … that was a kid you cursed at."

Dressed in all black and orange from head to toe, the elementary-aged kid jumped up and down, screaming obscenities.

"These hypocrites from Frederick. They pretend to live this life of aloofness. I mean, look around you."

County Road Twenty-Two morphed into High Street upon entering the town limits. In drastic contrast to South Heaven, Frederick was pristine. Victorian houses neighbored one another, each structure with a distinctive and radiant Caribbean color. Yards were manicured and bracketed by white picket fences. Oak trees were healthy, and shops were all occupied with tenants.

"Frederick's home to Cagel's Dairy and Summit Bicycles. They're always bragging about how clean their factories are."

Streamers and throngs of pedestrians indicated our passage to the school and the taut parking lot of Duvall Field. A single trip around the perimeter of the choked lot netted the buses a spot to hitch but did not expose the caravan to any parking possibilities.

Despite my protest, Miss Myra was insistent I exit the car while she strained to find a parking spot somewhere in the "craphole of a town." "And take your trash with you," she snapped, tossing the empty juice can through the window.

Pirates dominated the outskirts of Duvall Field. The traditional facsimile of a buccaneer was painted on the largest of structures: ticket booths, concession stands, and scoreboards. Frederick cheerleaders provided each and every child with a cheap pirate cap at the gate entrances. Some of the toddler swashbucklers also carried their own plastic sword.

"You for Frederick?" He was at least my age, accompanied by a television blonde who forced many a man passing by her to step over their tongues. With an impressive set of shoulders, hidden by the thick but single straps of a red tank top, he stood beside me in the line designated for hot dogs or hamburgers only.

The aroma from the grill enthralled the senses.

"I'm with the paper."

"Lima Sentinel?"

"Please."

Miss Myra, with all her disgust for Frederick faithful spewing, caught me just one spot shy of the counter.

"Then you're from South Heaven," my neighbor insisted.

"That's right!" Miss Myra stammered.

The crowd began separating from Miss Myra and me, as if we showed the effects of a plague.

"This concession stand's for Frederick fans," the blonde quipped. "There's a trailer on the other side of the field for South Heaven people."

"What difference…"

Miss Myra displayed her subtle and unexpected strength, yanking me from the line.

We heard a tame murmur of expletives from the Frederick faithful, following the degrading finger-arrows that directed us toward the visitor's section.

Duvall Field was the quintessential amateur stadium. The only concrete in existence held the flagpole in position. Bleachers and the press box were constructed of metal and wood. Although possessing a digital output, the scoreboard was primitive, with only a time, quarter, and score data entry.

A plush field where every fifth yard line was cut razor-thin and a white chalk line from a steady drunk's hand gave Duvall a sense of pride. Enough seating capacity to house two or three complete Catholic families gave Duvall a sense of charm. A government marker placed at the border of the cinder track and grass turf, a dozen yards behind one goalpost, dedicated the site as the former front gate to Fort Frederick and gave Duvall a sense of history. And the wafting stench of rotting fish gave Duvall a sense of the reason that Miss Myra despised all that was Frederick.

"What's that stench?"

Miss Myra pointed to the visitors' bleachers. "There's a creek back there."

We stopped at the trailer, a flea market contraption dressed in Pirate black and serving a limited menu.

"You aren't planning on stayin' for this entire game, are you?"

"It's only bad when there's no wind." She covered her nose and mouth.

"So, second quarter?" I dropped two dimes and a nickel into the open palm of a dark and hairy fellow who promptly handed me a dog wrapped in foil. "I was thinking maybe you could drop me off at the nearest bus station."

"Joining the Army, sport?'

"Probably be less painful than this."

"Aww." She grabbed my cheeks.

"Listen, I've played along. Tonight's it, though. Car or not, I've decided I'm heading home."

She walked away from me as if I were a toddler throwing a fit in the store aisle.

Perturbed, I chucked the wadded ball of foil into an open-top garbage barrel. "Wait!"

She fell into conversation with an older couple—he in his Ranger t-shirt and she carrying a cowbell.

"Hey!" I stepped between the couple and Miss Myra, then turned my head to ask forgiveness from the duo. "You promised me the story if I stayed. To this point, however, there appears to be not even a story, let alone the story. No matter, though. I submitted the piece I was sent here to write. You know the one I get paid for? My assignment is over."

"You wanna leave? Go ahead. Leave. But I'm staying for the entire game." She gloated before disappearing into the visiting crowd.

Two kids, smeared chocolate encasing the lower half of their faces, stood and stared, as if I were an amusing cartoon.

"I'll find my own way home!"

They had neither fear of nor any sympathy for me. Methodically, they moved from soda to candy then back to soda.

"I mean it! It's time to get my life back. She used me, you know? I am not a sports reporter, for crying out loud."

The smaller of the juvenile duo offered me, without a vocal utterance, a chunk of his chocolate bar, which had melted molted to the aluminum packaging.

Before I could offer any of my gratitude, the boys' guardian slipped in and whisked the two away. Instead of melted chocolate, I received a menacing glare from her.

The Pirates, wearing black tops, had vacated the field just in time for the visiting Rangers in all white. Through the glow of a falling sun, I read the winding game clock at twenty-nine minutes and a dozen seconds. There would be no consequences if I simply left town. So I would miss out on a few goodbyes. My car could always be retrieved later, or left for services rendered. My ambivalent editor was surely not about to chastise me for leaving the good people of South Heaven. I had nothing to lose but another night and day in this Corn Country Hades.

"Boy, thought I told ya the press box's where ya belong." Old Man Schmidt hobbled with the cane as a companion, the cigar as a friend, and an irascible tongue as a trusted confidant. His attention shifted sporadically from the American flag ensign snagged on its cord to the appearance of Big Pete from the general public entrance. "Whatya make of that? Sure hope he ain't vital to the pregame plannin'! Ya know that ol' boy coached down at Arkansas?"

"Big Pete?"

"Fired for strikin' a player in practice, don't ya know?" Again, as if it were a neurotic obligation, he offered me a smoke. "Heard you're lookin' for a quick ride to Lima."

I snapped my head toward the visitors' bleachers, searching for Miss Myra.

"Why don't ya just join me? I'm thinkin' we're in for a good one tonight."

"I don't care if this turns out to be the greatest game mankind has ever seen. I've seen my last South Heaven game, restaurant, pizza joint, and anything else that supports the Rangers."

"Ain't no one leaves a Ranger game early, so ya might as well pull up a chair next to Wally and me in Schmidt's Summit."

"Not tonight," I replied, making my way through the standing-room-only crowd in search of Miss Myra.

The Frederick faithful erupted into a crescendo as the Pirate band marched into position with the beat of their version of "On, Wisconsin!" Both teams had raucously gathered at opposite goalposts.

Without an eye on Miss Myra or an ally anywhere to be found, I found myself alone, once again, and cursed my existence, then reluctantly treaded in Old Man Schmidt's trail toward the press box and "Schmidt's Summit."

Amid a mad rush of Frederick students scurrying onto the field to form a temporary and crooked tunnel for the Pirates' entrance, Coach Waddell burst onto the midfield, leading the white-clad Rangers. The South Heaven faithful, packing the meager bleachers and hugging every inch of the fence surrounding the sidelines, exploded into a roar as their team hit midfield and wheeled left. The Rangers fell into a heap, jumping on one another as if attempting to do bodily harm to the unlucky souls at the center of the pile.

Not to be upstaged, the black shirts of Frederick rushed through the goalpost and into the tunnel that stretched nearly fifty yards.

Entering the first tier of the "Pirate Wheelhouse," the quixotic label attached to the press box, I was immediately accosted by one of the ten men jammed into the wooden coffin.

Ill-bred and laconic, the man, dressed in Pirate black with gorilla shoulders, demanded to know my identity.

"Um, I'm here to meet someone."

With the exception of the two men in shirts and ties yapping into headsets and microphones, inhospitable eyes were all over me.

"I'm looking for Old Man ... I mean Schmidt. Ira Schmidt. I glanced toward the field to see the captains of both teams meeting at the face of the buccaneer painted on the midfield grass.

With a thick and stumpy hand at the small of my back, the man in black forced me toward the door. "If you ain't from Frederick, you don't belong here." He slammed the door behind me.

Aghast and stupefied, I stood at the landing then grabbed the handle, but the man in black had locked the entrance. Three months prior, I was being graciously admitted into the offices of the Cleveland mayor, state senators, and the verandas of the wealthy of northeast Ohio. Now, I was being removed from the press box of Duvall Field in the obscurity of Frederick, Ohio.

"Hey, buddy."

I looked around but failed to locate the voice.

"Up here!"

I didn't recognize the face calling me from directly above. The man the face belonged to pointed toward a ladder affixed to the aft end of the press box.

The soccer-style kicker for South Heaven grounded his kick a mere thirty yards down the field. If it was a strategy, the grounded kick worked, and the Pirate receiver returned the ball only to the 35-yard line.

To navigate the ladder, I had to push two heavy black cables out of my way. With my foot on the sixth rung, I got a visual of Schmidt's Summit.

In two simple folding chairs, without a desk to offer any support, Old Man Schmidt and his crony were propped up, wearing headsets with microphones and holding binoculars. Old Man Schmidt, in mid-sentence, pointed toward a folded chair resting on the wood-structure deck.

"What's all this?" I hesitantly inquired, uncrating the metal seat.

A fumble by the Pirate quarterback and subsequent Ranger lineman recovery allowed Old Man Schmidt to remove his headset.

"WSHV." Old Man Schmidt directed his broadcast partner to assume control then handed me a set of binoculars. "Here ... sport."

"What?"

"Players. Numbers? Should've been up here for the coin toss."

Through the lenses, I caught the Ranger tailback, Lamont Dickies, tear off left tackle for six yards. He possessed a quick first step.

"Daggone captains for Frederick gave our boys black roses."

"You saw that number on the tackle, right?" The crony was a little too demanding.

My head was spinning, as if I were caught in a freakish daydreaming haze.

"Looks like Berkman on the tackle," he chirped into the microphone. "Run good for a first down for South Heaven." He vigorously relieved me of the distance spectacles, choosing to complete the task himself and wasting little energy in expressing dissatisfaction with my lack of ability.

For the past month, I was oblivious to any indications that South Heaven possessed a radio station and expressed my lack of knowledge to Old Man Schmidt.

"Since 1960." There was a sense of prostration in his proud statement.

Behind the strong interior line-rushing of Lamont Dickies, the Rangers churned up the turf, moving methodically to the Pirate thirty-two. Little noise was engendered from the Pirate faithful. With the exception of an occasional defensive chant, Frederick remained sitting on their hands. Another quick hitter off left guard by fullback Ricky Green earned not only South Heaven a first down, but also a berating of class-structure epithets from a Frederick man in the first few rows of the stands.

Old Man Schmidt was wallowing in the displeasure and ire of the Frederick crowd. "Yessuh. Wally Utley here joined me in '65."

"How did the two of you get up that ladder?" I asked after Dickies tore off another seven to push the ball inside the Pirate ten-yard line.

Old Man Schmidt was skittish and insisted that Frederick could not stop Dickies or the Ranger offense. "Just up to the defense now."

I could not bring myself to root for anything South Heaven. I found myself rooting against Lamont Dickies, and my pettiness was rewarded, when in a designed play, the much maligned but senior leader of the Rangers, Gary Redding, faked a give to Dickies then rolled opposite to pass.

Old Man Schmidt's moan of disapproval was overwhelming but pleasing to my spiteful ears.

Failing to recognize his tight end drag open at the back of the end zone, Redding panicked and threw underneath to his flanker.

"Shelley intercepted Redding's pass!" Wally cried into the microphone. Hardly a man of distinction or scholar, Wally was marked by unsightly and anecdotal scars, both red and pale in color, pestering his complexion. One of these obvious blemishes was the length of a knuckle and stretched diagonally from eyelash to scalp. Given that hardened exterior, however, Wally had all the qualities of a young man, many years younger than his radio partner , suggesting that Old Man Schmidt was off several years in recalling the date of the beginning of their partnership.

Old Man Schmidt beat his cane twice on the wood surface. "That kid's worse than his daddy or brother ever was!" He spoke furiously over the thunder of cowbells and horns littering the air on the Frederick side.

"Had Chris Durning in the back of the end zone. He needs to quit dancin' and just throw the ball!" Wally secured his headset and, without missing a stride, fell back into the beat of the broadcast.

I felt a little vindication.

With the interception, momentum dramatically shifted leeward toward the buccaneer brigade. On the initial play following the turnover, Frederick employed a gut-wrenching double-reverse, netting them fifty-two yards. A shoestring tackle by the Ranger safety, Eddie Marshall, saved a certain six points. Two more plays, a pass and one run, energized the Frederick faithful into a mere frenzy as the ball was advanced inside the South Heaven twenty.

"By the way, how far have you ever taken that Caddy of yours? Say Lima, maybe?"

Old Man Schmidt tersely shook his head, encouraging the defensive line to get penetration. "That veer option'll kill us if we can't rush up the field."

With the first quarter clock wound down to a ten-second mark, following a run out of bounds, Frederick came to the line of scrimmage with a fullhouse backfield and a split end extended to quarterback Dale Ritchie's left.

As Ritchie studied the defense and barked cadence, Old Man Schmidt uttered, "Boy, I'll drive ya all the way to Cleveland if we getta stop right here."

Ritchie's fake to the fullback on a dive off the right side suckered in all three of South Heaven's linebackers, opening a passing lane. He spun inside, then threw a dart to his split end on a perfectly run slant route.

The Pirate band erupted in fight song as number eighty-one crossed the goal line with the Ranger cornerback, Luke Post, liberally draped over his shoulders like syrup on a thick stack of pancakes.

A smile complemented a small iota of satisfaction, despite a loss of promise from Old Man Schmidt.

The joyous gathering in the end zone brought two more cane raps and an end to the first quarter, but not before luck was drizzled upon the South Heaven faithful. Ritchie's "wounded duck" fell behind its intended target, and the two-point conversion failed.

A layman would have been convinced that another American war was doomed to begin, with a study of the sodden fear on the faces of both Old Man Schmidt and Wally. As the kicker for Frederick measured his steps behind the tee, Wally repeated three times that the Rangers were in serious jeopardy of losing control of the game.

"You're only down by one score." There was conjecture of cheap wisdom in my comment.

"Don't remind me." Wally injected the body language of a possessed man into the flight of the kicked ball as it landed precariously into the breadbasket of Redding. Despite the projection of the forced body language, Wally fidgeted like a toddler at a wedding.

The second quarter broadcast belonged to Old Man Schmidt. Wally, on the other hand, requested that I not speak to him, on account that it might bring further misfortune to the Rangers.

Redding appeared to be driving a horse cart without wheels. After the Frederick score, the Ranger attack was harmless. Toying with Lamont Dickies, the interior defensive line of Frederick owned the line of scrimmage.

Only feet from the boisterous Frederick crowd, I could not help but blush at the barrages emanating from fans at the sight of an injured Ranger. Initially, a clipping penalty on a Pirate punt return caught Ranger long snapper, Kelly Cochran, by surprise. The tall kid fell, clutching his knee, and was subsequently carried from the field on the shoulders of teammates. Of course, that failed to halt the taunting. Two other Rangers, through hard blocks and high-impact tackles, departed the field woozy or with limps and joined other members of the walking wounded.

The atmosphere in the Summit was sullen. With every cramp, injured knee, and case of seeing stars, Wally moaned and predicted doom for the Rangers. Old Man Schmidt continued to thump the cane. I scanned the South Heaven fan base in search of anyone familiar, anyone who could be convinced to provide me a lift to Lima.

A roar cascaded from one end of the Frederick stands to the other as a lawn tractor crept along the cinder track at an arrogant pace. The pristine green John Deere hauled a small cart with The Rifle trophy supplying the load. Two cheerleaders stood beside the prize while the Pirate mascot drove the tractor.

"Trophy ain't supposed to be shown like that!" With a time-out on the field, Old Man Schmidt tore off the headset. "Show some respect!"

"Dang! We need that trophy back!" barked Wally.

"What you need are points." I gleamed.

On cue, Redding tossed another wayward and incomplete pass, prompting a fourth down. Without an active long snapper, the Rangers assumed a five-yard delay-of-game penalty. It appeared that Coach Waddell had no answer for the loss of Cochran. Then, a familiar, although cloaked, face trotted onto the field.

"Ain't that your kin?" Old Man Schmidt patted his partner on the shoulder.

Into the opening of the circled huddle squeezed number sixty-one, the same kid I met a week earlier in Frankie's. It was Stu, the backup lineman, and he was finally touching the field of play.

"God help the boy pass this ball cleanly." Wally removed his green Skoal ball cap and scratched at his coal-black top, a thick head of hair tooled to a neat flattop.

It was answered with kindness—for the most part. Wally's kin, Stu Ginnette, managed well the task of sending the ball through open legs.

I stood from my seat as Gary Redding scooped the pass on the second skip, in his forearms rather than cleanly in his hands. The couple of seconds required to compensate for the poor snap cost Redding dearly. Before South Heaven's captain could step forward, three Pirates were on him. A juke left avoided one would-be tackler, but also subjected a knee to severe strain. Redding buckled and dropped quickly, clutching at his left knee and willingly relinquishing the ball.

As Wally buried his face, Old Man Schmidt told all the farm hands and shop owners that Frederick was but a few yards and less than two minutes from entering halftime up by two scores.

Meanwhile, a throng of players had gathered around a reeling Redding.

"Here comes Papa Redding," Wally chimed as the quarterback's father jogged onto the field.

The collection of medical "experts" tending to Redding all shot to their feet and waved across the field at the two men lounging atop the hood of Frederick's lone ambulance.

Like a dog walking in heavy snow, the brick-red goliath crept from one end of the field to the other.

Both squads migrated to their respective sidelines. Through the binoculars, Big Pete could be seen slapping the helmets of his team, displaying some sort of an emphatic rant, while Coach Waddell stood astray, keeping a steady eye on his wounded quarterback.

"Waddell's got either Durning or the freshman Boyd now to play quarterback. "Course, Durning's the only good tight end we got."

Redding was loaded on a gurney and whisked away, under the auspices of flashing lights and a whining siren ... and the vision of the red machine carting off an injured boy either sapped the motivation from the Rangers or jolted the offense of Frederick. As soon as officials began play once again, Dale Ritchie hit his flanker on a flag pattern at the front corner of the end zone. Donny Blaint, number eighty-one and the recipient of Ritchie's first touchdown throw, leaped higher than the two Ranger defenders sandwiching him. Blaint snatched the ball at its highest point, stiff-armed one would-be tackler, then fell across the goal line.

As the late-summer sun fell below the tree line and the squad of offensive ten stormed onto the back of Blaint, the Frederick fans and band erupted once again.

The trophy was again paraded by the home-team stands. As the tractor reached the midfield portion of the track, half a dozen Frederick players broke from the exuberant mob scene of celebration and began to huddle around the trailer and tractor, posing with The Rifle.

Wally littered the air with a four-letter barrage, not indigenous to Western Ohio. He was provided some hope, however, when an attempt at an extra point sailed wide right of the H-shaped uprights.

With Redding out of the game, Coach Waddell dropped only Dickies deep to return the Frederick kick. A rich boot took the Ranger runner back to the ten-yard line. With his wall of blockers decimated, Dickies completely halted forward momentum and wheeled right, shaking off two tackles and juking a third. His right foot cutting into the turf, , he headed up field at the eighteen. Ten yards along the sidelines, and with Frederick lane discipline gone, Dickies pushed all frame weight on his right ankle and cut left into a gaping hole in the defense. In a severe diagonal, close to paralleling the goal line, Dickies sprinted toward the opposite sideline.

I swallowed hard, urging, under my breath, for someone to stop him.

Old Man Schmidt inched to the edge of his seat then excitedly called to his audience, "Dickies has two men in tow and three to beat!"

The closer Dickies got to the Frederick sideline, the more Pirate fans rose and encouraged their team to tackle and stop him—and the more concerned I became.

Spurning the opposing fans, Dickies leaped over a defender who dove at his ankles, clearing the kid like a gazelle. The landing, however, nearly cost him his balance, and he stumbled twice.

"He's still on his feet and stiff-arms another!" Old Man Schmidt was so far forward of the chair that his buttocks assumed less than a couple of inches of the metal seat. I was certain he would topple it.

Marching through the feeble attempt by the kicker, Dickies found himself in a foot race for pay dirt. As he crossed the fifty, there were three defenders within five yards of him. Forward progress became suddenly more difficult to achieve, but Dickies' resolve maintained distance between himself and his pursuers.

"Dickies is at the thirty! He may go!" Old Man Schmidt barked. "No, from way over there comes number twenty-six!"

The excitement in Old Man Schmidt's tones paled in comparison to the roars of the crowd at the sight of Frederick's Ricky Bonèt rapidly closing the angle on Dickies.

"Run!" Wally waved his right arm like the windmill action of a third-base coach.

"He's at the fifteen!" Old Man Schmidt told the world.

Dickies swung his head to the right to catch a view behind him. Bonèt was inching closer.

"At the ten!"

To advance the ball the length of the field, Dickies probably ran nearly two-hundred yards with heavy legs. Alas, he could not outlast Bonèt and was caught two yards shy of the prize.

"Thank God." I took a breath.

Both Old Man Schmidt and Wally fell back in exhaustion as the cowbells rang a tone of relief from the home crowd.

"Just a couple more yards, folks."

It was Durning who led the Rangers onto the field, without an obviously exhausted Lamont Dickies.

"Looks like it'll be Durning under center, folks."

Chris Durning's first play as quarterback was a portent of events to come. A pitch to the substitute tailback, Rex King, was behind the runner. South Heaven lost two yards on first down.

The clock wound under a minute as Dickies trotted in from the sidelines. Second and third downs netted a single yard for the Ranger offense. Two poor center-quarterback exchanges resulted in two Durning fumbles and a chuckle from yours truly.

With the time-out, Old Man Schmidt scratched at his scalp with both hands. "We're in trouble."

"Waddell needs to kick here." Wally was insistent that the Rangers put three on the board.

Three yards from six points, Coach Waddell sent Durning back onto the field.

"Mistake." The disappointment overwhelmed Wally's cool blue eyes.

On the second count, Durning successfully took the ball from center, then spun right to left and pitched the ball to Dickies on a sweep.

In turn, Dickies rolled left, looking to pass rather than run. Despite the rush, Dickies held his ground, scanning the end zone for a white jersey. White was covered by black, and Dickies tucked the ball away for his own jaunt to pay dirt—albeit futilely.

"One yard shy! One yard!" cried Old Man Schmidt.

With thirty seconds hanging on the game clock, Frederick took over on downs, ninety-nine yards from their opponent's goal line. Ritchie shocked the Frederick faithful when, on first down, he faked a dive, dropped five steps, and launched a laser down the sidelines to a streaking Blaint. Fortunately for the luck-ridden Rangers, his ball flight pulled Blaint out of bounds. Luke Post had lost all sense of bearing when Blaint executed the "out and up." Otherwise, halftime would have been extremely ugly for South Heaven.

With amazement to the broadcasters of WSHV, Ritchie threw again on second down. The wobble on the thrown ball was too much to overcome, and the slant pass sailed over the receiver's head and into the arms of Kyle Knause, a surprised South Heaven linebacker. Fortunately, the junior linebacker had the finesse of a bricklayer and neglected to clamp the ball.

Sixteen seconds remained when Ritchie brought his Pirate teammates to the line for a third-down situation. A fake dive suckered no one on the South Heaven defense. Ritchie scampered down the left side of his line, searching for a hole to exploit, but there was none to be found.

Knause and his backer pals strung out Ritchie, dropping him a mere inch or two from the debarkation line for a safety. Quickly, the South Heaven players shot to their feet and screamed to the referees with a time-out request.

"Just a few seconds to go. What's he planin' on doin here?" Old Man Schmidt asked the audience.

"Smart play here would be to go for it on fourth," said Wally. "Burn off as many seconds before handing the ball over. We ain't gonna score with Durning under center."

When the officials blew the whistle to trigger the play clock, Frederick was still in the huddle. South Heaven, however, had broken theirs and strung out ten players along the line of scrimmage.

"Looks like the Rangers are comin' after this punt, folks."

The binoculars projected a view that had the Frederick punter only centimeters from the back edge of the end zone.

While the Frederick crowd had fallen silent, the Ranger mass of fans had filled the void.

The pass from center was too high for comfort and forced the Frederick punter off the ground to retrieve the ball. Two Ranger players broke free from the same hole within the interior line. Unmolested, they made a beeline for the Frederick punter, who chose to catch and kick without employing the obligatory steps into the punt.

With deadened momentum, the booted ball traveled the length a backyard swimming pool to the Frederick fifteen, where the South Heaven receiver signaled for a fair catch.

"Well, I'll be! That's genius."

Coach Waddell hustled his kicking unit onto the playing surface, with three seconds showing on the clock. From twenty-five yards out, Bo Baddey steadied the ball on an oversized orange tee then spread his confused teammates along the twenty-seven-yard line.

As Frederick steadied their actual defensive unit, Coach Waddell stormed the field to reach the referee.

"It's a free kick!" blurted Wally.

"What in the world you talkin' about, Wally?" Old Man Schmidt cried above the ruckus being stirred among the Frederick fans.

"Fair catch! We get a free kick." Given his diminutive stature, Wally probably depended heavily on his rough "bite," one that appeared to develop straight from the diaphragm.

It sounded as if the rule were formalized during a sandlot contest, but nonetheless, the officials agreed with Old Man Schmidt's partner. The official in charge apparently knew neither fear nor common sense. He was pelted with confusion and disbelief, in the form of tasty language, as he ordered the Frederick defensive unit to retreat ten yards from the line of scrimmage. He left Bo Baddey with only himself to battle.

Once reality struck, the stadium erupted into a crescendo of incoherent noise. Fortunately for Baddey and the Rangers, the length of the kick was no longer than a hiccup.

As the horn sounded, the ball hit the cross-beam of the H-shaped goalpost and bounded over for a successful attempt.

I wasted no time in finding the exit. As the Pride of South Heaven marched onto the field, I was lost among the throngs of packs of three, groups of four, and other fans clustered around the visitors' concession trailer.

"Still no closer to Lima, I see." Miss Myra, all smiles, had latched onto the arm of Butch Boyd.

"Your team's losing." I was sheepish in my retort. "It's halftime." I sidestepped the junior high couple locked at the hip and impervious to anyone around them.

Miss Myra was irritatingly giddy and giggled at the joke Boyd mustered. "So?"

The adolescent, working the concession stand and dressed in a Pee Wee Pirate black jersey, had enough energy to play every position on the field at one time. "Here ya are, ma'am." He was chipper, handing Miss Myra a single cup of soda.

"So, halftime. Leaving, remember?" My intimidating stare was obliterated, embarrassingly enough, by the blindsiding thump of a free-falling Nerf football. Shaking the skull of cobwebs, I could feel the laughter around me. Instant ire drew my hand to the Nerf that had come to rest at my left foot. I squeezed the life out of the sponge ball and was a mere second from launching it, when…

"Hey, buddy!" The brat wore his black jersey with angry pride. "Gimme back my ball!"

Cat-like reflexes and the fact I stood an entire foot-and-a-half taller than he was kept the boy from getting back his prized toy. "That's the second time I've been hit by one of these things!"

My tirade brought raucous joy to his posse of six.

"How about I wash your mouth out with soap?"

Miss Myra asked for the ball with a disquieting finger snap. "Before you lose an argument to a group of third-graders, sport…" She tossed the Nerf back to the posse. "I'd hate to see you lose anymore dignity." She winked and then proceeded to tell me, again, that she was staying for the entire game.

My inquiries into potential rides out of town engendered too many negative responses from the end-zone crowd. With tail between legs, I wandered from person to person but received only odd glares, a few words of sympathy, and an uncomfortable proposal.

Frederick's finest wrapped up the last note and marched to a completion on their home team's sideline as both squads huddled at respective end zones.

Old Man Schmidt cloaked himself with the headset. "No ride?"

"By chance, does everyone in Corn Country have it in for me. And why are you kicking to start this half?"

With adrenaline carried over from the first half, Bo Baddey drilled his kick-off to the Frederick five, where the oblong ball bounded oddly to a stop, just on the playing side of the goal line. Like a Little League infielder lifting his head as the grounder rolled toward the glove, the Frederick receiver was more concerned with the oncoming rush of Ranger defenders. He inadvertently kicked the ball forward. A pile of white and black jerseys fell on the loose ball. Two referees joined the stack, tossing the naysayers aside to reach the fighters.

"Our ball!" yelled Wally.

The man in the striped shirt and black hat confirmed Wally's assessment, hopping up from the pile and pointing in favor of the Rangers.

And suddenly, a ghostly white appeared on the faces of the Frederick faithful— the same pale color of death that had no doubt engulfed my complexion.

Excitement dissipated from the South Heaven stands as a lanky and awkward kid trotted onto the field. He joined the circular huddle formed by the remainder of his offensive teammates. The lanky kid wore a nontraditional number five and was assuming control, with the football only a few yards from striking a notch on the scoreboard. The lanky kid was the freshman Duane Boyd.

As he looked about his enemies across the line and called cadence, I felt my chest tighten. Of course, the tension overcoming me, in my hoping that the kid failed miserably, probably paled in comparison to that in each of the Ranger faithful. His initial snap from center produced a slight smile.

"Fumble on the play! He got it back!" barked Old Man Schmidt.

In an unusual and bizarre move, Coach Waddell called a time-out and casually strode to his offensive huddle. He opted not to speak with anyone but Boyd.

Old Man Schmidt took advantage of the break in the action to remind his listeners of the importance of auto insurance and how the Dick Overton Agency could help.

"This kid's not ready," I chirped.

Whether it was related to a pep talk or a scolding, Coach Waddell inspired his quarterback and his offense. On second down, Boyd induced all three Frederick linebackers to commit forward with a fake to Dickies. A slot formation left pulled the Pirate safety toward the dual receivers. Chris Durning filled the gap in the defense, slipping behind the linebackers. Duane Boyd's first official high school pass fell into his tight end's hands.

"You-know-where's frozen over, folks! A freshman's done thrown a touchdown! Good God Almighty!"

"Where's that trophy now?" Wally stood at the edge of the Summit and chastised the Frederick faithful, like an incensed deacon to his transgressed flock.

The excitement of the moment soon waned, however, following the failed two-point conversion.

The game fell into a trench-warfare grudge match. South Heaven's defense assumed center stage, with Knause and his pals stuffing the Pirate offense. After sleeping through most of their first half, allowing Ritchie to run and throw amok, the Ranger front eight forced Frederick into two consecutive punts.

The second Frederick punt came with three minutes remaining in the third quarter and with the line of scrimmage at the South Heaven thirty-six. Coach Waddell pulled back his troops from a block formation, prompting Wally to guess a return to Dickies' right side. Two of us in the Summit fell outright for the punter's fake. At the snap of the ball, with binoculars in hand, Old Man Schmidt and I followed the Frederick punter as he appeared to frantically chase down a misguided center toss. After the surge of the Frederick crowd rising to their feet, we reversed course and suddenly found a Pirate back breaking into the open.

Number thirty-four, Aaron James, the Frederick starting fullback, rumbled into South Heaven territory with a trio of blockers two steps in front of him.

Lamont Dickies held his ground on the thirty then attacked the wall of blockers. He sidestepped a lunge by the first blocker and accepted the full brunt of the remaining two. Dickies was forced backwards a few steps but was on his feet—although, more his heels.

James, with runner instincts and fleet of foot, slyly avoided the collision and veered toward the sideline, switching the ball from his left to his right arm.

Dickies threw off his blockers, regained balance, and sprinted after the Frederick fullback, who was nearly 15 yards beyond him. He closed the distance quickly, but no one in the Summit believed in him.

"Daggonit!" yelled Wally.

"Go!" My hatred made a brief appearance.

James was at the five when Dickies lunged for him. He caught the ankles and brought the Pirate down inches shy of a score. James leaped high, with arms outstretched, but the referee insisted he was down prior to the goal line.

It took all my will to hold back my displeasure at the referee's call.

Several members of the Frederick staff stormed the field, but to no avail, as the fearless head referee refused to endure the rant and marked the ball shy of the goal line.

Old Man Schmidt lauded Dickies for his hustle and heart.

The coaching staff for Frederick did not relent and stole more time from the game.

Coach Waddell and Big Pete had the opportunity to muster their defensive troops before the Frederick offense meandered onto the field. Big Pete moved ten of his men into the box as the Pirates lined up in a full-house backfield with no flanker.

The uproarious fan base gradually calmed as Ritchie brought the Pirates to the line. Unfortunately, the down lineman of South Heaven "submarined" the Frederick front seven. Ritchie tripped on his own center and barely got the ball to his halfback, who then smashed into the line but went nowhere.

To my dismay, the entire bleacher section for South Heaven rose to their feet. Cow bells clanged, and whistles blared.

The Frederick Pirates' coaching staff ran the same play. Knause found a seam and busted the running back with a helmet-to-helmet blast that prevented the ball from crossing the goal line.

I bit at the bottom of my lip.

The Frederick staff initiated a time-out. Through the binoculars, the Frederick head coach, face blazing in crimson, screamed at his kids, jumping up and down and jerking at facemasks.

In contrast, Big Pete did little but pat the kids on the shoulders.

Frederick ran at the trench on third down with an isolation play off left tackle.

"They got him! Got him again!" Old Man Schmidt pumped his fist.

Another surge by South Heaven pushed the offensive line backwards, forcing the halfback laterally. Luke Post came off the corner and submitted a perfect-form tackle. Fourth down.

"You gotta be kidding! Three straight runs?" I complemented the eerie hush of the Frederick crowd.

"Frederick's gotta put the ball in the hands of Ritchie," Old Man Schmidt told his audience. "Coach Waddell's gotta key on Ritchie."

The scholarship-bound Ritchie took an extra few seconds to bark out signals, again to a full-house backfield.

The Frederick crowd stomped and chattered with uneasy excitement.

Ritchie took the snap, faked a dive to James, reversed his field, and headed down the line for an apparent option. Big Pete's defense failed to get a push, but Knause knifed through the gap created by his defensive end, Bobby Wiggins. The Ranger linebacker grabbed whatever he could of Ritchie. Struggling to free himself from Knause's grip, Ritchie pitched the ball back, but too far forward of his halfback.

"Fumble! Fumble! It's on the ground."

I grunted at Old Man Schmidt.

"Our ball!" yelled Wally as the South Heaven side erupted and the band broke into song.

Random but legitimate boos peppered the field, and I ingested every heart-burning one of them.

South Heaven took the ball and momentum into the fourth quarter, trailing by three. Carrying the brunt of the load, Lamont Dickies led his team on a grinding drive reminiscent of football lore—off-tackle right and off-tackle left.

"Dickies may beat Jim Westerman's rushing record this year," Old Man Schmidt commented. "Keep's runnin' like this, and he'll get them twelve-hundred yards."

"Westerman on the wall?"

"Career rushin' mark's stood for nearly thirty years."

Four more yards for Dickies netted another first down as the clock melted toward the eight-minute mark.

"Westerman graduated in '50 with Donald Carey," Old Man Schmidt continued. "Carey played quarterback and wound up at the Naval Academy. Jimmy found his way to West Point."

An option play by the freshman brought the South Heaven faithful to their feet as Boyd broke a tackle and tore off a ten-yard gain.

"Westerman and Carey played against one another in '52 and '53."

With the clock draining below the six-minute mark, Dickies chugged forward to the Frederick ten.

On first down and ten, with a mere eight yards to travel for six points and the lead, Coach Waddell put the game in the hands of his freshman.

A professional fake to Dickies on an off-tackle run, and Boyd set up to throw. With feet dancing, he held the ball directly below his right ear in a cocked position—a few seconds past any window of opportunity. The freshman missed a wide-open Durning and opted to fire across his body to his second receiver, who was so well blanketed that a jersey number could not be discerned.

I did not want to admit my sensation of satisfaction, but the corners of my mouth had to be creeping skyward. A large exhale finally relieved me of the threat of a South Heaven win. I could at least go home with some sense of satisfaction.

Cheers and screams radiated from South Heaven to Frederick. Ritchie and his Pirates regained possession and had but five minutes to kill the clock. In a surprise to the Summit, Ritchie took to the air and completed three straight passes to Blaint that pushed the ball thirty yards to his own forty-two.

Wally had the top few buttons of his shirt undone, unfortunately, displaying a large portion of his overgrown chest hair. "Folks, we need your prayers to get the ball back."

The chanting was becoming more cohesive and energetic. The Frederick faithful had to be sensing victory. With the help of the Pirate cheerleaders, the home crowd was spelling out the letters "R-I-F-L-E."

Unfortunately, as it was my luck, Ritchie and Frederick dug into the well once too often, and Knause blitzed from the inside and was unblocked. The South Heaven linebacker caught Ritchie blindside and jarred the ball loose.

"He got it! Knause got the ball!"

"The Almighty hates me." I gritted my teeth, struggling to watch the Ranger impromptu celebration.

Protecting their turf and possession of The Rifle, Frederick, with the jeers and sneers of the faithful behind them, moved eight men within two yards of the ball.

"They're gonna make Boyd throw." Old Man Schmidt displayed little confidence in the freshman.

Dickies crashed into the line but traveled nowhere. A second-down play brought the same result.

Coach Waddell opted not to stop the clock, but instead, he substituted two receivers for Dickies and Ricky Green.

I was beginning to regain some assurance of hope.

"Uh-oh," moaned Old Man Schmidt. "This move never works…"

At the snap, Boyd sprinted to his right, toward the triple-receiver formation. He danced and then dodged an oncoming rusher. The freshman pulled the ball down from its cocked position and began to run. Spinning out of a would-be tackle at the line of scrimmage, Boyd got two blocks downfield. He cut back toward the middle of the field, spun out of another tackle, and dove forward.

"Unbelievable!" cried Wally. "He got the first down!"

Dickies then ran twice for another first down.

"He's gotta call time-out soon," insisted Old Man Schmidt.

Ignoring the logic from the Summit, Coach Waddell ran Dickies to the left one more time, allowing the clock to fall below a half-minute.

"Come on." Old Man Schmidt chomped on his cigar, gnawing at the end.

I had the same demand, albeit for a different reason.

Boyd quickly pushed his team to the line of scrimmage and barked signals then handed to Green on a straight dive.

"Call time-out!"

With a feeble ten seconds remaining, the clock was mercifully stopped. Again, unlike his counterpart, Coach Waddell graced the field, with hands in pockets, to speak with his quarterback.

"Looks like he may be tryin' to win it." Wally was pacing as far as the headset cord could stretch. He bit at his nails as if they were a late-night snack. "Coach Waddell heads off the field. Here we go, folks."

The throbbing in my chest was unbearable.

No quiet voice existed in the stadium. The few hundred jamming the bleachers stomped on the wood footboards, while those without a ticket to sit had nearly surrounded the action end of the field. Fans were five to six feet deep, with toes touching the sidelines and the end zone.

From under center, Boyd took the snap and sprinted right. Still on the run, he heaved the ball toward the corner of the end zone. The crowd was so thick surrounding the end zone that, even from our vantage point, we completely lost sight of receiver and defender.

"There's no signal yet! Is he in? Is he in?"

Negative was the reply from the side judge.

Chris Durning, the Ranger receiver, protested and was supported vigorously by Wally. "That ref's gotta call fan interference, folks! They were on the field! He's gotta give Durning the catch!"

Frederick fans in that particular corner of the end zone cheered the side judge and went so far as to pat him on the back. Despite time remaining on the clock and South Heaven still possessing one more snap of the ball, bearing and all discipline were overwhelmed with emotion as dozens of fans poured onto the field, some reaching the twenty-yard line.

"That's gotta be a penalty, folks!"

Incredulously, the Pirate mascot followed suit and sped the John Deere toward midfield. Chaos was a pandemic.

"Still need that ride?" Old Man Schmidt asked me.

"What?"

"They kick the ball, and you stay in South Heaven." He was nearly oblivious to the confusion and disorder occurring on the field. Following a deep drag on his smoke, Old Man Schmidt insisted that Coach Waddell would kick a field goal and settle for a tie.

Agonizingly, referees restored discipline, forcing everyone to the edges of the field. Players stood in opposing huddles. Between the two teams was a yellow hankie clinging to a patch of turf.

"Tell ya what, he goes for the win, and I'll drive you all the way to Cleveland. When we kick that ball, though, you stay here."

I laughed, watching the referee walk off the penalty against Frederick and their fans. I laughed because of the pettiness in which my life had now been mired. "I suppose a betting man would say you go for the win on the road."

With his starting offensive unit huddled, Coach Waddell used his last time-out and strolled onto the field, without his kicker.

"Well? You a bettin' man, boy?" Old Man Schmidt asked.

"Only on sure things…"

His head held a flag position for several seconds. Coach Waddell was a man in deep thought. His offensive eleven waited for word. Suddenly, the binoculars showed Coach Waddell exhale a huge breath, then motion for his kicker.

Old Man Schmidt gleamed, "It's easier to be second-guessed with a tie than a loss."

Bo Baddey received a shoulder pad knock from Coach Waddell, then fell into huddle with his teammates.

"He's two yards from victory," I protested.

At the nine-yard line, Durning secured the black rubber tee to the turf. A good snap, placement, and kick would close the game at 12 apiece.

With palms saturated, I felt the tension of the entire stadium. Scanning both sets of bleachers, I could find no one sitting.

The Pirate faithful boomed with cheers as their unit trotted onto the field.

I began making promises to the Lord, in exchange for any event that would prevent the ball from traveling through the uprights.

Before lining up on defense, Frederick called a time-out of their own.

Old Man Schmidt wiped the perspiration from his brow.

Cochran, the Ranger center, returned to the field, stealing any thunder and redemption from Stu Ginnette. Nevertheless, the kick depended on the pass from center.

"Here we go, folks," Wally told the audience. "Last play of the game. Two seconds remain. Baddey needs a short one to tie this game … He lines up … Snap to Durning. Baddey steps and kicks. Holy … The ball hit a lineman! It's in the air!"

I shot to my feet in exultation.

Fluttering in the air, as if suspended on a thin wire, the ball was snagged by Chris Durning.

"Durning's got it! He scrambles right! Shue's out there. Touchdown! Touchdown! Touchdown! Good God Almighty, Chris Durning picked it off in mid-air and threw it to Shue. Rangers win! Rangers win!"

Ranger players stormed the field, contributing their bodies to a massive pile building atop the reserve wide receiver named Pete Shue.

I fell back into my chair in disbelief.

Uncontrollable fans disregarded sheriff deputies and poured onto the field. A small group of them did not wait around for any presentation. From out of nowhere, the John Deere was hijacked and driven at top speed toward the jubilant celebration.

Coach Waddell was tossed on top of the shoulders of a trio of players and triumphantly carried to the center of the field. With scores of fans in tow, the Ranger band bled onto the field, absorbing much of the green sod with maroon and white.

"Unbelievable!" Wally was uncontrollable. "Rangers win! Rangers win! The Rifle's ours!"

CHAPTER TWELVE
Just a Bad Snap, That's All

Lima

    Miss Myra relished in my agony. She had no haste in her drive to Lima and my freedom. Despite her injection of guilt, I refused to relent and demanded to be taken to the bus station. We left in mid-celebration of the Ranger win.

    "You do know, sport, Lima only has a few buses running daily." Miss Myra parked the car nearest the terminal entrance, about ten to fifteen yards behind a gray passenger bus spewing coal-black exhaust.

    "I need only one, a direct line to downtown Cleveland."

    Miss Myra inquired about the condition of my car, to which I requested she call the paper—after, of course, Beefy found the missing part.

    "Well, it's been real, and it's been fun, but it hasn't been real fun." I was relieved South Heaven was about to become a distant memory.

    "Tell me something. Is precociousness the bedrock of your family's foundation?"

    "Look who's talking!"

    She maintained a grin that underplayed an irritated tone, stepping on the clutch and popping her car into gear. "Goodbye, sport."

    Three miniscule pews of seats were aligned neatly behind each other and parallel to the ticket booth window. Fashioned after and stolen from the outside of a '40s-genre theater, the ticket booth contained just enough room for a cash register and a person to operate it.

    I spoke through the baffled hole notched into double-plated glass.

    The sports section of the *Lima Daily News* failed to reply. The only human signs of life were two hands clasping the sides of the paper.

    "Excuse me." I added a double-rap on the window to my repertoire.

    Like a heavy cotton curtain being pulled to cover a stage, the paper gradually lowered to reveal a miserly man with a hairline in full gray recession and ears the size of snare drums. "Yes?" Bob had been stenciled into his blue shirt. He was more concerned with an article on the right section of the paper than helping me. His reading glasses clung precariously to the tip of his nose.

"Is the bus full-up outside?" I dug into my back pocket to retrieve my wallet.

"Nope." Bob's alto voice was muffled through the voice plate in the glass.

I requested one seat then the price of said trip, estimating in my head three years of inflation from the last bus ride I took.

"One to Chicago."

"Chicago?"

His attention was diverted away from manually creating a ticket stub. "Chicago to Milwaukee to Omaha."

"No. I need to get to Cleveland."

"Ain't goin' to Cleveland," he replied, returning to his paper.

Anxiety beginning to fester, I asked for the next bus to my home.

"That'd be number forty-two."

I scanned the empty lobby of the terminal. "And what? It leaves later tonight? Tomorrow morning?"

"It's on the board." Bob pointed to his left.

To the right of the ticket booth, a classroom-size chalkboard, lined with tape, designated a grid of bus numbers, destinations, and days of the week.

"Tuesday is the first bus to Cleveland?"

Bob moistened his fingers then flipped to the next page of sports. "Every Tuesday and Friday." He opened the brass cover of a large pocket watch. "Should've been here at five."

"No, no. I couldn't be here at five. Ranger game, ya know?"

Another turn of pages netted a yawn. "Number twenty-nine be runnin' to Columbus on Sunday morning. I'm sure you could get a ride to Cleveland from there."

"What am I supposed to do in the meantime?"

"Motel down the road…"

I inquired as to the location of the nearest train stop, but Bob was either ignorant or annoyed by me. He was steadfastly insistent, however, that his shift ended at midnight, and at that time, the bus station would close.

"Great." Without a bed or ride, I wandered to a pew, kicking my bags along instead of carrying them. My luck—what there was of it—and my dignity had all but evaporated. The cherry wood of the pews was uncomfortable at best, and my stomach offered up extreme displeasure. Of course, rather than hunger, that pain could have been overall queasiness at the thought of being held captive in Western Ohio. A scan of my surroundings brought neither sympathy nor comfort: downtown Lima and unfamiliar territory.

The only attestation of life was the string of vending machines standing guard outside of a closed newsstand.

A line of four payphones caught my attention, a potential oasis to my predicament. I had retrieved a dime from my pocket and was scouring through the tattered phonebook tenuously attached to the wall-mounted phone, when a mother and daughter suddenly appeared from behind the closed female-bathroom door next to me. Each carried a single suitcase and startled me as much as I, them.

"Come along, Samantha." The mom nudged the back of her daughter. "We mustn't be late."

Miraculously, Bob appeared from behind the ticket booth. He was a runt of a man who walked with slumped shoulders and pigeon toes.

Another gentleman, probably Bob's age and dressed in the same blue shirt, came in from the outside. He held a cigarette in one hand and a coffee thermos in the other.

"Manifest is clear." Bob handed the man a couple of sheets of paper. "Have a good trip."

Through a heavy drag on his smoke, the other man studied the manifest then huffed, "Headin' out west after this."

Before Bob could disappear back into the booth, I accosted him. "Is there a taxi in this town?"

Supplying the cigarette machine with coins, Bob called, "There's Spartan Taxi."

I quickly shuffled through the alphabet of Lima businesses.

When I called them, Spartan Taxi mentioned again and again that the time was past midnight Reluctantly, the less-than-congenial dispatcher relented, although he did suggest that I merely walk across the street to the nearest motel.

Bidding Bob a good night, I hastened to the parking lot to wait out the fifteen-minute lead time for the taxi.

Munching on a sandwich wrapped in wax paper, Miss Myra was still there in the parking lot, reclined on the hood of her car. "Did I ever tell you I was offered the opportunity to be the speech writer for Senator Grimms? Could have been in the inner circle of the Beltway."

I threw my bags into the backseat like a scolded pre-teen being retrieved from after-school detention.

Monday, Afternoon Tennis

For dinner, Miss Myra challenged me to a tennis match. Fortunately, Lesaint Park was devoid of other players, and we walked onto the green painted asphalt court with no audience.

Crouching to stretch my sore and tight thigh muscles, I heard a swoosh of air buzz my head.

She blasted another serve by me. "Fifteen-love."

Two more quick points were stolen from me before I managed to return serve—a merger strike that forced the ball to the net but not over it.

She tempted me with an invite to her father's place for swordfish. Miss Myra ensured me that if I beat her on the court, a place setting would be reserved with my name on it.

Displaying that innate lesion of vulnerability my father decried as an Achilles' heel, I did not question her when she stated tennis was only mere exercise, not a sport for her. I could adopt to most sports. But tennis? Tennis, for me, was more similar to figure skating: unbearable to watch, and even less tempting to play.

I had soiled my shirt with sweat before mustering my initial point. Two games in the hole, and I had finally effectively returned her serve.

"Sure hope you know a good steakhouse in Cleveland." She laughed, bouncing the ball twice before drawing her racket to strike at the yellow object. Hers was not a professional stroke by any stretch. However, Miss Myra glided gracefully on the court.

Without too much pace, the ball bounded toward my forehand.

"Two in a row in the net!" I boldly called, believing her weakness had been discovered: lateral movement to her left.

My end of the deal involved dinner at a Cleveland restaurant—in case Miss Myra ever visited the city by the lake. I assured her a good steak and baked potato could be had in Cuyahoga County. Of course, she would first be required to rid herself of those purple velour sweatpants.

By the start of our fourth game, a crowd had begun to gather. Both the boys' and girls' teams from South Heaven High, dolled up in uniforms, matriculated onto the court as if Miss Myra and I had no existence.

"Excuse me!" Miss Myra cleared the perspiration on her forehead with a swipe of the wristband attached to her right forearm. "We're in the middle of a game." Despite that impressive athleticism of hers, Miss Myra appeared to be very much winded. Her hair had long since lost its foundation from the ponytail position, with several strands milling about her face.

A rather pretentious and awkwardly tall and thick blonde girl callously suggested we vacate the court. "We have a match with, like, Elk's Creek." She tied her mid-back-length hair into a ponytail. The only one of the five girls in shorts rather than a skirt, she was incredibly abrasive, not only with the two of us, but also with her teammates. "We have this court after school."

"Well, we have two more games."

"Well, I have, like, an important match in an hour and really need to warm up."

Despite Miss Myra's insistence on retaining the court, we reached a compromise: Blondie became my partner, and Miss Myra inherited a senior from the boys' doubles team.

I introduced myself but received only a snipe from the blue-eyed girl, right before she stole the ball out of my hand to serve.

"Like, just stay outta my way."

"She can't move to her left," I advised.

Out of certain spite, she served to Miss Myra's forehand.

I got nothing more than the rim of the racket on the ball, so my response to the return of serve traveled directly into the net.

"You've got to be kidding!" exploded Blondie. "Like, just let me hit the ball!"

Hearing the snickers from Miss Myra and her partner, I casually strode to the baseline. "Listen, I have dinner riding on this game!"

"Well, in that case, like, let me do the work."

Following my blonde coach's instructions, I left my racket in the ready position and did not even offer a whiff at the yellow ball. As a result, we knotted the set at two, then proceeded to steal the fifth game. Unfortunately, game number six fell on my serve.

Soon, the bus from Elk's Creek pulled into the lot, and a handful of fans began trickling into the stands.

My first two serves put our duo down by a point, with both striking my favorite target: the net.

Blondie retreated to the baseline, red in the face. "I don't, like, ever lose. Get it?"

Petrified my partner might explode, I managed to muscle the next serve into play.

Miss Myra's partner rocketed a return out of the reach of Blondie and therefore forced my hand. Again, net ball.

"Jeez!" Blondie gritted.

A sparse crowd was now into our match. And I did not fail to provide amusing entertainment, costing my team the next two points and the game.

"All tied up, sport. I can taste that steak now!"

Blondie grunted and grumbled as she passed me upon exchanging positions.

"Sorry."

Despite my lack of prowess and my partner's bubbling into a juvenile tirade, we held serve and then, with the fans chanting "C-I-T-Y-B-O-Y," defeated Miss Myra with a Blondie drop-shot in front of the person who owed me a reservation at her father's table.

Blondie refused to shake my hand, gifting me with only an invite to vacate the court.

Miss Myra, too, shunned me, opting instead to visit with South Heaven's female tennis coach.

I was spent and positive my insides were near an ugly expulsion. Stealing a towel from a gym bag Miss Myra must have retrieved from a local garage sale, I wiped down the perspiration from my forehead and headed toward the only drinking fountain in the park, located under a shelter some fifty-plus yards from the court.

A lone figure sat on one of a dozen picnic tables the shelter housed. As I entered the shelter, the face of the figure became clear: Stu Ginnette. "Hey. How's it going?"

His face was tinted with a hint of an unforgiving nature and appeared to lack an ally.

"Shouldn't you be at practice?" I wandered toward the drinking fountain. The fountain barely offered a stream from which to drink, and the water that trickled out was lukewarm.

Stu pushed himself up and began to walk away, toward the pedestrian entrance and the playground.

"Hey! I saw you get in the game on Friday."

"Then you saw me screw up?"

"Screw up? You got into the game. I thought that's what you wanted?"

Two tykes from the tennis crowd raced one another toward the swing set. They appeared to be oblivious to the two of us. With two of the swings caught and twisted on the overhead crossbar, the kids hastily moved to the steep metal slide.

"You guys won, right? Got that Rifle back."

Stu walked to the kids as they buzzed back to the swing set. Like a big brother, he maximized his wingspan and was the impetus for setting the two girls in motion. Stu had some mass to him, although by no means was he either pudgy or muscular. He had little trouble keeping both tots in a perpetual swing.

In the distance, Miss Myra was loading the trunk of her car.

Lost in a baby-face complexion, Stu manufactured a smile for the two girls. Unfortunately, there was no merriness in the brown eyes to accompany the compelled grin.

"Listen, I gotta be going. Don't beat yourself up about that play."

He helped the two kids down from the swings but declined to offer them assistance with the merry-go-round.

The tykes came after my person, running around me twice while smacking me in the back.

"Ain't never gonna play again, ya know?" Stu flopped on the black rubber seat of a swing. "That'll be the last play anyone will ever remember."

Out of the corner of my eye, I saw Miss Myra approach. Hardly this kid's therapist, I had no intention of spewing advice. Still, though, I could feel for him.

"Hey, we gotta go!" Miss Myra barked.

"It's not gonna matter now. We ain't got no money in our house. Dad can't find a job, and my mom, she's sick." Stu shook his head vehemently, then shot to his feet, forcing Miss Myra and me to flinch and fall back on our heels. "My mom's got cancer, don't ya see? I gotta pick up more hours at the grocery. I can't play no more." Stu collapsed into the swing seat. "Man, I just wanna leave here!"

Miss Myra attempted a ploy at utilizing her memorization of notes from her Psychology 101 class. "It'll be all right, Stu. You'll see…"

He wiped at his welling eyes as if the act would prevent any formulation of tears. "When I was little, all I wanted to be was a Ranger. Then when I was older, just wanted to be like Blue Laces, you know? Get outta here." He grabbed at the silver chain hanging loosely around his neck. "Wound up bein' no good at football, though."

"I think you're being too hard on yourself, man," I said. "It was just one play."

"Yeah. My one and only play."

Wednesday, A Cookout

With their team having upset their first opponent, South Heaven's fans had succumbed to the hope for the implausible and surreal: reaching the playoffs. Excitement was gushing. The impending Friday-night matchup was with Austin, several miles to the north and east. Out of guilt, Miss Myra was convinced, I wrote two articles for the Sun. One covered the Frederick game, while the second was filled with quotes from fans and a brief description of the impending Pickle Bowl. In reality, it was a swan song.

From Willie Tee, of all people, I learned that Austin was home to Kesselring Pickles, one of the largest fermented cucumber producers in the country. Every year, the Jaycees of Austin hosted the Pickle Festival, a weeklong celebration culminating in the Pickle Bowl on Friday evening. South Heaven had never been invited to play in the bowl game. Invitations were usually reserved for schools with a closer proximity to Austin. However, over the past few years, Austin football had fallen on hard times, and with the inception of computer rankings to determine a school's worthiness for entering the playoffs, teams had opted not to accept the invite—fear of losing prestige, supposedly.

While occupying the end of a concrete bench, I was admiring real journalistic work of those employed by the Columbus Herald when Stephanie found her way to the garden area.

"Myra's still not here." Miss Myra's younger sister adjusted the white headband that stretched horizontally across her scalp. With the coercion of the plastic device, her hair was pulled taut over an unbecoming brow. "Daddy's gotta liquor up the guests." She was hardly abiding by the rules of abstinence herself, with all fingers in her right hand wrapped around the circumference of a highball glass that was three-quarters full of an auburn-colored liquid. Her all-white sundress accentuated the physique of a co-ed.

"I thought you were due back at school?" I snapped the paper back into its original four-fold shape.

"And I thought you'd be sick of this place by now?" By the aroma of alcohol polluting her person, the drink she cuddled was not the first of the evening.

I inquired as to the nature of the dinner.

Sipping away, she sighed. "Bunch of my father's college buddies." She maintained composure in speech, failing to stumble or cross any word, like an experienced alcoholic. She ran her finger up and down my exposed right arm. "I hope you're not thinking Myra is the one for you?"

"I beg your pardon?"

With heavy eyelids trying desperately to conceal the pale green trait assumed from her mother, and leaning on a rickety right arm, she gave every indication the next morning would be a rough one. "Because ... Daddy, he invited Johnny tonight."

"I heard they have your car done, sport." Miss Myra appeared from behind a row of rose bushes resplendent in pink and red. "Stephie, Daddy wants you in the parlor."

She winked at me then climbed to her feet, careful not to spill a drop, and the ice cubes aggressively clanked against the bulkheads of the glass. "Daddy's a fan—of Johnny, that is." Stumbling gracefully, with the impetus of a shove from Miss Myra, Stephanie disappeared into the house.

I suggested to Miss Myra that her sister was well on her way toward a liver transplant.

"Admiring the work of others, I see," she said, reaching for the paper.

I inquired of the Epstein menu and made room for her on the bench.

"Surf and turf, I suppose." Miss Myra was hardly dressed for an evening of entertaining, again with barely a dusting of makeup and in red and white plaid trousers and tennis shoes. "Whatever you do tonight, don't talk unless spoken to."

I laughed.

"So I'm assuming you'll be on the road come tomorrow?" She stretched out her short legs to dig into a front pants pocket. "Gum?"

"Myra?" A tall and graying man found his way to the garden.

Miss Myra surged to her feet to hug the man. "Uncle Bruce." She kissed him on the cheek, and her sullen disposition immediately reversed.

I stood to join the niece and uncle.

"Bruce Worth." Uncle Bruce had huge hands. He also had an abused and scarred chin that added up to a rugged face.

Miss Myra continued the introduction with a few more details. She clung to her relative as if she'd just found a forgotten doll. "How long are you here for?"

Soft-spoken with an articulate tone, Uncle Bruce suggested intellect and sophistication. By his dress, however, I assumed that he was either colorblind or on the verge of senility. Uncle Bruce wore a purple sweater with the Northwestern University mascot embroidered on the left breast, a purple undershirt with collar, and purple trousers. "Shall we?" he suggested, motioning us towards the house.

Instead of enjoying the unseasonably cool September evening, we were seated in the formal dining room, all fourteen of us. My reserved seat was at the corner of the table, next to Miss Myra and one of the serving carts.

"I called your editor, told him you'd be returning tomorrow." Miss Myra passed me a glass boat filled with melted butter. "Unless you want me to tell him you'll be there tonight?" She slid a knife through an extremely rare but thick porterhouse slab of steak.

Conversation was plentiful around the table, but not one pertained to the other. Three female servants filled glasses of wine and water and catered to the needs of the picky and demanding.

The lobster tail needed not a drop of butter. It melted as soon as it touched the tongue. Vintage northeastern Ohio, the wine was light but dry and delicate. "I told him I would see him in the office on Monday." I said.

Miss Myra added four heaping dollops of butter to her baked potato. "Cashing in on a vacation?"

"Just getting him back for a couple of past … indiscretions." I became indulged in the conversation across the table, between Epstein and another gentleman whom Miss Myra referred to as One Big Jerk.

"Whole town," said Senior Epstein, after an abbreviated but painful coughing episode. "Whole town has taken stock in Charlie Van Wert." He injected two large folds into the table napkin used to hide his cough.

"They think Van Wert can be some sort of savior. Hell, Butch Boyd had a Japanese company all lined up for a tour of the AGM site."

"Foreign cars in Ohio?" Butter disparagingly slid down my chin and onto my lap. My napkin, of course, still maintained a placement on the dining table.

The Big Jerk glared at me over the rim of his condescending bifocal glasses, giving the nightmare image of my seventh-grade social studies teacher. "Epstein, who are you inviting to your home anymore?" He had a definite aloofness to his tone and a slight femininity to his facial features.

Senior Epstein insisted a server refill my wine glass, then proceeded to introduce me to the Big Jerk—a.k.a. Benji Schloss. Epstein painted a colorful montage in describing my credentials to Schloss.

"I've never read a paper out of Cleveland." Schloss commented. According to Miss Myra, Schloss was a best-selling author and columnist for the New York Daily. He tended to his steak with all the dramatics of a spiteful food critic.

"Union is the only body that will supply labor." Senior Epstein continued stirring his whiskey with a loose finger. "Boyd can work as hard as he wants to bring business in, but the Japanese companies are no fans of the union."

A distinctively excited but distant female shrill preceded the entrance of the former Dallas football star.

As if suddenly blessed by the sacrament of youth or the magical touch of an evangelist, Senior Epstein, upon seeing Blue Laces enter the dining room, lifted himself quickly to his feet.

Without an entourage or the snakeskin boots and black cowboy hat, Blue Laces, one could have assumed, was nothing more than mortal, like the rest of us. Johnny Sarian, however, was anything but ordinary, particularly in the eyes of the Ranger faithful. Despite a powerfully handsome presence, with parted blond locks and an exaggeratedly cleft chin, which, in itself, would have opened any door of opportunity, Johnny had reserved a comfortable position in the memory of the South Heaven fan.

"Mister Epstein." He stood a few inches taller than his host, latching onto the extended hand of Senior Epstein. Sarian wore an impressive silver ring on his right hand. The gaudy blue gem in the middle suggested it represented an accomplishment.

"Benji, Bruce, this here is one of the greatest Rangers of all time: Johnny Sarian." Senior Epstein, drenched in a childish and giddy grin, leaned on the football star with a hand on his shoulder.

Only Uncle Bruce stood to acknowledge Blue Laces, his purple sweater now stained with a splotch of yellow. "Saw you in the playoffs last year."

Miss Myra created a commotion with a sigh as she collected silverware and plates like a talented busboy.

"Myra," said Sarian.

A laconic and disingenuous head nod prompted Miss Myra's departure, arms loaded with stained dinner plates.

Senior Epstein provided an excuse for his daughter's behavior. "Sit down, son. You're just in time for dessert."

Sarian had little humility as he quickly assumed a spot at the table and willingly accepted a bourbon and Coke.

With dessert, all conversation focused around the one-time Dallas star. War stories and anecdotes littered the dining room with a foul stench of cheap admiration for athletic exploits. Along with Uncle Bruce and Schloss, Senior Epstein sang the praises of Blue Laces to a man he referred to as Woody.

Once again, I assumed, Sarian's ego absorbed every ounce of the attention being dumped upon him.

My stomach's recent contents were beginning to churn with the disgust of the homage being paid to him. "So, whattaya think the chances are of Dallas making the playoffs?" I asked.

Laughter abruptly halted, and the glare from five sets of eyes was extremely intimidating.

"Let's go, sport." Miss Myra tapped on my shoulder, then tugged at my shirt. "You've worn out your welcome."

As we cleared the dining room, I commented on Senior Epstein's overt intoxication with Sarian. "Are you sure he's not a son?"

Miss Myra removed a cigarette from a fresh pack, prompting the obvious question from me, concerning her habit. "Don't judge me, sport."

"Nervous with the ex-boyfriend back in town?"

"I've long since passed on Johnny Sarian." Miss Myra led the way to the oversized three-car garage.

"So I guess Johnny calls South Heaven home?"

Beefy may have repaired the engine, but he did nothing to rectify the squeaking problem in my door hinge.

"I suppose he came back for the next game. You know, sport, the one you could stay for?"

"I thought about visiting family in London."

"I hear Austin has the only official optometry museum in the Midwest."

"Well, I've always been a fan of obscure medicine." As I slid into the driver's seat, the thumbprint-sized dark-brown stain on the lambskin cover snatched my attention. "What the…"

A barrage of unpleasantries could be heard from across the driveway. Stephanie, in her stupor, struggled to insert a key into the door of her red convertible.

Miss Myra pulled up her hair into a ball before pulling it tight with a pencil.

"You know," I said, futilely attempting to wipe the spot clear with a magic finger. "You don't have to stay here either…"

"Sport, are you in a position to offer me a job at The Republic?" Miss Myra unscrewed my car antenna from its base. "Sorry…" She quickly secured the radio receptor back to its original location.

I turned the key in the ignition, just far enough clockwise to utilize my accessory function. "If I was, would you take the job?" My radio was tuned to a country and western station.

"Why don't you stay here?"

"Are there any other stations here besides country?" I tuned the knob to something more pleasurable to the ear.

"I'm afraid that's all we have to offer."

"Well, in that case, I'll have to pass."

"If you won't stay here on your own free will…"

I interrupted by suggesting Miss Myra attend to her sister, who had dropped her keys and was on her knees searching for the lost articles.

"You're paid in advance, sport. I'm afraid I'm gonna have to play boss here and force you to work through your contract."

Despite the rumbling of the 325 engine, I was certain my laughter could be heard.

"I'm serious. You owe me one more game."

Friday, A Very Humid Evening

For the first quarter-century of my life, I had—mostly—made correct choices. Exposed and prone to yet another mistake however, without the guidance and assistance of the caravan, I left South Heaven in search of Austin and the Pickle Bowl. On the advice of an adamant Willie Tee, who was riding shotgun, we followed the maze of the county road infrastructure. Thirty minutes from kick-off and two-hours after debarking, we found Austin High School after, of course, traversing the festivities in the downtown area.

We had to park on a side street, a couple of blocks' walk from the stadium, and the gummy evening air was evident in my sodden shirt. I offered my displeasure to Willie Tee, but he only retorted with a request for two quarters to buy a soda. Out of guilt, supposedly, or just a sap for that cute face and pretty voice, I followed through with my obligation to Miss Myra: one more game.

Austin's stadium assumed the name of Kesselring. The school itself had an aged and relic appearance. Tucked neatly but tritely behind the brick school building, Kesselring Stadium had an aura of claustrophobia, with one end zone buttressing a parking lot and the other hugging the tennis court. The home stands were large in number and size, made from wood and aluminum painted church white, and mere inches from the rear facade of the school. South Heaven and her faithful had been given acceptable accommodations, albeit not as plush. Along the edges of large trees, the visitors' bleachers cushioned the grove of maples and elms.

While in line at a ticket booth, I lost Willie Tee. "One adult." I requested from the lone but jovial attendant.

Two booths no larger than an expensive armoire welcomed fans to the gates of the stadium. Both wooden box structures had been decorated with caricatures of smiling pickles. In fact, the entire stadium was engulfed in pickles. The same cartoon kosher dill, with arms, legs, and a gleaming face, was painted on sidewalks, fences, scoreboards, bleachers, and, of all things, the black cinder track. It was the Pickle Bowl.

The crowd was not as numerous as the week before, but nonetheless, I still had to circumnavigate the field to reach Austin's version of Schmidt's Summit: sturdy scaffolding rising a few feet above the height of the bleachers.

"Holy cow. I don't know how the two of you get up to these places." I was nearly out of breath after scaling the last step to reach the platform. I had swallowed another gulp of pride in showing my face to Old Man Schmidt.

With the game clock showing ten minutes to kick-off, Wally was in the driver's chair, welcoming radio fans to another "Ranger Friday Night." The night's broadcast was brought to the South Heaven fans by Value Autos, at the corner of Broad and Sycamore Streets. In bizarre contrast to his typical game conduct, Wally sat motionless and staring into nowhere.

"Darn field's got pickles painted all over it." He was in his prime, on the perch, pushing the flame from his chrome lighter to a full cigar, and decked out in all white. "You a fan of them pickles, boy?"

Smiling Pickle had his face plastered sporadically on the field of play. His olive green stood in contrast to the field itself. Both end zones advertised the Pickle Bowl in bold white letters.

Above the crowd noise, the booming voice of the public address announcer directed our attention to the south end zone. One by one, the starting offensive unit for the South Heaven Rangers was introduced, an anomalistic but welcoming gesture from the host.

Once Duane Boyd hustled onto the field, the announcer focused his attention and that of ours toward the Austin defensive unit, riling up the fervor of the home crowd. The Austin team wore green jerseys with white pants. The team had a smaller number of players on the roster than South Heaven.

Old Man Schmidt bemoaned, "Couldn't stay away? Dun told ya South Heaven got sumthin' special to it."

"This is nothing but a swan song."

The thumping of a half-dozen bass drums and the whaling of the large horns serenaded the game's prelude, leading the Austin kicker toward the tee.

Around the thirty-five, Lamont Dickies picked the ball off the bounce and darted straight up the field.

"He's stopped around the forty-two," Wally told his audience. "Wait a minute, folks! Looks like … agggh."

The home stands erupted with emotion as the referee pointed in the direction of Austin. With the initial disappointment of the turnover, few people noticed Lamont Dickies struggling to leave the field of play.

"Looks like he's holding his hand." I dialed in the binoculars and followed Dickies to the sidelines and toward the comfort of the team doctor.

Dickies did not remain on the sidelines but a few seconds. He was rushed to the south end zone and into an ambulance.

"That can't be good for the mighty Rangers."

It took only three plays to force an inept power-I offense to punt the ball back to South Heaven. It also took only three plays for Lamont Dickies' return. With his left hand wrapped in white, Dickies was escorted back to his team, but not to the field. Coach Waddell sent his offensive unit onto the field, with his only weapon being a freshman quarterback.

"Folks, we may be in trouble here with Dickies on the bench."

Boyd and his offense reflected Wally's sorrow.

As the punt team migrated onto the field, I could hardly think of much more than Stu Ginnette. I had nothing to offer the kid to get him beyond his disappointment and dejection.

Angelo Pezzotta, the reserve punter, stunned the South Heaven crowd with a booming kick that forced the Austin receiver to retreat several yards. With his back to the defense, the Austin returner fielded the ball over his shoulder, planted his feet, spun around, and sprinted to his right. A perfect wall had been built for him, a wall that contained all eleven Rangers.

"He's got the corner!" Wally inched to the edge of his chair. "Agggh! He's in the tunnel!"

My heart skipped a beat as the Austin runner bolted free down the sidelines.

Lost in obscurity, both literally and figuratively, the kid who began the play, Angelo Pezzotta, was the only Ranger who had the opportunity to end the play.

"He's at the twenty! But here comes Angelo."

"Angelo's got him!" barked Old Man Schmidt.

At the eight-yard line, the Ranger sophomore left his feet and dove, preventing a touchdown just two yards from the goal line.

The uproar from Austin fans was controlled and subtle, even when their big fullback plowed across the goal line for the game's first score.

"Packers lead it, folks."

"Wait a minute," I said, as Wally fell into commercial. "The Austin Packers?"

"Pickle Packers," Old Man Schmidt replied.

I smiled, thinking of no better sign-off from South Heaven than seeing the mighty Rangers lose to a team named for a vinegar-soaked cucumber.

The return team for Coach Waddell lacked the lead of Dickies. I scanned the sidelines and found him surrounded by the doctor and a couple of coaches.

"What's he doing?" Old Man Schmidt huffed.

With half a quarter gone and at a moment in the game that most, if not all, cynics would question, Coach Waddell requested a time-out. The perplexed hush from the Ranger fans suddenly morphed into a relieved excitement when Coach Waddell thumped his star running back on the shoulder pads and sent him into the game.

"He ain't gonna be able to field the ball with that thing wrapped 'round his hand," insisted Old Man Schmidt.

Another weak kick fluttered aimlessly toward the turf, near the Ranger thirty-five. Dodging the ball as if it were a grenade, the upbacks for South Heaven cleared the way for Dickies to retrieve the kick. The Ranger back defied traditional means and moved laterally to his left. Without an opening, he reversed field, looped backwards to lose positive yards, caught a block, then pulled up a chunk of turf with his cleat and headed up the South Heaven sideline.

In a wave pattern, fans rose to their feet, from one end of the stands to the other. Lamont Dickies was striding by them. The South Heaven players flooded the edges of the sidelines, arms waving their teammate forward.

At the Austin thirty, with pursuit a few yards behind him and an ally and two defenders in front of him, Dickies barely lost stride as he cut back to the middle of the field.

"He's runnin' all the way to the other side of the field!"

Cowbells and claxon horns penetrated my last nerve.

"One defender to beat! He's got him. No! Dickies breaks free. He's gonna score! Touchdown! Touchdown! Good God Almighty, what a run by Lamont Dickies!" Wally was dancing about the platform, albeit with an unrecognizable step. "From one side of the field to the other and back again, Lamont Dickies—whew, boy! He's tied the score."

To add extra fuel to the fire of excitement, Bo Baddey followed up his last kick attempt by bouncing the extra point off the right goalpost upright. He sucked the breath out of every fan when the ball bounced from the upright, onto the crossbar, and finally over for a successful try.

"Man, that boy's gonna give me a coronary," Old Man Schmidt said.

"Who, Dickies?"

"No, that darn kicker!"

Apparently, not fulfilled with the previous dramatic moment, Baddey failed to strike the ball cleanly and drilled a "worm-burner" toward the Austin receiver. With the kick that could not have cleared more than two inches of turf, the South Heaven defense sagged and relaxed.

The Packer receiver fielded the kick like a second baseman then bolted to his left. With the cobwebs cleared, South Heaven reacted and pursued aggressively toward the ball—with all eleven players.

As if the play were a routine drill in practice, Austin completed a reverse with absolute perfection.

"A reverse!" I shot to my feet.

He had nothing but green grass to prevent him from scoring. All eleven defenders were bunched within ten yards of one another, prompting Big

Pete to chuck his clipboard a good discus throw behind him. No pursuers close, the Packers Brandt Cooley, number thirty-six, raced seventy yards to steal the lead from South Heaven.

"Ain't how you're s'posta cover a kick." Wally removed his headset momentarily then let loose his own version of the Lord's Prayer.

With his team trailing again, and still probably catching his breath from the previous exploit, Lamont Dickies retreated to his twenty in preparation for the kick. To the best of his ability, the Austin kicker forced Dickies to the sidelines.

The lead tacklers for the Packers broke through blocks and struck Dickies simultaneously, knocking the Ranger runner backwards. Unfortunately, though, they neglected to wrap their arms around him.

Dickies rebounded from the double blow, juked another would-be tackler, and headed into a cavernous hole in the defense, created by a wedge of four Rangers.

"He's to the forty and still on his feet!" Wally had inched to the edge of his chair. "Dickies breaks another tackle!"

With his hand pressed against a teammate's back, Dickies remained one step behind his last line of defense.

"He's got Ruhl in front of him!"

Austin siphoned Dickies and Ruhl toward the sideline. The entire episode evolved in slow motion, like a junior high dance. Pushing Ruhl into one defender, Dickies bounded off his blocker's left shoulder and took on the last man standing in the way of another six points. Number seventeen in green and white, much smaller than Dickies, did not stand a chance. With head and shoulders lowered, Dickies leveled the poor kid, treading over the top of him like a tank laying waste to a decrepit outhouse.

"He's got five, maybe six guys on his tail!"

At the fifteen, the Austin pursuers had significantly closed the gap on Dickies.

"He's at the ten, shakes off one tackle … At the five, breaks through another! He's got one on his shoulder!"

Despite the resistance, Dickies leaped for the goal line.

"Touchdown! Touchdown! Good God Almighty! Are you kiddin' me? What a run by Dickies!"

Amid the mass hysteria being generated by the Ranger fans, Old Man Schmidt uttered, "Four touchdowns in less than a minute!"

"Folks, that's got to be some sort of a record!" Wally suggested. "Two kick-off returns by the same person in the same quarter—in the same minute." Wally's excitement was genuine, and I was certain it was conveyed to his audience. Despite possessing a face only a mother could love, accented by a craggy nose, pugnacious chin, and straight-seamed lips that hardly ever generated any hint of a grin, Wally appeared to relish in the opportunity to bring Ranger football to the faithful.

The Austin Pickle Packers had employed all their surprise tactics—and energy. Throughout the remainder of the turbulent first quarter and insipid second, their offense proved to be even more inept than had been predicted. Even though they maintained control of the ball, their repertoire was run right, run left, run outside, then punt.

South Heaven, with Dickies in the backfield, deployed a similar offensive strategy. However, their fourth step never included a punt. Coach Waddell mixed up the plays, hitting the Packers with Dickies inside and sprinting the young Boyd outside beyond the line of scrimmage with the option. Three sustaining drives earned South Heaven two touchdowns and a try at a short field goal, right before half. In pure form, similar to my use of the driver off the tee, Baddey ripped a dead hook on the twenty-two-yard attempt, with the ball barely inching above the helmets of his own lineman.

"You know, boy," Old Man Schmidt lit his halftime cigar with his chrome prize, "Austin here claims to have had the first soccer-style kicker."

I acknowledged him with an unconcerned shrug. His trivia was nothing more than a bore.

Attention and focus angled toward midfield and the arrangement of nominees for the Pickle Queen.

"There's a plaque over next to the school. It says in '52, a German exchange student kicked for Austin."

The parade of ten was dwindled down to three as the excitement started to build.

"Berger was his name. Kicked ten extra points in 1952."

Drowning the diatribe from Old Man Schmidt was the announcement claiming Molly Higgins as the Pickle Queen for 1980.

No sooner had the winner been crowned, the court was shuffled from the field to give the stage back to the gridiron participants. A double-reverse on the first play from the line of scrimmage had garnered Austin the element of surprise once again. Unfortunately for the Packer faithful desperate to remain a part of the game, the predetermined recipient of the touchdown run shifted his concentration from the handoff to the wide-open field in front of him.

"Fumble!" barked Wally.

Both the giver and taker for Austin, some fifteen yards behind the line of scrimmage, dove for the loose ball. Destined for a blooper highlight, the two players crashed together, striking helmet on helmet.

Knause, standing flat-footed and some half-dozen yards from the ball, was the only Ranger witness to the Packer faux pas.

"Holy...Knause picks up the ball!"

With twenty yards of unprotected pasture in front of him and two defenders lying on the turf, Kyle Knause chugged toward the goal line, exposing a weakness of his own: lack of pure speed.

"Knause is at the five ... touchdown! Touchdown! Touchdown Rangers! Good God Almighty, Knause picks up the fumble and lugs in for a score!"

With the score by the South Heaven linebacker, the heart was sucked out of Austin's players and fans. A major emigration nearly depleted the home- side stands.

By the start of the fourth, South Heaven had posted another six and was threatening with a first-and-goal from the two.

"What's the record for most points scored in a game?"

"You kiddin' me?" Wally belittled my lack of Ranger knowledge. "Ain't even close. Coach Foxx's first team beat Hickam one-oh-six ta twelve."

With a break in the on-field action, Old Man Schmidt interjected that Hickam was a first-year program, with only fourteen boys on the team.

"Yeah, but back then, we only had twenty-five. That was the game that Bucky Clemmons scored eight touchdowns." Wally added.

Dickies broke over right tackle to extend the Ranger lead to thirty-three points.

Wally assumed I was still interested in his story. "Bucky Clemmons went on to play guard for Wittenberg's basketball team. You'll never see another high-scorin' game again, in my opinion. Back then, a team had only so many players to substitute. Nowadays, if you getta big lead on someone, you can bring in reserves."

By the middle of the fourth, South Heaven had replaced ten of its eleven starters, with the lone exception being Boyd. Scoring ground to a halt, and boredom was accelerated. Coach Waddell refused to allow his freshman quarterback to throw, opting instead to utilize his backup tailback, Rex King.

Wally proposed, "How many of us would've said this team'd be unbeaten after two games, with Boyd at quarterback?"

"We must be blessed there, Wally." Old Man Schmidt replied with a smile.

"S'pose we gotta wait for two weeks against Bisum. Dexter ain't got much next week," said Wally.

As Coach Waddell gathered his troops in the end zone nearest the parking lot and Wally began securing the equipment, I asked how to find Willie Tee.

"He snooker ya inta givin' him a ride here?"

"Snooker?"

Old Man Schmidt convinced me not to worry about Willie Tee. "He'll find his way home. Always does."

"You're kidding, right? He got us lost on the way here."

"Lemme guess, you bought him dinner? He convinced you that he couldn't go much longer without food?" Old Man Schmidt consoled me. "You ain't gotta worry 'bout Willie Tee. He's done found himself another ride home."

Handing the binoculars to Wally, I offered a hint of gratitude to the two old men for allowing me to be a part of Schmidt's Summit and the broadcast team. "I'm heading back home over the weekend."

"Boy, we're two and oh. You sure you wanna be leavin' now?"

"Two and oh, or ten wins and no losses … Home is home."

Old Man Schmidt dug in the front right pocket of his trousers. "In that case…" He handed me his chrome lighter. "You take it, boy. Remind you of all of us."

"I can't take this."

"AGM had 'em made for us. You keep it."

On the front of the chrome piece was a picture of a Roadster Sport—vintage AGM. On the rear side was a picture of the Harper County courthouse.

"You just never forget us back here in the middle of nowhere, eh, boy?"

CHAPTER THIRTEEN
A National Tragedy

Sunday, Morning Departure

"You come to see me off?"

Miss Myra had little life to her, with macabre face with darkening patches under her eyes.

"I'll be sure to write." My stay had come to an end, and I was immensely pleased to be bidding South Heaven adieu.

With the call of religion dominating, South Heaven was empty on a mid-Sunday morning. My plan was to find Parma and my apartment by at least four in the afternoon. I could feel the satisfying sensation of Cleveland and was as excited as a child would be the night before a favored vacation trip. "You look like you haven't slept in a while?" My keychain held only three visitors: car ignition, trunk, and apartment. I flipped the trio of aluminum and steel keys around my right forefinger.

"Message came across the wire about an hour ago. A suicide bomber flew a hijacked plane into one of our aircraft carriers."

My rear fell against the car door.

"Several hundred are feared dead or missing."

Suddenly, my needs and desires were hardly a necessity or even trivial. "Where?"

"Haifa." Miss Myra looked at me without asking for answers then turned and walked down the sidewalk toward the paper's office.

I climbed into my car but could not find the passion or motivation to insert the key into the dashboard ignition. Cleveland held my life and future, but the present was suddenly overwhelming. As Miss Myra disappeared from sight, I chunked two quarters into the parking meter that feebly protected the curb in front of The Ranger Roost ... and made a beeline for the newspaper office.

"It sank." Miss Myra carried a single type sheet of paper and caressed a mug of steaming liquid. "Tea?"

"How does a carrier just sink?"

"You should get on the road, sport, before mass lets out." Miss Myra unloaded several spoonfuls of sugar into her mug but did not bother to stir.

"I could give you, you know, a few more days of help—I suppose, with this story and all."

"The hubbub won't be here, sport. You're not gonna be a hero here. But if you wanna stick around, I got that staff coming in here in about twenty minutes."

Monday

It was not until the morning after the wire when the word of the attack finally stretched to every corner of the town. South Heaven offered isolation and protection for her people but also an opportunity to breathe life and liberty. South Heaven was also the soul of America, and her people were stunned and immensely saddened yet irate at the loss of a U.S. carrier and the murder of hundreds of her military men. Throughout town, flags had been lowered to half-mast, the usual halted, businesses closed early, traffic decreased, and people became glued to their media outlets.

Coach Waddell, two wins in his pocket, felt compelled to cancel his initial practice of the week. That postponement gifted me an opportunity to speak with him and Big Pete. Both were in the coaches' lounge when I found them.

The lounge was an oversized shop supervisor's office with two rickety desks. One housed a couple of heaping stacks of paper while the other played host to an 8mm projector. A lone desk lamp provided just enough light.

Coach Waddell, winding film and labeling cases, never saw me enter … and bang my knee against the edge of the desk.

Big Pete was adjusting the face mask of the helmet, using a thick-handled screwdriver. A stump of a cigarette hung from his lips. "Reporter's here, Coach."

Coach Waddell wore a set of bifocals. To see me, he tipped his head downward. "You made me famous yet, Newspapuh Man?"

My pain was intense.

Big Pete labored to retrieve the ashtray holding shelter under the lamp. "Training room's down the hall, case you need some ice."

I found refuge on a desk corner, flexing my knee to alleviate some pain.

Coach Waddell secured a reel to the rickety projector and asked me to switch off the lamplight. "Just in time for game film. Dexter's been runnin' the same offense for thirty-some years now."

Big Pete broke from his equipment maintenance to retrieve me a bag of ice. Hoisting my pant leg to the top of my knee, I pressed the bag to my injury.

With the sound of grinding, the projector displayed its age and state of decay, exposing a black and white film of second quality: Dexter versus Farnsworth.

Coach Waddell convinced Big Pete it would be Dexter's fullback that could cause problems with the Ranger defense. "Boys need to hit him low."

The Dexter fullback appeared to have his way with Farnsworth, and he accounted for nine out of ten plays it took his offense to score on the drive. I inquired about the level of competition in Farnsworth.

"Oh and two," replied Coach Waddell. "That don't matter anyhow. Coach Brewer's gonna have his kids ready to play. This'll be his last year to coach. Thirty-three of 'em with Dexter. Guy started up the Monarch program."

A rap was heard on the door, but without much light, only a shadow could be discerned at the threshold.

"Coach?" a bellowed voice asked.

The table lamp exposed a stout figure in shirt and tie, with a jacket draped over the left shoulder.

"Mistuh Ross," acknowledged Coach Waddell.

"Coach. Pete." Exhausted, Mister Ross leaned against the doorframe, extracting a cigarette from a crumpled and near-empty pack. The act of smoking did not appear to be habitual for him.

Without much sincerity, Coach Waddell asked what the football team could do for the principal of the school.

Big Pete checked the contents of three used spray paint cans, vigorously shaking to vibrate the ball inside the aluminum can.

Principal Ross dug into his wallet and retrieved a five-dollar bill. "Here. Donation for paint. School board's liable to question my sanity if I send them another requisition for the football team." He had the appearance of a tax accountant during the first week of April: slacked tie knot, sweat stains seeping from under his arms, and eyeglasses perched on the crown of his head.

I asked if the donation was tax deductable.

"Son, I've been on the phone all day with the Ohio High School Athletic Board." Ross borrowed the glass-block ashtray from Big Pete.

Coach Waddell pulled open the door of an under-the-counter refrigerator and grabbed a bottle of pink stomach medicine.

"Athletic Board has requested every school consider suspending all games." Ross further loosened his olive-drab tie and unsecured the top button of his NASA engineer white shirt. With impressive shoulders and awkwardly bulging chest, Ross was a Saturday afternoon pro-wrestler masked in a costume of reality.

"We got some momentum now," Coach Waddell moaned, grimacing squeamishly as he choked down a spoonful of the pink concoction.

"Ain't a whole lot we can do in South Heaven, no way." Big Pete tossed a used can of spray paint at the waste can. He mumbled his displeasure at the sight of the can rimming the edge of the receptacle.

"People need to be remembered, Big Pete." With an unkempt fingernail, Ross scratched at the peeling paint of a helmet. "Those boys over there didn't deserve to die that way."

"Rememberin' ain't gonna do much," Big Pete said.

Ross informed us that Dexter suggested the game be cancelled. He had spoken to both the high school principal and the athletic director, neither of whom he thought deserved a complimentary word.

Coach Waddell laced up his black coaching spikes. "Ain't no fan of cancellin' no game. Like I said, we got some momentum now."

Although he lacked the appearance of a devout fan, Ross leaned toward a postponement. "I believe it to be the best."

Coach Waddell began, "Ya just can't do that. A two and oh record…"

"Why don't you leave it up to the players?" I asked.

Big Pete smothered both elbows in an obnoxiously pungent dull-gray muscle cream. "They're just kids. Besides, it's our team to…"

"No, Pete. This team belongs to me." Ross borrowed a dollop of the muscle cream. He applied it to his left forearm. "I'd actually like a vote from the team. They wanna play, and I'll call Dexter."

A huff preceded Big Pete's departure from the coach's office. He followed Ross out of the room.

"Ain't cancellin' no game." Coach Waddell tossed down the remaining stomach liquid.

"It's just high school football."

"No! No, Newspapuh Man. To you, it's just a high school game." Coach Waddell obliterated a minor but neat stack of boxes of athletic tape with a single yet swift kick from a size 11.

"Look, I'm just…"

"No, you look, Newspapuh Man. I thought you's gonna do sumthin' for me, with that article. You said a lot of folks dun read your paper. Where's that story?"

Although I had written quite a bit on that story, I had allowed too many naysayers to trump my idea. Truth be known, however, I had allowed my desire for getting out of Dodge to superimpose its will on altruism.

"I gave ya my life in a thirty-minute meetin', Newspapuh Man. Thirty-minutes, you said you get me back into the college game." Without much compassion for the eraser, Coach Waddell annihilated the chalk design of Xs and Os disorderly displayed on the wall-mounted green board. "You dun been 'round here long enough to know." He held the full-length piece of chalk like an illiterate, scribbling some sort of daily schedule toward the top of the chalkboard. "Long enough to know this be my last year coaching here at South Heaven. I'm goin' out on my own terms, though. And I'll take anything I can get—publicity, two-and-oh record, a story—anything to get me out of here. I got people comin' to see me on Friday. Ain't cancellin' no game."

Wednesday, Let Us Meet Marty

He was not overtly upset with me. However, he was neither understanding of nor did he condone my decision to remain for a longer period of time in South Haven. Of course, I told my editor there was a problem at the Sun that required my help. Had there not been an ongoing major crisis in the realm of national security occupying the day in the life of Esposito, I had the sickening feeling that my job in Cleveland would have just been a note on my resume. He granted me another week, although I was certain he would ask for penance.

With the office key that Miss Myra gave me as the honorary and very much temporary co-editor, at least in covering the attack, I arrived earlier than any other. Tuesday was a late evening for all who worked for Miss Myra. In direct contradiction to the major city papers, the Sun gave a perspective that presented factual data of the event, versus the cause-and-effect version. Ours was the job of providing information rather than stirring emotion: A French Airbus, upon take-off from Cairo, was hijacked and then flown directly into the USS Langley near Haifa, Israel. At the time we sent the paper to press, at least twelve-hundred sailors were either dead or unaccounted for.

Although still not up to par with my desire, Aunt Jenny had improved her tea brewing, despite insistence that I switch to coffee. In front of me, on the lobby counter, was a fulfilling breakfast of tea and a cheese omelet. Krisp's had managed to supply me copies of the Lima Daily News and the Columbus Herald, both rungs below The Republic, however. More advanced than the periodical from Lima, the Columbus paper was announced there were two local men who victims of the attack.

The cowbell attached to the front door warned me of a visitor.

"Where's Myra?" The visitor was actually the paper's photographer, Marty Workman. Without much need or budget for a full-time photojournalist, Miss Myra could only employ Marty on a need-only basis. Therefore, Marty worked sporadically for the paper. Just a kid, Marty had the misfortune of being a dreamer, believing that a degree in photography from a nearby junior college would send him on the fast track out of town. He had been working for Miss Myra since his sophomore year in high school. Thus far, his biggest self-prescribed work to date was the picture of Senator Todd Walker during the politician's visit to the abandoned auto facility.

Four eggs and copious amounts of cheddar calmed my growling stomach. "Something I can help you with?"

Marty could have been a holdover from the peak days of Haight-Ashbury. Teaming with a ragged olive-drab U.S. Army jacket, he wore hole-ridden blue jeans and moccasins. A red plaid bandanna stretched like a sweatband amid a disheveled mess of hair that extended to his upper back. "You got seventy bucks?"

"On me?"

"My tuition's coming due." A tall kid, Marty had a book bag around one of his vacant shoulders and two cameras around the other. His societal naiveté complemented succinctly the boyish face sprouting the mere hint of facial hair.

I offered him the three dollars in my wallet, at the same time encouraging him to drop his penny-ante job and enroll at an "authentic" institution to pursue a real degree.

"I should've just stayed with my mom at Saint Anthony's. They were having a vigil to pray for jobs. I suppose I could've asked the Lord for tuition money."

Miss Myra entered with an open magazine in her face. "I gave you an advance last month, Marty."

Despite a soft and level voice that suggested little to no personal motivation, Marty insisted that the college raised his tuition, referring to the administration as selfish capitalists. Like a child following his mother throughout the house, he trailed behind Miss Myra into the reporter's "bullpen."

"That advance I gave you got lost in the nostrils of your girlfriend." Miss Myra tuned a transistor radio to a news station in time for a weather update. "I'm not giving you another. Besides, I thought you were taking shots of babies and kids?"

"I needed the money for Stacey's car." Marty dug into his book bag to retrieve two slugs of film then slid each into the same number of 35mm cameras. "Her Nova had to get new brakes."

"Did you actually see her buy those brakes, Marty?"

"No."

Miss Myra disappeared into her office.

"You sure you don't want my three bucks?" I tossed a whole packet of salt onto the remaining portions of my omelet.

Confident that Miss Myra was not an ally, Marty wandered out, carrying his tools instead of hauling them.

I asked her if she had received any feedback from the locals on the recent edition of the paper.

"Why? You looking for an atta-boy, sport?"

With the appearance of Senior Epstein, the cowbell clanged twice.

"Daddy?"

Epstein was troubled, beyond his laggard gait and ghostly paleness. I stood to acknowledge him, but he merely muddled by me.

"Myra." Epstein grasped his daughter's hand. "Davey Bryant was onboard the Langley."

Friday

September had introduced summer to autumn, and there was transition in the air.

I had been asked to prepare myself for the festivities of opening night. Willie Tee tried to convince me to believe in the power of the first home game. An hour and a half before the Dexter game, a parking spot could not be found remotely close to the stadium. Fortunately, the evening was comfortable, and my walk from Aunt Jenny's was just short of proclaimed exercise.

By an overwhelming vote, Coach Waddell's troops opted to play the game.

South Heaven, although generations behind mainstream America, was taking the terrorist attack personally. The townsfolk had a reason to move beyond shock. Davey Bryant had been and would always be a Ranger.

Marty was just inside the gate to Gottmann Field, bent at the waist and retrieving a dime from the matted grass. He shot upward. "You scared me." He added the dime to a collection of coins in his palm. Strangely, without being prompted, he shared his disdain for sports.

"Doesn't the paper pay you to take pictures of games?" I sidestepped the detachment of JROTC members carrying the nation's ensign, the flag of Ohio, and the symbol of the Air Force.

"I take them only when I need the money." He ensured that I understood his high school years were torturous, having been hazed by the jocks. Stocked with his usual book bag and camera, Marty huffed a last snort toward his bullies then disappeared into the crowd.

The obligatory throng of admirers had encircled Sarian once again.

The crowd was thick and milling about outside of the stadium, several minutes prior to kick-off. The number of Nerf games had multiplied three-fold since the scrimmage in August. Five-on-five to three-on-three, kids were engrossed in their individual games and ill-concerned about the space and well-being of bystanders. Both bands began committing treason, socializing with one another—South Heaven in dress maroon and white, while Dexter was without headgear in royal blue and gold.

For the first instance since arriving in South Heaven, I actually had to fend off an emotion of excitement. Then, Willie Tee found me.

Willie Tee was in an obnoxious scarlet satin jacket with gold buttons running up and down the sternum. The jacket nearly consumed his emaciated frame. "You gottuh quarter?"

I found his request among three dimes and two pennies. "How do you manage to get into the gate with no money?"

"Bless ya, man. Bless ya," he said, caressing the coin. He pulled close to me, scanning the area for spies, I assumed. Willie Tee, apparently, snuck into all games. "Da good Lord, he get me in ovuhr that there fence, behind da visituhs' side."

With the sun descending and obligatory anticipation pushing to a crescendo, both the Monarchs and home Rangers relinquished control of the field, heeding to the Pride of South Heaven and an adequate rendition of "Ol' Man River." With the last note to "Yankee Doodle

Dandy," the band broke from a disciplined bearing and mustered slowly into a bunched formation.

A powerful and distinctive tone, P.T. Bailey, the genuine voice of the Ranger band, asked the audience for attention then requested that everyone rise to their feet.

To honor those fallen sailors and Marines, the Ranger band slowly fell into "God Bless America."

In uniform procession, one player after another, the South Heaven Rangers streamed onto the field from the locker room entrance. Carrying an American flag attached to a four-foot pole, Lamont Dickies led his team down the sidelines, directly in front of the South Heaven faithful. It held the crowd breathless and spellbound.

From my sideline position, steps from the playing field, I was but one of the captivated onlookers.

Only one man in the stadium seemed ill-concerned about the spectacle occurring on the field: Marty. On one knee, he was rummaging apathetically through his book bag. Spread on the turf around him were two cameras and a few film cases.

"Marty!" I quickly closed the dozen yards between us. "Marty!"

"Yeah?"

"Are you gonna get a shot of this?"

"Of what?"

I snatched one of his cameras and pointed emphatically toward the procession. "This!"

Laboring arduously, he fitted a small lens onto the black and silver camera, focused for too many seconds, and snapped the shutter.

On the last note of "America the Beautiful," P.T. Bailey asked, in a simple and solemn voice, for a moment of silence—and the moment was powerful. Nerf games paused, jittering among fans ceased, a toying breeze allowed the American flag a sigh of relief, and both teams, aligned on their respective sidelines, bowed their heads. "Thank you."

"Where you going?" I demanded of Marty as he collected his working gear and headed for the end zone.

Apparently, Marty had a proclaimed station in the end zone, among the South Heaven band and former high school friends.

"Develop that photo." I was late for my appointment in the Summit. "Put it onto the front page."

Marty tossed me aside with a single arm wave. "I've been on the front page before."

I could have used my newly ordained authority to demand Marty develop his photo, but kickoff was near and the teams were finding their appropriate positions on the field.

By the time I found the Summit, the kick-off had come and gone, and I missed two passes by Dexter quarterback Quinten Robinson.

"You see that?" Wally gleamed. "Dexter quarterback threw that ball some sixty yards."

On the air, Old Man Schmidt preached the gospel of South Heaven's defense and their halt of the Monarchs in three plays. "No nerves from the defense. Let's see if the offense can contain their first-home-game jitters, folks."

Wally informed me that Quinten Robinson was Coach Hank Brewer's grandson. "Brewer graduated from Ohio State and played for Paul Brown," said Wally as Dickies crashed through the left side of the Dexter defense to gain six yards.

Old Man Schmidt barked to his audience, with more excitement than clarity, that Boyd had laid a perfect corner pass to Durning. "First down Rangers!"

"For all the times we played Dexter, Brewer never put the ball in the air. Now, he's got his grandson."

With the ball at the Dexter twenty-nine and the down marker registering three, Duane Boyd faked a dive to his fullback then rolled down the left side of his offensive line. Dickies followed him in a pitch relationship.

Believing the play to be an option, every linebacker and defensive back for the Monarchs stepped forward to defend the play.

At his tackle's outside shoulder, Boyd pulled up and dropped straight back to throw.

"He's got Scott Marsh wide open!" yelled Old Man Schmidt.

Marsh, a Ranger split end, was running an unmolested, uncontested, and unguarded post pattern.

Boyd's ball could hardly have been called a spiral, but it was in the air and leading Marsh toward the end zone.

Anticipation pulled the South Heaven faithful to their feet, while fear of the potential unknown forced some to hide their faces inside palms of hands.

It was simply backyard pitch-and-catch for Boyd and the senior Marsh. Simple—as the ball painfully migrated through the air. Simple—to put six points on the board. Simple—until the goal line tripped up the Ranger split end. Marsh dropped to the turf like he had been shot in the back. Boyd's wobbly spiral bounded off his receiver's helmet. It was fourth down.

"Aggh! Unbelievable, folks!"

I choked back a snicker.

As if the botched touchdown pass were not enough for a heart to handle, Kyle Knause insisted he fill the South Heaven faithful with a tad more excitement. On Dexter's first play from scrimmage following the Ranger punt, the Monarch fullback, vaunted Toby Rust, blasted through the "two-hole," looking to expose a sag in the defense. Reacting to the Monarch surge, Knause filled the hole and leveled a helmet hit on the lowered Rust. Both boys fell backwards like two horned rams. The football flew out of Rust's hands and into the opportune arms of a player who, according to Old Man Schmidt, had suffered through a debilitating birth defect as an infant that required extensive and numerous surgeries and several purposeful breaks of leg bones: Bobby Wiggins.

A roar erupted among the Ranger fans.

"Bone's got the ball at the ten!" Old Man Schmidt rapped his cane with every lumbering step Wiggins took.

"Run!"

"Bobby Bones," as he was known by his teammates, was making use of a convoy gradually breaking down around the four. That decaying convoy allowed two smaller Monarchs to climb onto the defensive end. Despite his blocker's ineptitude, Bobby Bones carried those two Monarchs on his back and into the end zone.

"Touchdown! Bones scores!" Old Man Schmidt could hardly control his excitement for the young man.

The Ranger defensive end was mauled by his defensive teammates in the end zone, prompting Big Pete to storm the field to yank his kids back to the sidelines.

Meanwhile, as the celebration continued, Kyle Knause lay prone on the field, just a few yards from his fellow combatant. His violent collision required the presence of the South Heaven doctors.

The ruckus of the crowd diminished as the severity of the situation was revealed.

"Folks, Kyle Knause is still on the field."

Rust showed signs of life and more as he rose to his feet under the guidance of a staff of three. He staggered toward the visitors' bench but received not an ounce of applause of appreciation from the South Heaven fans because Knause was still down.

Both Coach Waddell and Big Pete shuffled onto the field. Coach Waddell paced around the circle attending to Knause, while Big Pete pushed his way into the inner sanctum. The count had barley hit ten before Big Pete had pulled Knause to a seated position. The crowd responded with reluctant applause. Leaving the medical staff and Coach Waddell in tow, Knause and Big Pete jogged into the waiting arms of appreciative teammates.

After Baddey pull-hooked the extra point, Coach Waddell stunned both sides of the field by electing to squib-kick. Playing into Baddey's strength of poor kicking, Coach Waddell must have ordered his kicker to drill a line-drive into number seventy-seven of Dexter's front five.

Proving the theory that linemen have hands like street signs, seventy-seven permitted the oblong ball to attack him first, and Baddey's kick took one bounce and struck the lineman squarely in the numbers.

My shoulders slumped and head flagged.

Like piranhas on decaying flesh, eleven Rangers bounded for the loose ball, creating a bastardized scrum.

"Folks, they're fightin' for the ball!" Old Man Schmidt said. "Durning's got it!"

The South Heaven tight end freed himself from the scrum and leaped in celebration, with the ball held above him.

Devouring the crowd's enthusiasm, the Ranger offense needed only one play to post a second score in less than fifteen game-time seconds. On the first down, Boyd took three steps into the pocket then swung a pass to Dickies, who was circling out of the backfield. The five-yard throw resulted in a fifty-two-yard touchdown pass and put South Heaven up by twelve.

"That's number eleven," said Wally.

Watching Baddey use every inch of the ten-yard width of the goalpost to secure the extra point, I inquired as to why Wally was so giddy.

"That was Dickies' eleventh career touchdown against Dexter, one shy of the record against one opponent."

With three minutes to go in the quarter, Old Man Schmidt asked Wally to relieve him of the headset then, unfortunately for me, expounded on Dickies' potential record. "It was his first game two years ago. Lance Poulter got hurt on the first or second play of the game. Dickies came into replace him. He'd go on to score six touchdowns against Dexter. Heck, last year at Dexter, Dickies scored four times and rushed for three-hundred yards. Record's now held by Blue Laces, against Edina."

"Why do you guys bother broadcasting home games?"

"Not every person in South Heaven goes to the games. Fact is, first game we ever done was a home game. Taped the game on Friday and broadcasted it on Saturday, right out of the basement."

Of the two combatants who attacked one another earlier, only Kyle Knause returned to battle. And without the threat of a ground game from Rust, Dexter was completely limited in execution. Young Robinson displayed his arm strength, completing a couple of passes, but he had little support and spent much of the first and second quarter on his back.

With three minutes remaining in the first half, and with the South Heaven offense stagnant, holding onto the thirteen-point lead, Coach Waddell debunked conventional wisdom and directed his freshman quarterback into a shotgun formation.

Old Man Schmidt moaned at the sight of Duane Boyd readying himself four yards behind center.

Boyd nearly expired his allotted time, directing and barking cadence, which dropped the Dexter defenders onto their heels. His receivers were spread, and only one back remained with the quarterback.

"You gotta be kiddin' me," clamored Old Man Schmidt.

Everyone in Schmidt's Summit and all who purchased tickets—cynics and experts alike— agreed with Old Man Schmidt.

I, too, jumped on the bandwagon, but my stomach was not churning. Not churning, that is, until the group of fans standing along the south end zone began jumping up and down with amazed excitement.

"Good God Almighty!" Wally spit out his bite of hot dog. "It's a fake! Dickies has the ball. He's at the twenty!"

Lamont Dickies, somehow, had received a short snap from center and was all but alone as he crossed the goal line for a forty-nine-yard run and his second touchdown of the night.

"Unbeeleevable!" Wally fell back into his chair as if he had just completed a two-mile swim.

Old Man Schmidt grinned. "New record, by golly."

Halftime could not arrive soon enough, and it brought a twenty-point lead and much confidence for the South Heaven faithful. Like the setting of a sun—clockwork, as some would call it—the Nerf football games restarted, and crowds swelled around the concession stand. Although crude and almost comical, halftime was a ritual unto itself, for the fans of the game. The concession structure was more than simply an omnipresent physical entity. It seemed to serve as the paragon of gathering places for the South Heaven fans, for collective commiseration, spewing cynicism, or, on occasion, congratulating a father on a boy's exploits in the first half. Food, for the average fan, appeared to be of secondary importance.

Peculiarly, Sarian was alone, however. With both head and back flushed against the red brick, he had found a secluded spot along the exterior of the high school, near the entrance to the gymnasium. He lacked any representation of a man worshipped by many, with a dangling cigarette and an opened can of beer.

On my way to the lavatory, outside of the stadium, I stopped. "Hey."

"I don't have a pen or paper, Big Guy." He exhaled a cloud of smoke through his nostrils.

"I ... already..." I flashed him the prized page from my notebook containing the mark of Blue Laces.

With his athletic prowess, he flicked the butt an impressive distance.

Obvious sarcasm was pasted all over my inquiry into the rules of alcohol consumption on school grounds.

After a swig, Sarian suggested curtly that I move along.

"I understand Lamont Dickies broke a record of yours tonight?"

"Records," he sighed, shielding his eyes from the lamplight that popped on out of the blue. "This is high school, pal."

As quickly as the light illuminated the gym entrance, it flickered and fizzled out.

"I s'pose it'd be good for my fans to see me shake the boy's hand..."

A duo of adolescents wandered near us but given the lack of light, paid little attention to the two of us. They were preoccupied with gestures of puppy love.

"I still have two more records, you know?" Sarian interjected. "And he ain't gonna break them." Like an eighth-grader trying to impress his buddies, Sarian stomped on the top of the beer can, crushing it flat against the asphalt. "I 's'pose it's time to go give the fans more of Blue Laces." The injury that had apparently dismissed him from stardom was obvious as he made his way back toward the stadium. The bum knee meshed awkwardly with his bowlegged gait.

I outpaced him on my way back to the experts in the Summit. As soon as I arrived, those experts had little in terms of accolades to offer the Monarchs. The season was only two games old, but credit should have been granted to Coach Brewer. By the time the Monarchs received the ball in the second half, Rust was back, and Robinson was on target. His first three passes found their mark, and Rust was gaining five to six yards with every carry of the football.

South Heaven, the heavyweight champ, had come out in the sixth round and taken a couple of shots in the chops. The defense was hesitant to force the attack, no longer willing to mix it up. Kyle Knause and his comrades were surrendering yardage in huge chunks. Big Pete, the corner man, made a dire attempt to stem the first Dexter drive of the second half by substituting here and there. Robinson and the Monarchs were on Big Pete's ten-yard line.

"Looks like we're still in the locker room here," piped Old Man Schmidt.

Two plays later, Robinson lifted my confidence when he hit his flanker on a slant for six and completely silenced the home crowd.

I rubbed my hands together vigorously, as if preparing to cut into my main meal course.

Coach Waddell, with arms crossed, eyeballed each one of his defenders as they muddled toward the sidelines, following the converted extra point. Big Pete grouped the defensive unit on the bench and proceeded to nearly self-induce a heart attack. His rant echoed through the silent home stands.

Despite Big Pete's overload, the momentum had clearly shifted to the visitor. Two running plays to Dickies netted the Rangers a mere three yards. Boyd took the third-down snap but pitched the option behind his tailback, resulting in a fourth down. The subsequent punt from Pezzotta spiraled to a landing around the forty and rolled another fifteen yards across midfield.

Coach Brewer pushed a shotgun offense in the game. Along with Robinson in the backfield, a lone runner crouched in a three-point stance. South Heaven gambled with a four-four zone defense.

Robinson took the snap on a quick count, rolled to his left, and hit a wide-open receiver on a ten-yard curl. Fortunately for the home faithful, two Rangers reacted quickly to avert a big gain. On the second play from scrimmage, Robinson spread his receivers again, forcing the South Heaven backers to match the split formation. Robinson faked a quick throw then handed the ball to Rust, who broke through the line and found open territory. He demanded three Rangers bring him down on the South Heaven twenty-five.

Big Pete substituted frantically, enticing ridicule of the Summit.

Four new defenders, however, did not do much to stop Rust. In a tight formation, Robinson called his fullback's number on four consecutive plays. Rust lumbered forward for twenty-one yards.

Wally yanked off the headset, covered the mouthpiece with his hand, and swore until his voice became hoarse.

The horn to end the third could not be heard above the roar of the visitors. Rust scored on a two-yard plunge to pull his team within six points.

"It's the Dexter curse," Old Man Schmidt moaned. Over the span of halftime and the third quarter, he had worn out his cigar and began munching on a nub.

"That curse's hogwash!" Wally waved off Old Man Schmidt. "Bunch of barbershop talk."

"You wait and see, Wally."

Despite an argument from my conscience to avoid the topic, I inquired.

"Back in '73." Old Man Schmidt obliged, despite Wally's heckling. "Playin' at Dexter and had 'em down twenty-zip in the second half."

The Monarch kick fluttered to an upback who proceeded to step left—directly into a fellow Ranger. Like precision clockwork, the ball squirted from Ranger hands onto the ground, winding up in the surprised but unwelcoming arms of the blue and white.

"See, Wally!"

Enthusiasm and lust for the win were distinct and evident in the manner in which the two teams entered the field. Dexter's offense sprinted to the huddle while South Heaven meandered, some players donning equipment as they piddled onto the field.

"They came back on us, tied the score. Then, with ten seconds left, their quarterback Eli Wetzel threw a touchdown pass to win."

Rust continued to punish the Ranger defenders. He had forced the overflowing South Heaven crowd into stunned disbelief.

"In '74, back at our place," Old Man Schmidt continued. "Same score to start the second half. They came back again to tie the game at twenty. This time, with half a minute to go, that darn Wetzel threw another pass to win the game. Cursed, I'm tellin' ya."

"Don't listen to him. There ain't no curse!"

Curse or not, Rust hauled his team down to the South Heaven eight-yard line with just over nine minutes to play.

"They score here and kick the point, and we're cooked." Old Man Schmidt chastised himself for not packing an extra smoke. He tossed his stub aside then obliterated it with the bottom of his cane.

First and second downs acquired four yards for Rust and his Monarchs. The time on the clock continued to disappear at an agonizingly slow pace, however. On third down, the sage Brewer elected to implement his spread formation—two split left and two right. Robinson scanned the defense, an improvised four-three with four defenders man-up on receivers. The Dexter quarterback received a shotgun snap and dropped a couple of steps to the rear. Rust slid to his quarterback's blind side. In steady and professional composure, despite blitzing linebackers bearing down on him, Robinson lofted the ball to his right and the corner of the end zone. The perfect pass fell into the outstretched arms of his target.

"He's outta bounds! Piper caught it, but he's outta bounds. Good God Almighty!" Wally's body language surely played a part in guiding the spiral out of the field of play.

Dexter settled for three points, placing them the same number in the hole.

Old Man Schmidt's plea and the crowd's chant for some sort of offense fell on deaf ears. A run by Dickies and two incomplete passes by the freshman forced another South Heaven punt.

With just under six minutes to play, Robinson and Rust took over possession. Methodically, they marched the Monarchs into Ranger territory. Rust carried five times, with each run stealing dozens of seconds from the game clock.

Old Man Schmidt spoke of Coach Brewer like he would of a despised brother-in-law. "He's gonna eat up all the clock."

A quarterback keeper around left end by Robinson nestled the ball near a first down and burned another thirty seconds, and the clock fell below two minutes.

"Daggonit!" Wally paced as far as the cord would allow.

For those of us on the rooting side of Dexter, one could feel the inevitability of victory.

"It's the curse," hollered Wally."

Coach Waddell elected not to stop the clock, despite a Rust run to his five.

The emotion and gravity of the situation coursed through the South Heaven fans. Both sides, visitors and Rangers, stood on tippy-toes, probably praying to the Lord for salvation, yelling encouragement, or simply ingesting the aura.

As soon as the clock dragged to the half-minute mark, Robinson took the second-down snap and rolled past the tackle box to his right.

"Ah Lord, here we go," chimed Old Man Schmidt.

Squaring his shoulders to the line of scrimmage with Knause only steps away, Robinson fired toward the back of the end zone.

A collective gasp from the South Heaven faithful shook the Summit as the pass sailed over its target. South Heaven was still alive—and I was near wearing out my welcome.

"Wally, I knew this two-and-naught record was too good to be true."

The ruckus resumed as Robinson brought the Monarchs to the line on third down. He surveyed a four-four defense and appeared to begin an audible.

I suggested play options to Robinson.

Knause and his men held their ground, failing to bite on the quarterback's change of plans. Robinson took the snap and darted for right end, a sprint option with Rust as his pitch man. A seam appeared at the void, granted by the Ranger defensive backer, and the quarterback assumed the advantage, planting a cleat and tucking the ball.

We lost sight of Robinson and the ball. Our eyes shot to the line judge … no touchdown signal. Fourth down.

Providing relief for those of us whose heart, mind, and soul had been punished by the pounding waves of emotion, Coach Brewer signaled for a stoppage of the clock. His staff attempted frantically to retrieve the Monarch players who had stormed the field in anticipation of raised arms by the referee.

Ten headache-engendering seconds remained in a game of two separate halves. South Heaven, the team that the second half had abandoned, had boots in the seawater, protecting precarious inches of beachhead they called home. Dexter, with either a makeup change or butt-chewing under their belt, charged out of the locker room and was one yard away from not only completely owning the second half, but winning the battle and justifying Old Man Schmidt's belief in the curse.

No one sat.

Robinson brought to the line two tight ends and a full-house backfield. He faced an odd eight-man front, harboring three linebackers within feet of the line of scrimmage. Two bruising formations of football years past were set to do battle, two foes whose participants dug their cleats deeper and deeper into the chewed turf of the trenches. Staring down the defense, Robinson's head bobbed with the cadence calls.

I could feel the overwhelming thud of my heart rattle its cage.

The noise bursting from the home stands grew atrocious and overbearing as hundreds of feet thumped the concrete and cowbells poisoned the air.

Suddenly, a commotion stirred in the center of the line. Robinson scoured the turf in search of a loose football, and the ends of the lines collapsed into a heap. The pigskin was lost, until out of nowhere emerged the boy who would become the hero of the night for the Rangers.

Like a devastating earthquake, a roar vibrated Gottmann Field.

Chugging and churning, bumbling and stumbling, Blaine "Teddy Bear" Manning, the largest member of Coach Waddell's team, had a pair of blockers with him and turned the entire sidelines and grandstands into one lump of mass hysteria. Without height and at two-hundred and sixty-five pounds, Manning had the physique of a swollen water balloon. He carried the ball like a ticking bomb and had to be pushed along by teammates.

"Good God Almighty, Bear's got the ball!"

By the time any Monarch sensed his surroundings, it was far too late.

"We're gonna win! We're gonna win! Teddy Bear stole the ball!"

I was certain Blaine had never run farther than the length of the diving board to complete a cannon ball. By the time he reached the Dexter thirty, he was being held up by his lead blockers.

"He's at the twenty!"

Once he reached the fifteen, Manning's only pursuers had relented, but his teammates on the bench were streaming down the sidelines with helmets swinging in the air.

"He's at the ten! He's ... at the five! Touchdown! Touchdown! Touchdown Manning!" Wally was done.

The moment Manning crossed the goal line, he fell to the turf. The entire South Heaven team leaped on the big boy in celebration. From every corner of the stadium, fans flooded the field.

CHAPTER FOURTEEN
Home At Last—Or Am I?

Thursday

I returned to my career. Understanding wholeheartedly the ultimatum from my editor and enforcer of my employment, I provided little effort in convincing myself there was no choice. Common sense overruled and placed me back at an organized but dusty desk and among people who had no concern for anyone but their own person. Each reporter and writer surrounding me professed to know and understand people and the world, simply because they reported on behavior or submitted an editorial on emotional consequence. Truth be told, though, most never ventured out from behind their typewriter. They lived the job of The Republic, entering and leaving the office under the cover of darkness with their only human contact being fellow martini men at a corner bar. Of course, they were still my heroes and aspiration, and the paper was my home.

As for the position Miss Myra promised me at the Sun, I could not see myself scraping enough together on a monthly basis to even afford the apartment above the Ranger Roost.

Regarding Old Man Schmidt, I thought if we did not meet on my way out of town, I was destined to leave South Heaven.

"Hey. Welcome back." Gavin Gray, a peer of mine even though his degree read Baldwin-Wallace, worked as a beat reporter covering the Cleveland Indians—a macho job to compensate his ineptitude in height at five feet and four inches. "Some of us are meeting at Barney's in an hour for beers then headin' down to a Tribe game."

In the past, I humored the group, tagging along to the trendy bar on Euclid. The gatherings were nothing more than a pressing of egos.

"We got the boss's box seats, man." Gavin had earned a spot on the bench of the Baldwin-Wallace baseball team. Despite self-proclaimed accolades, actual records indicated Gavin swung the bat a grand total of ten times in his four years with the Yellow Jackets. However, the third-string infielder for B-W was extremely content with his life. "Tribe's on a roll—three in a row."

Fortunately, my desk phone interrupted and pushed Gavin to continue conversing in the cubicle next to me.

"Metro." I retrieved the receiver after the third ring.

"I suppose you're glad to be back in the big city?" For the short period of time I knew him, Senior Epstein rarely offered any man an initial word of kindness.

"Yeah."

The mail clerk, Wizard, a curmudgeon of an old man who despised the presence of others, had logged forty-three years with the paper and looked every bit as if each day of his past had punished him in some manner. He pushed his cart by my cubicle and offered me criticism for the lack of a mailbox on my desk. He tossed two envelopes at me.

"Listen here, Wright. You need to be back in South Heaven." He had no need for wasted energy, including idle conversation. "I need you back here…"

Scanning over a press release from the mayor's office concerning the hiring of police officers, I failed to oblige what must have been some sort of tasteless joke. "My plate's kind of full now—a shooting last night on the east end."

"My daughter's selling my paper, Wright. I can feel it."

My pen halted and began a line of scribbles. I was intrigued. "Well, Sir, I can honestly tell you that I am not the buyer."

"No, you fool."

The consistently accurate and efficient clattering of electronic keys disturbed our conversation. Connie Morovski occupied an adjacent desk. The newest reporter to our department was just four months removed from Kent State and assigned to "Parks and Recreation." Since my return, she had pestered me for an opinion on a new pen name. The tradition and respect of her father's family surname lacked flair.

"How about an assistant editor job?" Senior Epstein barked. "Come back here and keep an eye on things for me."

"I'm but a few minutes from finding a stool in a bar, enjoying a microbrew only found here in the heart of Cleveland. Then, of course, it's box seats at Cleveland Stadium to catch an Indians game—all because I have a good—no, check that, great entry-level job with the largest paper in the state. Besides, Miss Myra already tried to offer me an ops manager spot."

Senior Epstein retorted that it would take me many moons before I could even whiff an editor position at The Republic.

"As flattering as all that sounds…"

With the clock passing four, the ever-impatient Gavin, both brown locks and moustache teased with gel, reappeared and insisted that he give me a ride to Barney's. "Everybody's waiting, man." Gavin's playboy and Club 54 attire did little to compensate for his lack of prowess in stature.

"Mister Epstein, I appreciate the offer, but…"

"I got something else for you."

Wednesday, Lunch Outside Krisp's

I missed the Saturday afternoon contest, either considered the game of a lifetime or a wickedly anomalistic event, rivaling that of a snowstorm in June or accidentally exploding one's own garage.

The Blue Devils of Bisum did not own a home field. Instead, they borrowed the playing surface of Mullen College, a hometown four-year school of less than two-thousand students. With an unbeaten record, Bisum welcomed the Rangers for a Pioneer and Explorer league contest without the glamour of Friday night lights. The weekend brought an early fall storm, a deluge of rain that began some two hours prior to the noon kick-off. Said deluge emulsified a perfectly sodded field, creating a small lake approximately one-hundred and twenty yards in length, fifty-two yards wide, and a few inches deep.

The sports headline for the Sun was simple yet explicit. Miss Myra or some other artisan at the paper captured the entire game with three words: "Ugly. Ugly. Ugly."

In stretches of time marked in single-digit minutes or scores of seconds, the rain relented. Beyond that, Mother Nature tortured and abused everyone inside the Mullen stadium complex. With first place in the conference on the line, the game came down to turnovers, turnovers, and more turnovers. Both squads combined managed to post an astonishing 23 transgressions. In four grueling quarters of what resembled football, the offense of the Blue Devils contributed thirteen fumbles to the record book, while the Rangers chipped in seven of their own. Both teams, despite the rain, attempted to throw the ball—three interceptions. Contributing to the bizarre nature of the contest, both defenses put up two goal-line stands a piece, completely denying the opposition a lone score.

Those unfortunate souls who braved the rainstorm were treated only once in the game. Through the slop and turnover-ridden contest came a play epitomizing the Ranger season. With a couple dozen yards of total offense netted for both teams in three and one-half quarters, Bisum committed to a successful drive beginning at midfield. In response to one bad Ranger punt, Bisum played on a short field for the entire second half. Several generous dive plays pushed the ball to the Ranger thirteen-yard line. With just over two minutes to play, a break was forced in the clouds, and with the halt in the deluge, Bisum instituted a surprise pass play. Luke Post jumped the route of the Bisum receiver, intercepted the pass, and returned the ball seventy yards.

From the twenty-five, South Heaven exhausted the remainder of the game clock, but not before Lamont Dickies scored the lone and winning touchdown.

I held a precarious spot on the park bench outside of Krisp's. The security of steel into concrete was speculative, at best, since the support of the bench had broken from its support base. The bench had become a rocking one. A day earlier, on Pearl Road in Parma, I had turned my apartment key in to Mister Nowak, my landlord—the same man rarely with a shirt or without a Korean War story. For three years, I had collected enough of the trivial and material to own a corner museum along Main Street, and that collection required a twenty-foot box truck to move all of it back into my parents' garage. Despite their protests, they accepted everything from my lounge chair to a set of six dinner plates. I did, however, move my awards, degrees, and other accolade trinkets with my person to South

Heaven. I convinced my boss to extend me a leave of absence—sort of. I had either gone completely astray of reality or was lured by Senior Epstein's offer. Maybe I had a bit of compassion for Miss Myra.

"Anybody here readin' this paper?" A passer-by asked me. Without approval, the middle-aged man, with a ragged and dirty face that balanced well with a filthy set of blue overalls, began fingering my paper as it rested on the bench. Apparently, his vision was not interrupted by the dark-tinted sunglasses he wore. While glancing through the classifieds, he chewed on a long and narrow piece of hay.

"I think the library's down the street. I'm sure they'll have a couple of copies."

"This one here will do just fine."

"But that's my copy," I said, watching in perturbed amazement as the stranger casually strolled up Main Street with my paper in hand.

The lunchtime sun was warm on the skin, not overbearing but enough to be uncomfortable given a durable exposure. My extra-large soda committed admirably to combating the perspiration on my forehead. I had asked for two weeks of leave from The Republic, thinking in that time period that I would be able to decide the value of Senior Epstein's offer. To say my editor was less than reticent to the idea would be to insult his innate ability to engender wall-vibrating rants and episodes. In one taciturn blurt, he demanded a choice: status quo or the unknown. Within an hour of digesting ridicule from my editor, I had my desk cleared of belongings.

Before leaving The Republic, I had smuggled Marty's photos of the pregame versus Dexter into the hands of a good friend, Britt Policy. As a sports photographer, Britt had only a half-dozen years under his belt and lived a life in obscurity. But Britt knew the business. A fellow Oberlin graduate, Britt took two of Marty's photos and suggested potential. The day my personal belongings were stowed into my parents' garage, I received a frantic call from Britt—frantic being relative, considering he generally had the demeanor of a man on his death bed. Sport World Weekly picked up one of Marty's photos and decided to submit it in their next issue.

Marty was still oblivious to the recognition, and I had every desire to be the one to surprise him. I camped outside of Krisp's and waited for the delivery truck. Krisp's was undergoing a slight overhaul to its exterior. Two employees of Caleb Brothers were replacing a red awning with a white one. The awning shaded the storefront window of Krisp's, particularly during the evening hours. The original awning had fallen victim to pranksters who, apparently, had viewed it as canvas for spray paint.

The barrel horn of what appeared to be an 18-wheeler polluted the area with three blasts. "Hey, boy!" In reality, it was not a truck but Old Man Schmidt's Cadillac. Without concern for other vehicles, Old Man Schmidt lumbered the convertible along the curb, occupying two rather than the one obligatory parallel parking spot.

An evergreen enclosed delivery truck followed Old Man Schmidt. Its driver opted to double-park alongside the Caddy.

A burly figure of a woman, in olive shirt, shorts, and cap, bounded from the loading deck of the box, with a hefty stack of periodicals on her shoulder.

"Sport World?" I stared at the stack wrapped in grocery-bag brown paper and held together by string.

"Yup," she replied, disappearing into the store.

Struggling with the cane, Old Man Schmidt lowered his frame to the bench seat. "Thought you was gone?" He sighed with a gasp of relief as he reclined.

"I was."

As I crept closer to the store's entrance, Old Man Schmidt asked me to fetch him a root beer. "Not that cheap stuff he's got in front of the chill box, neither."

To secure the privilege of being the first in South Heaven to see Marty's photo in nationwide print, I was asked to help uncrate the stack of magazines and stock the shelves. Keeping my own promise, I did not lead on to the shopkeeper as to the reason for my anxiousness at reading the first SWW issue for the month of October 1980.

"Holy Jesus, boy. I thought you left me." Old Man Schmidt polished his lenses with a red plaid handkerchief.

I apologized and popped the cap from his 12-ounce bottle of root beer. Unable to control my eagerness, I unrolled the copy of the magazine, exposing the front cover. "You gotta see this."

"Marty's photo?" he asked, deflating excitement before complaining the root beer was the cheap brand.

"How do you..."

"The good stuff is in the back cooler."

Marty's photo was a brilliant color shot of Lamont Dickies proudly displaying the flag while standing in front of three band members whose heads were flagged. I was a little upset that Old Man Schmidt had stolen my thunder. "How did you know about this?" I showed him the picture that appeared on page five.

Remarking that he should have stopped at Frankie's for a soda, Old Man Schmidt commented on his supposed sources.

"Your source work for the magazine?" I demanded.

"No. Just a wise man."

Emphatically, I rolled the magazine into a cylinder shape then slapped it into my open left palm.

"You come back just to brag to Marty that you got him into this here magazine?" He snipped the end of his cigar. Although a neat and full white beard would have suited the man well, his face was taut and shaved closely, as usual. "If you're here for material things, boy, you ain't gonna be happy." He commented vehemently on the overbearing noise of a car stereo from a primered hulk of a GTO that passed by. "If you're here because your heart brings ya, happiness'll be with ya."

"Your right front tire is low." I pointed to the Caddy.

Through a harsh cough, he directed me to help him to his feet. Old Man Schmidt had but two keys on his chain. He opened the passenger-side door then slid across the bench seat to start the big-barreled engine. "We will see you Friday night," he said, handing me a nearly full bottle of root beer.

I dug in my right front pocket. "Here. Get rid of that plastic thing you got there."

The AGM chrome lighter bounced off the backrest of the front seat before coming to rest a few inches from Old Man Schmidt.

"Guess I don't need it to remember you guys."

The Office

Marty was not to be found, when I entered the office, neither was Miss Myra. Monitoring the fort, however, was someone foreign to me. He was adamantly rearranging the objects and trinkets on a desk that had been unoccupied during my last visit, and was completely enthralled in his own endeavor. "Hey, you can't go in there," he told me, as I attempted to stash my belongings in Miss Myra's office.

"I'm sorry."

"Who are you?" My newly found antagonist wore a thin ring of hair from one side to the other but nothing above ear level.

"Where's Miss Myra?"

"I asked you who you are." He had miserly and watchful dark eyes hidden behind a pair of horn-rimmed glasses and was dressed in brown corduroys that nearly matched the color of his herringbone jacket.

"I'm a new editor."

"You must be that person. How much do you know about sports, anyway? Bet you don't know anything about Saint John, do ya? I do. I know everything about them. Know about their quarterback Drew Magoteaux, third-generation Cardinal. He only needs a few more yards to break his dad's records."

"Relax, man."

"Bet you don't know that St. John has a sportsmanship award called the Sister Mo Award, given to the football player who demonstrates the best example of sportsmanship. Do you?" He held up two books that resembled scholastic yearbooks. In the middle of his lecture or rant, his fellow reporters returned from lunch in a clan of three. However, that interruption hardly stopped him. "Way back in '29, Saint John played at Werley High. Back then, the home team was required to supply referees. Most of the time, the refs were parents or coaches. By halftime, Saint John was losing, and Sister Mo took exception to one of the referees, attacking him with the purse of one of the Cardinal players' mothers."

"Should have gone with us to lunch, Phil," one of the other reporters said. "Salisbury steak special." She stared me down, like any driver accosting a meter maid, resentful but leery of consequences.

All four gathered near one another in a gang-mentality move. A couple whispered and pointed, as if I had forgotten my lines in the school play.

Arms laboring to hold two paper boxes, Miss Myra momentarily saved me from the mob. "Can one of you guys give me a hand?" She dropped the two boxes to the floor. Initially, she missed me on the visual scan.

Despite his non-athletic, almost emaciated build, Phil somehow muscled both boxes the short distance Miss Myra needed. He sniped that he and only he could cover the Friday night games, being a true Ranger.

"When Daddy said he hired a new assistant editor, I'm thinking some wannabee from a two-bit country town."

"Always have to win an argument?" I asked her.

With no fanfare and paying little homage to my credentials, she proceeded to introduce me to the staff as their new editor.

There were no questions for me. There was plenty of conjecture, however.

"So Myra, does this mean none of us have a shot at manager now?" She could not have been much older than Marty. With no makeup, hers was a homely appearance. However, she did hold the consensus vote with a couple of second notions.

"Seriously?"

I then decided to alleviate tension with my issue of Sport World Weekly. I handed the photo to Miss Myra.

"Sport World? You gotta be kidding me!" Miss Myra barely explored the photo before disparaging the moment and throwing the magazine onto the desktop as if it were some porn publication.

Like a bowl of potpourri, the magazine passed from one person to the next. Each took a deep whiff to inhale the contents, pleasant to the senses or not.

Phil, the apparent resident cynic, refused to believe Marty offered such work. "He's just a kid. I've been working for twenty-five years in journalism. Marty is out of school for one year, and..." He snatched the sides of the magazine and squeezed. The balding scalp blistered. "This is unbelievable!" he exploded, before astonishingly ripping the magazine into chunks of loose paper.

"What are you doing?"

The remainder of his peers systematically ignored Phil, as if the tantrum were commonplace, like a spring rain shower.

As he burst out the door, Phil cursed the photo and vowed some incoherent revenge against all who doubted his abilities as one of Western Ohio's top ten sportswriters.

"I can't believe that little Communist got a picture in a national magazine." Miss Myra appeared to be lost in her own tantrum. Suddenly oblivious to the remainder of us in the office, as if under a magician's spell, Miss Myra walked by me, stepping on and further scattering pieces of the picture. She opened the office door and followed Phil.

"I guess this means Marty's the new celebrity in town." Nate, the paper's advertising department, stood over my bent frame. "Suppose we do all get fifteen minutes." Nate had been introduced to me on my previous trip to South Heaven and, amazingly enough, was still wearing the same short-sleeved white dress shirt and spearmint-green tie. It was his breath that watered eyes, brought down birds in flight, and superimposed its will on an overall innocent disposition. "You think it's more luck or skill that gets you those fifteen minutes?"

"You wouldn't happen to know where Marty is now, would ya?" The objective of any man accosted by Nate was few questions asked and a quick departure.

"School," replied Nate. "I think. But, he may be…"

"Hey, thanks."

Fame, without a recent football star, had skipped over the downtrodden town. Big-city Ohio papers and sports magazines had, at one time, visited South Heaven. With the downturn of the football program and the void of emotion, the citizens were fortunate to see their town mentioned in the Lima paper anymore. Thanks to Marty, the guy who enjoyed sports as much as Brussels sprouts with cheese, the same person who had to be prodded to snap the shutter—Marty, a kid with a makeshift photo studio in his parents' garage. Thanks to Marty, South Heaven was once again a part of national media.

At dinner, I ordered in a couple of pies from Frankie, who, by the way, begged Marty to autograph a framed copy of the photo. Marty, gleaming with excitement and pride, accepted Frankie's offer. All but Phil joined the staff and several of the townsfolk in the celebration. It resembled a festive wedding. As people filed into the office, they carried in dishes of food. Marty had become a genuine hero, one title he never dreamed of wearing.

Miss Myra and I kept the corner of the desk occupied. She struggled to force a smile to all those who passed by and spoke of Marty's accomplishment.

"So, do you think Marty will be asking for a raise?"

On cue, Marty decided to join our twosome. "Man, it's a good thing you told me to snap that picture." Just a hair beyond the legal drinking age, he savored a plastic cup filled with beer. "This is great. My photo in Sports Magazine. Imagine that."

"Sport World Weekly." I was amused by Marty.

"I'm gonna need you to take a few shots at the town council meeting tomorrow night." Miss Myra's unexpected snootinesswas comically juvenile. To her credit, though, she was cognizant of my recognition of her disposition.

I asked Marty if he had acquired the services of an agent.

Wiping the dribble from his chin, Marty insisted he had not given any thought to anything. "It's all happenin' so fast. Heck, my mom probably'll kick my butt for havin' this beer."

"Speaking of beer, why don't you grab me one?" Miss Myra asked Marty. "I don't need a cup, though."

"What is your problem?"

"Don't encourage him, sport. It's one picture, for crying out loud. The boy's never been out of South Heaven. He wouldn't know how to function…"

Marty returned quickly with two cans of beer then fell back into celebration with the group.

Popping open the tab, Miss Myra wiped away the residual liquid pooling on the lid of the beer can. "South Heaven, really? It's only the assistant editor job, sport."

"Well ... and something else, according to Senior Epstein," I mumbled.

She insisted South Heaven was no two-editor town but was glad to see me nonetheless. Her tame inquisition then led to the pathetic topic of compensation.

"I won't be putting a down payment on a Bentley anytime soon, if that's what you're asking."

"What I'm asking here, sport, is what are you really doing back here? I mean, it was just last week that you were happy to leave here."

"So where should I be looking for those adrenaline-pumping stories here in Corn Country?" I asked if South Heaven had any scandals yet to be uncovered. "Does the sheriff have unpaid parking tickets? Maybe we could ask the postman, or possibly the dentist?"

"Are you done?" Miss Myra stood and took one last sip of her beer.

Thursday

The first cup of coffee had yet to settle before and controversy enthralled the town. The adrenaline-pumping story had emerged within the first week of my return—sort of. A steady stream of fodder fed the rumor mill. Two South Heaven's Rangers were in trouble.

Among a group of South Heaven students, Todd Veeble and Chris Scheve, the linebacker partners of one Kyle Knause, snuck onto the campus grounds of St. John High School many minutes before sunrise. In a prank that radiated out of control, Veeble, Scheve, and the group tipped a statue of the Virgin Mary to the ground. Apparently, Veeble and Scheve were implicated by a comrade who rolled under pressure from Principal Ross.

As the paper staff mustered for the morning agenda meeting, the rumors of punishment ranged from complete expulsion, which Phil vehemently protested, to a slap on the wrist for paying retribution to a prank St. John pulled several years back. Local historians recalled a few students from St. John breaking into the South Heaven trophy case and kidnapping an entire cache of football awards.

I called the gang to attention. "Let's…"

"This is the only story that matters. If they suspend Veeble and Scheve, we stand a chance of losing to Saint John," interrupted Phil. "People, we should be over at the school now! Not here in some meeting." Phil stood at the table like a lead juror, unable to convince the other eleven of a guilty verdict.

Megan Grimsley, the paper's Metro and newly assigned entertainment writer, patronized Phil, asking him to pass the sugar.

In turn and on cue, Phil excused himself from the staff meeting and stormed out of the lobby and building.

"Is that a daily occurrence for Phil?" I helped myself to the last white cream-filled donut in the carton. A dozen had shrunk to four, considering it was everyone's favorite type of food: free.

"Phil's the uncle on your dad's side you want to feel sorry for because he's a widow or he just lost his job or his house burned down." Neurotically, Megan picked off every speckle of coconut from her donut, eating each one before consuming a bite of the cake. "Only you can't because he's so darn annoying."

Nate sat alone at the end of the table. He had a friend in the ashtray that was already harboring what seemed to be an entire pack of smoked butts. "You probably ain't had the pleasure of a Phil diatribe on football yet, have ya?"

Megan handed me three typed pages that were held together by an oversized paperclip, pink in color. Her lethargic motion was matched only by the descent of a falling tree leaf. "Ann Arbor News, South Bend Register, Lexington Daily News… Anyplace with a college—and a football team." The dime-store romance novel she guarded like a child's stuffed animal held a leather strap two-thirds into the book.

"Better study them papers," suggested Nate. He was tapping his chin with the eraser end of a pencil, and studying a page from a crossword puzzle book.

Peeking over his shoulder, I took notice that Nate's approach to puzzle resolution started on the bottom right.

"You need to know the recaps of the college games," said Nate. Through a yawn, he added, "Pay close attention to the Notre Dame score."

I laughed as if it was obvious I was being pranked. "Why on earth would I do that?"

"Phil will quiz you, don't you know?" replied Megan.

"Well, given the wide range of important news topics from the meeting--plans to refurbish the statue of Jeremiah Harper, the recent discovery of arson as the cause of a fire that destroyed the Hatchets' barn, and the poor cabbage harvest figures for the past season, we have other needs besides game recaps," I suggested.

"Suit yourself," said Nate. "You're the new guy, though. Fresh meat for Phil. He'll be expecting you to contribute to his typical one-sided discussion on how other teams compare to his beloved Buckeyes."

In retort, I asked if anyone else had studied the recaps.

"Don't need to," replied Nate, setting to the side his puzzle book. "You see, Phil's intimidated by the female species. So, Megan and Myra get a pass on Phil's lecture." As quickly as he relinquished the puzzle book, Nate snatched it back and hastily began to scribble. "Friend and Mentor," he blurted. "Confidant."

"Hey, I appreciate you wanting to include me in this charade, but I have better things to do."

"Well," said Nate. "Phil won't talk to Marty, as he don't like to associates with hippies. As for me, Phil knows I am die-hard Michigan fan." Nate penciled in another answer. "So, that just leaves you."

Friday, Afternoon Laps

The playing surface appeared to be pristine, smartly and appropriately marked and chalked. The Ranger mascot caricature held his position at midfield. I was impressed with the depth of care South Heaven input into the facility. Gottmann Field was the one piece of property the people still had in their control. AGM was once a gleam of pride, but the skeletal building had become nothing more than an eyesore.

Without taking notice of me, another would-be athlete entered from the opposite end zone. He was silhouetted against a depreciating sun. As I started a relaxed pace around the first turn of the track, my focus kept returning to the kid on the field. He was placing a football on a tee and kicking field goals, and as I completed one half of a lap, he had not yet noticed me.

"Dang!" he huffed when the ball sailed to the left of the upright.

I made the left turn and slowed an already weakened pace, recognizing the face of the kicker. "Stu!"

Retrieving the ball, Stu Ginnette turned toward me. His was not a look of joy but more of disappointment.

"Whattaya doin' out here?"

Stu pressed the sides of a leather Wilson ball, both white stripes worn to near oblivion. Despite the warmth, he was in heavy sweatpants and red sweatshirt to match. On his left foot was a canvas-white high-top tennis shoe, but his right sported an oversized and homely-looking black cleat with a square toe.

"Kicking shoe has some years to it?"

He squinted into the sun, heeling the nick on the ball nearest the seam. "My dad's." He wandered back to the orange rubber tee placed along the chalk that highlighted the ten-yard line.

"Your dad play ball?"

Stu precariously laid the ball against the upright prongs of the orange tee. "My Dad's a drunk."

I jogged to a position some fifteen yards beyond the goalpost— perfect spot to retrieve the kick. "I've heard that no one cares much for this St. John team you guys are playing tonight." In response to his call for the ball, I threw a spiral back to him.

Stu squatted to lace his shoe before moving the tee back another five yards. He ripped into the ball with a crisp smack from the steel toe.

"You ever ask Coach Waddell for another chance?" I jogged after the ball.

"I bring home eighty bucks a week and groceries. Ain't got time for ball."

I held onto the ball with my last two fingers on the seams and my index finger reaching the apex. "Dad still hasn't found work?"

"Ain't no matter." Stu snatched the ball from my grasp. "Mom needs me to bring home money. Can't do that playin' football."

"I suppose you've given up on college, too?"

He engendered a smile, albeit attenuated. "I'll be turnin' eighteen in January. I'll be able to work full-time. Thought 'bout goin' to Chestertown—applyin' at the gun plant." His kick was a huge effort, but the ball fell a couple of yards short.

Neither team had yet to gather in the end zone for their march onto the field. It was nearing game time, Stu had long since completed his last kick, and I was perched yet again in the Summit. Two hot dogs, adorned in mustard; a pretzel also dressed neatly with the yellow condiment; and the largest of soda cups accompanied me. The ballpark platter had to supplant the evening meal missed at Aunt Jenny's.

"Don't think I could've imagined four and oh." The headset clung tightly around Old Man Schmidt's stocky neck like some sort of lifesaving medical device, and he puffed on a stogie. "Heard you're back. I knew this sport'd grow on ya."

"Football's something to do on Friday nights, and not why I'm back." With the luck of a dead man, I dropped a glob of mustard onto my lap and relatively new pair of blue jeans.

Of course, instead of a napkin, Wally handed me what appeared to be some sort of a flier advertisement. "First Baptist and Saint Brendan's havin' some Bingo thing tomorrow. Getta free board with a Ranger win. Just more money that none of us have."

"Sounds to me like you may be a sore loser?"

The advertisement indicated activities were to start at five o'clock and that each family should bring a covered dish of dinner food.

"Church dun got all the folks thinkin' only the Lord can help 'em." It appeared Wally had no argument without the accompanying hand gestures—finger-pointing and contortions, as if he were directing a squad of men through enemy territory.

"But not you?" I put a few amateurish folds into the advertisement before sliding it under the right foot of my folding chair to improve equilibrium.

"Don't get me wrong, me and the Lord have a good relationship and all. But I ain't never seen the Lord get no one a job."

The Cardinal team was dressed in bed-sheet white, from helmet to shoelace, and gathered in the end zone to our left. From just outside of Lima, the visiting team traveled well, bringing a respectable crowd with them. Those fans were on their feet as the two-win and two-loss team darted onto the field.

"Miss Myra got you under her spell?" Old Man Schmidt asked.

"Hardly."

Wally and Old Man Schmidt laughed harmoniously.

"I will have both of you know I am co-editor of the paper. That's an opportunity I wouldn't have in Cleveland."

The crowd erupted, rising to their feet and cheering, as their beloved Rangers gathered under the goalpost at the north end zone.

"South Heaven before heart and pleasure," Old Man Schmidt remarked. He pulled the headset on, the band broke into the fight song, and the Rangers roared onto the field.

Todd Veeble and Chris Scheve, instead of celebrating with the mass of players on the South Heaven sidelines for the obligatory pregame leap, wore the Scarlet A of street clothes, relegated to the task of handling the water bottles.

"Looks like South Heaven's lost the toss, folks. Baddey will line up to kick it away," Old Man Schmidt told his audience.

On a kick that fluttered only to the twenty-two, Benny Romano fielded the ball cleanly then broke straight up the gut of the defense. At the moment of crucial impact, it seemed every Ranger defender, except Baddey, had made some sort of contact with him, but Romano broke containment and fled past the initial wall of Rangers.

I shot to my feet.

It was Baddey who stood as the last defender of the South Heaven goal line. Backpedaling to his rear and left, the Ranger kicker steadied himself directly in the path of the oncoming rush.

Only ten yards from Baddey, Romano expired most, if not all, of his energy with a series of jukes and stutter-steps to try and elude the tackler instead of outracing him. Even with the extra and wasted effort, he nearly stepped by Baddey, but the Ranger kicker saved the moment with an uninspiring and uncoordinated shoestring tackle.

With a tired Romano resting in the I-back position, St. John's quarterback, Drew Magoteaux, connected with his slot back on a fifteen-yard flag pattern to push the ball down near the Ranger ten.

"Good Lord," quipped Wally.

Magoteaux brought his troops to the line and ran a quick count, calling his own number on an option left. Without defensive end pressure from Wiggins, Magoteaux turned the corner and found no resistance until Luke Post met him at the four, at which time he simply flipped the ball back to his trailer, Romano, for an easy score.

"Well, that took all of a minute." I was gloating.

Following a successful PAT, South Heaven assumed control of the ball on their own twenty-nine. Duane Boyd followed his men to the line, only to discover that St. John was throwing nine in the box.

"Looks like they're forcin' us to pass, folks. They got them three linebackers way up on the line."

Taking the handoff, Dickies crashed into a negligent six-hole.

"Outside! Outside!" Wally had covertly swiped my pretzel from the floor. In three bites, he had mostly consumed the salty treat.

Coach Waddell apparently heard Wally's pleas and ordered a sweep to the left.

"Holy… they're quicker than I thought," said Wally.

"Number forty-three of the Cardinals, Benny Romano, tracked down Dickies and dropped him after only two yards." Old Man Schmidt adjusted the left ear muzzle of the headset.

On third down, Boyd faked a quick dive to his fullback, spun inside, and fired a pass to Durning, who had broken past the trio of linebackers.

"Ha! Dropped it." I cried.

With no one in front of him, Chris Durning could not handle the bullet from Boyd, and the ball bounced off his fingertips.

Any momentum garnered with the pregame festivities was completely lost. Pezzotta failed to handle a higher-than-normal center snap, even though it clipped his outstretched hands.

"Get the ball!"

"And the Cardinals pick it up. Touchdown! Touchdown, Saint John."

Before the home fans comfortably settled into Gottmann Field, they trailed the much-despised Catholic school by fourteen. The Pride of South Heaven pulled a few to their feet with a rendition of the fight song, but most fans must have been in a state of shock.

"Well, folks," Old Man Schmidt bemoaned. "Barely a couple minutes gone, and Dickies is back to retrieve a second kick after touchdown."

A mediocre return epitomized the South Heaven effort up to that point. However, the "nine-in-the-box" policy was summarily rebuked by a steady diet of sweeps, ends-around, and sprint options. The Ranger offense melted most of the first-quarter clock, churning up chunks of turf in a seventy-three-yard march.

"Handoff right ... Touchdown Dickies!"

The end of the quarter found the cheerleaders canvassing the stands and selling raffle tickets for a chance to win the game ball. It also brought an exchange of the headset, and an earful from Old Man Schmidt.

"Ya know, in all these years, I ain't yet won that darn game ball." That chrome lighter seemed magical, as it was never without flints. "Betya I donated a few hundred dollars to those aluminum pails."

The cheerleaders migrated in sets of two, one carrying a roll of tickets and the other hauling a milk pail to collect money.

On a second-down play, Magoteaux faded back in the pocket.

"Holy..." I blurted.

"Ya ain't gonna believe this one, folks, but, we just lost a huge section of lights on the visitors' side of the north end zone. By God, lemme tell ya, it never was all that bright over there, even with the lights on."

Play halted while the referees caucused and presented their findings to both Coach Waddell and the St. John coach. Meanwhile, Veeble and Scheve jogged onto the field to greet their defensive mates with water bottles and a few motivational slaps.

"Well, it looks like, folks ... we're gonna keep playin.' Both squads are back in their huddles."

Dark corner withstanding, Romano owned the Ranger defense—five yards off-tackle then eight yards outside. To spite the partisan crowd, the Cardinals methodically mowed through a hampered defense and pushed six more points on the scoreboard when Romano broke three tackles on a supposed sweep to the left that melted into a cutback and a turn up the center of the field.

"Folks, never thought we'd be down by fourteen."

What the defense failed to bring to the table, the offense for South Heaven filled the gap. Lamont Dickies steadily wore on the Cardinal defensive front. Despite the nine-in-the-box theory, Dickies found holes in the interior line. He carried the Rangers eighty-two yards to the Cardinal five-yard line, pushing his team into the teeth of the blackout darkness.

All players were visible to the naked eye, despite the missing bank of lights.

With two minutes on the clock, the freshman Boyd induced a sucker's grin in the entire South Heaven faithful, and we all followed Dickies into the line.

I was relieved with the apparent tackle.

"Good God Almighty!" Wally shot to his feet and pointed toward a lone figure in the dark. "Boyd's in the end zone!"

The freshman had executed a naked bootleg, fooling everyone but Coach Waddell and the other offensive ten.

"Whattaya think about that, boy?"

Bo Baddey knocked Old Man Schmidt down a few pegs when he pull-hooked the extra point attempt.

"Waddell's liable to start goin' for two if the kid keeps missin' the uprights," bemoaned Wally.

I empathized with the Ranger kicker, who was forced to ingest the verbal wrath of the home crowd. Certainly, he had no intention of missing any field goal attempt or extra point try. However, it appeared the armchair quarterbacks had no ability to comprehend failure—or just refused to accept it.

Apparently consumed by the displeasure of the crowd, Baddey came within inches of whiffing his kick. As it was, he topped the ball and pushed it just beyond the ten-yard limit—a moment of failure that changed the game.

As Baddey approached the ball, the front five for St. John turned and began retreating. Not one saw the ball trickle past the required ten yards.

"Ranger ball! It's ours!"

I squeezed the life out of the binoculars.

On first down and with less than two minutes to play in the half, St. John finally reversed out of their previous defensive strategy.

However, the change favored Dickies and his line mates. Without the extra defender off the line of scrimmage, Lamont Dickies tore off twelve yards. Before the referees could whistle the next down, Coach Waddell stopped the clock.

"Folks, Waddell usually has some odd play set up after a time-out."

For the listeners of WSHV, Wally was as prophetic as he was in need of a trip to the dentist, thanks in no small part to a set of chomps pestered with chips and breaks.

Boyd sent his fullback, Ricky Green, into a slot position. He nearly exhausted the play clock before accepting the snap then dropping back five steps.

"He's gotta screen pass on," said Old Man Schmidt.

Sure enough, the freshman fell back a few more steps and allowed an unmolested defensive line to converge on him. More resembling the response of panic than the actions of a seasoned quarterback, Boyd dropped a wobbly and looping pass into the arms of Dickies.

With five defenders chasing Boyd and three others occupied with two South Heaven receivers on the opposite side of the field, Dickies had a convoy in front of him. It was a mere sprint to the goal line.

"Dickies is at the five ... Touchdown!"

As if starring in a cheesy and feel-good Saturday-afternoon flick, the entire offensive unit sprinted after their star tailback and mobbed him with a gang tackling celebration.

"Dickies pulls us to within two!" Wally commiserated with Old Man Schmidt the moment Baddey trotted onto the field. "Why aren't we goin' for two?"

In short, Baddey missed the kick.

As great of a call as the screen pass was, the squib kick, apparently ordered by Coach Waddell, was just as bad. Romano ran up to the thirty-five to field the bounding ball. He stuttered then bounded right and up the sidelines, casually avoiding would-be tacklers as if they were milk-cows grazing. For the ordained Rangers, Romano appeared to be running with cement shoes. My body language and subsequent grunts failed to help the Cardinal runner, however. Romano was caught from behind, near the five-yard line.

"Daggonit!" blurted Wally. "How do we let that happen?"

A quarterback keeper to the right netted three yards and a Cardinal time-out.

"Am I chalking up six more points for the visitors?" Neither man found comfort in my humor.

Before second down was whistled to begin, Big Pete departed the playing field, walking in retreat and barking instructions to his eleven. I zeroed the binoculars in on the coach, who also had a few words of departure for the line judge.

"Second down, folks." Wally rocked himself, sitting at the edge of his chair. "Magoteaux fades back. He fires ... Incomplete! Whew. That there was close, folks!"

Third down pushed the limits of logic, and St. John decided, with a mere three yards needed, to run a double-reverse play.

"What the..."

Initially, the trickery frazzled Kyle Knause and his mates, but as the play developed deeper behind the line of scrimmage, South Heaven gathered senses. The Cardinal runner was smothered near the eight-yard line.

"What was that?" I begged.

Fourth down brought just enough time for one more play. Big Pete was shooed from the field once the time was allotted for the stoppage of play. As the Ranger coach made the sidelines, Magoteaux sprinted on a roll to the left and his strong receiver side.

The Ranger faithful groaned as each of their defenders appeared to be allergic to Magoteaux.

"Ohh … He's open," sighed Old Man Schmidt.

"Throw it!" I demanded.

Magoteaux spotted the open receiver, squared his shoulders, and fired.

"Incomplete!" Wally breathed a huge thunder of relief.

Magoteaux's ball had sailed high, over the outstretched arms of his open receiver.

South Heaven wandered to the locker room, down by two.

I climbed from the perch in the middle of Wally's rant criticizing everything from Bo Baddey to Boyd's inexperience at hitting receivers.

The familiar commotion of Willie Tee was creating a disturbance at one of the concession stand windows. He was arguing with a humorless Boy Scout leader about the virtues of trust. "I dun paid y'all a dolluh." Dinner was being withheld from Willie Tee.

"A soda and hot dog is seventy-five cents." The Scout leader had a neat and organized full beard and a pair of peers taking his side.

Willie Tee, on the other hand, lacked any obvious crony. "I dun laid my dolluh down here, right here on the countuh!" He thumped his fist on the extended wood counter. His tantrum dislodged a condiment container and garnered the interest of a Harper County Sheriff's deputy.

Despite the darkness of an early evening, the deputy was hiding behind Hollywood aviator sunglasses. "Is there a problem here?"

"Well, Ray." The humorless Scout leader neurotically adjusted the condiment containers to their original position. "This man here does not seem to want to pay for his food."

"That true?" Deputy Ray seemed to adore the supposed authority that the badge provided him. With genuine condescension, he scanned Willie Tee from head to toe.

A paradox of the man that I had come to know, Willie Tee was timid, head flagged and mumbling.

"Tell ya what." Deputy Ray tucked his glasses into a shirt pocket. "Why don't you just find your way out of the stadium?"

The quasi-order jettisoned Willie Tee from his funk. "What ya sayin'?"

"I believe the deputy is asking you to leave." The humorless Scout leader, ironically, asked for no money for the soda he handed Deputy Ray.

"Ranguhs can't be playin' without me. I gotta be here."

Deputy Ray was hardly amused when Willie Tee pulled away from his grip. "Now, I'm sure you don't want any trouble here, do ya?"

"Uh. Excuse me." I was able get in between Deputy Ray and Willie Tee. "How much does he owe?"

Deputy Ray was insistent the matter was none of my business.

I dug into my pocket and retrieved enough coinage to cover a dollar charge. "Keep the change…"

"Bless ya, man. Bless ya."

After shaking the hand of Willie Tee, I bid adieu, and found my way to the Summit.

In a snippet of perceived spite, the Cardinal players migrated onto the field while the Pride of South Heaven was still in mid-form. They warmed up within a few simple yards of the band.

Coach Waddell, though, refused to heed the time clock. Seconds clicked away.

"Folks, we're ready to go here, but ain't yet seen one Ranger come out of the locker room." Old Man Schmidt glared through the binoculars toward the north end zone.

"Cardinals linin' up for the kick, folks. They ain't got nobody to kick it to, though. Don't know what we're doin' here."

Then, Coach Waddell led his players onto the field, in single file at a walking pace.

The crowd stood in an awkward silence. The ruffling breeze created more noise than the packed house. It was like watching a defeated army stagger through the city of their conqueror.

Unappreciative of Coach Waddell's maneuver, the head referee slapped the Rangers with a penalty for unsportsmanlike conduct, which moved the Cardinal tee placement beyond midfield. The kick forced a South Heaven drive to start inside their own ten.

The South Heaven offensive line apparently had taken Waddell's maneuver to heart. Dickies waltzed through cavernous holes that permitted him to tear off ten to twelve yards in chunks. After only five plays, South Heaven was already crossing midfield and reclaiming most of their momentum. Despite the penalty, Coach Waddell's intimidation ploy seemed to be working as planned. Four plays later, the ball rested only two yards from the goal line. One play later, Dickies carried for the sixth straight time over the right side and through a gaping hole.

The South Heaven faithful reacted half-heartedly, as if confused or so impressed with their team's dominance that they felt embarrassed to applaud.

Not risking another lost opportunity for points, Coach Waddell ordered his offensive unit to remain on the field.

After an isolation play, Dickies entered pay dirt again, untouched, for the two-point conversion.

"Folks, I dunno what Coach Waddell told dem boys, but they came out here and took it to Saint John. Rangers now lead twenty-seven ta twenty-one." Old Man Schmidt muddled an approval for Coach Waddell but hailed Lamont Dickies with a deluge of accolades. "Reminds us all of the service you get from Leo's Propane. Remember winter'll be here before ya know it. Let Leo's be your propane source."

"Just gotta see if the defense can step it up," Wally said.

First and second downs left little doubt in anyone's mind that the game was now controlled by South Heaven. However, with their possession on their own twenty-five, the Cardinals, sensing momentum swapping sidelines, injected the game with yet another shot of trickery. On top of the double-reverse play that failed miserably toward the end of half one, St. John added a pass to the repertoire. The play developed quickly, and all eleven Rangers reacted toward the ball carrier.

"Aggh." Wally moaned in reply to seeing the wide-open Cardinal receiver.

Although not resembling a pristine spiral, the ball still fluttered into the hands of…

"O'Malley's got it." Old Man Schmidt hid his eyes behind his palm.

Number eighty-nine, Billy O'Malley, despite his lack of speed, was thirty-five yards ahead of his nearest pursuer before any defender could react. He outlasted the three who chased him the entire length of the field, putting the Cardinals back in the game.

"Sandlot plays!" exclaimed Wally. "We ain't getting' beat on no sandlot play."

"They work," I retorted.

Unfortunately, even though the Cardinals had stolen some enthusiasm and the lead, Dickies continued to gouge his defensive foes for huge gains. Sucking the life out of the time clock, Dickies and his partners sustained another ground-pounding drive that carried them from their twenty to the St. John thirteen and into the fourth quarter.

"All right, folks, we start the fourth quarter down by one. Boyd brings 'em up to the line. He barks signals. Takes the snap; fakes to Dickies. He's gonna throooow! He's got Durning at the eight. Good God Almighty, Durning flipped the ball back to Dickies. He's gonna score! Touchdown Rangers!"

The South Heaven crowd erupted into complete hysteria at the sight of the hook and lateral. As two defenders closed in on the South Heaven receiver, Durning flipped the ball back to a trailing Dickies, and, at full gallop, the tailback entered the end zone unmolested.

Wally was flabbergasted and permitted awkward silence to litter his airways. "Whew. Sorry 'bout that, folks."

"Talk about sandlot, said Old Man Schmidt."

A two-point conversion pushed the Rangers ahead by a seven gap, and finally the South Heaven defense began to feed off the home crowd's energy. On three successive plays, Kyle Knause and company stopped Romano for a loss. With just over eight minutes to play, St. John was forced to attempt their initial punt of the game.

"This is Ranger football," Old Man Schmidt lauded the defense as they exited the field. "That's what I'm talkin' about."

Over and above the crowd noise, Big Pete could be heard hollering at his punt-receiving team to be aware of the potential fake.

The snap from center went directly into the hands of the Cardinal upback, who promptly skirted around left end and followed a bevy of blockers for a first down.

I was on my feet, waving the kid forward.

The fake punt poked a hole in the sail of the Ranger defense. Romano gained his first-half form and composure. He ran four times for nearly forty-five yards, pushing the ball deep into Ranger territory, and deeper into the fourth quarter.

Wally's broadcast was muddled. He fidgeted from nerves. Old Man Schmidt, on the other hand, sat in silence, refusing to light the flint of his chrome lighter. Both men gave off an aura of defeat.

Romano festered with that aura. Two more runs moved the ball down to the Ranger fifteen.

"Two minutes and twenty-two seconds, folks. Magoteaux takes the snap and rolls left."

The St. John quarterback had a pulling guard in front of him to fend off would-be tacklers. He rested and collected himself momentarily before rifling a perfect shot to the numbers of O'Malley.

"Touchdown St. John."

The St. John coach beat Big Pete in the race to call a time-out. Unlike the previous four scores, he was going for the win with a two-point conversion. It was Magoteaux nominated to receive the Cardinal coach's instruction, and he met his superior on the field, halfway between the huddle and the sideline.

Big Pete, once again, hobbled out to his defense.

"They gotta be expectin' pass," said Old Man Schmidt. "Nuthin' more."

Wally juiced his audience with an obligatory "all or nothing" comment, foregoing the choice to tell the listeners about the advantages of service from the Redding Agency. "Magoteaux brings 'em to the line. He's got two receivers to his left."

The Cardinals were heading into the teeth of the dark end zone.

"Magoteaux takes the snap ... looks right. He throws left."

From an elevation and the opposite sideline, we only saw the ball leave Magoteaux's hand. It was a high-lofted pass. We then heard a buzz from the visitors' bleachers and didn't need to see the resulting catch to know that South Heaven trailed in the game.

I offered a hint of a grin.

The Ranger partisans looked as if they were attending a funeral. It was to be the initial loss of the season for the Rangers. It was to be a loss to the despised Saint John. It appeared to be just another season of unfulfilled hope for the faithful.

With a subpar return of the kick, Dickies failed to remove the crowd from the wake. South Heaven had one minute and fifty seconds to negotiate seventy-five yards.

Refusing to concede to Lamont Dickies, St. John pushed nine players up on the line of scrimmage. Two players stood as safety valves, several yards from the ball.

South Heaven, with assumed lumps in throats, lined up in a tight formation, with a slot back just to the rear and right of Durning. Boyd did not have much defense to study, so signals were quick.

Old Man Schmidt moaned at the sight of Dickies smacking into the garbled line to pick up two yards. "What are we doin' here?"

Apparently with two plays called from the huddle, Duane Boyd got his unit quickly to the line of scrimmage. The second-down snap had the freshman pitching the ball to his tailback.

Against excellent pursuing coverage, Dickies shuffled initially then stutter-stepped behind the line of scrimmage. He forced a commitment from the defenders by dipping into the line two steps before spinning inside out and finding a hole along the sideline.

"Dickie's got the sideline. He's at the thirty-five ... breaks a tackle. To the forty! Dickies is to the forty-five! He's pushed down at the fifty. First down Rangers!"

And suddenly, I was no longer relaxed.

The crowd pulled hands from backsides and exponentially increased the noise in the stadium bowl.

The whistle from the referee set the clock in motion and pulled Boyd to the line. When the timepiece fell under one minute, the freshman took the snap, faked a two-handed straight dive to his fullback, spun outside, and then tossed a dart to Chris Durning, who had cleared the linebackers.

"Good God Almighty, Durning caught the dump pass! And he's at the forty! He's to the thirty-five and brought down. What a play call—a pass just beyond the linebackers!"

Coach Waddell visited his entire unit with a time-out. Despite the frenzy of the crowd, Waddell appeared extremely calm, given the situation.

Boyd's teammates were antsy, jumping up and down and bounding on toes.

"Helluva spot for a freshman. I hope he fails," I mumbled.

Duane Boyd must have felt my ephemeral anger. He fumbled the snap and immediately dropped to the turf to cover the loose ball.

It was then Dickies who stepped forward to stop the game clock. He patted the kid on the shoulder for either encouragement or a tongue-lashing.

Old Man Schmidt still had yet to light his cigar, although the tobacco stick had lost half its size.

On second down, Boyd faced a different defense: four defensive backs and four down linemen. No matter, though. He took a clean snap, faintly instituted a fake dive, reversed course, and sprinted down the line on an option play.

"He's got the corner!" Wally leaped forward.

Boyd turned the end and didn't bother to keep Dickies on his tail. He tucked the ball under his arm and dodged tackler after tackler, until finally picking up a first down and more.

At the twenty-three-yard line, Boyd hustled his team back to the line, and, with the clock dropping to twenty-eight seconds, he took the snap and heaved a pass out of bounds to stop the clock—so far out of bounds that the ball landed a half-dozen rows into the stands.

Old Man Schmidt got a chuckle out of Boyd's tension-mounted heave.

Coach Waddell pulled the freshman to the sideline for a brief meeting.

"Back comes the kid…"

My posture changed with every blink of the eye and perturbed breath, and I struggled to find a position of luck. Muscles were clenched to the point of cramping.

"Folks, we're down tuh twenty-four seconds, and Boyd, he brings 'em to the line. He checks the defense. There's the snap!"

Boyd tossed a sweep pitch to his tailback. In turn, Dickies tucked the ball away and sprinted for the left corner. It must have been the legs-crossed position that kept him from reaching the corner. Dickies was hauled down after only a gain of two yards.

"Oh boy, folks, we're now outta time-outs and still twenty yards away," said Wally.

"I dunno if Boyd can get us twenty yards for a score, Wally," replied Old Man Schmidt.

Coach Waddell departed his huddle, scratching his head and kicking at the turf. With deliberate pace, Boyd brought the team to the line.

I found a new position and begged for the clock to wind down.

"Here we go, folks! Boyd gets the snap and drops back. He looks left then moves to his right. He ain't got no one open. Boyd scrambles, and now he throooows … Durning's got it! Durning caught the ball. First down!"

Even before the referee placed the ball in play, Boyd had his unit ready to go.

"Boyd gets the ball. He fades back and throoows!"

"Yes! He's out of bounds. Game's over!"

"No way!" With a younger soul's vigor, Old Man Schmidt thumped the cane on the wood-planked floor.

One second, inexplicably, remained on the scoreboard, and but a few remained in the life of my vigorously pulsating veins.

"Holy… He's sending Baddey in for a field goal!"

A collective withdrawal resonated from the crowd as the Ranger kicker trotted on for a twenty-five yard field goal.

"Well, folks. I dunno 'bout this decision."

The despair and desperation that was rapidly engulfing the souls of Old Man Schmidt and Wally filled me with petty joy and immense relief.

I was able to breathe, without gasping, knowing the game hinged on the inaccurate foot of Bo Baddey.

The Saint John faithful stomped on the boards that held their seats. Meanwhile, the South Heaven fan base sucked in a collective gasp.

The maligned Bo Baddey followed a perfect snap with a strike of the foot. I suppose if a dog is given a chance to dig long enough, he will eventually find a bone.

"It's good! It's good! Good God Almighty, South Heaven wins!"

Saturday, A Fall From Joy

As great of an emotional high as it had to be for the seventeen-year-old to win a game for his teammates, coach, and fans, especially in light of harsh criticism for his inability to convert an extra point, Bo Baddey had little opportunity to relish in the moment. Just minutes after his kick slid through the left upright, Bo Baddey's father suffered a massive heart attack.

Instead of a trip to Lima and the action of the junior varsity game, I wandered into the office with the news of the Baddey tragedy weighing on my mind.

Miss Myra was engrossed in the crossword puzzle from the Columbus paper. "Didn't take you for the overtime type of guy, sport."

I balanced a school-cafeteria-size milk carton on a library book that precariously rested on a box of a dozen donuts.

"I need an eleven-letter word for subject." She bit on the eraser end of the pencil.

"Did ya try mathematics?" My milk had increased in temperature but was tasty nonetheless.

"I think it's in terms of subservience." Miss Myra appeared to be as comfortable as one could be, stretched between three chairs.

"How's Bo Baddey doing? Anyone heard?"

"Subordinate." She fell forward then tossed the folded entertainment section on the desk. Miss Myra asked if my box of a dozen contained any custard crème.

I handed her an open box, with a missing glaze.

She licked the powdered sugar from her fingertips. "Bo's at his grandparents."

The horizontal blinds clapped wickedly as they smacked against an opening door. Phil had been the impetus. Without much grace, he struggled to carry a transistor radio, a couple of legal writing pads, an aluminum lunch box decorated with the helmets of all professional football teams, and a red plaid thermos. "What are you guys doin' in here?" Hastily, he found his desk.

"Morning, Phil. Need a hand?"

"Certainly not from you." He knocked over the thermos with a flailing elbow. On cue, the heavy-gauged thermos careened into the pencil holder, scattering the dozen or so writing utensils like a full rack of pins being struck in the pocket by a sixteen-pound ball. "See what you have done!" Immediately, Phil fell to the floor to gather his possessions.

"What about a five-letter name for a Cadet Heisman winner?" Miss Myra had decided upon a chocolate concoction.

"Davis!" blurted Phil, right before he caught the crown of his head squarely on the extended corner of his desk. "Owwww!" He fell into a fetal position, with both hands clasped around the spot of the mishap.

Although against stout opposition, I fought back laughter. "You okay, Phil?"

"Shut up!"

"Shoot. I guess my answer to forty-four across—serendipitous—is not correct." Miss Myra stepped over Phil as if he were a downed tree on a forest floor, concerned only with getting to the other side

Gradually, Phil worked his way to an upright position.

Miss Myra retrieved one of the fallen pencils from underneath Phil's desk. "Phil, I'm not gonna tell you again: Stop taking Megan's stuff."

"What?"

"This pencil belongs to Megan. See?" She displayed the purple writing utensil. "It has her name stenciled on it."

Phil hugged his cranium, retrieving a couple of feed sheets from the news blotter. "Are you kidding me?" The lone sheet of type paper, apparently, had medicinal qualities to it, because Phil's immediate life concern quickly departed from the pain in his head and radiated to the paper. He shoved it into Miss Myra's face.

"For God's sake, Phil."

"It's the computer rankings, don't you know. We're at five! Five, Myra. Do you know what that means?"

With all the pleasure of self-surgery on a wood splinter ground deep into the palm of your hand, Miss Myra obliged Phil by reading aloud from the blotter sheet. "What am I reading here? And why should I care?"

"It's the new computer rankings thing."

"Phil, I told you not to bring that science fiction stuff to work."

"This ain't that, Myra." Phil tore the sheet from Miss Myra's hand. "State's now ranking teams on a computer. They determine who makes the playoffs. We're at five."

"So?"

"It means we got three spots to climb." Phil was the prototypical psychopath in the average B-list thriller: maniacally possessive, ill-concerned with personal appearance, and with a tendency to have incoherent rants. "Frederick's ranked above us! We beat them. They'll only take two teams from this region. And Frederick's ahead of us! These other three teams are city schools." Without asking, Phil helped himself to the donut carton, siphoning out three, but only after fingering each and every pastry. "Maybe I will contact the state." Phil's brown herringbone jacket stood guard for his light blue University of Dayton t-shirt, preventing powdered sugar from reaching the precious piece of clothing. "Maybe I will." He folded his computer ranking sheet into sixths, beginning laterally, then uncovered his typewriter. "This is my lead for Tuesday."

"Aren't you supposed to be covering the JV game this morning?"

His laugh was hardly genuine. "Please. It's Saturday."

"Right. The day of the JV game." I flashed him my watch. "In fact, I think you may be late."

Grabbing me by the arm, Miss Myra pulled me toward the door, insisting I get my notebook. "We ought go, sport."

From his lap drawer, Phil retrieved a half-dozen pill bottles.

"So you're not covering the JV game?" I asked, while Phil tweaked the dial on his transistor.

We left Phil to struggle alone with a stuck typewriter carriage return and escaped to the Ranger Roost. We entered just ahead of the lunch crowd.

"At least Phil is dedicated." Miss Myra snaked in between tables to find the one nearest the bar.

Aunt Jenny had a simple menu: the special of the day and the beer tap.

"Did you say dedicated or demented?" I retrieved the small menu card from the center of the table before sitting down. "Special's meatloaf."

"The Buckeyes are on at noon. Phil recaps the radio broadcast."

"Why?"

Instead of appearing from behind the bar, Aunt Jenny called for our order.

"I'll have the meatloaf and an iced tea."

"So ... demented?"

"In a way, I'd say dedicated." Miss Myra opened her Time magazine to near the middle, wrapping the one section behind the other. "He's got a mission in life, at least, sport." She lacked attention to detail and often failed to either observe or concern herself with the obvious. Despite several dozens of scores of salt crystals scattered on the tabletop, she laid the magazine on top of the spill. "Phil thinks that some paper will hire him as a college football writer."

Aunt Jenny called at me, "You eatin' today?"

"How about a fried egg sandwich?"

"How about the special?"

Without much congeniality, Miss Myra waved in response to the greeting by two of South Heaven's law enforcement officers. "He sends the Ohio State recap every week to papers around the country where there is a college football presence."

"And you approve of this?"

She pushed the open magazine to me, pointing toward the name of the author of an article on Beirut. "See this, sport? I graduated from Penn with him. He's a hack." Muttering unpleasantries about the writer's incompetence and amateurism, Miss Myra stomped toward the bar, grabbing the stool next to Big Pete.

Sitting alone at the bar, Big Pete was an awkwardly imposing figure. His conversation with Aunt Jenny involved Bo Baddey. Two empty shot glasses held positions on top of the bar in front of Big Pete. A beer mug, mostly depleted of contents, had become partner to the assistant coach. With one last gulp, Big Pete devoured the remainder of his beer then asked Aunt Jenny for a plate of the special. "All I know of Bo is that he won't be back to school for a while."

I inspected a black zipper folder that was allied with Big Pete.

His grip was engrossing and masonry rough. With the mechanical precision of a crane claw, he compressed my hand in a painful vice. "I didn't ask for company at lunch."

He hadn't bothered to fully conceal the contents of the folder. Between grimaces and squints of pain, I noticed what appeared to be a resume of sorts peeking out from the folder.

"He must be off-duty, sport, because Aunt Jenny would never put up with a coach partaking at the bar."

On a small, round platform tray, Aunt Jenny carried a lone plate of the special, which included fries and coleslaw, and a large and extra-wide tumbler of iced tea. "Honey, if you're referin' to that drunken fool who coached basketball here the past couppla years, this here's different. He deserved to be run outta town."

"Seems to me you lead the charge." Miss Myra maintained a sheepish grin as she layered the inside of her sandwich with several squirts from the ketchup bottle.

"Myra, if I didn't know any better, I'd swear you were my own flesh and blood." Aunt Jenny returned to her perch, wrapped her person in a butcher's white smock, and poured Big Pete another, without much foam. "Besides, my bar's always open to Marines." She slipped back into the grill area.

"Buy ya a beer?" asked Big Pete. Despite the cool morning, he was weathering the temperature in coaching shorts and a t-shirt. On top of massive forearms, he wore tattoos. The left held the Marine Corps symbol, and the right bore the word "Chosin." Both were nearly illegible with the fading of age.

I declined, claiming alcohol at lunch was a certain step toward a bad day. "So Bo won't be back with the team?"

"Afraid not," he responded.

"So Myra, I hear the town council don't want to refurbish the grain elevators?" Jenny momentarily disappeared, only to come out from the grill with my fried egg sandwich on wheat bread.

I asked of the topic of the conversation.

Aunt Jenny donned a pair of pink horn-rimmed spectacles and lost herself in a ledger book.

"Outside of town. Cahill used to operate several large elevators. I'd say they employed a couple of hundred people," said Miss Myra. "Have not been used in a few years now. They've become rusting hulks of metal."

With the table manners of a convict just released from solitary confinement, Big Pete finished an oversized bite.

Just like the dozen other times I ordered the fried egg sandwich, Aunt Jenny failed to disappoint. "They can't be used again?"

"Too much effort to get the elevators going again, I guess, sport."

Big Pete devoured his saucer bowl of coleslaw then commented, "Looks like we're outta kicker now. Ain't got anyone else who can get the ball in the air."

The light of the late-morning sun suddenly shone through the bar's entrance, like a flashlight beam in a cryptic hallway. The newest patron to the Ranger Roost was an intimidating figure, at the very least. He appeared to have no purpose, though, standing close to the threshold and scanning the bar.

"Looking for someone, pal?" Miss Myra's favorite police officer offered up his skills as a card-carrying member of the welcoming committee.

"Me. He's looking for me." He managed the extrication from the bar stool like a well-drilled social drunk. Big Pete referred to the bald man as Mister Shelton. Along with a welcoming hand, Big Pete offered Shelton the contents of his folder.

In the middle of my third bite, the idea overwhelmed like a migraine headache. "Hey!" I choked on my food as the idea struck me. "I gotta kicker for you guys."

"I think you're playing days have already expired, sport." She engendered a laugh from the coach.

Of course, I had to salvage some dignity by pointing out the dribble of ketchup on her gray sweatshirt.

To spite me, Miss Myra ignored it and continued to eat.

"Stu Ginnette."

"Stu quit," replied Big Pete, dispensing a smoke from his pack.

"I saw him just the other day booming kicks from thirty-yards." Of course, I was hardly a salesman, having escaped with a passing grade in my only business class of my undergraduate education. "Come on, you said there's no one left to kick."

Big Pete borrowed a green pack of matches from Aunt Jenny. "Coach's already decided to try two points, and it takes too much to change his mind."

Tuesday

With the general election just weeks away and his political future on the line, the U.S. president launched a series of bombing raids on perceived terrorist strongholds throughout the Middle East. As debate intensified in Congress over the course of action of retaliation and the efforts to salvage the sunken Langley, and as America saw her sailors filter back home from hospitals abroad, the president was assuming daily barrages of harsh criticism for his pacifist foreign policies. Despite possessing a small percentage lead over his conservative challenger prior to the terrorist attack in Israel, the president, in mere days, sank dramatically in opinion polls.

The world had become a cauldron of hatred and retaliation. America had grown quickly into an anchorage of embarrassment. Of course, the lead story for the weekly South Heaven Sun was a potential buyer for one of the AGM abandoned buildings. A German auto parts maker had expressed interest in South Heaven, and our crack news team was on top of the story. Instead of reporting the reality of turmoil and the inevitable crumble of a presidency, I approved the submission of a story on the remote possibility of a new employer. In all honesty, though, it made not a difference in what was reported, at least for the diehards of South Heaven. In spite of a local economy that pushed the unemployment rate to 20%, and in light of world events that had tarnished their country, these were not depressing times for the citizens of Nowhere, Ohio. The Rangers were unbeaten after five games, and it was Homecoming Week.

Festivities began at 4:30 p.m., with the freshman-versus-sophomore Powder-Puff football game. With football practice and a volleyball tournament ongoing, the crowd at the stadium to witness the matchup of underclassmen was paltry.

Miss Myra and I found an undisturbed seat in an empty press box.

"Heard Coach Waddell let Stu back on the team," she commented.

Most of the action, not to dismay the efforts of the girls on the field, was occurring outside of the stadium, though. Pickup truck after pickup truck entered the parking lot and the gates surrounding the ticket booth, hauling piles of various types of wood, from 2x4s to broken shipping pallets. With every trip inside the gates, each truck deposited its load onto an ever-increasingly growing heap.

"Hey, sport! I think they're adding an addition onto the elementary school, if you enjoy wood construction that much," said Miss Myra. She appeared to be enjoying the game on the field and took offense to my lack of concern.

"Why don't we go grab some dinner?" I snuck back into the press box just as a fleet-footed tiny thing in a ponytail flew past the sophomore eleven to score six for the freshman team.

"Did you see that?" Miss Myra hollered and cheered.

I repeated my question.

"Can't, sport" she said, before welcoming two men into the press box, each with a hug and peck on the cheek.

The two were no more my senior than by a couple of years, and both had features that coordinated well with their expensive clothing and accessories. Miss Myra knew both—one more than the other, though.

"Myra, unusual business setting." The taller of the two pulled out a metal folding chair from underneath the writing counter. "Clandestine?" Miss Myra referred to him as Mickey. He carried a hardbound black briefcase.

"What's up here, Myra?" I asked. "Couple of good fellows?"

Mickey coughed a laugh, adjusting the dial of the timepiece of his gold wrist watch. "Is it my Italian leather shoes or the gun in my jacket that gives me away?"

"Relax, sport."

Dialing in both combinations for the two locks, Mickey popped open the briefcase. He retrieved one of a few yellow envelopes then handed it to Miss Myra. "You're positive about this?" He pulled the letter-size envelope out of Miss Myra's reach before she could lay claim to it.

"I didn't know you had a conscience, Mickey." Miss Myra, with possession of the envelope, caressed it against her chest, as if the paper object were a love letter from a soldier fighting overseas. Her smile was actually true, and her brown eyes seemed to lighten with the gleam of satisfaction. "When did you actually fall victim to altruism?"

Mickey professed a feigned squeamish contortion of the face. "That's sacrilegious. Money makes life, Myra, and you know how much I love money. I'm simply looking out for a friend." He brushed the foreign objects from the cufflinks of his navy blue sport jacket then handed his partner one of the other two envelopes from his briefcase.

"What, uh … what's going on here, Myra?" Intently, I watched her break the seal on the envelope.

She, of course, was like a homeowner opening the deed to one's property after years of mortgage payments—deliberate and cherishing every moment.

"Don't worry, brother." Mickey's friend possessed average size but an oversized East Coast bark. "We're what you call venture capitalists. You see…"

"I know what a venture capitalist is." I relieved Miss Myra of the check she had removed from the envelope. "But, I'm curious to know what the going rate is for a newspaper."

"Thirty-five thousand to be exact," quipped Mickey's friend, cinching his power red tie.

Miss Myra took control of the expensive piece of paper. "Stay out of this, sport. Mickey, you're welcome to stay. There's another game after this one."

"Appreciate the invite, but I never include pleasure with business. It makes for a less lucrative deal." He retrieved a cigarette from a hardbound case engraved with gold "MM" initials. "Besides, we have reservations in Indianapolis for the night. Meeting tomorrow."

Like Saturday morning superheroes or a July thunderstorm, as quickly as the duo appeared, they were gone, having vacated the press box to me and Miss Myra.

"Are we upgrading the paper?"

Miss Myra savored the check.

The sophomore team tied the score of the game when their quarterback broke a long run for a touchdown.

"Does your father have any idea you just sold the paper?"

An argument had ensued on the field. A penalty, and a questionable call at that, had negated the touchdown.

Folding the check into three equal segments, Miss Myra neatly tucked the draft notice in her purse. "I prefer to call it an investment."

"Please," I quipped, implying her two friends were nothing more than vultures. I told her my experience suggested accepting the check was a bad idea. "They own you now."

"It's an investment, sport. I could care less if they own the paper or not. The Sun is so far in debt…" Miss Myra, face turning a second shade of red, stopped herself from shedding a tear.

The commotion on the field stole our attention—another argument.

"No one has managed the finances of this paper for years now."

"So, what, you're the savior?"

"No, I'm just the chosen one of the Epstein daughters."

"Family before career? I didn't know you were so giving."

Miss Myra pointed toward the girl carrying the football, indicating she was the daughter of the mayor. "Daddy's sick," she said. "Doesn't have much time left. And I, well … I left this town once."

Thursday

The offensive the military launched against a terrorist campsite in southeastern Iran had backfired for the president. Army special forces penetrated a suspected terrorist cell interwoven among the civilians in a town just larger than South Heaven. Once the initial assault wave began to take fire, they counter-punched, and a bloody fight ensued. When the last trigger was squeezed in the battle, fourteen Americans and sixty-one non-Americans, both combatant and civilian, were among the dead. For an embattled president, the television pictures of burned and downed helicopters and those of dead American soldiers could have been the last nail in the political coffin. Prior to the post-meal gathering of fans at the annual Homecoming Pandemonium, the scenes of battle appeared on the nightly news, and many carried those images with them to the field. The Thursday night celebration therefore began with a subdued atmosphere.

After speaking for nearly an hour with a friend at The Republic, I expressed my envy of his position of foreign correspondent and calmed my disappointment before making my way to the stadium to catch the rhubarb pie-eating contest. It was won, hands down, by a freshman boy of impressive size, who polished off five to everyone else's two.

The pie-eating contest bordered a mudwrestling mess and the football toss. In the midst of the Nerf field used by the kids on Friday evenings, a ten-foot by ten-foot pit had been created and filled with thick mud. Eight kids committed three minutes, battling one another in a single-elimination tournament. By the end, two men, both covered in dark clay, slopped their way to a draw, despite the rowdy and noisy crowd. The football toss continued to covet the drama of the evening, with Debbie Logan, a senior basketball player, throwing a ball just as far as Duane Boyd did. On the last throw, it was the Ranger tight end, Chris Durning, who ousted his female classmate, though.

Family counseling was neither my trade nor a topic of editorial discussion. Given my recent choice in career path, however, I had become mired, voluntarily or not, in the Epstein dilemma. From the onset of the conversation with Senior Epstein, I provided him little credence in his outright accusation against his daughter. Still, although I felt for her and the family, my overwhelming concern was my future.

Standing on the top row of the home bleachers, I felt awkward and unsure if my decision to join the South Heaven staff was either morally justified or career-enhancing, for that matter. Unfortunately, the Sun had become my only means of employment. The bridge between The Republic and me had been burned beyond recognition, given my decision to abruptly part ways.

As manmade lighting became a necessity, I, without any destination in life, migrated toward the bonfire stack along with the crowd. There was, however, little conversation about the upcoming Ranger opponent, Chestertown. A Pioneer and Explorer Conference opponent, Chestertown was unbeaten in league play and, according to Phil, only two points behind South Heaven in the state computer rankings.

Several gallons of gasoline and a few unauthorized Molotov cocktails ignited the huge stack of wood. Fans were several deep, encircling the perimeter of the bonfire, and broke into song when the Pride of South Heaven played "Across the Field." One of South Heaven's cherry-red fire engines occupied a spot of turf a couple dozen yards behind the crowd and contributed to the foray with lights and whistles.

"Little loud, eh?" I asked of the family of four standing next to me. The two small kids, a boy and girl, protected their ears with palms, the girl tugging at her mom's jacket.

"You folks going to the game tomorrow?" The cessation of whistles allowed me to speak at normal levels.

"Playing the Stuebbings." A man with the appearance of little means, the father raised his boy onto a set of stout shoulders. "We never miss a game."

"The Stuebbings? Like the guns?" I handed the girl the last caramel from my candy box.

"Yeah. Made in Chestertown."

Covetous of his sister, the boy begged me for a piece of candy. Fortunately, I had a stick of gum to offer him. "You a Ranger fan?"

"My brother plays." The boy's smile widened further, unraveling the gum wrapper. "He's gonna be a Buckeye." He tore open his jacket to show me his scarlet Ohio State mesh jersey. "My brother's gonna be a Buckeye."

The father appeared embedded in humility. He wanted to offer his boy a few words of encouragement but, instead, apologized to me. "Sometimes he gets a little carried away, you know?" In thanking me for the candy, he introduced himself as Chris Durning, Senior.

"Wow. Yeah. The tight end? I've seen your boy play. He's pretty good."

"He's great!" the little brother exclaimed.

Again, the father was almost embarrassed by his little boy's enthusiasm, as if he knew his oldest son had little to no chance of every playing for the state's team.

From the pile of burning wood, a thunderous crack stole everyone's attention.

"I just wanna see the best for my boy, college or not. But we just don't got the money right now, though. Jobs ain't been too kind to us. We got faith, though. The Lord'll see to it that I get back on my feet." He waved in response to a call to his wife. "It was nice meeting you."

"Take care of that family. I'll be looking for your son on the field—maybe on Saturdays in Columbus…"

Friday

The good people of the National Weather Service in Frederick office predicted correctly when they assumed a dramatic shift in weather from the beginning of the week to the end. By dinnertime of game day, the temperature had sunk into the lower 40s. The expected drop was to reach the freezing mark by game time. Confirming, albeit without professional admission, the suspicions of The Farmer's Almanac, which called for an unseasonably cold latter half of October, the NWS predicted the potential for the coldest tenth month on record.

Years of lake-effect snow and windchills had thickened my blood and hardened my spirit, prepping me for winter survival. Draped in a Cleveland Police Department parka, which was bestowed upon me by a captain while researching my article on cleansing the streets of heroine, and my Browns beanie, I faced the wrath of gibes and crude comments from the students and fans of Chestertown.

A trio of school buses hauled rowdy and game-fitted fans into the confines of the South Heaven streets. Lodged behind foot traffic and some of the vehicular variety, the buses came to a halt, allowing me to bring up the rear. Of course, the three kids hanging out the open windows in the back of the trailing bus decided it was easy to be brave while hiding behind a bright yellow fort.

"Hey buddy, did that hat come with the jacket?"

"You always keep your hands in your pockets?"

Par for the course, I thought: humiliation and embarrassment. I pulled my cap further down on the forehead, closer to a hiding place.

On static display, aligned bumper-to-bumper around the edges of the parking lot, were eight convertible muscle and sports cars to be used, presumably, as the chariots for the Homecoming Court. The vehicles were of various makes and models, but all glistened with a fresh coat of wax. Their owners stood proudly by, hand polishing and posing for pictures. A dark green '69 Camaro caught my eye.

"Can I help ya?" His receding hairline was glaring, glistening nearly as much as his black satin jacket, which struggled vigorously to cover an impressive beer gut.

"Great ride," I said, peeking into the cab.

The Camaro had a wood-paneled console, both along the dash and manual shift. White vinyl bucket seats clashed slightly with said wood grain, however.

I mentioned my '67 model but was rebuffed by the driver for Melody Samson.

The corner of the cardboard sign displaying Melody's name in glitter and pink was peeling from the passenger's door of the green Camaro.

"Hey, Reportuh Man!" Willie Tee was in his Cincinnati Reds jacket. He had a handful of pretzel rods, at least a half a dozen wrapped in fingers and one between his teeth. "You gotta dollah?" Willie Tee had a pal with him who, apparently, also enjoyed the taste of the pretzel rods.

With the appearance of Willie Tee and his partner, the Camaro owner started his car and reversed course a few dozen yards. Willie Tee, though, appeared to be oblivious to the blatant endeavor. He simply held his famous grin in a loaded position.

Concerned for his health on such a crisp evening, I asked Willie Tee if he would be warm enough in his thin jacket.

"Bless ya, man. Bless ya." Counting the change I gave him, he replied, "You's 'bout to see a great game. I ain't needin' no more warmth dan dat." Willie Tee distributed a few of the coins to his partner. "Besides, this here jacket's got some luck in it still."

By the time I climbed my way to the Summit, the thermometer was reading below forty, Willie Tee and has pal were finding their vantage points, and the '60s muscle cars were planting rubber on cinder track. The wind, although slight, was just harsh enough to make the perched position above the press box an uncomfortable one.

"D'ya bring this here cold with ya from Cleveland?" Old Man Schmidt was bundled in a thermal camouflage hunting jacket. "Never been a big fan of that place, ya know."

A score of minutes before kick-off, the class banners were paraded in front of the growing home crowd. Two kids from each class hauled opposite ends of a 2x4 that supported the heavy plywood banners. Each banner was painted in red and white with various Ranger caricatures.

"I'm goin' with the sophomores' banner." Wally dialed the lens pieces of the binoculars. I am not sure how, up to that point, my perceptiveness had missed the malady in Wally's right hand. His ring and small finger were shortened by a knuckle. He was to man the headset for the impending first quarter.

I asked Old Man Schmidt his prediction for the game, baiting him with the fact that Chestertown was unbeaten in the league.

"Well, Stuebbings don't have much except a quarterback."

"They gotta be unbeaten for a reason."

"Ain't gonna matter, if we put a rush on 'em. Chestertown's been givin' up too many points" Old Man Schmidt was pouring liquid from a small flask into his thermal coffee mug. He passed the flask to Wally, as if it were simply a section of the daily newspaper.

Chestertown fans traveled well, and they filled not only the visitors' stands, but also the fence along their sidelines. With thunderous applause, they welcomed the appearance of their Stuebbings in the south end zone. The team wore white jerseys with jet-black pants and helmets with a "C" emblazoned on the side.

The two bands did battle as both broke into their respective fight songs when their teams stormed the field at the same time. From the perch, our senses were drowned by "Across the Field." We caught a snippet of Chestertown's fight song, an unrecognized tune.

Oddly, I found solace in the Summit, despite the cold and my, up to that point, complete disdain for Ranger football. Uncertainty had suddenly become a shipmate of mine, and I was wallowing in paranoia without a desired future. I was hoping a Ranger loss would, at the very least, soothe some frustration.

"Folks, looks like we're kickin' off to start." Wally began his broadcast. "It's a chilly one today, but Homecomin' and two unbeaten teams should warm up the air tonight." At the receiving end of the WSHV broadcast, Wally's grainy inflection had to be ingratiating and difficult to pocket. It was a voice that could only be appreciated at a family picnic.

Trotting out with the kick team, dragging his square-toe shoe, was Stu Ginnette. His initial boot of the ball, loaded with adrenaline, soared end-over-end to a receiver around the twenty-five. Truth be told, I had no trouble rooting against the kid. After all, he was a Ranger.

"Stuebbings'll take over up around the thirty-two." Wally added an extra shot to his coffee, licking the drip dangling from the side of the cup. "And Chestertown comes out with five receivers and only Timmy Rolf in the backfield."

Chestertown's quarterback, Rolf, a gangling left-hander, had posted eighteen touchdown passes for the first half of the season. His initial throw, from the shotgun, was a swing pass to a flanker, which netted the Stuebbings eleven yards.

Big Pete, throwing a standard five-two formation at Rolf, left one receiver uncovered. With that, on the second play from the line, Rolf found the uncovered man for another first down.

"Folks, this is simple pitch and catch. Stuebbings're already across the fifty."

Rolf took another shotgun snap and rolled to his left. His was not a classic athletic gait. Squaring his shoulders, though, he popped a pass to a receiver on a curl, who promptly avoided two tacklers to pick up twenty-two yards. The play had silenced the home crowd.

"You recognize that name, don't ya, boy? Rolf?"

I chose not to oblige him.

"Bill Rolf? Basketball coach at Toledo," added Old Man Schmidt.

The Ranger defense yielded another completed pass and first down. It appeared as if Kyle Knause and comrades were laying the red carpet for Rolf, and I was feeling a positive vibe.

"Touchdown Chestertown," sighed Wally.

Rolf had hit Rick Hamm for a twenty-yard touchdown strike.

"These guys predicted to win the league?" Apparently, I had found the key to silencing him as the Stuebbings' kick fell into the hands of Lamont Dickies.

"Well, folks, it didn't take long for us to get the ball back. But we're now down seven."

Lamont Dickies' first run, off-tackle, reiterated Old Man Schmidt's prognostication on Chestertown's soft defense. Through a huge hole, Dickies was never touched until fifteen yards clear of the line of scrimmage. The run juiced the home crowd and my nerves.

Off the opposite tackle, Coach Waddell sent Dickies on the second play. Again, a huge hole was generated, and the South Heaven back bolted for another seventeen yards.

As bad as Knause, Veeble, Scheve, and the boys looked defending the pass, the Stuebbings were that atrocious at halting the run. It took only five plays to move the ball seventy-one yards to the Chestertown two.

"Wow, folks, Lamont Dickies has run right over Chestertown."

The Chestertown staff moved nine men up to within a yard-and-a-half of the ball. The move halted Dickies at the line of scrimmage. Unfortunately for the Stuebbings, Duane Boyd failed to give the tailback the ball. Not one defender saw the freshman stroll into the end zone on a bootleg play.

Following a successful PAT, Stu's second kick was not much to brag about with his teammates. The ball never got off the ground and bounded to a slow death around the Chestertown thirty-five-yard line. Kyle Knause, but a few yards behind the ball, immediately drew a beat on the Stuebbings runner.

"Fumble!" Wally jumped from his chair at the sight of the ball sailing from the arms of the Chestertown runner. "We got it! Our ball."

"Are you kidding me?" Suddenly, the solace I had been seeking radiated into an extreme throb in my forehead.

At the forty-one, Dickies took another handoff and quickly pushed the ball ahead twelve yards.

Coach Waddell shifted strategy and called for a swing pass. That change-up caught Chestertown napping. Catching the pass in stride, Dickies turned the end then cut farther outside and up the field. Untouched, he skated into the end zone.

"He's a superstar!" Old Man Schmidt exclaimed.

Rolf took back control of the ball with but a couple minutes to go in the first quarter. Again, from the shotgun and facing a six-man line with only Knause as a backer, he took the snap.

Knause blitzed straight up the middle and flushed the quarterback out of the pocket. He planted and cut left to pursue and push Rolf directly into the arms of Bobby Bones. Big Pete, on his second defensive series, found the solution to disrupting the quick pass offense of Chestertown: push the defensive backs right up against the opposing receivers and rush seven. Second and third downs resulted in an incomplete and another sack, respectively. Rolf was not athletic enough to sidestep pass rushers.

"Only the second time that team's punted all season," Old Man Schmidt said proudly.

Despite Chestertown crowding the defensive line, Lamont Dickies pounded away at the undersized defenders, chewing up chunks of turf in ten- to twelve-yard patches. A five-minute drive pushed the Rangers ahead by fourteen points, prompting the South Heaven crowd to chant the acronym for the conference, "P-E-C."

"Folks," Old Man Schmidt spoke to the radio crowd. "Lamont Dickies, he's already over a hundred yards for the night and, as it stands now, only about two-hundred and fifty from the record."

With the chant continuing, Knause and his defenders harassed Rolf the remainder of the half. The Ranger middle linebacker blitzed on every down. Rolf was able to complete a few passes, but for insignificant yardage.

On the other side of the ball, Lamont Dickies swept cleanly through cavernous holes in the line without effort. By the end of the first half, he had posted another score for the Rangers and pulled within one-hundred and seventy-five yards of the all-time rushing record for South Heaven. Stu Ginnette was a perfect four-for-four on extra point attempts.

Anger had forced my mind flush out of common sense and rationale thought. "I cannot believe I'm sitting here watching this…"

"Yep," replied Old Man Schmidt. "Sure gonna be a cold one for them girls on the Court."

With the cooler weather, the eight queen candidates were unable to expose their Court attire. Jackets hid dresses that probably set parents back a few dollars. Despite the cold, all eight took positions on top of the rear bucket seats of the appropriate convertible.

Along with Dickies, Gary Redding, dressed in sweatpants, made the traditional appearance as the football captain. Both captains held bouquets as the candidates exited their vehicles and formed a semicircle toward the South Heaven sidelines at midfield. Few in the crowd had departed their seats, in anticipation of the announcement.

Samantha Ritz was named the second runner-up. Apparently, Samantha's true calling on Friday nights was being an active participant of the eight-member cheer squad. Her seven teammates cheered widely with the announcement, two of them braving the circumstances to run onto the field for a group hug.

"The first runner-up, as voted by your student body," piped the student council president, Heidi Fossitt. "Rene Issacs."

A petite girl with a giant of an escort finished first runner-up. She received the smaller of the bouquets from Lamont Dickies, who politely reached over to peck her on the cheek.

"And now, the moment we've all been waitin' for … this year's South Heaven Homecoming Queen is … Melody Samson!"

Melody must have been the crowd favorite. At the moment of announcement, the South Heaven faithful burst into screaming applause.

"Figures." Old Man Schmidt commented.

"What's your problem?" I asked.

"You think the Redding boy would be huggin' and kissin' any girl that won, boy? Them two be goin' out since they were toddlers, it seems. Whole darn thing's probably rigged."

I escaped the perch just long enough to nab any type of hot liquid refreshment. The unmistakable boisterous laugh of one Papa Redding could be discerned without much effort as I stood in line.

Once again, Papa Redding was coveting the attention of Johnny Sarian. Ironically, though, there were few in the crowd of laymen who shared the same sentiments of Johnny Sarian. The legions of Ranger fans seemed to be more concerned with a snack and soda to tide them over to the second half, rather than with heaping admiration onto the former star. Rumor had it that Johnny Sarian was destined to become one of the laymen, as he had been hired by the Redding Agency.

Of course, without the luxury of a cup of tea and with the hot chocolate machine incapable of dispensing anything else but frustration, I had the choice of coffee or soda with no ice. Armed with a small cup of black death laced with five-plus spoonfuls of sugar, I climbed back up the ladder in time to see Chestertown boot a ground-hugger just deep enough for Durning to retrieve and return to the Ranger forty.

"Five bucks, Wally. Five bucks says Dickies breaks the record tonight." Old Man Schmidt was confident.

Wally glared brazenly at his partner then turned his head to spit. "They score again here and Waddell'l probably call off the dogs, folks." He peeled open his wallet and handed me a crisp five-dollar bill.

"Here, boy." Old Man Schmidt passed me one of his own bills. "Hold 'em."

Six yards off-tackle to the right. Eight yards on a sweep around end. Ten yards on a counter. Dickies continued to run unabated as the Rangers moved first down after first down methodically toward another score. "First and goal for the Rangers, on the Chestertown four-yard line. Handoff … No! Fake to Dickies. Boyd looks into the end zone. Touchdown! Touchdown Durning!"

Lamont Dickies stood only a buck and a quarter from supposed South Heaven immortality when Ginnette booted deep to Chestertown.

"Waddell ain't called off the dogs yet, Wally. Still first-team defense out there." Old Man Schmidt gleamed.

The sage must have seen the immediate future in predicting he would gain five dollars. Although a complete nonfactor, from the first drive onward, Rolf gave an all-conference performance, hitting his first four passes.

"Every second half, we have a lapse," said Old Man Schmidt.

Rolf took that cue and hit his man on a post-pattern, netting some thirty yards.

I edged to my seat. The coffee became a little easier to stomach.

The offensive starters for South Heaven, after departing the field from their last score, had undressed a portion of the uniform. As Rolf crept closer to a score, though, the pads were refastened.

"Rolf's got his four-receiver formation. He takes the shotgun snap and lofts the ball toward … touchdown!"

Not comfortable with a mere three-touchdown lead, Coach Waddell sent the first team back onto the field. Unfortunately, the brief respite did little harm to the South Heaven momentum. Lamont Dickies took a pitch on a sweep left from his own thirty-one, rounded the end with a full head of steam, picked up two key blocks, and closed in on his record-breaking goal by another sixty-nine yards.

"Touchdown Dickies! Good God Almighty, Lamont Dickies was untouched!"

Playing as if he believed in my misery, Rolf, through snap passes, harassed the Ranger defense from his own thirty-eight until the opposing ten.

"Well, folks, whatever the Ranger defense did well in the first half, they've done forgotten it here in the second, 'cause Chestertown's got the ball ten yards away from a score. Rolf takes the snap, pump fakes, now throooows. You gotta be kiddin' me! What's happenin' here? Folks, Rolf's pulled his team back to within three scores."

It was doubtful that all in the South Heaven stands were cognizant that Dickies was half a field away from the rushing record. With a 42-21 lead, Coach Waddell sent the tailback into the game on first down and the ball resting on the Ranger forty-two. To the amazement of all except his staff, Coach Waddell directed his quarterback to induce the defense with an off-tackle fake to Dickies. After pulling every defender two steps toward the line, Duane Boyd cocked the ball next to his ear then lofted a stout spiral to a wide-open Chris Durning, who promptly spun around and sprinted toward the goal line.

"Old Man, I'll be taking that five from ya. Waddell's gonna bring in second string in the fourth."

Following his seventh successful extra point, Stu Ginnette laid into a boot that carried over the heads of the Chestertown receivers, bounding into the end zone for a touchback.

With two minutes left in the third quarter, Big Pete finally opted to man-up every Stuebbings receiver. When Rolf brought his team to the line, he looked over a five-man line, his favorite target double-teamed and the other four receivers covered. On the first snap, Rolf found himself, similar to the backyard Nerf games, with all day to survey the field in front of him. He looked to his right, then to his left.

The Ranger line pushed forward but could not shed blockers, until Teddy Bear Manning collared Rolf with a talon.

The Chestertown quarterback tried to pull free but could not, and as he realized the inevitability of the sack, the ball flew from his hand, directly into the arms of Luke Post.

With his offense starting from the twenty-two, Lamont Dickies chugged onto the field.

"Even if he runs the distance, still gonna be short," chimed Wally.

Beyond demoralized, the Stuebbings' defense was bulldozed by Dickies, who took the initial play of the drive and stormed off right tackle. A cutback across field allowed Dickies to advance the ball to the six. Following two more off-tackle runs, Lamont Dickies was across the line for yet another six points.

The Ranger tailback would not receive another opportunity to break the record, however. As the temperature dropped to near-record lows, with a cloudless sky to harbor ground warmth, Coach Waddell liberally substituted on both offense and defense. Rolf enjoyed the luxury of a second-string defense, taking full advantage on the drive following Dickies' last touchdown.

Giving little to no credence to the Chestertown effort, the South Heaven faithful expressed their displeasure with the Stuebbings' complete first-team offense dismantling the Ranger reserve defense.

Rolf knifed through the Rangers, completing nine of ten, en route to a seventy-yard scoring drive. His awkward run for a successful two-point conversion closed the deficit to twenty-seven.

"We got eight minutes to go here, folks." Old Man Schmidt was ringing his finger around the rim of his flask, stealing any loose drops. "Ow! Onside kick. We got it? Who's got it?"

"Daggonit!" blasted Wally. "Chestertown."

Coach Waddell refused to relent to the crowd's demands and ordered the reserve defense back onto the field. With that, of course, it required only a half-dozen plays from Rolf before the defense caved again.

It was awkward, but I hardly felt guilty that Coach Waddell was gifting me.

In an offense that featured no running back and two called quarterback keepers for the entire evening, Rolf had thrown the ball forty-nine times, completing thirty tosses, prior to the Stuebbings' recovery of another onside kick.

With a nineteen-point cushion and less than five minutes to play, Coach Waddell insisted upon keeping the second-string on the field.

Boos and displeasure multiplied.

The Ranger second-team defense put up a fight on first and second downs but could not withstand the Rolf aerial attack. Third down netted the Stuebbings thirteen yards, which precipitated four more successful passes, the last of which was an eight-yard slant that generated six points. Two minutes to play, and the deficit was only thirteen.

"Folks," sighed Old Man Schmidt. "I'm only believin' this 'cause I'm seein' it firsthand."

Wally's daily demeanor did not seem to have the ability to handle even the slightest bit of change. With that being said, he paced frantically, kicking at whatever he could find and mumbling incoherently.

"Here we go again, folks. Another onside kick, I'd guess here. He boots it along the ground. The ball bounces in the air."

A monster pile was built around and on the ball.

"Oh Lord, please make it ours." Wally was more expecting than hoping for divine intervention.

Out of my chair, I pointed in the opposite direction of Old Man Schmidt and Wally.

Three referees jumped into the scrum and began pulling superfluous players from those who were fighting for the ball.

"Can't tell yet, folks!"

Several seconds into the dismantling of the scrum, the head referee climbed to his feet and sucked the lump out of every South Heaven fan by pointing in the direction of the Rangers.

"Good God Almighty, I think it's finally over, folks."

CHAPTER FIFTEEN
Hall of Fame, Who Knew?

Monday

Indeed, the game was over with the last attempt at an onside kick as South Heaven dried out the clock—with, of course, the second-team offense on the field. By the time the clock mercifully came to a stop on Friday, the 1980 matchup between the Rangers and the Stuebbings had shattered no fewer than three league records, four Chestertown team records, and four South Heaven bests, both positive and negative: most points in one game for two teams combined (101), most passing yards by an opponent (395), most rushing yards in a quarter by a South Heaven runner (164), and most consecutively made extra points by kick in one game (8).

Although not due for another day, Phil had submitted his articles for the week. While enjoying an early lunch, I was critiquing Phil's work and editing with my comments. Phil possessed a knack for the obvious. Whenever one read his synopsis of the game, he or she received a scripted play-by-play recount of Friday's big events. Unfortunately, he lacked any and all abilities to tell a story, leaving his work insipid and colorless. For a game that introduced an unknown as the Ranger kicker and played witness to fourteen touchdowns, I expected to sense some sort of emotion from Phil. Apparently, he garnered all that passion on a one-page editorial on the injustice of the state's computer rankings. In a piece reminding me more of a legal brief, Phil outlined, with detailed examples, the reasons South Heaven should be ranked ahead of the other four schools in line: Frederick, Toledo East Catholic, Cold Springs, and Farmington.

"Boy, it's a tad cold to be out here, isn't it?" Old Man Schmidt had found me again. He had tracked me down to the park bench, just outside of Krisp's.

I slid my boxed lunch closer to me so Old Man Schmidt could make use of the other end of the bench.

"Only gonna be fifty today, boy." His body moaned as the cane assisted him to a seated position. "Don't care if there's a wind or not. It's cold. Park benches are for summer, boy. Don't you have an office to do work?"

The city, I assumed, had supplied a little damage control to the bench that had started to rock. A new batch of concrete had been poured around the one leg of bench structure that had broken free from the base. Unfortunately, it appeared that no one bothered to make use of a level before the concrete had had time to harden. The bench listed to starboard.

I showed him Phil's editorial and requested that he read it.

"Why don't ya just enlighten me?" He removed a cigar from the inside of his brown herringbone jacket.

"Phil's a little upset about this new type of rankings the state's doing for the playoffs." I contended Phil must not have been witness to the game on Friday. "It appears as if all his energy went into the op-ed piece."

"Phil's still looking for the train to take him out of Dodge. Have you found his articles on the Buckeyes?"

"I've been introduced to the phenomenon."

A trio of older women straggled by, without acknowledging the two of us. One pushed a baby stroller.

"Heard Miss Myra had visitors the other day."

I took a couple of steps to the open-top public garbage barrel, which was pristine in condition compared to the other city-owned properties. "You know something I don't?"

"Don't let nuthin' happen' to the paper, boy. The story's the team now. Paper needs to be followin' the team." He could not serve a smile with his diatribe. "Whattaya make of that?" He pointed across the street.

In front of the large shop window of the Redding Agency, Johnny Sarian adjusted the string tie supposedly complementing his Texas orange suit. He occupied one of two chairs at an elongated folding table adorned with a white banner. Except for a collection of a handful of black binders and accordion-like folders, Sarian sat alone.

In maroon block letters, the banner indicated the Redding Agency was hosting Blue Laces Day.

"Don't let the paper leave us, boy."

Wednesday

A red tie and gray jacket were required attire for dinner. My decision to leave Cleveland was weakly combatting homesickness and the guilt of self-disappointment. Regret had become extreme, and I had just completed the dialing of the tenth number to the receptionist at The Republic when Miss Myra knocked.

Frankie's played host to the fifth annual athletic department hall of fame dinner. From its simple inception, the dinner had become, in a short period of time, a major endeavor of importance to the Ranger faithful and a front page headline for the paper.

Speaking of the paper, Phil, sporting a pad and pencil and a Santa red tuxedo, had been spotted at a table not far from ours, berating the wife of Teddy Foxx with some sort of diatribe on the criteria for selection into the hall of fame.

"What are we doing here?" I asked, upon seeing Myra.

Full, but not packed, the dining room was moderately decorated in maroon and white. Social hour began the evening's festivities and said dining area found most attendees milling about with their choice of beverage in hand.

"So, how was Chicago?"

"Pretentious and cold, sport." Uncharacteristically, Miss Myra was without some sort of a gray college sweatshirt. Tattered and well-worn jeans had given way to a red and white striped strapless dress that fitted well to Miss Myra's athletic physique and appealed to the very fiber of the male species—single, married, or otherwise. It required little for her to shed the everyday tomboy look.

"You weren't, by chance, interviewing, you know, for one of those big-city paper jobs?"

"And leave South Heaven? Come on, sport." She was consumed in the reflection from her pocket mirror, adjusting depths of make-up.

I interjected, asking if she believed it would be beneficial for me to tag along next time. "Maybe check out those big-city papers?"

"Don't ya think you oughta pad the resume, sport?" Her wave toward a taller woman twice her age was accompanied with an unsure smirk. "I know The Cleveland Republic is the best paper in northeast Ohio, but…"

"Do I need to look for another means of paying for my meager lifestyle?"

"Mister Eichs." Miss Myra acknowledged a gentleman, receiving a peck on the cheek.

"Only the third woman to be elected." A man with way too many years in his face, Mister Eichs was not nearly as gleaming or genuine as his smile. "You must be happy." A pronounced and methodic German accent rolled from his tongue. "Is your father here? He must be proud?"

Miss Myra politely and respectfully informed him that Senior Epstein had made a trip to Pittsburgh. "Believe it or not, Mister Eichs was our track coach." On her second gin and tonic, slyly enjoying the moment, she led me by the hand back to our table.

"Pittsburgh?" I asked her, assuming my assigned seat next to the former South Heaven boys' basketball coach, Mel Long. "Didn't know he had any dealings in Pittsburgh."

Frankie had laid a basket of breadsticks on each table, and Miss Myra took advantage.

"Are you leaving the paper?" With a little grace, I draped the red napkin over my lap.

She struggled with an uncooperative corsage, repositioning and pinning the blue and white flowered collection to the top of her dress.

With the prompting of the evening's emcee, all attendees found their way to seats and tables. "I think we'll get started with the buffet dinner." Teddy Foxx, the emcee, appeared more concerned with being one of the first in the food line than maintaining proper order.

Our table was among the second group of tables to make the trip to the cafeteria-sized buffet server holding half a dozen sunken stainless steel tubs of food. Frankie left three pies on top of the counter, filling the tubs with ziti, manicotti, and pasta alike.

"So, here with Myra?" Mel Long asked. "She been bragging about her exploits?"

"What?"

"One of the best we've had." Corpulent and as athletically imposing as a manhole cover, Mel did not release a radiance of basketball, horseshoes, or any event of athleticism beyond the daily newspaper word search. He did, however, wear a loud and obnoxious green plaid jacket that made every attempt at coordinating with navy pants.

Miss Myra avoided my inquiry, concentrating more on her baked ziti and enjoying a conversation with Mel.

No sooner had we dusted our pasta with Parmesan cheese, it seemed, than Foxx had consumed his meal and assumed his perch at the microphone.

"Okay, I'd like to get started by welcoming all of you to the fifth annual hall of fame dinner and induction ceremony. I'm Ted Foxx, the AD, and I am very excited about tonight. We have five amazing athletes we're bringing into the hall of fame family."

The first two candidates Teddy introduced were not present at the ceremony. The grandson of Carl Berger enjoyed the moment, however, accepting the award for the two-sport star. Carl Berger excelled in baseball as a pitcher, basketball as a guard, and represented the graduating class of 1939. The wife of Raymond Coy accepted the induction for the all-state track star. Coy, in 1955, held the school, conference, and county records for the mile. For four years, Coy starred at the University of Toledo.

"Our next inductee was a two-sport star from the graduating class of 1969. A three-time all-conference performer for the Ranger volleyball team, she led her squad to three PEC titles and two sectional championships. Her records for assists and kills are still records for the PEC and ones that may not be topped by any Ranger anytime soon. During the spring season, this Ranger swung a bat, and she also killed the volleyball. In four years as a second baseman and shortstop, she batted over six-hundred three different years to record the highest average for a South Heaven player. In her senior year, she led the team to a sectional and district title. Ladies and gentlemen, Myra Epstein."

Friday

Events and circumstances worldwide had further denigrated the campaign of the incumbent U.S. president. Unprovoked, the "Evil Empire" of the Soviet Union had invaded a small sovereign neighboring nation. Hours following the initial invasion, the news found its way to Corn Country. Political laymen everywhere began to lay blame on the U.S. administration. For the afternoon on game day, the Soviet invasion was the topic of discussion—until the reality of the impending matchup with Lincoln set in.

Hapless, hopeless, and winless, the Lincoln Huskers had been walloped the week previous by Bisum. They were prime targets of prey for the craving South Heaven fans. Setting aside the international foray of news and disaster, the Ranger faithful were building up for a celebration, a blow-out of a victory that could pull the team closer to number one in the computer rankings. Few, however, were excited about the possibility and inevitability of Lamont Dickies breaking the all-time rushing record. Despite the fact that he was a kid who had grown up playing on the streets of South Heaven, some could hardly stomach the thought of a black player breaking the cherished record of a white player.

After all, Jim Westerman came from a well-respected South Heaven family and was a decorated U.S. Army colonel. It was the irony of the situation that the cultured and socially educated shed a tear for the citizenry of South Heaven and their economic plight. The town rooted for the senior running back, provided his exploits brought the team wins. However, the same fan base could not step beyond and out of the mindset of closet racism and suppress the urge to root against destiny.

Desperately, I wanted to attend the game and be witness to the record-breaking rush of Dickies. Unfortunately for my confidants in the Summit, I could not simply turn the channel from event to event like a cheap television. In the remaining two years of my college career, I had developed an obsessive interest in the policy and history of the Soviet Union and had parlayed enough credits to earn a minor in Soviet studies. Thus, I bypassed the field and traveled back home. With the Secretary of State addressing the UN at 7 p.m. and the president set to speak to America in prime time, I needed to quench my thirst for legitimate news on the Soviet invasion. I found my former colleagues bellied-up to the bar of a local Parma dive.

"The wayward son comes back home?" No fan of mine, Paul Quantrill was a senior statesman of Washington correspondents, among Ohio newsmen, and of those six of us scattered at Mark's Pub and Grub. He had no obligation to associate with us. Tenure and years of awards granted him stature beyond greenhorn "news kids." Quantrill was a mouse of a man and either ignorant of the social ladder of success or completely incompetent outside of the newsroom. "Missed reality a little bit, did we, Melvin?"

"It definitely wasn't you," I mumbled, retrieving a laugh from the guy next to me, Kirk Lemasters.

The scotch and water Paul sipped hardly meshed with the watering hole establishment. Driven by ego, his presence at a blue-collar bar was probably to merely browbeat our intellect. "Covering crop yields not paying the bills, or did you just come back to see Mom and Dad?"

"Two of the larger foreign policy stories in the past decade, and The Republic's top correspondent is massaging his ego in the metropolis of Parma, Ohio?" I plucked the last pretzel from the bowl in front of Kirk and me. The lack of salt only served to further agitate me.

"I don't think I had the chance to congratulate you on your new job, Melvin."

The pub was beginning to lose patrons. The first-shift regulars at the nearby tire plant were concluding their post-shift work and leaving for home. Meanwhile, a few hours still remained before the bowling league wrapped up the third game across the street.

"Of course, that's a moot point now." His body movements and twitches were simple but neurotic and every bit a disturbance to an observer. Nearly every ten seconds, Paul either pushed on the piece of eyeglass frame covering the bridge of his nose or loosened and then secured the cufflink on his taupe leisure suit. "Your misadventure didn't last long. I could have warned you, no one in their right mind leaves a big city circulation for Podunkville." On a roll, Paul opted not to accept Kirk's advice to cease and desist. "I think your job has already been filled back here, right, Kirk?"

"Paul, you're an…"

"For your information, Paul," I interrupted Kirk, sliding the empty beer mug toward the bartender, Tony—Kirk's cousin. "My stay back here is only temporary." I asked Tony for another pour from the tap. "I thought I could come back and discuss a few things without being subject to inquiry."

"Another scotch and water?" Tony was within earshot of our conversation. He was the local hero of the bar's populace, a star for Parma South High who played linebacker for Mount Union College.

"I have a plane to catch—the redeye to Washington." He insisted that Kirk supply him with a smoke. "Care to join me, Melvin? I could always use an assistant."

After Tony fed me a full mug, he adjusted the volume on the small black and white TV hanging above the liquor selection—the evening news.

"Journalistic wannabees." I suppose to either compensate for his void of a manly stature or to perhaps finally convince a member of the opposite sex, Paul had recently undertaken a superficial change in his outward appearance. Black horn-rims were replaced with gold rims that housed glass pieces the size of ping-pong paddles, and a neckerchief had been added. "I suppose if covering the farm does not work out for you, Melvin, there's always television."

Despite the video coverage of Soviet tanks rolling through foreign territory, I fell victim, once again, to Paul's obvious trap, like a big brother taking the bait from his little sibling. "Outside of Playboy's 'Girls From the Country' edition, have you ever seen a farm, Paul, or ventured beyond concrete and asphalt?"

With the smirk of an easy victory, Paul said, "Don't need to. I can read about the trivial from you."

Both Kirk and Dale Chernisky played referee, Dale with beer in hand.

Handling the obnoxious one in a scuffle would have hardly been a challenge for me, as Paul carried just enough mass to remain planted on the surface during a durable wind storm. However, I simply threw a few dollar bills on the table. "I got this round."

"Good luck in farm country, Melvin."

"For your information, as if you cared, Paul, farm country actually has a name: South Heaven."

Paul tugged the front and back edges of his camel-brown racing cap to ensure they were secured to the top of his pea-size head. "You're right. I don't care."

Monday

I suppose it was more than spite for Paul Quantrill that pushed me back to South Heaven. The overabundance of underwhelming appreciation from my former peers and my father, for that matter, had been more than humbling. However, I should not have expected anything more. There was excitement stirring at The Republic, and the staff had been engrossed in it. As for my father—without remorse, he peppered me with questions about the senility of a move to Western Ohio and the stability of my future.

The first shift of the mid-day meal began at the high school around 10:45, and its monitor was none other than Coach Waddell. Reclining on the hind legs of a folding chair, he held a shepherd's perch on the wood floor of a stage at one end of the cafeteria. "Here for the Johnny Marzetti, Newspapuh Man?"

The aroma of pasta and canned tomato sauce was surprisingly pleasing. "I missed the game on Friday."

According to eyewitnesses, the Lincoln Huskers played the bill of lonesome loser to perfection. A complete lack of offense paled in futility to a defense that yielded seventy points and over four-hundred yards to the Rangers, of which Lamont Dickies owned two-hundred and fifty. The Husker defenders surrendered touchdowns on the first eight drives by South Heaven. Although not overshadowed by the win, Lamont Dickies broke the heralded rushing mark. The celebration, apparently, was cautious, at best.

"I've done given the wrap-up to Phil," he replied, before barking at a group of boys. Two had decided to use an apple as a baseball. "One of these days, them Huskers'll be stickin' it to us. Things happen that way in high school."

The cafeteria filled quickly, with the vast majority of two-dozen large round tables occupied by many or at least a few. Natural light grazed the area, thanks to the two sky windows and dozens of the wall variety on one side that opened to the school's faculty parking lot.

"Seven down. Only three to go. Phil tells me you guys are up to four in the computer rankings."

Coach Waddell climbed down from the stage, tugged at the black belt that maintained his trousers on a fit waist, then proceeded to search out a table. With his vice-like grip, he latched onto the collar of a stocky boy and pulled the kid to his feet. For a solid thirty seconds, Coach Waddell dressed down the boy before relinquishing his grip and swiping a couple of french fries.

Female students, assumed to be cheerleaders, were replacing "Shuck the Huskers'" pep signs with those reading more along the lines of "Derail the Truckers," the next opponent.

"That boy Knause's got the greatest football knowledge of anyone I've ever coached." Coach Waddell resumed his spot. "Off the field, he's a knucklehead. Amazes me how he gets through every day without killin' himself or someone else."

I asked him for a minute of his time.

"I'm working here." Coach Waddell munched on a thick wooden toothpick. He now wore a full and well-groomed moustache. At the foot of one leg of the chair rested an abused paper copy of a crossword thesaurus and a daily copy of the Lima Sentinel.

"It's about Lamont." One of the girls asked me to hold an edge of a long sign to be hung on the bottom front of the stage.

"What about him?" Coach Waddell sighed, peeling off strips of silver electrical tape for the girls to use. He bellowed a warning to a smaller boy who was running from a larger kid.

Once the girls completed their task and moved on to another station, I brazenly quipped that there was no outpouring of celebration for the kid.

He gritted his teeth, and his powerful jaw muscles flexed with annoyance. "So?"

"So? The record deserves more recognition than a simple article in the local paper."

"Whatya plannin' on doin'? Havin' a parade or sumthin'?"

In scanning the cafeteria, ironically, I found Lamont.

The Ranger star was among a throng of other players, doing more lounging than eating.

"Record's stood for almost thirty years."

"So? And thirty years from now, somebody else be breakin' it. Is that all you wanted? Talk about Lamont?"

I was severely agitating him and could feel an uneasiness gradually overcome me. "Just thought I'd get the coach's thoughts…"

"You want my thoughts? I'll give ya my thoughts, but you ain't quotin' me. Reason there ain't been no celebration, it's been a white boy's record, up tuh now. Folks round here, they like wins, and they like any player who'll get them those wins. But there's a fine line between likin' what a black player does on the field and holdin' him up as some sort of a hero." Coach Waddell retreated from the chair to retrieve a piece of trash discarded by a wayward student.

"All the reason to cherish the accomplishment."

A sequence of bells signaled the rush of another group of lunch goers.

Coach Waddell wore his familiar bitter grin. "Leave it alone. Lamont, he don't care about no celebration. He knows what's best for everyone involved. Besides, I ain't got time to be thinkin' about that, anyway. Got…"

"That's right. You got other things on your mind. Don't ya, Coach?"

"You're right. You exactly right." From a kid passing by, Coach Waddell snatched a maroon ball cap from the boy's head and told him he would hold it for the remainder of the day. "I gotta get forty-seven kids ready for the next game."

"Edina Truckers?"

One of the cheerleaders had found a male companion. The two decided sharing affection, on the stage and only several feet from Coach Waddell, was worth the risk and not the least bit inappropriate.

From a black binder, I produced a single sheet of yellow legal-sized notebook paper. "Apparently, to my surprise, of course, Phil has friends…"

"Mistah Shay, this ain't the place for that." He dismissed the lovebirds, directing them back to fourth period, and advising the boy to be as attentive in English as he was to Jill.

"I found this," I said, handing him the note. "Found it on Phil's desk."

"Shouldn't be snoopin' 'round other's stuff." He creased and folded the paper then pushed it back onto me.

"Does the school know?"

"What? That I'm interviewin' somewhere's else?"

"I would think…"

"Didn't ask for your opinion."

An awkwardly and disturbingly lanky gentleman, with an overall lost disposition and bushy grayish hair that had not seen the likes of a comb in several months, stopped on his stroll to the cafeteria. He carried a brown paper sack and rather large green thermos. "Coach," he said, barely audible over an engrossingly nasal voice. "One of your players failed my exam." He employed every ounce of the ephemeral advantage he had at that time. "I would fathom a guess that this score may affect eligibility this week."

"You got ham salad today, Mistah Sims?"

"That's none of your business, Coach." His affront on Coach Waddell and football had will, but began to crumble, when the red apple fell from the tear in his paper lunch sack and rolled a few feet—ironically, like a punted football.

Coach Waddell and I both leaned forward to see Mister Sims, the algebra teacher, scramble for the stray fruit.

"There!" Sims blurted, before marching toward the teachers' lounge.

Grabbing his book, Coach Waddell climbed down from the stage. "My shift's up." He glanced at the clock on the wall above the entrance to the food line, then at his own time piece. "Ya know, ain't nobody wants you when you can't win, not even your own town. But a few wins in a row, and you get some people lookin' at ya."

Wednesday

During the season bestowed by the Lord, football, the South Heaven Sun expanded the paper to include a separate sports section, which maintained articles on college games from Saturday and a few blurbs from the pro contests on Sunday. Under normal circumstances, from November through July, sports were actually an afterthought and meshed in with other local news, somewhere within the first and only section and relegated to pages seven, eight, etc. With the separate football section, Miss Myra rarely permitted any sporting-related story to appear in the front section, let alone the front page.

It took some prodding, but I was able to secure a front-page spread on Lamont Dickies. When the paper appeared on people's porches, driveways, yards, or wherever the paper skidded to a rest, it displayed a photo of Lamont hugging his mom, immediately after his record-breaking rush. The article-accompanying photo contained only positives and no mention of any underlying cynicism for the breaking of a white man's record. The only jabs I could get in against those cowards were my repeated entries of Lamont breaking, smashing, and/or obliterating the long-standing and cherished record. I was, however, able to score a coup over the traditionalists and purists: a quote from the revered Jim Westerman. The former record holder was retired from the military and living in Kansas. He offered a genuine attaboy to Lamont.

With a copy of the Columbus paper, I followed Miss Myra into the chambers of the local union hall. The Columbus news fed my hunger for keeping up with the Soviet invasion.

The union hall was filled to capacity with people, smoke, and the stench of stale beer. Surrounding the podium at the lead of several rows of folding chairs were two long rectangular tables playing host to about ten men.

"The two men in blue pinstripes are with the state." Miss Myra led me toward a ubiquitous coffee urn outside the kitchenette of the hall. "This'll hit the spot, sport. I can't believe how cold it is for October." She was insistent that the state reps would have no impact on or any new information on the settlement with AGM.

As far as the panacea of the settlement, rumor had it that AGM would sink $2.5 million into the coffers of the city. The one unknown was when.

Along with the two in blue pinstripes, there were four others in suit and tie, three of whom were most assuredly foreign to South Heaven. All in suits took seats to the right of the podium, while two in union satin jackets—the mayor of the town and Butch Boyd—owned the table to the left.

One of South Heaven's councilmen, a former auto worker named Lyle Hempstead, banged the gavel on the podium to bring the meeting to order. Not the most eloquent of public speakers, Lyle possessed an ugly elementary accent. He also, according to Miss Myra, was as crooked as an Augusta National dogleg. With some jeers from an unappreciative few in the crowd, Lyle introduced two men from the state economic development board, then men from the manufacturer Phoenix Toys. "We wanna announce we may have us a tenant for the auto plants." Lyle grinned through his bushy and unkempt moustache. Unfortunately for his egoless public speaking skills, he received a reserved hush from the crowd. "These men here are from Phoenix Toys, and they're interested in comin' to South Heaven."

Before Lyle could produce the utterance of another sentence, half a dozen in the crowd stood and piped questions aloud at the tables. Their ruckus radiated through more in the crowd and created a manageable disturbance.

Butch Boyd stepped to the podium, gradually displacing Lyle. "All right, all right! Everyone calm down. You'll all have a chance to ask questions, one at a time. We simply need a little order."

The crowd, mostly former employees of AGM, responded to Boyd and complied with his suggestions.

"As Lyle pointed out, South Heaven has a few distinguished guests today. They're executives with a company out of New Jersey, looking to expand in the Midwest. We've been in touch with the company for a few weeks now…"

"We heard these guys ain't about the union?" He was an average man with circus reddish-orange hair.

"Greg, I understand your concern. But Phoenix could bring six hundred jobs to us."

"Six hundred!" blurted a healthy and plump man. "AGM had it at four thousand."

Butch could not help but concur. "They don't make cars though, Frank."

"What about wages?"

"Yeah!"

"Would ya rather have no jobs?"

"You're a traitor, Lyle!"

"That's enough," Boyd insisted. "Listen. Listen to me, everyone. Phoenix Toys hasn't settled on anywhere yet in the Midwest. We're only on a list of potential cities.. We need to sell these gentlemen on the viability of South Heaven. We need to show these folks South Heaven can produce the best in this country."

"We heard they don't operate under no contract!" Greg created an explosion of four-letter forays from the crowd. The cacophony echoed in the smoke-induced room.

With the unsettling appearance of the visitors from Phoenix, Boyd waited for a moment of calm then started again. "Let me repeat: We're only in a preliminary stage of discussion. Nothing has been settled upon. Not wages. Not contracts. Nothing."

"We can't be livin' without contract wages!" Greg demanded to hear from the Phoenix representatives, which prompted a chorus of "yeahs."

Boyd fended off the request by claiming that the Phoenix reps were not going to field any questions related to contracts and wages. "Gentlemen, this is the present. The past has doomed us. The present will give us a future." Boyd had discarded his calming demeanor and began enunciating the words that would emphasize the outstanding point.

"When am I going to start being included in the future of this paper?" I asked Miss Myra.

"Jeez, sport, what job do you want now? Procurement? Accounting?"

"Send 'em back to Jersey!"

Miss Myra appeared less than comfortable, as if she too were fending off the punches being thrown at Boyd. "They don't realize the opportunity."

"Are you leaving South Heaven?"

Lyle jumped forward amid the commotion. "People, people! This is the best opportunity we've had in a long time!" He slammed his fist on the podium.

"You just nailed the coffin shut on your election, Lyle!"

With the impending election, Lyle's seat on council was up, and he was combatting a former teacher in the school system.

"Myra, are you leaving South Heaven?"

The Office

We were invited by Boyd and the representatives from Phoenix to lunch and a tour of the plants. However, we opted to return to the office and were met promptly and abruptly by the lone occupant: Phil.

"You guys know this Ambrose kid at New Jefferson is only thirty-eight points away from the all-time scorin' record for Ohio? All-time." Phil was reading from an out-of-town sports page.

Again, Miss Myra nonchalantly passed him, ignoring our lovable sports writer to ask me about lunch.

"What's his name?" Seeing that no one was offering Phil the attention he sought, I began to feel little sorry for Phil.

"Ambrose. He plays tailback for New Jefferson." Phil made sure I saw the article from New Jefferson's previously played game.

Miss Myra read from two different takeout menus. "I feel like Frankie's."

"I like Frankie's. Love the meatball hoagie." He had an awkward flat-footed walk. Phil was a prototypical sports geek.

"Maybe we should do Chinese?"

"Myra." Phil waddled to his desk to retrieve a letter. "Got a letter from the Prognosticator. He's back."

"Chinese sounds good, sport."

"He's been missing for a few years now." Phil was excited, beyond his normal paranoia.

Miss Myra glanced at the letter then placed her order with me.

"I say we go with a new column for him. He's got fans, ya know?"

"You need to talk to your boss." Miss Myra pointed to me.

"He don't know about the Prognosticator," retorted Phil.

"I've heard a little about him." I shrugged.

"He needs to be put back in the paper."

Miss Myra finally offered some attention to her reporter. "Did he say where he's been for the past five years, Phil?"

"No, but he's ready to restart his column again. Come on, Myra," Phil pleaded.

"And we have no idea who this guy is?" I asked.

"Nobody knows who he is. Nobody. Sure, there were guesses, but nobody ever found out who he was. That's what made the column so great," Phil insisted. You see, every week, the Prognosticator would submit a cartoon and a column on the impending game. His cartoon character was always a Ranger doing battle against the week's opponent. He never ever predicted a loss for South Heaven. It was great."

Miss Myra stole Phil's thunder. "We're but two days from the eighth game of the season. Perhaps, Phil, it's a little too late for people to get excited about our mystery writer?"

"No, on the contrary. This town, these fans are in awe of an unbeaten record. The Prognosticator will add to the excitement. Look, he already made his prediction for the Edina game!" He flashed the letter. "Rangers twenty-eight, Edina ten."

"Whattaya think, sport?"

"I don't know. I've never seen Edina."

"Come on Myra. One more year."

Friday

Just two weeks before the election, the president-initiated Operation Roadblock, the immediate shipment of supplies and foreign aid to the newest enemy of the Soviet Union: Afghanistan. His attempt to track down those responsible for the attack on the Langley was failing miserably. With a nationwide unemployment rate pushing double digits, following a recent Labor Department report, the president had only one trump card to play, and that was to employ whatever force possible against the Red Menace. By the time the caravan departed South Heaven High en route to Edina, the president had announced Roadblock to his constituency.

I doubted if any member of the posse in the car had any concern or opinion for the president's plan, the Soviet Union, or the impending election. Willie Tee and his consortium of three cousins and/or friends crammed into Senior Epstein's station wagon. Miss Myra borrowed Daddy's car and unfortunately offered the posse a ride.

"So, what's the scoop on Edina?" I asked from the middle position of the front bench seat, since Willie Tee had shotgun.

"They called the Truckers," responded J.P., one of Willie Tee's friends.

"Foh and three." Willie Tee was engrossed in a sports page. "But they only lost one in the league."

Cornered between the interstate and County Road Twenty-Two, Edina was home to a gargantuan truck stop, which the caravan decided to patron.

The string of cars, vans, and station wagons were decorated in maroon streamers and Ranger flags and drew mostly odd or unusual stares from the truck drivers and other patrons of Mo's Truck Stop.

Just south of Mo's but north of the town of Edina, we passed the major employer of Trucker parents: Harvester Exact. A plant that occupied several dozen acres, Harvester manufactured larger combustion engines.

"Ya know, like eighteen-wheelers and combines." J.P. was the tour guide. "Donny Wheeluh and Benji, they drive here six days a week to work."

"Must be good pay," I suggested.

"No moh than any othuh place." Willie Tee polished off his Mo's burger. With the last mouthful, he impolitely muttered, "Least they not closed."

The IGA grocery store and an anemic business district welcomed us to downtown Edina.

"Gotta turn right up here," J.P. told Miss Myra. "Past da circle."

The middle of town presented travelers with a classic European roundabout that hampered the progress of three different roads: County Roads Twenty-Two and Twenty-Eight and Edina Avenue. Inside the circle was a park setting, with aged and brown pear and cherry trees surrounding a gazebo shelter. Pristine white, the gazebo was large enough to house a small orchestra but had a circumference of only a third of the entire circle.

Miss Myra turned onto Edina Avenue, just past a service station.

J.P. held the director position as the lead car pulled the caravan into the beginning of a residential neighborhood before finding the marquee of Edina High School.

By the time Willie Tee and his posse disappeared through the back gate, a member of our caravan had latched onto Miss Myra. So I bid her adieu and meandered toward Old Man Schmidt's perch. From the gate to the grandstand on the home side, a walk of no more than thirty yards, I was accosted by no less than a dozen fuming and irate Ranger fans, cursing the very existence of the people of Edina. Gathering nothing more than incoherent rants about a wet field, I found my way to the top of the press box.

Neither Old Man Schmidt nor Wally was seated. They both had the same disposition as every other South Heaven fanatic.

"You see this, boy?"

Somewhat parched for breath following the climb, I asked the reason the entire town had suddenly become mentally unstable.

"Look at the field!" Wally's bulbous ears were stinging red.

I obliged Wally and caught a stunning glimpse of the field. "I know it was cloudy all day, but I don't recall any rain today, let alone a deluge."

Puddles, some three to four feet in diameter, consumed the field. There had to be two dozen of the water holes throughout the field of play. Both sidelines, near and around where players stood, were virtual ponds.

Old Man Schmidt, tiring of pacing, fell into his broadcast chair then moaned, "1959."

Neither team dared to enter the field of play. From our perch, I could see Coach Waddell and the Rangers simulating their offense on the playground of the Edina middle school, several hundred yards from the stadium.

"Back in '59," Old Man Schmidt started, retrieving his smoke. "Edina had themselves a star running back named Glaser. Unbeaten record, before they came to South Heaven." A terse breeze that had just developed toyed with the flame of his lighter. "Glaser was fast."

Through the pregame sounds of the home Truckers crowd, we could still discern a boisterous and vociferous argument between athletic directors. Ted Foxx was reserving a lengthy session in confessional with the number of four-letter bombs exploding in the press box.

"What's going on here?" I stammered.

"In '59, Henry Lyso was a kid helping out his granddad, Jack." Wally picked up on the story. Even without a temper, Wally was hardly the sage or narrator Old Man Schmidt was. "Jack, he was in charge of takin' care of the school grounds—cuttin' grass, buildin' fences. Ol' Henry, he dun left the sprinklers on overnight. When the game came around on Saturday, the field—soaked."

"Glaser didn't score a point," laughed Old Man Schmidt. "Thanks to Henry, we won that game and went on to win the league that year."

The gaggle of referees walked the perimeter of the midfield area, accompanied by officials from both schools. Transferring animation from the press box to the field, Foxx was providing the referee with an earful.

"Edina has never forgave us," insisted Wally.

"You mean to tell me this is due to sprinkler damage?" I asked.

"Boy, they left them sprinklers on all night."

In single file, marching methodically and without haste or purpose, the Rangers moved from the middle-school playground to the apron of the pole-vault pit, some few dozen yards beyond the west end zone. They displayed little emotion or energy as they grouped around Coach Waddell.

With an annoying but less-than-constant wind replacing the terse breeze, officials, despite the protest from South Heaven, decided to go ahead with kick-off.

Edina was in need of a few breaks to earn a share of the PEC title, and one of them involved a defeat of the Rangers. According to Willie

Tee, Edina had a great defense, which was only due to receive help from the soaked field.

To spite the home team, Coach Waddell, who was obviously not amused with the current field conditions, didn't march his Rangers directly toward his designated sideline. Instead, he took the circuitous route around the field. As the Truckers poured through the east-end goalpost amid an anxious crowd, Coach Waddell, with his team at a slow jog behind him, led the Rangers along the cinder track between the home stands and the Edina sideline. By committing to the endeavor, Coach Waddell completely exhausted the emotion from the Edina fans and players with a counterattack that stunned and silenced the enemy. As the team made the last turn home, they began to whoop and holler like an attacking rogue military formation. The single-file column broke all bearing as the team rushed their sidelines and piled onto one another.

Unfortunately for the shocked Edina team, the Truckers' coach was forced to send the weaker of his two units onto the field first.

In the muck, Edina's offense lost yardage on three consecutive plays and was forced to punt. And with each thwarted attempt, Old Man Schmidt and Wally added their own whoop of spite.

Dickies and the Ranger offense fared better than their counterparts, but only slightly. Five plays took the ball from the Truckers' forty-two to exactly midfield.

With only two offensive drives in the record book, the field had already degraded into muck, with no sight of grass. Ruts littered the middle of the field like an unkempt bean pasture during a wet spring.

"This is ridiculous," moaned Old Man Schmidt.

Receiving a poor snap from center, Angelo Pezzotta stepped forward to plant his left foot. That left foot, however, hit precariously in the mud, and Pezzotta slipped and slid as if he were negotiating with sleek ice. In a scene reminiscent of slapstick comedies, the football sailed from Angelo's hands as his body floated parallel to the ground. Gathering his senses, Angelo struggled to locate the loose ball.

I shot to my feet, waving on number eighty-two for Edina.

The pigskin was tucked in the arms of number eighty-two. Following two teammates, number eighty-two slopped and trudged through the mud and eventually crossed the goal line to the fanatic delight of the home crowd.

Wally covered the microphone during his rants and barrages of words not found in Webster's version of the English language.

"That's what ya get!" Old Man Schmidt pulled some satisfaction following the missed extra point, with their kicker suffering the same fate as the Ranger punter.

"Folks, down six to nuthin.' This ain't lookin' good. With a bad field and all, it may only take six to win this game."

It seemed Madame Fortune, all season long, had maintained a kind heart for Coach Waddell and his Rangers. However, when the ball from the kick-off fluttered in the breeze before sticking forthrightly in a clump of wet mud, she was either occupied somewhere else or had finally granted me some of that cherished luck.

"There's a pile on the field! Folks, I can't tell who's got the ball!"

I lost count of the number of players wrestling for the loose ball, but the pile included the student councils, the art club, and the kitchen sink.

"Dang!" Old Man Schmidt rapped his cane after the referee signaled for Edina.

The initial play from the line of scrimmage could have been the sickness that pulled the last breath from a perfect season. Willing the wet and mud-soaked ball to his wideout, Jack Rielding, the Edina quarterback, completed a quick pass. The famous number eighty-two practically dug the ball from the turf, juked left and right, and was gone up the field.

Madame Fortune had put Luke Post on the turf with a slip and fall.

"We're now down by twelve," Wally told his audience while nipping at his bottom lip.

Both men in the Summit were more perturbed than dejected. Despite the rhetoric that Wally was feeding his audience about the certain and impending South Heaven demise, neither man carried a defeatist appearance. Unfortunately for them, though, the Rangers limped into the second quarter with a two-touchdown deficit hanging over them.

Before Duane Boyd could bring his team out of the huddle to begin the second, however, we were distracted with the commotion behind the press box. From the parking lot and through the entrance gate came one of South Heaven's all-white police cruisers, kicking up stones and lights flashing. The vehicle screeched to a halt just behind the home crowd, a moment before Ted Foxx leaped from the passenger-side door. Foxx lugged a large mesh bag over his right shoulder. Inside the bag had to be a dozen or more footballs. As fast as he could, Foxx chugged around the track and toward the Ranger sideline.

"Looks like he's got ammunition, eh, Wally?"

After the first-down play in which Dickies gained three yards off right tackle, Coach Waddell stopped play momentarily and ran a dry ball onto the field.

With the clean ball in play, Coach Waddell sent Boyd back into the pocket. In turn, Boyd sent Durning on a ten-yard curl pattern. Two successive plays with dry balls netted completions to Durning for short yardage.

As his team progressed slowly down the field, on quick and short passes, Coach Waddell continued to send the ball boy on and off the field to swap wet football for dry one. The ploy worked, sucking minutes off the clock and moving the line of scrimmage from the Rangers' thirty-eight to the Truckers' ten.

"Boyd's got a flanker left, and Durning split out right." Old Man Schmidt focused the binoculars. "He takes the snap, pumps right, then hands off to Dickies. Dickies darts up the middle ... Touchdown! Touchdown Rangers! Duane Boyd faked a pass then handed a draw off to Lamont."

Despite treacherous footing, Stu Ginnette muscled through a successful extra-point attempt.

A meager drive by Edina and a lengthy one by Boyd and the Rangers drained the clock, without a change in the score.

"Whereya goin'?" he asked me as I stood with feet on the ladder. Old Man Schmidt placed his order for a Pepsi and a small basket of fried chips. "They serve the best chips here. Homemade."

The home-side concession stand was tucked neatly under the main grandstand. With the lines stretching beyond my patience level, I trudged to the visitors' side, as near to the edge of the end zone as possible without soiling my shoes.

Hustling by me, Willie Tee had two clean and newer footballs tucked under his elbows.

"Whoa!" I called after him. "Whattaya doing?"

Out of breath, Willie Tee halted his pace then scanned the area as if someone were tailing him. "Dem Truckers ain't gettin' away with this. Brand-new from the coaches' office."

"You stole these?"

"We be needin' dry balls!"

The heat from the locker room apparently did not radiate to the hands of Lamont Dickies. Catching the kick on the fly, Dickies headed straight up the gut of the defense. With one move to the right, and without a single hit from the opposing defender, the pigskin flew from Dickies' grasp and into the awaiting arms of number eighty-two.

"You gotta be kiddin' me!" moaned Old Man Schmidt, nearly dropping his basket of chips.

Dickies, head clasped in hands, dragged himself to the sidelines. He stood alone, away from the action of the field, refusing consolation. Kyle Knause, though, must have felt his teammate's pain. On three successive plays, Knause and his Rangers stuffed the Truckers' offense.

"Ya know, boy…" Old Man Schmidt began digging at his teeth with a makeshift pick. "Miss Myra, she ain't never been happy here. South Heaven just ain't never been her home, always wantin' to go elsewhere."

"Why are you…?"

"Just some advice, boy."

"It doesn't sound like you approve of Miss Myra's direction."

With a fresh cigar in one hand, he squinted through the binoculars. "Know that every kid who grows up a part of South Heaven wants to do everything they can to leave town. Some make it, but most of 'em don't." With his open index finger, Old Man Schmidt wiped up salt from the bottom of his basket. "Those that do make it out, through college or otherwise, usually yearn to come back. Nothing replaces a small town, not even no big city life."

"Except for Miss Myra?"

The play of the third quarter accomplished little more than adding to the muck and mire of what was once a manicured field. From helmet to cleats, every player with significant minutes was soaked in black and brown tar-like mud. Pride, tradition, and innocent school mascot colors were indistinguishable. It was, in a word, dreadful.

South Heaven took possession into the fourth quarter, but their first play was a punt.

"Folks, this daggum field's gonna cost us the playoffs. We ain't moved the ball at all here in the second half, and if we don't start, you all can kiss that unbeaten record bye-bye."

The weak link of the Edina chain put together a string of positive plays. Jack Rielding had slowly turned the dagger in the chest cavity of the South Heaven faithful. With the ball on the South Heaven thirty-nine and a fresh set of downs to manage, the Truckers' offense had enough momentum to melt the remaining five minutes of the game clock and steal a share of the lead in the PEC.

"Folks, this ain't pretty here. Rielding's taking his good ol' sweet time gettin' the team to the line. He takes the snap and hands on a quick-hitter to his fullback Stuckey. Stuckey's been carryin' the load here in the second half. He was stopped by Teddy Bear."

Based on his slouching posture in the chair, I assumed Wally had relegated himself to believing that the perfect season was soon to be an afterthought.

"Almost four minutes to play, and Rielding brings 'em to the line. There's the snap. Again, Stuckey carries. He's stopped after only a couple."

Wally began securing the extraneous equipment, practically ignoring the play on the field.

"Third down and about seven to go. Rielding brings 'em back to the line. He's got that number eighty-two flanked to his right. Three minutes and thirty seconds to go. Rielding takes the ball. He pump fakes to his left, turns, and throws to his right … Ohh my! Luke Post jumped the route. He's got the ball! He's racin' down the sidelines! Nobody's gonna catch him. He's at the thirty … the twenty! He's kickin' up mud. He's at the ten … Good God Almighty, Luke Post'll score! Touchdown Rangers! Touchdown Rangers!"

Wally fell to his knees to acknowledge his relationship to the Almighty as Knause and his fellow defenders mobbed Post in the end zone.

CHAPTER SIXTEEN
War Hill of Marlboro

Monday

Flurries welcomed the morning for the residents of South Heaven. The cold, however, was second on the mind of the Ranger faithful. When the state computer rankings became public on Monday, South Heaven had moved up one spot to number three. Thanks to a shocking loss by both Cold Springs and Farmington, Coach Waddell's crew inched one step closer to the playoffs for class AA. Heading into game nine, South Heaven was a full two points behind Toledo East Catholic and only a half a percentage point from the second-ranked team, Frederick.

A trek from my apartment to the office had been accompanied by dozens of cars migrating out of town, all heading to Lima. The whistle stop by the Republican candidate for the presidency had intrigued the constituency of South Heaven. Our reporters were mixed in with the cars traveling to Lima, making the office empty—almost.

Phil had several different sports pages spread out on his desk. He was propped in front of a typewriter.

"Do you always keep abreast on what's happening in … Dayton?" I asked, fingering the pages of The Dayton Journal and News.

"I'm gonna need you to edit this." Phil snapped the sheet of paper free from the typewriter carriage. "Here." Insistently, he traded the type sheet for the sports page then neurotically collected all the pages, folding them exactly along the predisposed creases. "By at least two o'clock…" Phil had little compassion for his fellow man, beyond what a peer or immediate supervisor could do to satisfy a pressing yet insignificant need. Despite my presence only arm's length from him, Phil snorted and huffed on a nasal inhaler.

I glanced over the typewritten work. "This looks like a letter?"

Phil had moved from nasal decongestant to comb in his hourly and compulsive ritual of hygiene and grooming. "Do you know we're still third in the computer rankings?" The comb was housed in its own vat of green barbershop germicide. Phil worked out his wrist and forearm muscles, screwing the cap onto the small cylinder. "It's a travesty."

From the third sentence of the first paragraph, I read, verbatim, those same words.

Phil's letter was addressed to Bud Scott, Commissioner of the Ohio Athletic Association, and was less than impressive grammatically.

"How many letters have you written like this?"

"To date, three." He was a wretched typist, the white-out tool his favorite weapon. "They got to respond one of these days."

"Phil, whattaya do—you know, for fun?"

Phil squinted toward me. "That's none of your business."

"Right…" I politely declined his request for me to edit the letter.

"You are the assistant editor of this paper—not by my choice, mind you. Be that as it may, however, it is your job to review my work."

"Work? Yes. Personal crusades? No."

Phil retrieved a rag and furniture polish from his desk. "You're jealous. I can see it," he chimed proudly, dousing his wooden picture frame with polish spray. "There can be only one sports writer here. Only one."

"Okay."

"No one knows more of the game of football than me. Take, for instance, this Friday's opponent: War Hill. They call themselves the Marauders. Stupid nickname, if you ask me. Did you know that back in the '50s, South Heaven was unbeaten and went up to War Hill? Snowed the entire day. At halftime, nobody had scored. War Hill scored right at the beginning of the second half." Phil removed his eyeglasses and a large bottle of glass cleaner. A hankie served as his cloth. "At the very end of the fourth, Gary Starcher busted through the middle and ran down the sidelines untouched. Couldn't tell where you were at on the field—Starcher thought he was past the goal line. He spiked the ball but was five yards from pay dirt. We lost."

"Here's a thought, instead of expending energy recapping the Ohio State game, make use of your South Heaven trivial expertise and submit something weekly. Readers would love it."

"Last anyone heard of Gary Starcher, he had moved to Cincinnati to live with his grandparents."

Thursday

High noon on the fourth day of the week was mayor's court in the town of South Heaven. Never would I have known that fact had it not been for Marty's unpaid parking tickets.

"Man, I'm glad you're here to help me out." Apparently, no one informed Marty of the proper appearance for court. Tattered blue jeans and an Aerosmith t-shirt wrapped in an olive-drab Army jacket probably could have been supplanted by a collared shirt and dress pants.

"You may want to take the hat off before you get up to the bench." Although engrossed in a copy of Newsweek, I still had an ear to the conversation occurring with the case in front of us.

In the small world of South Heaven, the defendant in the forward case was none other than the master of the petty scam, Willie Tee. Allegedly, he had been caught borrowing a vehicle from the lot of Tommy Totes Used Cars, despite possessing neither a license nor permission. Unrepresented by counsel, Willie Tee presented his own defense.

"Do you know the mayor?"

Marty wore sandals and was, well, relaxed in his seat. "He's a friend of my dad's."

Willie Tee's defense plea humored the mayor and his court recorder. Despite the plea, Officer Jerry Stump, the arresting officer, encouraged the mayor to impose a harsh punishment.

I closed the magazine to listen.

"C'mon Jerry, me and you go back a ways," insisted Willie Tee. "I know you since you's in school."

The mayor interrupted. "Willie, this is a second offense for you. We dismissed the first."

"And bless ya for dat. Bless ya."

The mayor introduced Tommy Totes, the used car salesman.

"Thank you, Mayor." Tommy was skeletal, with any exposed skin saturated in cheap lotion, and his jet-black top was drenched in oil or some type of dressing. His manufactured stench created false phlegm at the rear of your throat. "I now have three cars with extra amount of miles on 'em."

"Ya Honah, dem cars, they AGMs. I's just test drivin,' see if they had problems."

"All the way to Columbus?" Officer Jerry interrupted. "Watch the Buckeyes, I bet."

"That so, Willie Tee? You get up there to watch the game?" asked the mayor.

Without a word of defense to utter, Willie Tee simply hung his head.

"Mayor, I'm out mileage that I can't get back."

The mayor asked of Willie Tee if he had any other words to add. "In that case…"

"That's just a coincidence." Reacting to a racing heart, I stood to address the court. "You can't prove he borrowed the car to attend a ball game."

"Who are you?" The mayor peeked above his bifocals with a crinkled forehead.

"Just a friend."

"A friend does not a lawyer make. You also friends with the photographer celebrity there?" The mayor glanced at his docket.

I relented and returned to my seat, much to the dismay of Marty, who chastised me for getting him on the bad side of Mayor Montgomery.

After a brief meeting with brown leisure suit-laden Totes, the mayor returned a verdict and passed judgment on Willie Tee. "Willie Tee, I think it best you repay the car lot the mileage used. The way Tommy figures, that comes to almost a hundred bucks. Do you have that to repay?"

Willie Tee shook his head. His perpetual smile had evaporated.

"In that case, you will be ordered to appear every Friday, Saturday, and Sunday night for the next month at the used car lot, to work off your debt."

"But I miss Ranger games if I does dat." Small droplets of frustrated tears appeared on top of his gaunt and wasted cheekbones. "Please, Mayuh? We ain't been unbeaten in a longtime. We's gotta chance for dah playoffs."

The mayor cracked his gavel.

Outside of Court

It was probably more due to Marty's newly defaulted fame than his family connection with Mayor Montgomery that granted him a reprieve from his parking transgressions. Either way, however, Marty's sentence hardly compared to that given to Willie Tee.

"You ever been to Michigan?" Marty tugged a red stocking cap over his mess of hair.

The two of us stood ground outside of the city's maintenance office. "Why?"

Among gum wrappers, a couple of used pencils, and a key chain, Marty retrieved from his coat pocked a used envelope, folded several times, like a note sent home with a fifth-grader. "I got this from The Flint Messenger. They wanna offer me a job."

I snagged Marty by the shoulder and plucked the envelope from his hand. "Offer you ... a job?"

"Staff photographer, or sumthin' like that." Despite the news, Marty had the concern of a used car battery.

"Have you called these guys back?"

He replied through a bellowing yawn, "I don't even know where Flint is. Besides, I haven't told the other paper nothing neither."

Although shocked, I uttered the obvious question.

"I dunkow. Some place. I think Fort Wayne."

My pleas with Marty failed miserably to break the defense of immaturity. Words like future, opportunity, and fortune could hardly overcome the awesome force of effort, work, and moving, despite his previous desire to leave South Heaven.

Instead, Marty refolded his envelope, stuffed it back into an overcrowded pocket, and headed off to class—basic pre-calculus.

Friday

War Hill Military Academy was established in the summer of 1863 as a preparatory school to train young men for the Ohio regiments of the

Union Army. Thanks to fiduciary and political backing from one Robert Brownlee, Union Brigadier General, land tycoon, and U.S. Senator, the prep school remained open after the surrender at Appomattox.

In 1931, a retired colonel of the Army and former graduate of War Hill, Randolph Jolson, returned to Marlboro, Ohio, as an advisor to the school. Having been stationed along the Northeast coast following the First World War, Jolson learned and became enamored with the game of football. He brought the Ivy League-type of play with him to War Hill and began a program in the autumn of 1932. For half a decade following, War Hill struggled, winning only once. However, Jolson would eventually pass command of the watch over to a former Ohio State player, Fran Dressen.

With their enrollment increasing three-fold during the early '40s, the Marauders, under Dressen's direction, racked up three eight-win seasons and an overall record of 30-2. At the end of the war, Dressen would depart the school for the lure of college ball, leaving War Hill to suffer through mediocrity for decades to come.

As life entered the ninth decade of the twentieth century, War Hill's football squad was mired in futility, and the school itself was on the verge of being closed due to record-low enrollment.

Marlboro was a forty-minute drive for South Heaven fans—two or three county roads south, west, and south again. Hardly a ghost town but empty nonetheless, Marlboro possessed a score of houses, a post office, and a single blinking traffic light. The academy towered above the miniscule town, on a hill, beyond the southern border. Named after the spot where a group of settlers and militia ambushed a force of Shawnee warriors crossing the plains below the hill, War Hill Academy was a distant partner to the residents of Marlboro, much like the asylum at the edge of Anytown, USA.

A single-lane driveway led up War Hill to the school and the football field. There were hardly enough parking positions on the asphalt to hold all the vehicles of the caravan, let alone the entire crowd expected from South Heaven. Cadets in full garb hastened to the point of contention and began routing inbound cars onto the parade grounds behind the main campus building.

Jolson Stadium was a healthy walk from the parade grounds on a calm and comfortable evening. With the position on the hill and the temperature on the last day of October hovering just below freezing, the walk seemed to double in length.

"I hope they have coffee ready." Miss Myra was bundled in enough clothes, jackets, and caps to withstand the frigid temperatures on Mt. Everest. She had a scarf completely concealing the lower portion of her face.

With the throng of other South Heaven fans, Miss Myra and I scampered toward the stadium entrance, only to be caught in a line that appeared to have no sense of expediency to it. Like the feed end of a bridge toll, patrons painstakingly filed through the line.

"What's the holdup?" I asked rhetorically.

With the obligatory two dollars in hand, we worked our way to the front, only to discover no individual at the gate accepting money. Either heeding to progression or the ultimate regression, War Hill had replaced an individual ticket-taker with a cardboard sign and a five-gallon orange bucket. The handwritten letters on the sign asked fans to leave two dollars in the bucket. By the time Miss Myra and I dropped our fee into the pickle container, others had done the same. Several scores of single dollar bills filled the bucket.

Riddled with age, Jolson Stadium was mired in neglect. Although the grass on the field was lush and full, with few dirt patches, the concrete structure that held the wood bleachers was lousy with egregious cracks and leaning in on itself. With only one section of bleachers, the throng of South Heaven faithful had to use the decrepit seating structure.

The press box and the makeshift Summit leaned with the concrete stands. Footing was steady, but I walked with a very slight lean. Fortunately, there was a barrier at the rear, thus preventing our chairs from dropping off the edge.

Skies surrounding War Hill were a menacing gray, exacerbating the ever-approaching evening darkness. Painted against the background were the white road jerseys of the South Heaven Rangers—different, however, from the usual game attire. For the War Hill game, the team wore a grungy, almost cream-colored heavy jersey with black numbers.

"What is up with the jerseys?" I asked, pulling the ear flaps out from under my stocking cap.

"I'm guessin' a little motivation." With much frustration, Old Man Schmidt made attempt after attempt at balancing the four legs of his chair on the sloping deck.

Wally leaned some muscle to his radio buddy's problem then picked up on the story. "Waddell's coach, Ron Kusak, gave the pep talk today. These jerseys are from the '60s."

South Heaven took the field prior to the home Marauders, and, as they did, flurries became more and more prevalent. Not a Lake Erie-effect snow, by any stretch, but one that was assuredly aggravating.

Subtly, the team from War Hill assumed their sideline. They had meager numbers as compared to other members of the conference. Twenty-six were counted.

With only a single section of bleachers, it was difficult to discern South Heaven fans from those of War Hill. But there was little to no noise when the home team entered the field of play.

Stu Ginnette connected firmly with the ball, and the wind froze graciously, pushing the receiver back to his own five-yard line.

"Riley takes the ball to about the twenty-two," Wally told his listeners.

War Hill's first play was a mere embarrassment. The entire offensive line caved at the snap of the ball. A dive play from a full-house backfield resembled one from a Pee Wee game, netting a three-yard loss once the quarterback collided with his fullback and fell to the turf. Through his hands, the next snap popped from the quarterback's hands as he pulled away from center.

"No wonder they're winless." I felt guilty watching such ineptitude.

"He takes the snap and pitches—oh my! Fumble."

Once the War Hill back fell on the dropped pitch, the referee whistled fourth down, and both teams ordered their respective punt teams onto the field.

"Folks, I dunno if we were good, or they were just bad on that series."

From the eleven, the Marauder punter set back a few yards into his own end zone. Despite the futility of the first three plays, the snap reached the punter flawlessly.

Coach Waddell sent everyone but the water boy and the trainer to block the punt. The leaders of the rush were within mere inches when the War Hill punter pushed the ball from his right foot. Unfortunately, like a carrier traveling at full-flank speed, those lead rushers could not stop on a dime. At a dead sprint, three Rangers plowed into the punter, knocking the kid some five yards beyond the end zone line—and garnering a major penalty.

Instead of taking control of the ball just nineteen yards from pay dirt, the spot where the weak punt dropped dead, Coach Waddell was forced to send his defense back onto the field.

The play yielded only moaning from Old Man Schmidt and Wally.

On the next two consecutive plays, Knause and his mates toyed with the inferior Marauder offense. However, the Rangers did offer a couple of gifts to their enemy. War Hill advanced the ball twelve yards on a pass-interference call, and fifteen more yards on a facemask penalty.

Two yards across midfield, however, was the farthest War Hill moved the ball. Three more plays displayed more ineptitude.

The batch of light flurries blew through the academy grounds as the first legitimate snow of the latter part of 1980 seemed to conclude. But the cold did not leave with the precipitation.

No one bothered to awaken Boyd and his offense prior to South Heaven assuming their first possession. A delay-of-game penalty bled into a false-start foul, which infected the play immediately following and resulted in another error of lost yardage.

"Folks, readin' the ref's lips, that hold appeared to be on sixty-five, Schlicter. So instead of a twelve-yard gain by Dickies, Rangers now got the ball back at the eighteen."

"Too darn cold to sit up here and watch penalties," stammered Old Man Schmidt, his hand shaking too much to ignite the chrome lighter.

Dickies took the complaint to heart and rambled thirteen yards off right tackle on the exact next play. If at all possible, the Ranger tailback contributed to making the War Hill defense appear less competent than their offense. Another off-tackle run, to the opposite side, gained back fifteen yards. He dragged two or three Marauders with him before falling to the ground. Dickies was a man playing among boys, and he tore off ten and seventeen yards on two more successive plays, both within the interior line.

"Folks, Lamont Dickies heads to the sidelines for a much-deserved rest. On four plays, he's taken the ball from the eighteen all the way down to the War Hill twenty-seven."

With Dickies on the sidelines, Boyd lined his backs up in the I-formation. Backup tailback Rex King gave Dickies a breather. Opposing the conservative thought of the Summit, Coach Waddell ordered Boyd on an option right. Unfortunately, the freshman must not have conveyed the correct call to the sophomore backup. Duane Boyd faked the dive to his fullback then darted toward the defensive end. Suckering the defender perfectly, Boyd, assuming his tailback was trailing, pitched the ball backwards.

"God dawg! Folks, Boyd went one way, and King went the other."

An insignificant defender for War Hill, having been completely taken out of the play, found the loose ball on his team's thirty-four.

The very mid-section of the turf at Jolson was dirt, like a baseball diamond. It stood in sharp contrast to the other eighty percent of the field. Without significant precipitation, dust was a temporary enemy and nuisance to all field performers. Clouds of it hovered over the field after every skirmish, until they met their fate at the hands of the wind.

War Hill's offensive woes continued upon taking control of the ball. Despite being handed five yards on a Ranger penalty, the Marauder eleven managed an impressive one yard on three plays. It was like watching any given freshman squad do battle with the varsity. War Hill was being tossed around like undersized little brothers in a pickup game of backyard tackle. Still, as pathetic as their play was on the field, the embarrassment was solidly on the side of the Rangers. At the end of the first quarter, neither team had posted a single point.

Kicking into the breeze, the War Hill punter opted to add his own misfortune to the plague of Marauder football. Caught in the air, his kicked ball traveled a mighty fifteen yards from the point of contact, netting all of two yards.

"Aggh! You gotta be kiddin' me, folks!" complained Old Man Schmidt. "Ineligible player on the field for the Rangers. First down, War Hill."

Thus far, by pure luck, War Hill was subscribing to the theory that the best defense is a good offense—or penalties by your opponent. Even with the extra possession, they settled into their routine of three plays and a punt, losing a total of six yards.

"Numbah fifty-two lines up to punt ... again," Old Man Schmidt told the audience.

A gust whipped toward the line of scrimmage the moment the ball left the punter's foot. Smothering the kick, the wind halted the flight of the ball and drove it straight down, right on top of the helmet of an unsuspecting Ranger.

War Hill fell on the free ball.

"Folks, I sure hope someone's gonna tell me this here game's just a bad dream."

Stunningly, it was not until the five-minute mark of the half when Duane Boyd and Lamont Dickies repossessed the ball. From the Marauder forty, Boyd pitched back to Dickies on a sweep right.

"Great run by Lamont. He picks up some eighteen yards."

Three more dashes by Dickies, and a keeper by Boyd moved the ball down to the War Hill eight-yard line.

"Folks, we got only two and a half minutes to play here as Boyd brings them up to the line. Ahh no!"

Boyd's pass ricocheted off the helmet of one of his own lineman and into the arms of a War Hill defender.

With an unbeaten season on the line and a chance to keep slim playoff hopes alive, South Heaven wandered into the locker room, knotted with the Marauders at nil. In a game that most Ranger fans believed would be a cakewalk, the visiting team had nearly twice as many penalties as first downs, and three turnovers. Despite completely dominating the much-weaker War Hill, South Heaven had nothing but pure embarrassment to show for their efforts.

From the Summit, I left the subdued duo and detoured toward the entrance gate prior to the halftime concession stop. Without being disturbed, the bucket of money was in the same position as we found it earlier. Dollar bills consumed three-fourths of the bucket.

The leadership of War Hill Academy was either feeling generous or subtly implying that the shop was on the verge of closing. Either way, it was an inventory-reduction sale in the concession stand. With a lone quarter, I walked away with three cups of coffee, to the delight of my Summit mates.

"How 'bout a fire?" Wally welcomed the cup of coffee.

"Dese here boys lose this game…" Old Man Schmidt shook his head. "Dese boys lose, and South Heaven'll be gone forever."

A nil to nil score was generating nightmarish thoughts, forcing Wally to bite at his nails and Old Man Schmidt to light up his third cigar. However, the nightmare soon dissipated when Lamont Dickies fielded a short kick-off on his own thirty-eight and bolted directly up the middle of the dirt. The defense parted as if to make plenty of room for the royal party's parade.

"Dickies' to the thirty! He's at the twenty-five. No one's gonna touch him! Touchdown. Touchdown! Thank God Almighty, Lamont Dickies scores!"

Once Stu Ginnette connected with the extra-point kick, the Rangers completely turned the game and displayed the power of an unbeaten squad. Again, Knause and his mates stymied the War Hill offense on the very next possession, which led to another weak punt. Three runs later by Dickies, South Heaven was up by fourteen. By the end of the third quarter, Lamont Dickies had run for 150 yards, and his offensive mates had posted four touchdowns.

The evening's temperature continued to sink below the freezing mark, topping out at twenty-seven, by the middle of the fourth quarter. At the six-minute mark of the fourth, South Heaven was up by six touchdowns, and King had replaced Lamont Dickies. In the end, Coach Waddell's troops had out-gained the weak War Hill squad three-hundred and fifty yards to ten. South Heaven owned the Zugellder Trophy. They were PEC league champions.

CHAPTER SEVENTEEN
A Regime Change

Election Eve and a Rally

"We are the ones who got those thieves at American Genuine to pony-up money owed to us!" Covering his politically enhanced navy blue suit, the Ranger maroon jacket made Charlie Van Wert every bit South Heaven.

Despite the slight chill of the seasonable temperature, the council that represented South Heaven moved the rally for Charlie Van Wert from the high school gym to LeSaint Park.

"If not for us, those thieves at AGM would've walked away without even a nickel owed to you all." Charlie Van Wert didn't even need the podium that had been secured to the base of a hay trailer. Like a talk-show host, Van Wert was comfortable strolling on the make-shift stage and carrying a microphone. His towering presence in both stature and tone could instill confidence in the mind of an impending voter. A political handsomeness that included a full head of brown hair with a perfect middle part and a purebred and full-bodied complexion, one sure to attract any and all television viewers, bolstered a well-stocked cellar of charisma. "AGM left you high and dry—disgraceful. We secured for you a multi-million dollar settlement from those thieves. Money that will be used to rebuild this city. Money that will be used to help you."

The edges of the hay trailer had been outfitted in tasteful red, white, and blue banners. Two industrial and concert-size speakers, stuffed into the corners of the trailer, exacerbated the baritone vigor of Van Wert.

It was indeed a smart decision to move the rally. Although a jacket was required for comfort, the crowd of interested would have far exceeded gym capacity. Among the throng of onlookers, I stood several rows from the makeshift stage.

"We got AGM to pay for their mistakes, and we will do the same in Washington!" Van Wert paused to absorb the magnified ovation. As the youngest person to ever serve the people of South Heaven in the State House of Representatives, Van Wert was a man on the rise. He had been on the periphery of the negotiations of the settlement with AGM, just enough to attach his name to the project charter. "South Heaven deserves jobs, and I promise you that if you send me to Washington, I'll bring jobs to South Heaven!" Van Wert waved to calm down the crowd. "My opponent is nothing more than a lackey for those executives at companies like AGM. He supports tax breaks for business, tax breaks for companies like Phoenix Toys." Emphatically, he nodded his head, welcoming the chorus of Bronx cheers. "Phoenix Toys has no intention of paying you a prevailing wage. The jobs they have to offer are a pittance of what you had. Phoenix Toys is not concerned about you."

Unfortunately for the Republican Party, their candidate, Dick Barker, was an outsider to the people of Harper County, a carpetbagger who had migrated to Ohio to assume an executive role at the truck plant in Edina. Ivy League-educated, Barker professed a belief that union-dictated wages would continue to drive companies out of Harper County.

"My opponent has thrown his public support behind Phoenix Toys. He doesn't care about you! Would he ever support getting those execs at AGM to pay millions for their misdeeds? Never! Instead, my opponent believes we should bring any company into Harper County. I am the only one you can trust to bring real jobs back to your home."

Election Day

A polling site occupied the gym of the high school. At one end of said gym, I stood with pen and paper in hand as an exit pollster. The questions posed to residents, young and old alike, were simple but appeared to annoy all. Besides the occasional genuine responses of Republican or Democrat, I received mostly rude gibes and unsure glares. However, by noon, at least based upon my polling, it appeared as if the incumbent was near to being a lame duck—if South Heaven had any say in the matter.

"Pardon me…" He wore a black jacket and sweatpants and had both hands wrapped around the base of a trophy. "Can you point me to the athletic office?" A red moustache matched his curly top.

I caught a glimpse of the brass plate stuck to the base of the trophy: 1980 Pioneer and Explorer Conference Champions.

It was lunch break for the pollsters, so I opted to escort the man with the trophy to the office of Ted Foxx.

"You with the school?" The man was stocky in the shoulders, like an iceman of a bygone age. His inflection, however, failed to live up to the imposing bill.

"Not really," I replied, passing the men's locker room to reach an open office door. Knocking, I peeked into the reception area to find a petite and older lady assumed to be Foxx's secretary. "Is the AD around?"

With her bifocals clinging to the edge of her nose, she looked up from the black typewriter owning her desk. "He should be back from class shortly." Much less congenial than one would expect from a receptionist, she wore a flowery patterned dress. "You can wait in his office." Quaint and cramped, her work area guarded the entrance to her boss's office.

Foxx's open door was draped, top to bottom, with a maroon felt banner emblazoned with the figure of a Revolutionary War figure.

"Oh, hey!" Crammed against his chest, held with a forearm, was a wrecked stack of papers and folders, as if he had just scooped the mess from the floor. Foxx knew the man with the trophy and called him Dale.

"So, where's Coach Waddell?"

The South Heaven AD informed Dale that Coach Waddell was monitoring a fifth-period study hall. "Is that trophy ours?"

Dale rubbed the egg-shaped prize with his left hand, one harboring an overtly thick gold wedding band. "Hoping to give this to Coach Waddell."

"Are you the keeper of the cup?" I waved my hand over the dome as if it were a crystal ball.

"He's a newsman." Foxx introduced me to Dale Zugellder, the commissioner of the conference.

Zugellder passed the championship trophy to Foxx with a handshake. "Pass our congratulations onto Coach Waddell, will you, Ted?"

Foxx welcomed the commissioner to remain waiting for the coach to finish class, but Zugellder declined and left.

"Voted yet?" I followed Foxx into his office.

From his brown lunch bag, he retrieved a ham sandwich on rye, a batch of corn chips, and two foil-packaged snacks. "Line was too long this morning." Like a child, he ate the snack cakes first. "What about you?"

"The incumbent. Anything else would've been a sin for my family."

Admiring the Zugellder Trophy, Foxx had a sheen to him. I suppose, however, that Ted Foxx had earned that personal luster. Either by pure fortune or efficient strategy, Foxx had chosen his profession correctly. Education, when compared to the virtues of the auto industry, was recession-proof. Ted Foxx, a South Heaven schoolboy hero, had no need to leave his home to earn a comfortable living. Unlike most of South Heaven's recent schoolboy heroes, he could relish in his past endeavors and accolades with the security of a perpetual paycheck and a home in the Legendary Country Club section of the town. Still, though, I felt somewhat sorry for a man who had probably never ventured more than 50 miles outside of his small town.

Various bits and pieces of sporting equipment littered his office, giving the appearance of a cluttered garage.

Foxx cherished no other piece of equipment more than the newest addition of hardware. "His grandfather. This here trophy's named after Dale's grandfather. He saved the league way back when."

Mrs. Ellington, as Foxx referred to his secretary, was reluctant to announce the newest visitor: Johnny Sarian.

The former star hardly appeared coherent, and the stench of consumed alcohol was too much to ignore.

Foxx bounded toward the former Dallas star like an emergency-room nurse tending to a traffic-accident victim. In turn, he attempted to shelter Sarian and shooed me from the office.

Promptly, I found the parking lot, which, by that point had been depleted of vehicular customers. I caught up to the newest PEC champion coach. "I saw that Zugellder Trophy today," I said.

Coach Waddell was fingering through the keys on his chain, presumably searching for the one that would unlock the door to his Blazer. A full cigarette bobbed up and down as he spoke. "D'ya make sure you voted today, Newspapuh Man?"

My watch indicated fifteen minutes until five. "Practice a short one today?"

"Big Pete's got it today." The truck was raised higher than your average utility vehicle, but he had no trouble negotiating the obstacle. "Besides, only got another twenty minutes of light."

"I wouldn't think a coach of an unbeaten team would leave his team to practice without him, given the fact they have a shot at the playoffs and all…"

"Me, I didn't vote yet." He generated a tremendous amount of energy in slamming the car door.

However, I had just enough gumption or stupidity to reach and knock on the door. I felt his disgusted sigh sour my system.

As he rolled down the window, Coach Waddell flicked his cigarette. The butt whizzed by my left ear. "Can I get a quote for the paper?"

He sniffed twice, ingesting the chill of the air. "I'm thinkin' a change would be good. Country needs a new direction."

A fine mist began creeping onto the scene. It would have been unnoticeable without the cool air.

"I suppose it's a quote."

"Ever heard of Centerville College, Newspapuh Man?"

Wednesday

The rally the previous evening had pushed the capacity limits of the VFW hall. As the results of the first Tuesday in November rolled in, the rally became a celebratory cause for Charlie Van Wert, and the excess crowd absorbed every ounce of the excitement of a Democratic selectee to the United States Congress. With a super majority, Charlie Van Wert had become the newest representative for the people of South Heaven and Harper County. Having assumed the hopes of resurrection, Van Wert held the confidence of the South Heaven populace and their belief that prosperity could return if one of their own were in Washington. Van Wert, however, was one of only a handful of Democrats who either maintained or earned a seat in the nation's capital. Whether because of the terrorist attack or the sluggish economy, America had turned over its leadership the previous night.

The mood in the town, however, was ambivalent, and negotiations with Phoenix Toys had come to a virtual standstill. With an ultimatum from the company looming, the union had the sentiment of the town. Lower wages and a company without a need for organization were not resting well with the citizenry of South Heaven. Devoid of income for months and years, former auto workers could not survive if the manufacturer of plastic figurines opted not to fight the potential hassle. Still, those former auto workers refused to acquiesce and accept wages far below the level they had previously known. Most were energized by the rhetoric of Van Wert and holding out for his promised delivery of high-paying jobs.

To entertain myself at Frankie's, I carried a copy of our paper. Phil's sports section actually included a respectable effort in summarizing the War Hill game, two miniscule articles on the volleyball team's awards and the golf squad, and a half-page spread on the New Jefferson running back, Jacob Ambrose. Lauding the exploits of the seventeen-year-old kid, who was seven points shy of the state scoring record, Phil was adamant about the significance of a Western Ohio boy owning such a milestone. Apparently, a state record merited a feel-good story from Phil. For a school not in the PEC and some forty-plus miles from South Heaven, Phil had delved significantly into the background of the New Jefferson running back.

From a modest family, this New Jefferson back, like all of the kids in the rural town, was reared on a generational farm. In the article were a couple of quotes from Coach Waddell and Ambrose himself. The New Jefferson back took a reticent and diffident approach to the record, overtly acknowledging his teammates and coaches. The Ranger coach, on the other hand, told Phil that his defensive approach would not change.

My accolades for Phil lasted only until I opened an envelope with my name scribbled onto the face in pencil. It was a resume—of sorts, detailing the stellar career of the sportswriter for the Sun. Along with the resume, I found a small note—from Phil, of course—suggesting I review said resume.

"There you are." Relying heavily on an uncomfortable-looking will of spirit for movement, he fought his way through the maze of empty tables. "Certainly hope you at least made an attempt at keeping a Democrat in the office." Although feisty in spirit, Senior Epstein was hardly the paramount of health. Ashen had become his dominant color, and he still maintained an irritatingly deep chest cough. He struggled for a comfortable spot in the chair. "So how's that paper of mine, Wright?" It was a talent— overcoming the disturbing shakiness in his hands to push flame to pipe.

I leaned back in the chair and stuffed Phil's resume back into its envelope. "Reporting all the news that's fit to print in Western Ohio!"

As he scooted his increasingly feeble, thin body deeper into the green-vinyl booth bench seat, Senior Epstein asked at what point I intended on informing him of the visit from the Penn boys. "After they had the deed to my paper?" He had no good use for tobacco. Nonetheless, he nurtured the smoking utensil stuck between his teeth.

With a little guilt, I slid a block-glass ashtray toward him.

"Wright, you need to start feeding me this type of information." Reaching for the menu propped up against the stainless napkin holder and the ketchup bottle, Senior Epstein's hand shook mildly, as if he had just exited the car of a roller coaster. "I'm sure the missus will have a fit if I eat here." He flipped the two-sided laminated menu card to the sandwich side. "But I'm a sucker for the meatball."

"I'm no fan of playing spy, sir."

As if scolding a child, Sweetie, Frankie's flirtatious waitress, snatched the menu from his grip and scolded him. "Missus Epstein will not be havin' you ruinin' your dinner appetite."

Senior Epstein pleaded for an exception.

"Coffee is all you're getting. Take it or leave it."

He had a derogatory comment for the opposite sex.

"Shouldn't you be talking to your daughter?"

"I have, Wright. Oh hell, who am I kidding? I knew she had no interest in coming back home. But I'm a sick man, Wright."

I had no ally in the room in case Senior Epstein took to the offensive against me. I begged Sweetie for an explanation of the specials of the day—a sacrificial lamb, so to speak.

"Where's the cream?" asked Senior Epstein of Sweetie when she sat the mug and saucer in front of him.

"Missus Epstein said no."

"For you?"

I stalled. "Let's see. How many meatballs come with the spaghetti and meatball plate?"

She had a talent for snapping bubbles of chewing gum inside her mouth. "It says right there in the menu you're reading."

I wanted to tell her she wore too much green eye shadow, and her choice of flavor of bubble gum was nauseating: watermelon. Instead, I handed her the menu. "Just a couple of slices of pepperoni."

Senior Epstein fell into a coughing episode. Fortunately, the painful scene was short. "She didn't want to do this, but I had no one else."

"Why don't you just sell it?"

Without the necessary precision and dexterity, he struggled to open a small tin of aspirin. "I've owned four papers in my lifetime. Sold three of 'em. Estel..." he coughed. "Estel and I came here thirty years ago." He dispensed two of the aspirin into an unsteady and frail right palm. "Ain't left since." Two more rough coughing episodes followed the ingestion of the pills.

The crash of metal on a tile floor was a welcomed distraction.

"This town still has some life to it, Wright." Senior Epstein slumped forward in his seated posture, as if he were hauling large sacks of flour over each shoulder. It appeared the burden of sickness was too overwhelming for the man. "This is my home."

With some grace but no more hospitality than displayed at the time of order, our waitress returned with lunch. She carried a glass dispenser of Parmesan cheese and one of crushed red pepper in the pouch pockets of her apron. "Anything else for you?"

"This town needs the paper, Wright." Senior Epstein tucked a corner of a cloth napkin behind his collar.

"Don't you have other children?" The temperature of the pizza necessitated a knife and fork. Unfortunately, the latter was something I failed to possess. "I mean…"

"I wanted Myra to feel the same way about this town. My others—good kids, but couldn't run their own daily lives let alone my paper."

"Listen," I said through the remnants of a bite.

"And Wright, I think there's now a need for the Prognosticator." He struggled to his feet then dug into his wallet. From the middle crease, he removed a cut piece of newspaper that displayed the decay of age. "Remember the other thing I promised you?"

I was afraid to add another ailment to the stitch of yellowing newspaper, but obliged him and gingerly uncreased the folds.

"My first."

The paper remnant still possessed enough ink to display a cartoon Ranger football player spiking a cleat into the stomach of a Devil. "Your … first?"

"Wright, I want you to take over as the Prognosticator."

Friday

Opinion was mixed regarding Coach Waddell resubmitting his senior quarterback, Redding, as the starter. Willie Tee insisted that no one should mess with a win streak, while on the other side, some believed that the senior had much more talent than the freshman. With a week's worth of repetition, those on the side of Gary Redding were convinced his timing was steady enough not to harm the offense.

For Parents' Night, the cold weather broke, giving the home crowd a pleasant evening to watch the Rangers reach for the perfect season. But the air was thick with humidity, prompting the layman to believe in an inevitable rain.

A perfect season could have and should have enjoyed company with any football fan, but not in South Heaven. Despite the overachievement of its team and a season dominated with extreme fortune, the South Heaven faithful seemed to want more. The traditionalist had experienced unbeaten seasons in the past.

From my apartment to the stadium, the crowd of pedestrians was much thicker than normal. Without a miracle, it appeared that South Heaven had little opportunity to make the playoffs. Frederick and the Catholic school on the east side of Toledo both held leads on the Rangers, and both were playing cupcake teams for their last games. Still, that perfect season was well within reach, and the town was showing up in droves. Unfortunately, Phil had tagged along for the walk and, although resentful of the playoff structure, seemed to have relented and accepted the fact that his Rangers would not play beyond the New Jefferson game.

"Ambrose boy's only seven points away from the scoring record." Phil was genuinely excited for the New Jefferson back. "Too bad his team ain't that good."

The New Jefferson Comets had been carried solely by Ambrose, winning just over half of their games, and were clearly the underdog to the unbeaten Rangers. In a cartoon depicting the Ranger mascot lassoing the tail of a comet, Epstein submitted the most recent prediction of the Prognosticator: doom for both the Comets and Jacob Ambrose.

Instead of following the throngs of fans filing into Gottmann Field, I bypassed the bleachers and found my way to the Summit.

"Don't need a jacket tonight, boy."

While both teams occupied the field in warmups, Wally was setting up the equipment for WSHV, albeit late.

"Heard you voted for the lame duck? Should've listened to Wally."

"Just be prepared for four years of tax breaks for the wealthy." I opened my folding chair.

Coach Waddell, his secret still kept with me, led all but eighteen members of his team off the field and into the locker room. The eighteen were all seniors, and they mustered on the opposing sideline near midfield. Surrounding the eighteen was a plethora of adults, dressed in their Sunday best and topped with proud grins. Parents' Night, a special event for South Heaven, earned a full thirty minutes of pregame activity. It included not only football players, but also band members and cheerleaders.

Without its senior members, the Pride of South Heaven formed a tunnel to guide the students and their parent guests from one end of the field to the other.

Once through the periphery, the first senior football players to enter the tunnel were Lamont Dickies and Gary Redding. Most of the home crowd stood in ovation as Dickies entered with his mom under his arm.

"Hard to say which one of these guys is enjoyin' the spotlight more: Redding or his Daddy," Wally commented.

Stu Ginnette walked across the field unaccompanied. His mother was desperately ill, and his father was imbibing heavily. However, it was hard to feel sympathy for the kid. It was a season beyond imagination for Stu. In a quickened pace, he smiled and waved eagerlyto the crowd.

When the last player had escorted his parents across the field, they were all serenaded with the South Heaven alma mater and then given one more standing ovation.

New Jefferson wore white road uniforms trimmed in green, including helmets and numerals. They appeared first out of the locker room following the pregame ceremonies. Their crowd traveled well and erupted when the team of forty-plus stormed onto the field.

"There's at least half a dozen college scouts here tonight. All here to see this Ambrose kid. Ya ask me, boy, he ain't major college material."

"Sounds to me like he's pretty darn good—a few points away from a state record."

Old Man Schmidt insisted Ambrose was too small and played against meager competition.

"A record's a record."

"Those scouts'll find out exactly how good he is tonight."

The last home game of the season was designated as honorary captain night, a tradition that was nearly twenty years in existence. Along with Gary Redding and Lamont Dickies, Coach Waddell sent two other kids onto the field for the coin toss—one player and the other a student-manager.

To punctuate an unusually amazing season, Stu Ginnette had been picked to represent his team. Since assuming the role as kicker, he had yet to fail his coach or his teammates, with a perfect extra-point-kick record. A kid who was desperate to find answers just weeks earlier had found the top of the world.

Eddie Napier, on the other hand, was never without an amazing posture. On the outside, life had cursed Eddie with a Down syndrome malady that garnered pity from all. In his heart, though, Eddie felt pity for everyone else who did not enjoy life as much as he. As an equipment manager, Eddie had the chance to express his fanaticism for his favorite team. On his way to midfield, Eddie bounced around with pure excitement and energy. Unfortunately, the excitement did not garner South Heaven the winning toss.

And so, Jacob Ambrose was given a quick opportunity to claim his stake at immortality. From his own twenty-yard line, Ambrose raced toward the sidelines and up fifteen yards to retrieve a pop-up kick from Ginnette. South Heaven tried to pin the New Jefferson player back to the sideline, pushing all its defenders into that zone area. The ball fell from his grasp and onto the turf. Instead of pouncing on the fumble, though, Ambrose reached down in stride to regain control.

"Ambrose steps along the sidelines. He reverses field!"

Circling back some ten yards, Ambrose outpaced his nearest pursuers as he raced from one sideline to the other. He was quick like a jackrabbit.

"He stops again!"

At the thirty-two, Ambrose cut back, sidestepped a would-be tackler, ducked underneath another, then bolted through a small gap and up the field. Stu Ginnette and an obscure Ranger stood ten yards from Ambrose. A simple shimmy of the hips took care of the obscure Ranger.

Without much experience in the art of tackling, Ginnette dove at the feet of Ambrose.

The New Jefferson back tripped forward and appeared to be falling to the turf. With his free hand, however, Ambrose caught himself, bear-crawling a few yards.

"My Lord, this kid's still on his feet! Ambrose is to the thirty. He's to the twenty! No one's gonna catch him. He's gone. Touchdown!"

Big Pete flung his clipboard a solid twenty yards onto the field before charging a side judge to rant over an apparent missed call. Within seconds, the yellow hankie was out of the official's back pocket.

"You missed a clip, you blind fool!" yelled Old Man Schmidt.

"One point away," I laughed. "One point from the record."

Old Man Schmidt got some revenge, however, when Kyle Knause broke through the middle and tackled Ambrose behind the line, denying the extra-point attempt.

Big Pete's penalty allowed the Comets to kick off from the Ranger forty-five. In turn, they decided to squib-kick the ball along the ground.

The upback, Durning, promptly fielded the ball and fell forward to down the play at the twenty-one.

"Whattaya wanna bet, boy, that the kid doesn't break the record tonight?"

I offered up lunch or dinner, confident in Jacob Ambrose.

"Tell ya what, he breaks the record, and you got the keys to the Caddy."

"Please…"

"No, no. My Caddy against an article in the paper tellin' everyone that Western Ohio is a better place to live than the big city."

Wally bellowed a laugh between calls of Dickies' consecutive positive gains.

"Just a simple article?" asked Old Man Schmidt.

"I'll pass." I replied.

Dickies brought the home crowd to its feet when he gained thirty yards and a first down on a sprint around right end.

"Whattaya afraid of, boy?"

"You know what? You're on. Only, if I win, you stop calling me boy."

Jacob Ambrose would soon get another shot when Lamont Dickies broke off right tackle and bolted forty-five yards for a retaliatory touchdown, sparking mild pandemonium in the home stands.

Big Pete's game plan was contrary to Coach Waddell's statement to Phil earlier in the week. Instead of the standard five-man line, Big Pete pushed six down lineman up on the ball and moved in three linebackers. Jacob Ambrose, himself, was not about to beat South Heaven and ruin a perfect season.

The first play was a run off right tackle. Hardly a kid of football stature, relying obviously more on speed and agility than power, Ambrose was stuffed at the line. On second down, Ambrose took a pitch and bolted toward the wide side of the field, but Luke Post broke off his block and tripped up the New Jefferson tailback. Third down was a mere omen of events to come: an option play snuffed out by Knause for a loss.

Oddly, another star for the Comets was punter B.J. Nitkowski. He laced into a kick that forced Redding to turn and run.

"Good God Almighty, folks! That kick traveled some fifty yards in the air."

Redding finally retrieved the bounding ball around his own fifteen. He was able to return it twenty-five yards, with the punt outdistancing the coverage.

Thick humidity eventually mutated into a slight drizzle. Despite a break in the chill, it was still November, and the rain was uncomfortable. Umbrellas opened up throughout the stadium.

On a second-down play, following two runs by Lamont Dickies, Gary Redding faked a dive to his fullback then popped up and fired a pass—directly into the pads of a New Jefferson linebacker. The ball ricocheted off said pads, bounded off the helmet of another defender, and fell into the hands of a stunned New Jefferson defensive lineman, who simply dropped to a knee.

Uncomfortable jeers immediately began to resonate within the home stands.

"Folks, Jacob Ambrose has the ball now at the Ranger forty-nine."

The turnover, however, failed to deter the Ranger defense. Two consecutive runs by Ambrose, a sweep left and a counter right, netted little more than a yard of positive turf. The kid may have had an immediate burst in his first step, but without help from his front line, his night would be a long one.

"Folks, it looks like we got the Comets' number. Knause and the boys are pushin' around that offensive unit. Singer brings his team back to the line on third down. Four minutes to go here in the first. Singer takes the snap. It's an option … No…"

The New Jefferson quarterback suckered in the entire linebacker crew on the option fake. His flanker was twenty yards beyond the line of scrimmage and there was not a Ranger within eyeshot. In the midst of a rush, Singer let the pass fly—but the drizzle played havoc on both ends of the play. A wobbling spiral was slightly under-thrown, forcing the flanker to halt forward momentum.

"Sheppard's underneath it…"

Whether it was the mist or an inability to seize the moment, the wide-open Sheppard dropped the ball.

Redding, or one should say Dickies, carried the Rangers into the second with a slim one-point lead. Coach Waddell refrained from putting the ball in the air. Given a third-and-long situation, Coach Waddell refused to break alliance with the crowd and ran out the down with an option play. Redding's initial punt following his rehab engendered a time-out by Big Pete.

"Folks, he's gotta be talkin' to these kids about defendin' Ambrose once this ball's kicked," Old Man Schmidt spoke confidently.

New Jefferson posted only Ambrose to retrieve the punt. However, for those of us with money on the kid, Redding booted the ball out of bounds.

Word was broadcasted across the public address system that energized the crowd. At the end of the first quarter, Frederick trailed Lima Ross by seven points.

Like a table lamp connected to a wall switch, the crowd immediately merged from raucous roar to silent prayer. Jacob Ambrose hushed the home crowd, taking a swing pass and nabbing the corner. He weaved in then back toward the sidelines and was suddenly in the clear. Luke Post made a diving attempt at the fleeing back but failed to stop him.

Heads flagged in the home stands as Ambrose bolted toward the end zone. Jubilation, though, was tempered when I focused the binoculars on the side judge calling the play dead along the South Heaven thirty-eight. Ambrose had stepped out of bounds.

On three plays, Knause and his crew had relaxed slightly, allowing the Comets to advance the ball to the thirty.

"Folks, they're trottin' in their kicker. I don't know about this call. This a long kick…"

Big Pete left his first-team defense on the field to defend the kick.

"Folks, number nineteen, Nitkowski, is gonna try a forty-seven-yard field goal. There's the snap, and the kick. Holy … Plenty of distance. I'll be darn, it's good."

At a two-point deficit, following a record field goal for Gottmann Field, South Heaven took control of the ball on their own twenty-two. In a momentum-crushing drive, Dickies and Redding carried their squad and drained seven minutes from the game clock before pushing the Rangers ahead by four.

One minute and thirty seconds remained on the clock when Stu Ginnette marched on to extend his consecutive streak of successful PATs. It was Redding instead of Durning who would set the ball on the tee.

"There's the snap…"

Rifling through Redding's hands, the ball hit Ginnette in the knee. With the reaction time of a dead fish, Ginnette picked up the fumbled snap, tucked it under his arm, and dragged the kicking-shoe-laden feet toward the goal line. Unfortunately, he also had the speed of the same dead fish and was swarmed under by a half-dozen defenders.

Halftime brought an updated score from the Frederick game: Lima Ross, 16, and Frederick, 13.

"Hear the score from Frederick?" Phil was behind me in the concession line. "Frederick falls, and we're in."

"Unless you're actually posting for a job with the AP, Time, or Reuters, I don't want to see your resume anymore," I retorted, before ordering two hot dogs.

"You'll see. We'll be heading to the Glass Bowl in Toledo."

I escaped when Phil stepped up to the counter.

Nitkowski drilled the second-half kick-off near the goal line, prompting a sigh of awe from the Summit.

Coach Waddell held to his guns and sent Redding back onto the field, with a pass play.

"Oh, Lord," moaned Old Man Schmidt when the senior quarterback faded into the pocket.

From his own sixteen, Redding panicked when a linebacker broke through on a blitz. He pulled the ball from its cocked position and put a sidestep move on the defender, and, although he gracefully eluded the would-be tackler, Redding, somehow, lost control of the football.

"Fumble!" cried Wally.

On the South Heaven thirteen, New Jefferson took control of the ball.

The mist had halted, but the anxiety of the home crowd multiplied. Jacob Ambrose was a mere dozen yards from a touchdown, which would put the Rangers in the hole and establish himself as the new king of Ohio scoring.

"I'll be glad to take the bet off the table," I said, after Ambrose carried a swing-pass eight yards.

The visiting crowd cheered zealously as Ambrose pushed the Ranger defense back to its last morsel of protected ground.

"First and goal from the one, Old Man."

"Don't you worry none, boy. I ain't backin' down." His tone was much less arrogant then previously, but that superficial confidence received a slight boost when Ambrose hit a brick wall on a carry up-the-gut.

On second down, Singer pitched wide to his tailback, but nine defenders pursued the ball and pulled down Ambrose for a loss.

The New Jefferson coach stopped play to pull his entire offensive unit to the sidelines, providing enough time for WSHV to claim just what the Harper Credit Union could do for the people of South Heaven.

Third down and goal agitated the butterflies in the stomachs of fans. Both Wally and Old Man Schmidt sat on the edges of their chairs.

Bad knees and all, Big Pete hobbled off the field as the chief referee blew the whistle to begin the play clock.

Instead of the usual quick count, Singer took an extra few seconds to read Big Pete's defense. His count initially pulled an interior lineman off-sides, but no penalty was called.

"Singer's gonna throw!" called Wally.

The Comet quarterback mustered a rocket toward the back of the end zone, but the pass was a few inches too tall for his intended receiver.

"Fourth down, folks!"

By the time both teams approached the line for the last play of the drive, anticipation and excitement had compounded and morphed into a cacophony of thunderous whistles, cowbells, screams, and applause from both sets of fans.

"This is it, boy."

"Sure you don't wanna change your mind, Old Man?"

Everyone in attendance knew the ball could only go one to one player…

Giving his back the best option to score, Singer pitched the ball to Ambrose. The tailback headed for the wide side of the field.

"Ambrose drops inside … but he's back out!"

Knause and his crew gave chase.

"Ambrose dives. Can't tell, folks! There's a huge pileup. Is he in?"

Just feet from the sideline, Ambrose had cut back and then dove for the goal line.

Immediately, and on cue, the stadium fell silent while the referees scoured through the stack of players in search of the ball.

"Double or nothing?"

Despite the previous penalty, Big Pete had wandered some fifteen yards onto the field, pointing in the direction of his team. My binoculars quickly departed the coach and trained on the New Jefferson head coach, who was on the field as far as the cord of his headset would allow and holding his hands in the air to indicate a score.

"Our ball! Our ball! Good God Almighty, we held 'em!"

Old Man Schmidt was convinced Coach Waddell needed to sustain a drive and prevent Ambrose from touching the ball again. His theory was practical, logical, and possible, until Dickies took a handoff from Redding over right tackle.

"My Lord!" Wally shot to his feet, nearly falling forward after slipping on the wet surface.

Once Dickies broke through the initial contact, there was no defender between him and his goal-line target.

"No one's gonna catch him!"

By the time he reached his own forty, Dickies' nearest pursuer was a hefty twenty yards from his tail.

Wally suddenly fell hoarse while the home crowd jumped up and down in a maddening frenzy.

Wally pushed the microphone onto me, and I fumbled it in surprise, before donning it in just enough time to make my first touchdown call. "Uhhh … touchdown Dickies."

Old Man Schmidt relieved me of broadcast duties. "That's what I'm talkin' about. Lamont should calm alotta nerves with that run."

Deep into the fourth, both South Heaven and Lima Ross held leads, although the Rangers had an eighteen-point cushion. While Dickies posted another score, the Rams from Ross were desperately clinging to a three-point lead. When Redding lined up to kick away the Ranger fourth down, we received word through the Frederick radio network that the Pirates had possession of the ball and deep in Ross territory.

With only three minutes to play, I began to compile thoughts on my impending article, believing Knause would never allow the Comets to move seventy-five yards for a score.

A transistor against his ear, Wally listened intently to the Frederick broadcast.

"Minute-forty to play here, folks."

One player at a time, following each sequential down, Big Pete began substituting for his starters on defense. Suddenly, there was a flicker of hope for me—and Ambrose. The combination of the star tailback and Singer carried the Comets to the Ranger thirty-two. The New Jefferson coach opted neither to substitute nor stop the clock. With thirty seconds showing, Singer took a snap and darted down the line on an option. He cut the ball up field, though, without pitching it to Ambrose.

The first down stopped the clock at twenty-two seconds.

"Singer rushes 'em to the line. Takes the snap from center, fades back … and throws to the end zoooone … Incomplete!"

Although only fifteen seconds remained on the game clock, I had to believe the New Jefferson coach desired as much as anyone to see Jacob

Ambrose set the state scoring record. With at least a couple of time-outs, he had to be thinking two plays—at least. On the first, he failed to disappoint those of us wishing for the record and called for Singer to toss Ambrose a swing pass.

"Ambrose breaks across the twenty and is tripped up at the seventeen. New Jeff calls time-out, with six seconds to play. Seventeen yards and time for one last play, folks!"

"He's gotta throw the ball to him." Wally struggled with a raspy voice.

For the first time all game, Ambrose failed to align himself in the backfield. Instead, Jacob Ambrose was aligned in the slot position to the left of Singer.

"Singer takes the snap! Drops back and fires across the middle to Ambrose."

The New Jefferson back snared the pass just a hair beyond the reach of Kyle Knause.

"He cuts back to the sidelines! He's at the five … Ohh, Good God Almighty! Luke Post comes out of nowhere!"

Post fought off a block to reach Ambrose only steps before the tail-back-turned- flanker reached his destiny.

"Post knocked Ambrose out of bounds! Game over! No record. No record!"

CHAPTER EIGHTEEN
No Wait, You're In!

Sunday

Reality of life in South Heaven stole a large chunk of happiness and joy from the townspeople, who had asked for nothing more than an honest wage and a football team of caliber. By the end of the first week in November, there was still no new employer to assume control of the vacant auto plant, and a perfect season had come to an end.

As churches were letting out their flocks, Ranger players were filtering into the high school equipment room to give up possession of pads, helmets, and game jerseys. On a last-second play, the hated Pirates scored on a Hail Mary pass to beat Lima Ross and squash all hopes of South Heaven entering the state playoffs. For Stu Ginnette, the absolute in ultimate fantasy concluded with a record for consecutive extra-point kicks made, and the thrill of simply playing the game he loved. For Kyle Knause, it had been a season of momentum-building for another year to come, and more than likely, a shot at earning all-league. For Lamont Dickies, the season's end brought a cherished rushing record, over twenty touchdowns, and a legitimate argument to earn all-state honors.

Coach Waddell was serene and relaxed, as if relieved the season had concluded. He was actually welcoming of my presence. Balancing on the rear legs of a wooden chair, he held a clipboard containing an equipment inventory list.

"I wanted to thank you, again, for giving Stu a second chance." I added what assistance I could to Big Pete's task of removing thigh pads from game pants.

"Don't know whether to retire that kickin' shoe or pass it on to next year's kicker for good luck," laughed Big Pete.

Lamont Dickies entered the equipment room alone, dropped his equipment in front of Big Pete. Outside of a distant press box view at the beginning of the season, it was the first instance I saw the Ranger tailback without pads, helmet, and a jersey. In civilian garb, Lamont was not overly impressive in stature. He was just above an average man's height, with his most impressive feature being a powerful and defined set of thighs. Despite the chill, Lamont wore cut-off sweatpants and a hooded sweatshirt displaying the colors and logo of Centerville College. Unlike most of his teammates, Dickies had folded his jersey and pants neatly and had his pads wrapped with rubber bands or strapping tape.

"Gotta math test on Monday, right?"

"Yes, Coach."

"I don't wanna hear nuthin' from Miss Jacobsen 'bout no bad scores."

"Yes, Coach."

I commented on Lamont's Centerville sweatshirt. "Does he even know where Centerville is?"

Coach Waddell scribbled, in black ink, onto shreds of athletic tape, which were being affixed to single canisters of 8mm film. "You gotta reason for comin' down here on a Sunday?"

A gaggle of six players initiated the exit of Big Pete as he led the group to a neighboring helmet-storage room.

"Lamont ain't had much to brag about, ya know? Centerville be the best thing he's had—or will ever have." Coach Waddell munched on what appeared to be two oversized antacid pills. "This place'll just swallow him up. There ain't nuthin' for him here. South Heaven's like a sinkin' ship. It's gonna take everyone down with it—unless you jump."

"In that case, you're right. Centerville College is Lamont's only choice."

"Whattaya want from me? Huh? You want me to tell ya I hate this place? Ya want me to tell ya that as of eight tomorrow mornin,' I'll be the new defensive backs coach at Centerville College—and have no regrets?"

Monday, A Council Meeting

It was the second Monday of the month, the ritual setting for the South Heaven city council. Coincidentally, on the same day, the South Heaven representative for the U.S. Postal Service, the rusty and venerable Bert Nugent, delivered an oversized package to Mayor Montgomery.

"All right," Montgomery said with two knocks of the palm-size gavel. "Let's get started."

Given the impending discussion of the settlement money, all five council members were probably regretting the decision to open meetings to the public. Miss Myra and I sat among the news hawks, nosy neighbors, and genuinely bored and socially inept onlookers occupying the three rows of metal folding chairs designated for spectators.

All of the camel-brown chairs faced a continuous bench of sorts, in the shape of an incoherent semicircle and raised almost two feet above the deck. There were five apertures notched into the bench, like bank tellers' work stations, and each opening held a microphone and an elected official of the city.

"We need to vote on a couple of issues from the last meeting." Yet another man who had yet to venture outside the confines of South Heaven, Montgomery was a former AGM union man and a veteran of city politics, having spent the past decade on the council. As the mayor, he had been able to stop the bleeding but had not yet been able to mend the wound of a depressed and decrepit economy. "I've got an estimate here to work on the Jeremiah Harper statue: scrape, grind, and refurbish—two hundred dollars."

"Mel, I thought we decided to postpone that idea." She had a clown-red beehive hairdo. The excessive globs of makeup covering her narrow face failed to reverse the effects of aging. Instead, the chemicals created an unappealing mask of a woman who had known nothing but hatred.

"I agree with Myrtle." He occupied one of the outer positions on the bench and, according to Miss Myra, was a physician at the Harper County Hospital. "Two dollars or two thousand, it is money that should be used elsewhere. Can we not just get a group of volunteers together?"

"Volunteers ain't easy to come by, Doc." By a mere one-hundred votes, Lyle Hempstead had maintained his seat on the council. Unfortunately, the less-than-overwhelming endorsement failed to humble him. "This ain't the hospital. People just ain't gonna show up just because." Lyle occupied the chair to the immediate left of Montgomery.

"Fine." Montgomery smacked the gavel once. With every drag of his Marlboro, he grimaced as if the taste were abhorrent. "Let's move on to the theater." Montgomery was wasting a tremendous amount of energy brushing away the abundance of bangs from his eyes. "As you know, last month we got a request from Ethel's group to fix up the old theater. Hopefully, we have all had a chance to read their proposal?"

Ethel Buchanan, the president of the South Heaven Preservation Society, had petitioned the council for money to bring life back to the stately but vacant Norris Theater, in hopes that they could lure out-of-town entertainment to the city or even a big screen for movies. In her best schoolmaster dark-gray full-length dress, she stood to acknowledge Montgomery.

"I looked at that place a few days ago," Lyle insisted. "It's gonna take a whole lot of work—holes in the walls, torn seats, bricks falling apart. I say it ain't worth fixin,' Mel."

"I second that." Myrtle received a third notion from the other female on the council.

"Well, three nays. Motion is de…"

"Wait a minute, Mayor." Miss Myra shot to her feet. "What about the AGM money?"

My sly yet valid attempts to pull Miss Myra back to a seat were futile.

"We aren't about to spend that money on no theater!" exploded Lyle.

With his soft chin, thin-rimmed eyeglasses encasing timid and serene blue eyes, and longer-than-average sandy brown hair that brushed the top of his shoulder blade, Montgomery did not possess a look of authority. In fact, he mimicked the features of a Modern English Literature professor of mine at Oberlin. Still, though, as he rubbed at the glass pieces of his spectacles with a white handkerchief, Montgomery displayed obvious frustration with Miss Myra. "You're outta line there, Myra."

"Am I, Mel?"

"The motion to fund the Norris is denied," retorted Montgomery.

Miss Myra then demanded to know the ultimate disbursement of the money. "What are you planning on doing with the AGM money?" Whether intentional or not, she was beginning to stir some energy in the audience—and some agitation in the city council.

"You won't be complaining when you get your check, Myra!" Lyle was the container of aged egg salad in a fridge without deodorizer: all-consuming and lacking subtlety. He could not rid his sleeve of his heart.

"Lyle, please," Montgomery muttered.

Ethel joined Miss Myra, foregoing the chair. "What's going on here, Mel?"

Obviously sensing a pending eruption from Lyle, Montgomery interjected a preemptive strike. "We..." He cleared his throat.

"Every adult in this town will get almost five-hundred dollars!" Lyle shook his finger at Miss Myra. "Make sure that gets in the paper, Myra."

Montgomery attempted to hide behind a mug of coffee.

"Mel?" asked Miss Myra.

"We..." responded Montgomery, following a huge swill. "We decided to divide the money among everyone in the town who was eighteen or older..."

Tuesday

With feet propped, I was into the third page of the Columbus paper when Phil bolted into the office.

"They're in! They're in!" Without any more grace than a broken oscillating fan, he sprinted to his desk to grab a tape recorder from a desk drawer.

"What's going on?"

"We're in the playoffs!" He rifled through papers on his desk to find a clean pad and pen. "Frederick played an ineligible player. We're in! We're in!"

Practice Time

The decision was made to utilize the stadium field for practice, pleasing every fan in the town. By the time the Rangers completed warmups, hundreds of fans had filled the stands, bringing along dinner and jackets to combat the chill. The Rangers had made the playoffs! Their opponent would be the number-three-ranked team in the state of Ohio, the Crusaders of Toledo East Catholic. No doubt the Rangers would be heavy underdogs, but it was insignificant to the town faithful.

"Where have you been all day, sport?" Miss Myra nestled up to me on the bleachers. She did not carry the same overwhelming joy and enthusiasm her fellow citizens did.

Oddly, Big Pete stood out like a coffee stain on carpet. He screamed at and dressed down his defense, all while dressed in a light red shirt and ruby-red tie. He, too, must have been surprised with the announcement of the playoffs.

Coach Waddell had either returned, overnight, from the other side of the state or had not initially left. Whatever the case, he was back on the field and directing his Rangers.

"How about dinner tonight at my place, sport? I picked up a bottle of wine earlier."

"Dinner?"

"Hey dere, Miss Myra." Despite the chill, Willie Tee wore his red shorts. "You ain't gotta quarter to spare, do ya?"

I dug into my pocket and handed him a dollar. "What's the chances on Friday, Willie Tee?"

"Bless ya, man. Bless ya." He cherished the bill. "We gonna haveta throw the ball. Dickies ain't gonna beat East Catholic by hisself."

"So does the trail end on Friday?"

"Waddell stays with Redding, we lose. He's afraid to stay in da pocket." He pointed to Redding while the quarterback overshot receiver after receiver as the offense ran through plays. "See dat?" Willie Tee had a stench of alcohol surrounding him. "Miss Myra, you'd be drivin' up to Toledo on Friday, right?"

"Willie Tee, if I give you a ride on Friday, wouldn't I be abetting? I thought you had a sentence to carry out on the weekends."

Without concern for the appearance of his rotting and broken teeth, Willie Tee replied with a smile and a wink.

"You need to stop feeding him money, sport."

Ted Foxx was accompanied by Johnny Sarian. "Myra, you gonna lead the caravan north this Friday?"

"If that's what my duty calls for." She accepted a cup of coffee from the AD.

Johnny Sarian was no longer befriended by arrogance. He had the appearance of a travelling vacuum salesman who spent his mornings overcoming hangovers, his afternoons trying to convince housewives to endorse his product, and his evenings chasing his misery with cheap Kentucky whiskey. He acknowledged Miss Myra, but without a hint of a smile.

The buzz and commotion changed direction from the practice on the field to the two news vans that pulled into the parking lot in simultaneous fashion. Suddenly, everyone in the stands was gawking at the cameramen from Channel 13 in Lima and Channel 4 in Toledo as the news crews hugged the sidelines of the field.

Papa Redding and Ted raced to reach the camera first.

Sarian did not keep pace with the other two, however. He simply blended into the crowd.

Hordes of fans moved from their seated positions in the stands and onto the cinder track, like curious nomads gravitating towards a landed alien spacecraft.

"Good news travels fast."

"Speaking of news, what has become of the money from your Penn buddies?"

A fine mist had mutated into a diluted fog. Distant visibility was hampered slightly, but otherwise, the weather phenomenon had little effect.

One by one, banks of lights flickered to illumination.

In an obnoxious but shoddy attempt to avert attention from my inquiry, Miss Myra focused on the trivial of a few strings of lights that did not illuminate. She then, despite wearing what appeared to be more than enough clothing, insisted that the chill in the air was uncomfortable.

"Are you aware your dad knows about them?" I consumed the misty air with a deep inhale. The refreshment was crisp to the lungs.

Miss Myra tugged at the strings to pull the hood of her sweatshirt tighter.

"Myra, I'm not here to play mediator."

She waved at a couple sitting a few feet to our left and a few bleacher rows forward. "Family, sport." She indeed was shivering. "Do you think my two siblings would step up, help out when Daddy fell ill? No. It had to be Myra. Sure, Myra will leave Philly."

A long set of whistles reverberated throughout the stadium, the result of Coach Waddell's apparent displeasure with a play run by the offense.

"Those kids out there." Miss Myra pointed without specificity. "They spend their entire lives plotting on how to get out of this town."

One of the news crews was led to the Ranger sideline by Foxx. The reporter, a small thing, could barely reach the torso of the lanky Foxx.

"I got my chance to leave, and I vowed never to come back."

"And I'm guessing you got the chance to leave again?" I stood to relieve the numbness that had overcome my backside, thanks to the aluminum seat. The tug at my jacket zipper was, hopefully, emphatic enough to display a little frustration. "So … why am I here?"

"Don't worry, sport. Daddy took care of my deal."

Wednesday

The Rangers were in the playoffs! Talk in restaurants, hardware stores, and the barber shop was engrossed in the Rangers' chances against East Catholic. In the schools, there was discussion of an early dismissal time on Friday.

"What is this?" Miss Myra called from her office.

I had left Miss Myra sitting in the bleachers the previous evening. My frustrations were doused with a few pulls from the tap, opting not to hear her plans for the future.

"Uniforms!"

I followed a group of staff writers into Miss Myra's office to find her digging into one of the half-dozen large cardboard boxes.

Miss Myra removed white jersey after white jersey, each one decorated with maroon numerals and cuffs, both around the sleeves and collar.

Peeling at the tape securing the top of a box, I removed a pair of maroon pants, free of pads. "Looks like the wrong address or a bad joke." I then found an envelope that was attached to one of the boxes. "Here."

It was a simple letter.

"This," I read verbatim, massaging my left eye socket to relieve a throbbing pain, "is something we've been needing for a long time. Good Luck in the playoffs." I flipped to the back side of the paper. "There is no name or signature to say who it is from."

"These are brand-new uniforms," said Miss Myra, spinning jersey number seventy-five around to reveal the name of Ginnette.

Neither the current road nor home jerseys contained names of the Ranger players. However, what those current jerseys did contain was years of service.

"Well, at least we know one thing about this fan. He's well off," I suggested.

Miss Myra asked me to haul the boxes to her car.

Before complying, I slipped into jersey number twelve, stretching out the tightness around the chest. Inhaling, I took in the freshness of the mesh and the rubber emblazoned numerals with deep luxurious inhales. The maroon color in the pants and jerseys was an invitingly delicious color: dark lipstick red.

"Myra!"

The cawing of Phil stole me from the surreal. Unfortunately, I was in the middle of doffing the jersey.

" Where did you get that jersey?"

I surmised the dejection on Miss Myra's face meant she was not thrilled to see Phil.

"What is the meaning of all this, Myra?"

"Phil, I thought you were visiting your mom today?" She handed me her keys.

"She's having her eyes checked today."

Miss Myra snatched the jersey from Phil's hand. "Do not write about this, tell your pals over at the VFW, or speak about this to anyone." Stuffing all contents back into boxes, Miss Myra did her best to reseal the tape. "We're not sure Coach Waddell would even want this … gift."

"Gift?"

"Phil, I said don't say anything. As for you …" she demanded of me. "Help me load these in the car, like I asked you a few minutes ago."

I responded in kind.

Friday

To the Glass Bowl from caravan central in the high school parking lot was a solid hour and forty-five minutes. By playoff season, our caravan had swollen from the stable twenty cars to a massive forty-one. Upon reaching the interstate that stretched north, some thirty-plus minutes into the trip, the line of cars seemed to stretch for a mile or so. The caravan included a couple of school buses that hauled students. Both of the big yellow transports were decorated with a clash of red streamers and banners and stuck near the middle of the pack of cars. Along the interstate, dotted every few miles, we found pennants nailed to fences, affixed to road signs, or simply staked to the ground. Although each flag had its own unique personal flavor, the message conveyed was the same by all: Go Rangers!

Within the caravan, Miss Myra's vehicle was jammed from door to door and front to back with every conceivable member of the Willie Tee clan, except Willie Tee. I held the middle of the rear bench seat, hosting in my lap the discarded peanut shells from Willie Tee's kid nephew. Miss Myra enjoyed a laugh, continuously glancing in the rearview mirror.

As we entered the city limits of Toledo and eventually the university campus, the horns of the individual cars of the caravan began sounding and creating a nuisance. We found the Glass Bowl and bivouacked in the parking lot, some hour-and-a-half prior to game time. Like camping equipment necessary for comfort and survival during a cold night on the range, the portable grills appeared from vehicle trunks.

"Gotta like tailgaitin', don't ya?" Willie Tee found his way to a neighboring station wagon which also served as the closest place serving barbeque.

"How did you get here?" I asked.

"Ain't nobody keepin' me from dah playoffs. Nooobody."

"I don't think you understand the law…"

"I unduhstand. I unduhstand well enough 'bout da law. Be spendin' a few years in Marion. But I'd be riskin' my whole life in jail, if I's just tuh see one playoff game."

Although I never received official word on the evening's temperature, my quarter-century of experience told me that the mercury could not be above twenty-five degrees. As such, with the wind gusting and flurries blowing madly about, I passed on the parking lot party and made a beeline for the stadium.

The Crusaders from the home town, East Catholic, were already occupying a portion of the dull and pale green Astroturf field when I reached the press box. With their green and gold uniforms, the muster on the field looked more like lawn weeds than an intimidating team presence. Still, the Crusaders were unbeaten. Prior to Willie Tee's employment of cat-and-mouse to avoid the various law enforcement officers, he had informed me that the East Catholic defense had at least three or four major college recruits. Big up front with fast linebackers, the defense had yielded a paltry twelve points in ten games, only three away from the all-time state record. On the other side of the ball, the Crusaders' offense was led by a junior quarterback who could easily rein in all-state honors. It was Willie Tee's painful belief that the South Heaven dream would end in the Glass Bowl. There was definitely little promise for South Heaven. Any chance at beating the Crusaders appeared to be just shy of slim. After all, South Heaven had backed in to the playoffs and was facing a team whose talent would completely overwhelm that of any of the previous opponents of the Rangers.

Cresting the top of the west bleachers, the two-tiered press box was divided into three vertical sections. Stuffed into a corner on the second tier, Old Man Schmidt occupied the counter—without Wally.

"Ain't seen Wally, have ya?" Old Man Schmidt asked. He had three full cigars laid out on the table in front of him, all parallel to the other and the edge of the table.

Although sheltered from the flurries, the press box was open to the elements. Supposedly, we held an advantage over the saps in general admission.

"Where's the girl?"

"Who, Miss Myra? I dunno. Lost her on the way up here."

"Told ya. Only get involved if your heart's in it…" He pulled the brim of his snow-white fedora closer to his bushy and full eye brows. "Sometimes, boy, hope just leads to disappointment."

While East Catholic showed off to the crowd in executing specific drills, Coach Waddell's crew meandered onto the playing surface, like scores of small herds of wayward cattle. Dressed in game pants and sweatshirts or hooded jackets, many of the Rangers spent their superficial warmups feeling and touching the plastic grass, tracing the letters in the end zone, or rolling footballs down the pronounced crown of the turf. The antithesis of the professional Crusaders, South Heaven gave every appearance of a team from Corn Country. From the press box, it hardly appeared as if the unbeaten Rangers were prepared to do battle on this Friday in November.

Grumbling about the cold and the persona of the parochial-school dominance in the playoffs, Wally dragged himself into the Summit, bundled from head to toe in thermal camouflage hunting attire. "He's startin' Redding tonight."

Old Man Schmidt passed the thermos to his broadcast partner. "It's time the people of Toledo saw his boy play ball."

"What's that kid's future, anyway? Hopefully, it does not resemble that of his older brother."

Both bands descended upon the same entrance at the same time, creating a migraine for the security guard monitoring the authorized personnel gate. Neither combatants nor adversaries, per se, members of both bands mingled politely, desperately avoiding striking neighbor with brass or woodwind instrument. Fortunately, personalities mixed well enough to overcome the utter disgrace in the clash of uniform colors, with both bands in the dominant hue of the school—East Catholic in moss green, and South Heaven in maroon.

"They'll all be like Daddy, livin' on the past and hopin' every day to be the king of South Heaven." Wally insisted on adding liquid to his coffee to create an Irish concoction. Like some sort of fantasy cartoon character, his bulbous lobes anchored the edges of his orange hunting cap.

Both bands filed into the stadium, finding their appropriate sidelines. South Heaven was opposite of the press box.

Eventually, authority and organization overcame the gaggle of Rangers. As the Crusaders departed, leaving only their placekicker on the turf, Coach Waddell willed his offensive squad into drills of scripted plays. Unfortunately, though, the offense was not sharp. In fact, on three successive plays, Redding fumbled the snap from center, prior to Lamont Dickies tripping on the carpet on a failed swing pass.

Although each playoff game was supposed to be played on a neutral site, the Glass Bowl hosted all East Catholic home contests, prompting numerous complaints from the South Heaven faithful. Apparently, the ruling body of Ohio high school athletics could not find a spot in between Toledo and Corn Country to host the game.

Traditionally, East Catholic brought out the fans, not just their own faithful but many on the bandwagon. Knowing the South Heaven fans would travel, the ruling body moved the game to a facility that could handle the projected attendance of over ten grand. Old Man Schmidt was convinced that by game time, only a third of South Heaven's population would be remaining in town, despite his apprehension on the outcome of the game.

When the pregame clock struck thirty minutes on the downturn, the Pride of South Heaven took the field. Despite Coach Waddell's decision not to have his team don the gifted uniforms from the anonymous fan, the band director didn't hesitate to do so. His squad was also gifted with new uniforms, and the band was dressed in pageant maroon, with a superhero-emblazoned S and H on the chest. New black boots and white trumpeted head covers accompanied the outfits. With those new uniforms glistening in the lights of the Glass Bowl, the Pride of South Heaven concluded the four-song set with an additional tune that was not part of earlier performances: Kansas's "Point of Know Return."

The green of the East Catholic band's assumption of the field coincided with the mass influx of fans filing into the bleacher sections.

East Catholic's four songs were more classical in nature, rather than recognizable pop. When they concluded with a Gershwin number and subsequently marched to the Ranger sidelines, the squad of fifty-plus introduced their football brethren from the locker room.

The Crusaders' gridiron monsters gathered excitedly in the closest end zone.

With much haste, the East Catholic band trotted back onto the field and, in joining their cheerleaders, formed a makeshift tunnel. As soon as they formed the crooked and snaked path, they broke into "The Notre Dame Victory March." The football team burst onto the field and through the tunnel, leaping onto one another as they reached the sidelines.

No sooner had the East Catholic fans regained their seated positions than the South Heaven faithful erupted with the sight of their Rangers and the sounds of "Across the Field."

Redding's loss of the coin toss forced Stu Ginnette and his ten friends to start the game.

"Hold onto your seats, folks!" cried Wally. "We're about to be under way! Welcome to playoff football in Ohio." As the ball was struck, Wally peered directly outside the press box to steal a glance at the game-time temperature. "Twenty-four, folks."

Ginnette's kick was snared by the wind and fell harmlessly into the arms of an upback around the twenty-nine-yard line. Avoiding the first and second tackler, the return man was eventually subdued near the thirty-seven.

"So, folks, we've given this Jake Michaels a short field—and the wind."

The unfortunate number thirteen was assigned to Jake Michaels, the star quarterback of East Catholic. He brought a pro-style formation to the line, with two set-backs on either side of him and three wideouts—one on his left, and two in a slot on his right. A tall kid, Michaels had no trouble glaring over the front line as he set up in a deep pocket.

"Michael's fiiires … incomplete. He had a man open, but that wind gotta hold of the ball. He overshot number eighty-two—Man … Kavitch—by some five yards." Wally displayed his "talent" for pronouncing surnames, particularly those with more than two syllables.

Second down was not as fortunate for the South Heaven side. To combat the wind at his back, Michaels called for a quick strike to a slanting flanker.

"He's got Flannigan. Flannigan's to the forty-five, and down after midfield. Folks, that was on the money."

From a shotgun formation, Michaels flooded his right side with three receivers, finding Mankievitz on a corner pattern for sixteen yards. It appeared as if Michaels' actions were scripted. The Crusader quarterback took another long snap and sprinted left beyond the tackle. Without a defensive rush, Michaels drilled a bullet to Flannigan, who was crossing the field just below the twenty-yard line.

"Flannigan's down to the nine."

Knause and his comrades gave a perfect rendition of stationary toys with rotating heads, only able to stop the opposing offense when they accidentally got in the way. The next play from scrimmage was only academic, and Michaels found an open Flannigan some five yards deep in the end zone for the game's first score.

"Dang, I hate that song," groaned Old Man Schmidt at the sound of the East Catholic fight song.

"Folks, that looked too easy." Wally shook his head, not so much in disgust but more out of disappointment.

"And that wasn't the strength of this team?" I stared at all twelve cheerleaders for East Catholic, half of them male, rushing the end zone to complete a set of push-ups in unison.

With the wind, the East Catholic kicker pushed Dickies back to his own five. Having little support from his teammates, Dickies returned the kick only ten yards.

The auspicious beginning continued for the Rangers when six of them jumped on Redding's initial cadence for a five-yard penalty.

"Folks, we now start from the ten."

A run off-tackle was snuffed out by the massive Crusader line. Dickies lost two more. On second down, Coach Waddell ordered Redding to fake a dive to his fullback then pull up and toss a dump pass to Durning. Nothing of the play went as planned. Durning slipped coming off his block, and Redding threw the pass into the pads of a linebacker. Third down.

"Folks, the play was there. Redding brings 'em back up to the line. They got four men on the line against us. He gets the snap, fakes the dive. He's got the option … pitches it to Dickies. Wow!"

Willie Tee underestimated the speed of those major college prospects at linebacker. No sooner had Dickies received the pitch than two pursuing tacklers dropped the South Heaven tailback for a three-yard loss.

"Not a good spot to be kickin' from, folks. Redding's deep in our end zone, almost at the end line."

At least the snap arrived cleanly for Redding.

"Redding's kick gets caught up in the wind…"

The entire return unit for the Crusaders had to dodge the bounding ball as it fell dead near the fifteen. From there, it was a mere wedge to the green for Michaels. On a strike, he found Mankievitz in the corner of the end zone.

"Folks, we're six minutes into this game, and we're already down two full touchdowns."

For only a sixteen-year-old kid, Jacob Michaels had a command presence and mastery of the field and defense. Without the resemblance of even a hint of a rush, despite the South Heaven effort, Michaels had the extra second to wait for his target to clear. Unless Big Pete devised some sort of solution to repairing the wreck, Jacob Michaels was set to experience a glorious night. And only two minutes melted from the clock before he gripped the laces for a third possession. A draw, isolation, and sweep to Dickies netted the Rangers a shabby positive two yards. From the South Heaven thirty-nine, Michaels took a snap and gunned a quick pass to Flannigan, who promptly juked Luke Post and gained a Crusader first down.

Old Man Schmidt had yet to light his initial stogie. His mouth was filled with one too many denouncements for the play on the field.

As the clock fell below two minutes, Michaels dropped quickly into the pocket.

"Draw!" Wally waved his arms as if flagging down a tow truck, and as if the defense could see him in the press box. "Draw!"

The cawing failed to reach the field, however, and Kevin McFale tore through an open hole, past Kyle Knause, and into the end zone.

Silence deafened in the Summit and filled the radio airwaves. Time still remained in the first quarter, and South Heaven trailed by three touchdowns.

"Think we oughta pack it in, Wally? Get out of this cold?" Old Man Schmidt pulled two leather gloves from his coat pocket. "They didn't come to play tonight."

Shaunegsy, the Crusader kicker, opted not to allow Dickies to play, skidding the kick along the surface.

"Whattaya call here, boy? From our own twenty, we ain't seen much so far."

With no well to draw from, Coach Waddell remained with the plays that had won him ten games. Those isolations, counters, and sweeps fed the hunger of the defense. Dickies went nowhere. The three plays did, however, expire the remainder of the first quarter, which presented Redding with a cherished gift when he aligned himself for another punt. Redding had the wind behind him and took full advantage by catching a zephyr to drive the East Catholic return man back to his own forty.

Up to his fourth drive, Jacob Michaels had missed on only one pass, and it was the wind that foiled perfection. Although impossible to perfectly gauge the wind from the booth, there was enough debris and paper trash being tossed and swirled around on the field to indicate that gusting had not diminished. On his first play, traveling against the wind, Michaels' shoulder release was no match for one wicked gust.

"Well, folks, he was open again, but the wind just knocked the ball down like a wounded bird." The play was enough to generate a celebratory light of Old Man Schmidt's cigar. "We'll take anything at this point."

Michaels had no accord with the wind gusts. On second down, he rolled left on a quasi-bootleg before heaving the ball over the middle to Mankievitz, floating wide open.

"Well I'll be, if that wind didn't just knock that ball down again."

Big Pete brought the sink and kitchen on third down, blitzing ten players and leaving only Eddie Marshall, the safety, in the defensive backfield. With amazing fortune, the Crusaders ran a draw, and Knause sacked McFale for a three-yard loss.

"Folks, not sure if the tide's turnin', but at least we stopped 'em. Number nineteen back to kick, on fourth down. He's at his twenty-three. Good snap. There's the ki... Holy ... Good God Almighty, I never saw anything like ... All of a sudden ... Daggone, we got the ball! He kicked it behind himself. He kicked it straight up in the air, and the wind took it behind him! What's goin' on?"

Coach Waddell apparently tried to capitalize on the sudden momentum garnered from the freak play, sending Redding on a sprint option right.

A smudge in the sterling silver that was the Crusader defense appeared when containment fell apart, allowing Redding to turn the corner and sprint by the nearest linebacker. Breaking off the block, the Crusader cornerback attacked Redding, but the defense had already lost the upper hand.

Near the fifteen, Redding pitched the ball backwards. In stride, Lamont Dickies caught the pitch and bolted for the corner of the end zone.

"He's at the five ... the two ... dives for the end zone ... Touchdown! Touchdown!"

The celebration was childlike in the corner of the end zone. Maturity was hardly present in the stands, either, as the Ranger faithful littered the stadium air with cowbells and air horns.

A perturbed East Catholic team stormed on and off the field. The eleven-man return squad appeared to be overtly emotional in assuming their positions for the impending kick-off. I could feel their energy.

"Back deep to field the kick is McFale. Ginnette approaches the ball. It's uhn onside kick! Now, there's a pile on the ball..."

The sucker punch by Coach Waddell had worked, and the referee signaled that the ball belonged to the Rangers.

Fortunately, I no longer felt sick to my stomach when luck fell into the laps of the Rangers. Maybe I had graduated beyond pettiness. However,

I was a traditionalist and adamant one should earn all that he receives. An onside kick? Please.

Apparently believing in the value of shock, Coach Waddell sent Duane Boyd into the game for the first Ranger play after the kick.

"Folks, Boyd's in the game. He brings 'em up under center, with Durning split out right."

Receiving the snap on a quick cadence, the freshman tossed a shuttle pass back to his tailback, who trailed behind a convoy of blockers. Without attracting any attention to himself, Boyd snuck around the opposite end of Dickies and then turned up-field.

As the East Catholic linebackers closed in for the kill, Lamont Dickies halted his pace, flipped his shoulders in the opposite direction, and heaved a wobbly spiral down the field into the waiting hands of Boyd.

"Good God Almighty, Boyd caught it! He's at the twenty. The fifteen. The ten. He's gonna score! Touchdown Rangers! Touchdown Rangers!"

And suddenly, within a span of a minute, all had changed for me and for the Rangers.

The wind, however, was not abating. And the wind had become the worst of enemies for Michaels in the second period. On their next series, the Crusader strategy shifted one-eighty. Michaels pulled two receivers, including Mankievitz, much tighter to the line. The game plan slid from the arm of Michaels to the legs of McFale, who carried two straight plays on the drive. All for nothing, though.

The South Heaven defense held blocks and forced Michaels into a third-and-long situation.

"Third down, folks. Michaels takes a shotgun snap. Looks left, then right, and fiiires ... Oh my! Luke Post..."

As the ball hung in the wind, Luke Post jumped the out-route on Flannigan and had a certain touchdown run from an interception—until he dropped the ball.

In unison, the South Heaven faithful, who had shot to their feet in anticipation of a Post touchdown, slumped back into their seats.

Magic and miracles, it seemed, had expired for Coach Waddell and the Rangers. They slugged it out, play after play, with the Crusaders pushing the remainder of the game clock toward expiration.

"Folks, this'll be about a thirty-two-yard attempt for Ginnette. Rangers, just enough time for a couple a plays there, before getting Stu on the field. Not sure if he's got the leg here, though. There's the snap. Durning puts it down. The kiiiick iiiiss good! It's good!"

In a mock display of hero worship, the Ranger players mobbed their kicker, and all headed toward the locker room for halftime.

Despite the five touchdowns and one field goal, the most important "play" of the night occurred when Gary Redding and Lamont Dickies met the four captains of the Crusaders at midfield. The option belonged to South Heaven: possession of the ball to start the second half or possession of the wind in the fourth quarter. If they deferred possession of the ball, Jacob Michaels, with the wind, might post another three scores and push the game out of reach. If they kept the wind in the third quarter, Michaels would be given the opportunity to win the game in the fourth. With Coach Waddell gleaming on from the end zone, hands on hips, Gary Redding indicated to the referee that South Heaven wanted the ball to start half number two.

It was the University of Toledo band and a regional ceremony for the state's governing body of athletics that forced the two high school bands to perform at the beginning of the contest. Halftime was a lame break, yet it pushed me out of the Summit and into the passageway connecting the various segments of the large press box.

"You believe this crap?" He was another reporter and wore the same press badge I wore, only his was clipped to the front zipper of his ski jacket. "This game shouldn't even be close."

"Who do you write for?" I concurred with his assessment.

"This team from Podunk doesn't even belong in the playoffs. These games are reserved for real football teams. Not that school. Heck, any other time of the season, under normal conditions, East Catholic would destroy the ... whatever their name is."

"Rangers. They're called the Rangers."

"I don't care!" he blurted, tossing aside an extinguished match. "They don't belong here! Why would the state allow this to occur?"

One of the man's cronies appeared from the closed door of their section. He was taller and older than his fellow press-box mate and not dressed for the cold. "You gotta another smoke, Bob?"

Bob had an immature and plump face, a plump face that matched a nonathletic physique. "I tell ya what, Larry. I won't stand for anymore backyard plays from this team from the Sticks."

Larry scoured through the pockets of his dress shirt and suit pants but came up with nothing. "Don't worry. Michaels will light these farm kids up in the second half."

"South Heaven. The farm kids? They're from South Heaven."

"Well." Bob stomped on his smoke. "They need to get back on their tractors and combines and head south. We don't need them up here—or in this game…"

When the Ranger return squad broke the team huddle, sending Dickies back deep, it appeared that the innocence that was so prevalent during pregame had disappeared—from both the Rangers and the transplanted reporter. Bob and Larry had no right, and they had pulled from me an emotion that was nowhere to be found in the previous two-plus months: a desire to see the Rangers win.

On a kick that died slowly into the wind, Redding brought the offense into the second half, near the Crusader forty.

"We start four in the hole, folks," said Wally. "Redding fakes to Dickies and drops back. He fires toward Durning."

Another gust interrupted play, hoisting the ball above the outstretched arms of the Ranger tight end—and into the hands of a free safety wearing a green jersey.

"And he's finally brought down around the thirty-five. Dag gum, that wind got ahold and wouldn't let go."

A natural defender, like a river or mountain range guarding a city's entrance, the wind was a twelfth man protecting the goal line. No matter the play, plot, or ploy, Michaels could not combat the gusts. By sheer will only, he mustered three positive yards for his team. As his ten teammates trotted off the field, Michaels flagged his head and pulled himself to the sidelines in a dragged and frustrated gait.

South Heaven's most effective weapons in the third quarter were the punt and field position. Gary Redding could not pull the trigger on any completions, and his teammate, Lamont Dickies, failed to outmuscle or outrun the Crusader defense. And yet with the wind, South Heaven was able to push East Catholic farther and farther back toward their own goal line. By the time the third quarter neared an end, Redding caught the jet stream and punted the ball down toward the Crusader two-yard line.

"Michaels, from the shotgun formation, gets the snap. He looks right. Here comes Knause! He's got him. Knause's got him for a safety! He came on a blitz up the middle. Good God Almighty, whattuh play!"

The safety was the last play of the third and brought the Rangers to within two points of the lead—and into the wind. Taking control on their own thirty-two, following the free kick, the Rangers, along with their faithful, felt an uneasiness overcome them with the sight of Michaels warming up his arm on the sidelines. With the Crusader quarterback extended beyond his teammates' sideline boundaries, the thought of Michaels' allying with the bitterly cold wind was frightening and frustrating. But holes began to open, Redding found receivers, and Lamont Dickies slowly tamed those major college-talented linebackers. To the amazement of many, South Heaven assumed a drive directly out of any classic Big Ten school playbook: ground-pounding, smashmouth, frozen turf, lean on the big men up front. In the midst of an 18-play drive, seven minutes were exhausted, sixty-five yards were chewed up, confidence among the Rangers grew, and Michaels stopped throwing and became a mere spectator.

"Well, folks." Old Man Schmidt fidgeted. "It's come down to this: Fourth down and goal from the five, and it looks like Waddell's gonna send in Stu Ginnette. Don't know about this decision, against the wind and all, but I guess it's gonna be a field goal that wins or loses this game. Let's just hope the wind is kind to us."

I felt the sweat creep into my palms. The last thing I wanted for the kid now was to have a loss blamed on him.

To soften the Crusader rush, Coach Waddell sent in Gary Redding to hold for the kick, instead of Durning, giving the defense the distinct possibility of a fake.

"There's the snap."

I am quite certain there were numerous others in the Glass Bowl who were convinced that the kicked ball halted in midair, as if live action had been paused.

"Good! It's good. Stu Ginnette has kicked us into the lead!"

Unfortunately, the frenzy that huddled with the masses in the South Heaven stands abated when Michaels trotted into his circular huddle. Behind the Crusaders, the American flag, hoisted a score of feet in the air, was stiff from the wind. Two quarters free of the wind and a half a quarter away from the ball did not steal the quarterback's taste for the big play. Three straight completions—amazingly, all to Flannigan—pushed the Ranger defense back across midfield.

Knause and his comrades hugged their hips, as if preparing for the inevitable doom.

Lacking haste, Michaels was composed and occupying nearly every second of the play clock.

"First down for East Catholic. Michaels brings 'em up to the line. Ball on the forty-eight."

The shotgun snap to Michaels was high, but the quarterback handled it athletically then gunned a strike to Mankievitz for a nine-yard gain.

In chatting with his audience, Old Man Schmidt gnawed on the end of his cigar. Tension was evident in his inability to speak without utterances. "With the wind, folks, we can't seem to stop him."

And Old Man Schmidt was as prophetic as he was nervous when Michaels drilled Flannigan on an outside slant route that picked up yet another first down.

The game clock on the scoreboard had a couple of burned-out bulbs and registered two and one-half minutes when the quarterback set himself under center.

"There's the snap. Michaels swings it out to McFale. He cuts it up, all the way down to the seventeen."

In absolutely no hurry, Michaels, facing a second and short, brought his squad to the line and casually read the defense before retrieving the snap and rolling right.

"He's got Flannigan."

Luke Post got a paw on the foot of the Crusader flanker. Otherwise, East Catholic would have infused the home crowd with ultimate satisfaction.

The break in play came not from the team trailing but from Coach Waddell. He stopped the clock with fifty seconds to play.

"Folks, I've had just about enough of these last-minute games this year. But here we go again…"

On first and goal, Big Pete had his corners jam the two wideouts, refusing to allow an edge for the offense.

"Michaels got nobody open. He looks and throoows…"

Big Pete's strategy worked to perfection, forcing an incompletion, second down, and an exhale from the Ranger faithful.

"Wally, don't know if my heart can take this."

With the clocked stopped after the incompletion, Michaels brought his offense to the line with four wideouts and only one man in the backfield. Without a second to waste to read the defense, Michaels took the snap and handed the ball, for the first instance in the game, to his fullback, who smashed at full throttle into the line and into the arms of Blaine Manning.

"Whatta play by the big boy! Third down. Wow! Teddy Bear Manning stuffed the line, and now East Catholic calls a time-out."

Third down found the Crusaders four yards from victory. East Catholic posted two wideouts as Michaels brought his team to the line.

Knause only had a lone linebacker, Scheve, lined up with him along the goal line. South Heaven was guessing pass.

From the center, Michaels backpedaled five steps, deep into the pocket.

"Michaels looks. Ain't got no rush. Looks, looks … Fires into the end zone!"

"Out of bounds! He's out of bounds!" yelled Wally, after Flannigan leaped high above Luke Post to snatch a pass.

"Too darn close, folks!"

Big Pete initiated a time-out and again, pulled his squad to the sidelines. Just thirty seconds remained to be played.

The knot in my stomach was growing exponentially by the breath. My heart was thumping beyond control, piercing into the throat. Despite the cold, I was riddled with perspiration. I was tempted to run and hide, so my change in emotion had no witness.

"Here we go, folks. This is it!"

Michaels left nothing to chance when he brought three receivers to the line. In the shotgun, he was going to attempt to win the game on the strength of his arm. Toward the end of his cadence, he put McFale into motion.

"Good snap."

With all his receivers loaded to his right, Michaels paid no attention to his backside.

"Good God Almighty, here comes Luke Post off the corner!"

The entire Ranger crowd rose in unison.

At the very second before impact, Michaels caught a glimpse of his pursuer.

On a dead beeline sprint toward the Crusader quarterback, Post could hardly adjust his route when Michaels stepped forward. Amazingly, though, Post was able to latch onto the collar portion of the quarterback's shoulder pads.

"Post's got him! He slings him around."

In desperation, Michaels simply chucked the ball skyward toward the end zone. His ball flight traveled a miracle route: off the hands of Kyle Knause, then off the helmet of a Crusader lineman, and then into the chest of an ill-alert Flannigan before falling aimlessly to the ground.

CHAPTER NINETEEN
Without Any Respect

Tuesday

The media fervor was still present following an overwhelming Monday, during which no fewer than half a dozen outlets bombarded Coach Waddell and the school. Television cameras from the Columbus and Toledo areas could be found on the high school campus. Four teams remained with a chance to claim the AA football crown. Three of the four were supposed to be in contention: Wheelersville from the southeast, Mentor Lake from the Cleveland area, and Cincinnati Fort Washington. With all three holding spots in the top four of the state rankings, the most compelling of stories was that of the unranked Rangers from South Heaven. The win over East Catholic may have been a freak occurrence, but when it came to the media's thirst for the underdog, a win was a win.

The media, however, didn't have to be present to stir the excitement within the town. Banners and signs of all sorts were suspended in the windows of all downtown stores actually still in business. Many of the shops, in honoring the excitement, conducted sales and buy-one-get-one-free deals. City council members and vocational residents of city hall had rejected traditional and starch dress for maroon and white casual. Hardly a house could be found not decorated or flying a Ranger flag. Inside the glass-paneled marquee that welcomed visitors to the union hall, the words "See You in Columbus, Rangers" shown under lights. In the spirit of the week, Frankie's offered free sodas with the purchase of any-size pizza.

As such, we moved our staff meeting to the lunch hour and the pizza parlor. As an added bonus, by some probably unethical means, Frankie had secured a yellow and green East Catholic helmet for display. He was on the second-to-last rung of a stepladder, securing the abused headgear to the wall, when the lone holdout of the staff finally made his presence known.

"You guys already ordered!" Without invitation or prompting, Phil helped himself to the pitcher of soda and a few squares of sausage pie. He then turned around and clamored to Frankie for a dinner plate.

Obligingly, Frankie huffed in retaliation for Phil to use his hands.

Tucked into the back cover of the folder I carried was the latest edition of Phil's Ohio State recap. His sad endeavor was simply another reason for me to leave. Just pack up the bags and go. I should have done exactly that. I still felt a little homesick for Cleveland and the career I once knew, but the feeling was no longer overwhelming.

At the end of the two combined tables, nearest a trio of road workers in neon orange garb, Phil lined up six opaque brown pill bottles. He dispensed a pill from every bottle then, one by one, swallowed each of them before taking a bite of pizza.

"Regarding Phoenix Toys, no one needs to be reminded they're not coming. How about we keep it off the front pages?"

"Myra." Crumbs flew from Phil's mouthful of food. "Gotta friend in Dayton…" In reaching for another piece of pizza, he knocked a quarter-filled tumbler of soda directly into the lap of Rikki Sake.

"Phil!" barked Myra.

The recipient of the lap-wash jumped from her chair. "I'll be okay." Rikki Sake, a recent addition to the staff, was a graduate from a small college in Dayton, with a degree in photography. After Marty's exodus from South Heaven, Miss Myra was forced to work herself out of a bind and quickly hire a new photographer.

Offered a spot on a paper in Bloomington, Indiana, Marty weighed the opportunity then closed up shop in his garage and left us a simple note of resignation.

"It'll be all right." Phil continued with his lunch regimen as if nothing had occurred.

"Phil, get out! " Miss Myra walked around the table and sequentially removed every piece of pizza from the napkin in front of Phil then tossed them back onto the round baking dish. With lightning reflexes, she snatched the half-eaten piece from Phil's hand and offered it the same fate as the others. "Get out."

"You can't kick me out. This is Frankie's joint."

"Get out, Phil," Frankie called, leaping down from the ladder.

The paddled pooch, with a dumbfounded expression, begrudgingly waddled toward the exit of the restaurant. Phil looked back at the table then nodded for me to join him, with the subtlety of a hot cup of coffee poured over an ice cube.

Apparently, unfulfilled with my current level of self-destruction, I allowed myself to succumb to Phil's demand. "What?"

Phil scanned the vestibule foyer for prying eyes. "I've got something that's gonna blow the doors off any story that we've ever done." He could hardly whisper, as his voice was not capable of possessing such a physical gift.

I dropped a newer dime into one of the five gumball and candy machines sharing space in the lobby with two newspaper dispensers.

"Waddell." Phil searched the coin dispenser of the pay phone. "He's taking a job at some school on the other side of the state."

Despite the intoxicating sensation of sugar and gum paste, I halted in mid-chew. "What?"

"Waddell's leaving. Got it from a good source."

The glass door allowed the chillier outside air to seep into the foyer.

I sidestepped to avoid a would-be patron entering, an assumed man of importance in a three-piece dark blue suit.

"Gotta buddy who writes over in that area. He heard Waddell accepted the defensive backs position. But he's got to be on campus by this Friday." Phil peeked at his watch. "Thought I'd get over to the school before practice."

My wad of gum had lost its flavor. "No one is gonna say anything." I chucked the saturated mess of sugar and grape flavoring into the trash receptacle housed on the outside of the pizza joint.

"Are you kidding?"

"No one needs to know about this, Phil."

"Everyone needs to know!"

I halted Phil with resoundingly negative appreciation. "I said no…" Then I abased myself and offered a petty exchange: no mentioning of

Waddell, and I would forward Phil's recent Buckeye transcript to friends at other papers—in hiring positions.

Wednesday

It was a casually warm afternoon, and I was enjoying it on the park bench outside of Krisp's. The bench could hardly enjoy the fresh coat of paint covering the wood back and seat. After all, it appears as if the artist neglected to scrape the previous coat prior to applying the fresh layer. The lack of detail was destined to lead to further decay.

I was a mere chapter into the book Paper Lion when the bells of the military recruiting office door clanged with a grotesque annoyance. I turned and found Stu Ginnette exiting the shop adjacent to Krisp's. "Stu?"

With what seemed to be a late-June sky, there were few clouds to be found to combat a full sun. The hue was not a crisp blue, but pleasant nonetheless.

He held a plethora of brochures, folders, and papers like textbooks. Despite the success of his team and his own personal record of wins, Stu Ginnette was still a kid whose naiveté had been stolen and someone without positive energy.

"Whatta game Friday. Congrats on the winning kick."

"Thanks." He glanced up and down the street as if he were searching for a cab.

I looked back at the recruiting office then marked my page with a dog-ear before asking if he needed a lift.

"No thanks."

I could read the pamphlets he was holding, all with the words United States Navy. "Thinking about enlisting?"

Stu nodded.

"I thought you wanted to go to college?" Hardly a radical, I was still not a fan of the military, in general—something inherited, I guess.

"My buddy's brother's in the Navy. Says he's been all over the world."

"Yeah, that is Uncle Sam's selling point." I added, without much enthusiasm.

"Navy'll pay for my college." Stu displayed anomalistic yet tempered excitement, conveying the salesmanship of the recruiter and the opportunities available to him in the Navy. Stu expressed his desire to work with jets, following in the footsteps of an uncle who served aboard an aircraft carrier in the Pacific War.

"I thought you needed to be home to help out?"

His plan was logical: Send money home and use the government to pay for school. South Heaven offered no guarantee of income or a job, but the government did.

"Be that as it may, you sure you know what you'd be in for? I mean, there's no quitting the Navy. Once you sign up…"

He looked up and smiled. "It's a chance to leave here."

A burnt orange Nova, both as much a noise nuisance as an eyesore, welcomed Stu into the backseat then bolted out of the downtown area, running two yellow traffic signals.

Senior Epstein, stepping out of Alton's Drugs, took quick notice of my position from across Main Street.

Had I known he had intentions of jaywalking to join me, my return salute would not have been so hardy. Of course, given that he had the pace of southern pit BBQ, I had plenty of time to escape, if desired.

"Wright! I thought that was you." He maintained a death grip on a small ivory white pill sack and caught me ogling. "Heart pills," he replied, as if the paper sack contained an appointment card to a root canal. "I need a moment, Wright."

I suggested we return to the office. "It's probably empty."

"Too nice of a day, Wright. Park bench is fine." He nudged aside the remnants of my lunch to make room on the structure that, in addition to a fresh coat of paint, displayed a written advertisement for Nettle's Funeral Home. "Have you thought more about the offer?" He flipped through a handful of pages from my paperback before providing his critique.

"I'm sure Mister Plimpton will be glad to know you approve."

The inevitable but still unpleasant auspices of arthritis echoed as Senior Epstein took longer than the normal man to fall onto the bench. "Wright, none of these doctors have the guts to tell me how long I got."

Was he confessing? He suddenly had my sympathy, as I was little overwhelmed with discomfort at the eerie silence that followed each cough.

Alleviation came in the form of a convoy of three tractor trailers hauling mangled masses of wrecked vehicles.

"Wright, I've been watching you. You know enough about this game—this game of football."

"Listen, I'm not a cartoonist."

"It's not about drawing a cartoon, you fool. The Prognosticator is about the game. He's about the team, the town."

"Wait a minute. Weren't you the one who told me this town would know a fake?"

"The Prognosticator needs to carry on, Wright."

Friday

Indian summer weather continued to the end of the week, a complete paradox of the tundra conditions in the Glass Bowl.

Dayton and Welcome Stadium, on the banks of the Great Miami, were a compromised and supposed midpoint between Corn Country and the eastern side of Cincinnati. The Gem City would be home to the semifinal matchup between the Rangers and Cincinnati Fort Washington.

The Generals from Fort Washington had collected a storied tradition of victory, pride, and controversy in a short period of time. Fort Washington, formerly known as the East Cincinnati Academy of Physical Education, did not profess the typical core curriculum. Founded in 1970, the school, under the coaching of Vic Mancuso, had collected eighty-eight victories, three regional championships, and eight straight Cincinnati Seven Hills league titles. It was assumed by all in Cincinnati and many throughout the state that Fort Washington, in essence, recruited top talent with the physical education repertoire.

Nothing generated more satisfaction in opponents than defeating the Generals. Despite some success in the winter and spring sports, football was king at Fort Washington. Since the beginning of the football program, Fort Washington had sent dozens of players to top college teams and was already a member of the Ohio High School Hall of Fame, with over two-hundred and fifty victories. Coach Mancuso had retired from a small school powerhouse in Newark, Ohio, transferring back to his hometown of Cincinnati to generate another perpetual state contender in the Generals. Fort Washington operated from the full-house backfield, and according to Willie Tee, all four members of the wishbone were underclassmen.

Speaking of Willie Tee, I deposited only his entourage in the parking lot of the University of Dayton Arena. By order of Mayor Montgomery, Willie Tee had been placed under a simplistic form of house arrest. He would miss the second playoff game—we all assumed.

Welcome Stadium harbored fake turf, similar to the Glass Bowl. For practices and ten games, the Rangers had played on real grass and/or dirt, thus necessitating the need for spiked cleats. Leading up to the East Catholic contest, Coach Waddell and Big Pete scrambled to acquire turf footwear. Unfortunately, though, it came down to street tennis shoes, which actually had no effect on the outcome. For the semifinal match, the University of Dayton stepped forward and supplied the team with appropriate footwear. The white shoes with dark red stripes mixed perfectly with the new uniforms—gifted from the anonymous fan—that Coach Waddell finally decided to use.

I had not heard any news on whether Waddell accepted his new post or not. If indeed he was due to report to Centerville College, he would be late, at the very least.

The Prognosticator, for the time being, remained incognito. In Wednesday's paper, he swung hard with several jabs and the occasional left hook, claiming an unfair advantage for an academy of physical education. In the end, though, the Prognosticator predicted a Ranger victory. Although it would be close, he claimed that South Heaven would win by one.

Cincinnati was well represented in the media pen, with two separate radio broadcasts and a couple of news cameras. Once again, WSHV got bumped into a corner of the press box.

"This here team's the darling of Cincinnati," said Old Man Schmidt. "At least, until the big Catholic school plays tomorrow night."

Fort Washington and South Heaven held opposite ends of the field. With just over thirty minutes to kick-off, the Generals were drilling wishbone plays while the Rangers remained in several specific groups of a defensive attitude.

Old Man Schmidt threw some elbow grease at a dark brown stain on the writing counter of the press box. "You're 'bout to see a team that averages purdy near fifty points a game."

I offered him a hankie, but he just added a little saliva to the spot. "These guys beat Dayton Carrollton by forty-five last week."

Near the end zone where South Heaven practiced, a bank of lights suddenly fell silent, darkening twenty-plus percent of the field. As the team trotted into their locker room, a contagious disease struck all remaining banks of lights, and Welcome Stadium meshed with the color of the night.

It would be another twenty minutes before light was restored. A traffic accident nearby was to blame.

The darkness had become a metaphor for my career: no earth-shattering Pulitzer Prize-winning story, no job to return home to in Cleveland, and dwindling pride and soon-to-be loss of my only ally in South Heaven. Miss Myra was determined to leave her hometown. She was absent from the semifinal matchup. Hardly was she fooling anyone with a claim of a business trip to Philadelphia.

The surge delayed the start of the game, and each squad, apparently, completed warmups in their respective locker rooms.

"Well, folks, now that we got power back, the captains are meetin' for the toss. But before we get tuh that, like tuh tell ya'll 'bout Scheve's Feed and Seed. Get all your winter needs at Scheve's."

"New sponsor?"

Old Man Schmidt stoked the flint on his lighter. "Everybody wants onboard now, boy."

South Heaven won the toss, and Lamont Dickies indicated to the referee that he and his Rangers wanted the ball first.

"Kick-off tonight brought to you by the union. Your Auto Workers' Union will always be there for you. Fort Washington set to kick, with

Dickies back deep for your Rangers. There's the boot, and it's a line-drive that hits at the forty. It's picked up by Durning. He's up to the forty-three; not much of a return."

On the first play of their second playoff game, Redding initiated a perfect play fake to Dickies then set up to throw backside.

"He's got Durning—wide open!"

The spiral was perfect, but neither the touch nor the loft could match said perfection.

"Good God Almighty! Chris Durning was wide open. Nobody within ten yards, and Redding overthrows him!"

Redding's incomplete throw would be the best and only opportunity for positive yardage on the opening drive. A sweep to Dickies and a quarterback option were no match for the speed of Fort Washington.

"Numbah twenty-one, Bobbitt, back deep for the Generals. Redding's punt's high but short."

Darius Bobbitt collided with Luke Post and nearly lost control of the ball. Knocked backwards two steps, he regained balance then bolted left toward the sideline, the original position of his blocking wall. The wall provided enough of a seam to jettison Bobbitt down the field.

"Nobody's gonna catch him. Nobody. Touchdown Generals!"

Once again, South Heaven found itself in a hole early in a ball game. Darius Bobbitt had displayed speed and amazing quickness, the likes of which no Ranger player had seen in eleven previous games.

Fort Washington was unconventional in their extra-point attempt. Instead of a kicker, the offense lined up in the wishbone set. At the snap, the ball was pitched backward to Bobbitt, who, in turn, followed a plethora of blockers into the end zone without a hindrance of defense: 8-0.

"As Redding brings 'em up to the line, wanna tell ya'll 'bout Minnie's Toys. Minnie's on the corner of Main and Madison." Wally appeared to have a bad taste for advertising. "Handoff to Dickies, and he's goin' nowhere."

"Wally, these boys are fast. No wonder they're winnin' by so much. By the time they score four touchdowns, you finally get a glimpse of 'em."

A developing counter to Dickies generated the Rangers a significant gain of five yards. Until that point, pursuit had been the weapon of choice for Fort Washington. However, Coach Waddell had earned eleven victories counterattacking with his own unique weapon: opportune adaptability. On second and five, Redding pitched the ball to his tailback, helping to create the illusion of a mass sweep left. As pursuit ran with the play, the ball suddenly shifted direction when sophomore flanker Sammy Gwynn took an outside handoff from Dickies.

"Gwynn's to the fifty … the forty…"

Sammy Gwynn, rotating in and out with every play call, was not the most intimidating of football players, but he was quick. Indifferent in stature, Gwynn had an awesome first step. However, even with his track experience, quickness was no peer to pure speed.

"Gwynn's gonna be caught on the twenty-two. That boy came outta nowhere to catch Sammy! Wow."

From the reverse's end yardage, Lamont Dickies carried the brunt of the load, compiling a tough eight yards on three carries.

On fourth down, the newest future inductee into the U.S. Navy trotted onto the field. It would be thirty-two yards for Stu Ginnette's attempt.

"Folks, says here that Fort Washington's dun blocked four field goals this year. So I'd bet they'd be after this one."

The snap was perfect to Redding. Both sprinters on the end of the defensive line rushed toward the set ball. Stu Ginnette took his momentum forward, but before he struck the ball, Redding picked it up from the tee and flipped it to the squat Gwynn cutting across the line.

Neither spectator nor defender found the petite Gwynn until he was three yards beyond the line of scrimmage.

"It's a fake. Gwynn's got the ball!"

He was pulled down inside the ten-yard line, but not until the South Heaven drive was continued with a first down.

"Waddell ain't gonna win this game on gimmicks," insisted Old Man Schmidt. "They'll post fifty on us if he continues with this stuff."

On first down, Redding pitched back to Dickies, who was streaking to the left.

"Agghh! They're gonna pin him. No, Dickies throws ... Touchdown! Touchdown! Durning caught the ball in the corner of the end zone. Good God Almighty, whatta pass by Lamont!"

"Gimmick or not," I laughed. "It's working."

An actual kick by Ginnette brought the Rangers within one point.

With Darius Bobbitt deep for kick-retrieval duty, Coach Waddell had no taste for giving him another opportunity to score. Instead, Coach Waddell opted for another gimmick.

"Ginnette kicks onside! It's ours! It's ours! Luke Post's got it. First down Rangers!"

It truly appeared to the cynic within me that Coach Waddell was playing as if he had nothing to lose. Indeed, maybe he was a man coaching his last day at South Heaven. In which case, it wouldn't matter if he lost by two or fifty-two. Maybe, however, there was something more to this abrupt and complete alteration in his ultraconservative methods. Maybe this change was about winning.

Lamont Dickies had shouldered his team's offensive load for the entire season, and as the second quarter started in the semifinal match for class AA, he would welcome that task once again. Coach Waddell's line began to find the step needed to sustain open holes long enough for the tailback to squeeze through and gain significant ground.

Wally remained on the microphone into the second quarter. "Folks, appears as if we got Goliath on the ropes. Redding brings 'em up on first down, from the five. They ain't stopped Dickies on this drive yet."

Although a captain and the one player on the team who touched the ball every play, Gary Redding, since his return to the starting unit, had participated merely as a role player, yet to contribute to any game's outright outcome.

"Redding fakes a pitch to Lamont. Rolls out right. He looks ... into the end zone. He's got Hainesworth. Touchdown! Good God Almighty, Redding finally hits with a touchdown score!"

The kid they called "Soapbox," for his love of stealing conversations, Billy Hainesworth held the opposite end of Chris Durning and had yet to, unlike his fellow receiver, catch a pass in game competition. A sheer paradox of Sammy Gwynn, Hainesworth carried two XXs on his game jersey size tag and assumed his blocking assignment on the line without complaint. He hugged the touchdown-thrown ball, refusing to relinquish it to the referee until all his teammates patted him on the helmet or got a taste of his excitement.

With the Rangers leading by six points, Coach Waddell parked his kicker on a hash mark. Stu Ginnette's kick forced Darius Bobbitt to the sidelines.

"We got him down at the twenty-five."

Football, particularly amateur football, had a colorful tradition of names, both first and family titles. The quarterback for the Generals would, no doubt, be eventually listed in the annals of great names: Major Rider. On first down, Rider called his own number and displayed the speed that matched that of Bobbitt. Grasping the corner, Rider abolished the option and gained eight yards on a scamper. Only close to average height, Rider was as stout as a fireplug and was the reigning 100-meter state sprint champion.

Contrary to scouting reports, Fort Washington's offense was hardly disciplined or machine-like in the precision and movements of the wishbone offense. Pure speed subsidized such lack of precision. Unfortunately, discipline is much desired on a cross-buck action play.

"Ball's on the ground!"

With only twenty-three yards to an exclamation point on momentum, South Heaven's offense regained possession.

Major Rider and his crew had nearly lost their gait of confidence. Only a quarter and one half into the game and the Fort Washington offense was laboring off the field, dumbfounded or shocked at the progress or regression of the game this far. The kids from the country were getting the better of them. But the Generals' defense decided to push back the contender with a counterattack, blitzing all three linebackers on the first play from scrimmage.

Gary Redding's eyes had to be the size of buckets when four defenders broke free of blocks or shot straight through untouched. As the distance between him and the four Generals rapidly dissipated, Redding retreated, shuffling on a backpedal.

"They got him!"

With enemy hands on his jersey, Redding heaved the ball skyward to his left before being slammed to the Astroturf, backside first.

"Holy ... Dickies is out there. He's got it!"

From behind him, Lamont Dickies hauled in the pass then spun back toward the goal line.

"He's to the five ... touchdown Dickies! Touchdown! Good God Almighty, Redding just heaved the ball!"

The demeanor of the Fort Washington offense did not change as they took control of the ball on their own thirty-six. Football has always been simplistic for those who triumph. Major Rider called a straight dive to his fullback, Dexter Nuchols.

Before Knause could ready himself for a tackle, Nuchols was by him, and the Ranger backer had to dive behind his line of demarcation, only to trip up the Generals' fullback.

Major Rider went back to the well and called Nuchols' number once again.

"He's across the fifty and down to the forty-six. A pickup of nine. Folks, we soon oughta find an answer for that quick hitter."

Nuchols, not yet gassed, took another handoff on an X-block play off of right tackle.

"Ohhh ... Nuchols in the clear."

A great open-field stop by Eddie Marshall stopped a touchdown.

From the thirty-five, Major Rider suckered in the linebackers with the X-block off-tackle motion. He rode Nuchols into the hole but retrieved the ball at the last minute and stole the corner. At the thirty, Rider switched on the afterburners, duped Luke Post, and shot straight toward the end zone.

"He's to the five. Touchdown!"

It did not take long for the ball to fall back into the hands of Rider. South Heaven ran four plays and two minutes from the clock, and despite a first down, Redding booted the ball back to Fort Washington. And once

Rider regained possession, it was a mere moment in time until Darius Bobbitt put his team ahead by a point.

"Well, folks, lightning has struck and struck quickly for the men in the Navy blue. No sooner did we jump on 'em with two scores than they turn around and drop two on us." Wally shook his head. "Bobbitt took that pitch and, whew, he was gone for forty yards."

With plenty of time remaining in the half and South Heaven with the ball on their own forty, energy suddenly shifted from the action on the field to the immense commotion in the stands. Despite an incomplete pass by Redding, it appeared that the entire stadium rose to their feet—to view the fisticuffs between members of the South Heaven faithful and fans from Fort Washington.

Due to an abundance of South Heaven fans and the need to fit the Pride of South Heaven into bleacher seats on one side of the field, officials had to detour numerous South Heaven fans toward the end of another section—the same section that housed the crowd from Fort Washington.

We had a perfect vantage point to the debacle, which played out immediately below us and to our right. Shrills and screeches could be heard, and it appeared fans were invading other's sovereignty. Arms raised fists into the air, and grown men were piling onto one another—an obvious mass of confusion.

The drama on the playing surface, the actual play that all paid admission to see, stopped. Referees sent both teams to their respective sidelines and eventually into the locker rooms.

With as many law enforcement officers as there were game officials, cops converged on the scene of chaos, like corpsmen attending to a foxhole of wounded Marines.

All three of us in the Summit were on our feet and peering out of the press box. Wally maintained his broadcast, attempting not to give highlights of the debacle. Old Man Schmidt loused up the air with derogatory epithets at any Fort Washington fan within earshot.

Twenty plus minutes into the melee and every state official in the stadium, ten or so cops, and numerous Good Samaritans had their talons fully entrenched on said bullies, culprits, instigators, and perpetrators.

As more law-enforcement types arrived, more grown men and adults were being pulled down bleacher stairs under the care of a Montgomery County Sheriff's deputy.

"This is a travesty," repeated Wally several times to his audience. "This is terrible!"

A possible explanation was only a few days in the making. Despite the two schools never meeting before on any sports playing field, wretched karma had been created between Fort Washington and South Heaven. Throughout the entire week, most in the Generals' camp had incessantly repeated their disappointment in having to face inferior competition in South Heaven. Going so far as to refer to the Rangers as "hicks" and "hayseeds," those from Cincinnati surmised that an inevitable trip to Columbus and the state championship would have only been worthwhile with a victory over East Catholic. Even the revered Mancuso added his jab by declaring to have never heard of such a place as South Heaven. All those in the pen media who covered Cincinnati sports had predicted the most lopsided game in state playoff history.

Shock and astonishment were gradually upstaged by frustration and anger, and a loud chorus of boos escorted instigators from the stands. By the time the assistant director for Ohio sports, Fran Willis, took control of the PA system, the last of the presumed perpetrators were being walked away in handcuffs.

"Ladies and gentlemen," Willis spoke. "It is our obligation and ultimate responsibility to protect the safety of our athletes. Under current conditions, we cannot do that."

"Not quite certain what's goin' on here, folks. But it's been a while since the teams left the field."

Some thirty minutes after Willis' initial announcement, the Rangers and Generals migrated back onto the playing surface.

"Folks, here come the teams, and they look as shocked as us."

The referee's whistle blow echoed bluntly in the hush-ridden stadium as he signaled for play to begin. Neither team, however, was certain of themselves or the situation. As a result, the score remained status quo, with the advent of halftime.

The chatter among the Cincinnati media members in the booths next to us involved words not flattering toward the "hicks" from South Heaven.

Mancuso and his Generals were the first to reappear after halftime. They appeared reluctant and tepid in foot.

Wally continued with the microphone, owning up to yet another wager lost to Old Man Schmidt. Despite the warmer-than-normal temperatures, he had donned a navy blue windbreaker with the white letters of "WSHV" silkscreened on the upper back of the clothing piece.

As if allergic to aggression, almost shying away from their capabilities, Fort Washington was a shadow of the team that reeled off easy touchdowns in the first half. Only three plays into the second half, Major Rider had already turned the ball over to his punter.

Lamont Dickies and his Rangers were a little more inclined than their counterparts to employ strength and to neglect the thoughts of the melee. From their own forty, the Rangers' offensive line tore open a gaping hole for their tailback. Another nine yards came easy for Dickies on a counter play.

"Better get your tickets for Columbus, boy. This game's ours."

"Dickies up the middle, another six yards. South Heaven's to the thirty-seven."

The Ranger offense was in complete control, negating any emotion that was remaining in Fort Washington. Then, the roller coaster had overcome a peak to reach top downhill speed.

"Redding fakes a dive to Dickies. Back in the pocket. He looks to his right and fires."

Darius Bobbitt stepped in front of Chris Durning's post pattern and had an open field in front of him.

"He's to the forty…" Wally's confidence and excitement were shattered, and his voice fell into a plain tone.

Without a peer in speed, Bobbitt sprinted untouched ninety yards to score.

Cheers erupted from the Cincinnati press gallery.

Collectively, the breath was sucked out of us. I was ill with anger—angry with the Cincinnati press, the thugs in the stands, and anyone who believed the Rangers did not belong in the same game as the mighty Generals. Anger or not, however, we were trailing by eleven.

Emotion had not dissipated the Rangers. However, a kick that never departed the ground was muddled by one Ranger, who handled the ball like a minor-league journeyman third baseman, then muffed by a second South Heaven return man. The ball was blown dead on the eight-yard line.

Duane Boyd jogged onto the field to join the huddle.

Old Man Schmidt smiled.

Offering no time for the freshman to settle into the game, Coach Waddell called the kid's number with a waggle bootleg to the right.

With the rejuvenated energy of the Generals and the outright speed of the defense, Boyd's first option was not available. Instead of tucking the ball and running, however, the quarterback squared his shoulders and perfectly led his tight end over the middle.

"Eighteen yards," said Old Man Schmidt. "Bet Papa Redding's down there cursin' up a storm."

Coach Waddell called Boyd's number once more. Boyd tossed a slant pass between linebackers to Gwynn for another first down.

From the Ranger thirty-nine, after a couple of runs by Dickies, Boyd took a snap and bolted to his left, setting up to throw downfield. Some ten yards outside of his tackle and with two blitzing linebackers coming unscathed and full-force at him, Boyd turned and lofted a pass back to his right and into the hands of his fullback, Ricky Green.

The absolute unsung hero of the Ranger offense, Green excelled more as a wrestler than a football player. But the senior had spent the entire season opening up holes for Lamont Dickies. At the receiving end of the lengthy screen pass, Green secured the ball with hands of a lineman, but secured it nonetheless.

"He's got nothin' but Rangers in front of him!"

Green also had the footwork of a lineman. But speed was not a requirement, when no defender was within twenty yards of him.

"He's to the thirty."

Eventually, though, that dreaded lack of speed did catch up to Green, but the bubble of blockers surrounding the South Heaven fullback prevented any contact and halting of the inevitable.

"Touchdown! Touchdown Rangers! Good God Almighty, Ricky Green scores!"

A loud and long-lasting roar erupted from the Ranger side of the complex.

Half the third quarter had created an amazing sequence of events. Major Rider and Darius Bobbitt took turns carrying the ball on the option play. The duo tore off six to seven yards each time they touched the ball, marching down the Welcome Stadium turf like the team that was supposed to destroy the Rangers. Ten plays and five minutes were required before Bobbitt scored on a sweep around right end.

"Folks, we start the fourth with the ball on the forty-eight." Old Man Schmidt had lit his last cigar, finally taking over the microphone. "Boyd brings 'em up on second down, with Sammy Gwynn split right."

Searching the sidelines, I could not locate Gary Redding among his teammates. Word had not reached the press box as to the reason the freshman was still in the game. All in the Summit assumed the senior had just been benched.

"Pitch to Dickies … heads right. Ohhh, it's a reverse! Here comes Gwynn, and he's got room to run!"

Skirting along the turf, with his undocked mesh jersey flapping against his back, Gwynn was finally hauled down near the Fort Washington thirty-two.

South Heaven rushed to the line, and Boyd quickly received the snap, catching the Generals napping.

"Ricky Green's in the clear! He's down to the sixteen!"

Coach Waddell had the Fort Washington defenders arguing among themselves. He called his quarterback's number, once more with a bootleg.

Like a seasoned veteran, Boyd pulled the defense toward him then drilled Durning with a completion that pushed the ball down to the four.

Again, South Heaven failed to give their opponents time to set, rushing to the line. Boyd took the snap and rifled a bullet to Gwynn.

"Touchdown Gwynn! Touchdown Rangers!"

Nine minutes remained on the clock when Major Rider crossed midfield on an option run.

"Folks, I gotta believe that the last team to touch the ball's gonna win this game."

On yet another option, Rider stole the corner again then pulled Luke Post to him before pitching to Bobbitt some seven yards beyond the line of scrimmage.

"Ain't no one gonna catch him, folks."

Pursuit remained several yards behind the sprinter as he crossed the goal line for another Fort Washington score.

Perfection had been the mainstay in every extra-point attempt by the Generals to that point. It was either perfection on their part or a desire by Knause and the boys to appear completely inept.

"Well, folks, here we come out of the time-out. Generals up by eleven. Rider brings 'em up to the line in the 'bone.' Calls cadence. Looks like the Rangers gottuh six-man front. The snap. It's an option…"

On the sprint option, Rider pitched the ball to Bobbitt.

"He leaps. Don't think he got it. No! Kyle Knause stuffed him right at the goal line, and believe it or not, we've held 'em."

A few shrills and caws emanated from the South Heaven corners when, despite trailing in the game and with Boyd having moved the team successfully, Gary Redding trotted onto the field.

"First down Rangers, and we got it on the forty. Redding pitches the ball to Dickies. He crosses the line and gets up to the forty-four."

On second down, a lack in communication nearly turned the game in complete favor of Fort Washington, so we thought in the Summit. Redding appeared to carry a handoff back to Dickies, which brought the harshly pursuing defense to the line, stopping the Ranger tailback for no gain.

"Oh my! It's Bruce Morton with the ball. He's in the open!"

The "hidden ball" trick. The Ranger guard, Morton, retrieved the ball from the surface and subtly found wide-open running room around the right end.

"Big number sixty-six is rumblin' down the sidelines."

Before any General defender realized the magnitude of the situation, Morton was thirty-yards from the goal line.

"Go! Go!" yelled Wally. "Go!"

With cement shoes clinging to his feet, Morton eventually ran out of steam.

"Good God Almighty, I don't know where that call came from! Bruce Morton picked up the ball and ran all the way down to the ten-yard line. Unbelievable! We've seen it all tonight!"

Unfortunately, two runs by Dickies and an incomplete pass by Redding moved the ball only five yards closer to the goal line.

"Daggone, folks. We had 'em on the ropes."

Coach Waddell sent in Stu Ginnette to draw the team a few points closer.

"You'd think we're down too many points to kick a field goal. But here we go anyway."

The snap from center was perfect, and Stu Ginnette connected to push his team's point total to 38.

"Ain't a whole lotta time here, folks. We gotta hold these guys on this drive."

"Rider hands to Nuchols on a dive; short gain. Under six minutes to play. We need a stand, here."

On the sidelines, in front of their troops, the coaches were paradoxes of one another. The patriarch Mancuso, in blue ball cap and jacket, stood stoically, almost emotionless, with his arms folded over his chest and glaring onto the field. Across the turf, Coach Waddell had mustered his offensive unit and was animated in either his instructions or tongue-lashing.

"Rider hands to Bobbitt. He's up to the thirty-six. It'll be third down comin' up."

Fort Washington appeared poised and was egregiously deliberate between downs, draining as much clock as possible.

Up and pacing, despite an obvious tinge in the lower lumbar, Wally was on an island by himself, at times unable to observe any action on the field. "Hold 'em. Just hold 'em."

A quick snap and the Generals' quarterback surged parallel to the line of scrimmage for a sprint option. With Darius Bobbitt in tow, it appeared someone or something was determined to not allow a first down. Refer to it as divine intervention or just simply another case of dumb luck, but without being touched, Rider lost his footing—and fell straight to the turf.

The Summit erupted.

"Fourth down!" barked Old Man Schmidt.

"He'd be a fool to go for it here." Despite the broadcaster's self-professed knowledge of the game, Wally had not registered over two-hundred coaching victories like Mancuso.

After the time-out, the venerable Mancuso marched his offensive unit back onto the field. Because with just over four minutes to play, a first down would have probably sealed the game for Fort Washington. That, and Mancuso had a weak punter. I opted to believe in the theory of arrogance. Once and for all, Mancuso was determined to convince any potential doubter that his offensive unit was far superior to any team a hick school could field.

"Rider calls cadence. The snap!"

Coaxing the defense, I contorted myself with awkward body language, my stomach in knots and palms lousy with sweat.

Two of South Heaven's linebackers scraped up inside-out and strung the option beautifully.

"Rider stops and plants, cuts back!"

Major Rider lowered his shoulder and plowed his squat frame into a mass of defenders.

"He's short!" I jumped up and down like a kid who had just split open the piñata. "He's short!"

The entire South Heaven defensive unit, with helmets thrust into the air, charged off the field in celebration. They had forced a turnover, just a yard shy of a game-ending first down.

With a mere twenty-seven yards to negotiate for a score, Coach Waddell rolled the dice again, inserting his freshman quarterback. The substitution, however, did not immediately energize the offense. Lamont Dickies muscled his way back to the line of scrimmage on a first-down run.

"Folks, it doesn't appear as if Waddell's gonna stop the clock. We're closin' in on three minutes."

Boyd sent Sammy Gwynn right, Durning left, and kept Hainesworth in tight.

"Boyd swings it out tuh Dickies. He breaks a tackle ... breaks another, and is finally hauled down at the fifteen. First down Rangers!"

A simple play netted a gain on first down, basically moving the ball to the center of the field while picking up a couple of yards.

"We're now at the two-minute mark." Old Man Schmidt's hand was shaking, as if showing his age.

A quick fake to Green lured enough of the Fort Washington linebackers a step forward for Boyd to dump a quick-hitter to Durning.

"Durning's down to the seven!"

Neither Mancuso nor Coach Waddell opted to stop the clock as it passed the one-minute mark.

I had no emotional obligation to this team or town but suddenly could not recall a time when I was so nervous. As those who had befriended me were desperately finding avenues out of South Heaven and means to a life beyond the mundane and directionless, I was—unbelievably—wanting to be a Ranger.

With the clock ticking below twenty seconds and the team facing a third down, Boyd took the snap from center and bolted to his left.

"He's got no one open."

Boyd reversed field, avoiding pursuer after pursuer. Nearly reaching the sideline, he heaved a toss into the deep reaches of the end zone.

"Touchdown! Touchdown! Good God Almighty, Durning caught it!"

In the midst of pandemonium, both in the press box and on the field, the realization that South Heaven still trailed forced Coach Waddell and his staff to frantically regroup their players for the extra-point conversion. Players, team managers, and water boys alike had streamed onto the playing surface in celebration.

Old Man Schmidt smiled and winked, as if he knew I had become one with him. "Do ya throw for it here, boy?"

Mancuso had initiated a time-out to regroup his squad.

"Here we go, folks. Game on the line."

Of all formations, a shotgun, Boyd lined up his team for the two-yard conversion.

"I guess we're gonna throw." I reverted back to my contorted body language.

"Boyd gets the snap. He pump fakes a throw. No! It's a draw."

Dickies took the handoff and scurried around left tackle, only to find a wall of defenders. Having taken an initial hit, he maintained balance and reversed field.

"He cuts it up and diiiiives!"

I let loose with a huge sigh of relief and pushed my heart back down into my chest cavity. South Heaven had once again pulled out a miracle. The game was moving into an extra period.

Only in playoff football did high schools offer an extra session of play. A team could conceivably run through an entire season without a win or loss on their record. However, the playoff system was established to determine an eventual state champion. A clear winner had to come from either South Heaven or Fort Washington. And, unlike the pro game, the extra period was not a sudden-death situation.

In the overtime period, each team would be given the ball on their opponent's twenty-five yard line. Once the ball was whistled into play, the offense would be given four downs to gain ten yards, until such time as they either scored a touchdown or field goal or turned the ball over on downs. In turn, the second team on offense had to either match or improve upon the score offered up by the first team. Improvement netted a win. Match the score and continue playing. Any other option and the game ended, along with the season.

As the lower-seeded team, South Heaven got the call on the coin toss. Gary Redding joined his teammate at midfield. The whooping came from the Generals' sideline when the referee pointed in the direction of Fort Washington.

"Rider pitches."

Bobbitt found the corner of the defense but was only able to achieve a first down, pushing the ball to the twelve.

"Time no longer matters here, folks, unless you're needin' to see a new episode of Dallas." Old Man Schmidt hugged the microphone for the overtime period. "No sir, only thing matters in overtime is luck."

Making every attempt to end the game on his own, Darius Bobbitt clawed, crawled, and spun his way down to the four.

"These guys don't never kick the ball." Wally's frustration could not be concealed. "They'll go for two if they score."

It would be Nuchols launching himself over the goal line for six points.

"Well, they go for two here. There's the snap ... Rider on the option. He'll keep and score—easily. Too easy."

Hardly depleted, Boyd and offensive mates confidently strode to the twenty-five in preparation to overcome an eight-point deficit.

Given the nature of the unorthodox offense to that point for South Heaven, Fort Washington did not attack the line of scrimmage. The strategy worked, and they surrendered only a few yards to Dickies. Boyd took notice and sprinted at an angle into the pocket. He flipped his shoulders toward the line and tossed a strike to Hainesworth.

"Still gonna be a coupleuh yards shy of the first," added Old Man Schmidt.

From just beyond the seventeen, Boyd pitched back to Dickies.

"Ain't gonna do it. He's gonna be short of the first down. It'll be fourth for the Rangers comin' up."

A mere inches separated the ball from a fresh set of downs and continuing with play.

I blew on my hands in a meager attempt to halt the moisture. Having doused my interior clothing with perspiration, I was annoyed by my slight shivering.

"Here comes Boyd. He's got Gwynn on his right."

The meat of the South Heaven offense was Dickies off-tackle, which was the call Coach Waddell made.

"Dickies all the way down to the twelve! Whatta hole!"

On a slant, straight up the gut, Lamont Dickies broke into the secondary before being tripped up just inches from a touchdown.

"Good God Almighty, another huge hole for Dickies!"

It was an assumed formality with the next play. However, nothing in the game could be an assumption. Boyd faked to Dickies then rolled left and had nothing but the end zone in front of him.

"Touchdown Boyd!"

No player was more excited than the young freshman. He leaped into the arms of his tight end, Durning, as a crowd mobbed the two of them along the rear line of the end zone. Unfortunately, though, the celebration had to be interrupted prematurely. There was still a two-point conversion needed to tie the score.

Permitted one time-out per overtime period, Coach Waddell used his teams' stoppage of play to conceive a two-point ploy.

"Bootleg." Wally feigned a throw. "Gotta be a bootleg."

But again, Coach Waddell refused to acknowledge football logic for a given situation and rebuffed Wally's suggestion. Simple and basic would catch the defense off guard.

"Dickies through the middle. He's in!"

Total exhaustion could only describe the game. In the intermission between overtime periods, deep breaths filled the Summit, but no words were even whispered. Total exhaustion! Old Man Schmidt pulled the headphones from their perch and massaged the vein-infused edges of his ears. Wally repeatedly tugged at the black belt with which futility attempted to maintain his trousers at the correct level of a vacant waist.

Double-overtime would begin differently. South Heaven would get the ball first.

Old Man Schmidt was tardy in getting his audience back into the game, following an advertisement for snow shovels from Pistol's Hardware. Boyd was nearly under center before the WSHV airwaves were rekindled with the action of the game. He offered no apology and rolled with bucolic professionalism into the action, "Boyd gets the snap."

Dickies took a handoff and secured three tough yards, pushing the South Heaven tailback's total beyond two-hundred for the game.

"Second down."

The outside veer had been missing from the South Heaven repertoire—for most of the season, at least. On second down, with the ball just inside the twenty-two, Duane Boyd rode his fullback into the seven-hole. The motion pulled the defensive end toward the play. Boyd hopped over the commotion in the hole and cut up the field.

"He's to the eighteen."

Boyd held onto the ball as long as he could and took a thump from the Fort Washington cornerback, but only after he pitched the ball to Dickies.

"Dickies got the pitch! He's to the five. Touchdown! Touchdown Dickies! Good God Almighty, whatta play by Boyd!"

"They gotta go for two," insisted Wally. "Gotta go for two."

Coach Waddell used his lone time-out to pull not only his offensive unit into a huddle, but the entire Ranger team.

"Folks, here we go: the two-point conversion."

When the huddle broke on the South Heaven sideline, Coach Waddell held onto his quarterback, latching onto the youngster's facemask.

Boyd brought his team to the line and saw a six-man front for the first time in the game from Fort Washington.

"There's the snap. Give to, no…"

Boyd waggled to beyond the right of the line: Wally's bootleg.

"Boyd tucks it … No! He throws to the back of the end zone. Durning's got it! He caught the ball!"

With discipline among the Rangers non-existent, lost in the excitement, streams of players again careened onto the playing field to celebrate. Several mobbed their tight end. Despite the gravest of efforts from Coach Waddell and his staff to literally pull players back to the sidelines, a couple of yellow hankies sailed into the air. South Heaven was busted with a fifteen-yard major penalty.

"You gotta be kiddin,' folks."

I was indignant, not so much at the players, like my cohorts, but with the officials. A game at that level of competition, under the circumstances, should not be dictated by the call of an official. As our Cincinnati press brothers were screaming and applauding the referee's movement of the football from the twenty-five to a starting position at the ten, I lambasted the men in stripes.

"Well folks, the Generals only got ten yards to score. And with this offense, I don't like this."

Almost immediately, Rider took advantage, with an option left that netted him five yards.

"Come on!" barked Wally.

Nuchols blasted off center for another three on second down.

"Dang..." Wally buried his scarred chin into his chest.

"Third down, folks."

I was almost willing to concede the touchdown and then regroup for the extra-point attempt. Still, though, my blood coursed with anger in a vain attempt to halt Fort Washington.

"Rider gives to Bobbitt. He's over. Touchdown Generals."

The Cincinnati press corps erupted next door. Meanwhile, the perpetually calm Mancuso could be seen pumping his fist.

Wally kicked his folding chair but, without question, felt little to no pain with workman's steel-toed tarnished tan boots protecting his feet.

"Folks, they're still down by two!"

Mancuso didn't bother with a time-out to set up a conversion play. After a quick congratulatory hug of Bobbitt, Rider had his squad in the huddle.

Uncharacteristically, Kyle Knause took an inordinate amount of time in his defensive huddle, breaking just in time to meet the offense at the ball. He shuffled his linemen in and out of gaps as Rider called signals.

"Rider's gonna drop back to pass!"

To the surprise of all, and for only the second time in the game, Major Rider stood in the pocket to throw. Lacking a traditional passer's height, he appeared lost in the pocket.

A wideout took two steps forward then interjected an oblique cut toward the goalpost. On the cut, he was open, with Luke Post on his rear.

"Rider throws. It's batted in the air!"

In the Summit, we never saw the Ranger whose hand got in the way of the thrown ball's flight path.

"It falls to the deck! The ball's on the ground. Good God Almighty, Rangers win! Rangers win!"

CHAPTER TWENTY
Columbus and Ohio Stadium

Sunday, A Breakfast to Remember

The commander of VFW Post 315 had more than a simple vested interest in the South Heaven High football team. Hank Knause, a veteran of the Korean War, was the proud father of four, the youngest being Kyle. Elder Knause opened the doors to the VFW hall for a football fundraising pancake breakfast.

Despite his lack of an appearance, Old Man Schmidt suggested I donate my services to the fundraiser and serve sausage links. I had been asked to replace the new congressman, Charlie Van Wert. My position was next to Mrs. Rumsfeld.

Mrs. Rumsfeld held the syrup ladle. She was the mother of a junior varsity player who had not seen the playing field except for kick-off returns. Despite that, she was thrilled to be a mother of a member of the team. Giddy, Mrs. Rumsfeld could not stop chatting about the game with Fort Washington. "I can't believe we're in the championship game, can you?" With a simple voice and a majestically naïve smile, Mrs. Rumsfeld had a kind word to say to everyone who passed through the line.

Although battling the cold, throngs waited outside the hall for their chance to partake in the festivities. Three dollars bought one a hefty-sized portion of pancakes, two sausage links, and either coffee, milk, or orange juice.

Quite possibly the only people as excited about the Rangers' amazing trek to the title game as the residents of South Heaven were the football fans in the PEC and surrounding towns. Congratulatory and good-luck greetings poured into the athletic department on Saturday.

Not the right fit at the time was the word we received. Centerville College decided to move on—without one Coach Waddell. An overtime stop by the Ranger defense and a stunning upset of the heavily favored Generals exposed Coach Waddell to the cruel ironies of fate. Coaching like he had nothing to lose or prove to anyone, Coach Waddell had to believe he was finally playing his swan song to his soon-to-be former fellow citizens. Many, I am sure, questioned his means against Fort Washington. Was his motive genuine? No one will ever know. Maybe, in the not-so-distant future, another opportunity would present itself. For the time being, however, Coach Waddell was huddled at a corner table with other coaches, arms folded at his chest and offering few passers-by any sort of acknowledgement.

At the beginning of the food line, Big Pete, in control of the manual counter, had tallied ninety-eight. Most, but not every, table was occupied. Without a lead table, all of the cafeteria-style eating counters were aligned succinctly in military formation. Those of us serving food were placed, offset, just outside the small kitchenette.

"I think luck has shined on them thus far. Maybe just one more game," I replied to Mrs. Rumsfeld as Willie Tee stepped in front of me.

"Why don't ya be givin' me four sausages?" Willie Tee had already ripped into his pancakes, eating along the way to my station. His law enforcement escort for the weekend milled about among the patrons, allowing the Rangers' biggest fan a few moments of meager pride.

Despite insisting each customer only got two links, I could not convince the man and eventually relented. I felt pity for Willie Tee.

"We's got Wheelersville in da championship." Willie Tee decided not to be among the throng of commoners who were already eating at tables and instead, opted to stand next to me. He had missed the semifinal match, and unless he subdued the officer who was assigned to him, Willie Tee would miss the most significant game the Rangers had ever played. South Heaven's biggest fan would be deprived of ultimate satisfaction. "Unbeaten, ya know?" Without a hint of concern for or knowledge of offending those around him with his relatively uncouth manner of eating, he ignored the few unpleasant looks he received from other patrons. "They down along' the rivah."

"I heard it's way over on the other side of the state?" Mrs. Rumsfeld disingenuously asked.

"They called da Whippets?"

With a new pan full of links, I provided Willie Tee with the encyclopedia version of the definition of a Whippet.

"Figured dey be called sumthin' like Rivah People."

With tongs as weapons, I thwarted Willie Tee's attempt at swiping another link before insisting he find a table to consume the remainder of his breakfast. Although my heart ached for Willie Tee and his circumstance, I was quickly losing my ability to digest his cologne mixture of stale beer and body odor. "It's not very sanitary for you to be up here eating."

Many of the Ranger players served either as busboys or gatekeepers collecting money. The stars of the team, however, enjoyed their roles as ambassadors, migrating from table to table, shaking hands and sharing laughs.

"You's know," Willie Tee started, choking down a gulp of coffee. "Ain't nevuh been champs. Dey been darn good, but nevuh champs."

"And they ain't gonna be champs this year either. We're bringing the trophy home, here, to South Heaven." Mrs. Rumsfeld scooped syrup into small bowls for her son to distribute to the various tables.

In place of the military banners that represented the various divisions and squadrons from all four branches of the service, Elder Knause had displayed, temporarily, pennants and colors of the Rangers. Attached to the bulkheads were elongated signs created by the cheerleaders.

"Miss Myra?" said Mrs. Rumsfeld.

I snapped to attention, dropping both links from my tong forks. "I thought you weren't due back 'til tomorrow?"

She appeared tired and rather disheveled in dress, as if she'd just rolled out of bed for an early lecture course. "Morning, Willie Tee."

"Miss Myra. You's gotta car warmed up on Wednesday?"

Miss Myra had no tray of food. "I heard you were here, sport."

"You gotta place lined up to stay in Columbus, Reportuh Man?"

Miss Myra volunteered to relieve us of Willie Tee, escorting him to an open section of a table.

"Maggie, we're gonna need help with serving the Saint Michael's crowd."

Mrs. Rumsfeld received another pan of pancake syrup. "Valerie, I told you I had to leave by eleven. I'm working a shift at my regular job today."

Tall and narrow, with a face to match, Valerie Redding responded with an atrociously sarcastic roll of the eyes. "Maggie, we need your help. Period." In foreman-like precision, Valerie carried a clipboard under her left forearm but offered little help to any of the stations.

"Mass hasn't let out yet at Saint Michael's," Mrs. Rumsfeld commented.

Although the actual conversation could not be heard, the tone of it could most definitely be discerned when Valerie met Coach Waddell outside of the bathroom area.

"Besides, she and her hubby are still flamin' about Friday night," Mrs. Rumsfeld said with a hint of a mean but gratifying grin.

Gary Redding had not been benched due to injury on Friday night. And it had yet to be determined which quarterback would start the championship game on Thursday. Papa Redding was nowhere to be found inside the VFW hall. When asked, Valerie stumbled through an excuse for her husband's absence.

Before the St. Michael's rush hit the morning chow line, I enjoyed a quick break. By the time I found a seat next to Miss Myra, she was surrounded in conversation not only with Willie Tee, but also with Frankie and Aunt Jenny.

"Successful trip, Myra?"

"I heard I missed a classic, sport."

Two young adults, not more than a couple of years removed from high school, hastily approached our section of the table. Without offering too many words, they departed, but not before clandestinely handing Frankie a box.

"I'm sure we can find a spot for this one."

The white Generals helmet was lined down the spine with a blue stripe. Also in blue, affixed to only one side of the helmet, was a Roman emperor crown.

"Town's lost its mind on this team." Miss Myra dropped eye medicine into her right orifice. She blinked repeatedly, as if a metal object had hit her eye. "Can't stop to realize that Phoenix is gone, just like the luggage company and the textbook manufacturer. All settled elsewhere. We're going to die a slow but painful death, and yet all anyone can think about is just one more game."

"And you, Myra?" I rubbed at the red marks on the white helmet, thinking to myself that the previous owner of the helmet had either delivered or received a few good shots. "You dying a slow and painful death?"

Monday

With daylight disappearing earlier and earlier as winter approached, little time existed for outdoor practice.

As a member of the crowd of forty or fifty fans and reporters that hovered around the field, I stood in the mist and fog with Phil and Phil's college buddy who worked for a paper in Marietta.

"This the kid here?" Phil's buddy was another who probably never set foot onto any sports field of play. One would have thought him to be Phil's twin.

"Yeah. Lamont Dickies." Phil pointed toward the Ranger captain leading calisthenics.

"Wheelersville has a big D-line," said Phil's buddy. "Gonna be hard to run."

Phil refuted with a superlative about the Ranger line.

A vintage river city, Wheelersville built its existence on coal mining and water transportation. Similar to South Heaven, Wheelersville had fought for its life since its founding. The demise of mining had placed the town and her people in the same situation facing the Ranger faithful. The school's odd mascot name originated from a long-standing mayor, Russ Sermon, who had a love for the Whippet breed of dog.

In the middle of warmups, Big Pete and the team's line coach, George Linus, a barrel-chested man who served as the school's wrestling coach, approached all of us reporters. Big Pete cleared his throat. "You're all gonna have to leave. Practice is closed."

"What?" came a response from the crowd.

"This ain't right."

Despite the chill, George was in shorts, legs the girth of oak-tree trunks. He stepped forward, scattering the crowd. "You'll need to leave the premises, car and all."

"You can't make us leave."

Without sense, I stepped in between the crowd and the coaches. "Okay, I'm sure that, following practice, coaches and players will be available for any interview?"

Big Pete smiled and nodded.

Before leaving the field, Phil's buddy secured an interview with Coach Waddell. In the meantime, the three of us found an open booth at Frankie's. Monday's special was dedicated to the previous Friday victory: meatball sub, chips, and bottomless soda.

"Gotta place like this in Marietta." Phil's buddy was grotesquely irritating, from his shrill whine to an insatiable appetite to prove his intellect. "This place don't compare to the one back home."

I searched for the newest addition to Frankie's helmet collection.

"Our place back in Marietta's got all this, and more." Phil's buddy neurotically spun the ice in his soda with his chew-scarred straw.

"Yeah?" My acerbic tone could not be disguised. "This place—Frankie's, we call it—does not exist anywhere else in the state or world, for that matter." I ordered another cherry-flavored Pepsi before finding my way toward the bathroom. On the way, I found the Fort Washington helmet.

On top of a glass case, the Generals headgear rested next to the green and gold of East Catholic. The case stood my height and half as wide. With only three shelves, the glass case held a football and a half-dozen action photos of the two previous playoff games.

"Frankie?" I asked as the proprietor exited the men's head. "What is this?"

"Unfinished work."

"Great pictures." I admired the one from the end zone perspective with Lamont Dickies breaking through a hole. "Who's the artist?"

"Me."

"No kidding?"

Frankie offered up his personal complaints of Phil's buddy. "He's an arrogant…"

"You should sit next to him."

Frankie was subdued, almost depressed. "Been thinkin' about sellin' the place, ya know? Maybe retirin' somewhere else. Do some photography."

I stuttered, not knowing whether he was simply stating a fact or soliciting my opinion.

"My brother lives in Tampa. He wants me to come down and help him with his restaurant."

I suggested it would be hard for him, nearly impossible to leave a life one thoroughly enjoys. "I thought South Heaven was your life?" I followed him into a closet-size office, just out of the reach of the galley.

Frankie's office was all about angles and straight lines. Like a military formation, as if a drill instructor had taken a tape measure and ruler to align his subordinates, more than a score of photos were affixed to the wall: framed features of Frankie and local celebrities who had visited the establishment. There were also half a dozen of military bombers in flight.

He caught me staring at the military ones. "B-twenty-nines. Army Air Corps. Moved here after I left the service." Frankie retrieved two elongated and drained ledgers from a file cabinet. "Haven't made money in two years." Although there was no hue on the scale that would overshadow his dark, almost black pupils, irate streaks of blood governed the white of his eye. The redness appeared to bring about pain, and he continually rubbed at the corners of his eyes. "Doubt if I'd getta fair price, considering."

"This is a place of escape for some."

He found another log book and handed it to me. Written in white marker on the black book's cover were the letters I.O.U. "Years of freebies have put us in the red."

"What's going on with you?" Phil barged into the office with his buddy in tow. "You said you'd pick up the tab."

"It's on me," said Frankie.

"Great." Phil and his buddy quickly departed as I dug into my wallet.

"Here." I dropped a sawbuck on Frankie's desk.

He refused it. "Profit now doesn't really matter."

"Then consider it gas money for your trip to Florida."

Tuesday

Tradition, in football lore and days gone by, dictated high school games be played on Thanksgiving Day. In the cold and often snow, fans showed up in droves to watch their team play a rival. The holiday was never complete for folks in Ohio without the annual football game. Despite the criticism often levied against the domain that dominated Ohio high school athletics, the powers-that-be of that organization guessed correctly in establishing a schedule that put the three state championship games on the holiday. The last Thanksgiving in which a South Heaven team played was a game against War Hill in the mid-60s, for simply another PEC win. On Thanksgiving of 1980, the Rangers would contest the Wheelersville Whippets at ten in the morning, for a chance to bring home the ultimate prize in Ohio high school athletics.

By the time I found the paper's office, Butch Boyd was sharing a cup of coffee with Miss Myra.

"Morning, sport. We gotta another possible company to fill the auto plants."

I laid my own cup of coffee on the desk, the large cup only half-full. Aunt Jenny's brew actually tempted a conversion from tea to black coffee, although I included a couple scoops of sugar.

"A vegetable canning plant."

"Company officials are due here next week." Boyd, with the lid removed, blew a steady stream of breath into the steaming liquid.

Off the cuff, I asked if he broached the subject with the union, which stole the smile from Miss Myra and forced Boyd into an uncharacteristic sigh.

"Company only pays minimum wage. It could be our last opportunity."

"I don't think I'm the one who needs to be convinced." I asked.

Miss Myra wandered to my desk to find a perch next to my chair.

My handheld tape recorder had been existing on the same two batteries for several months. I was scouring through my desk drawers for any loose electrical containers. "Is Duane ready for Thursday?"

"Pardon?" he asked.

"Football, sport?" complained Miss Myra.

"Are you kidding? A freshman starting a championship game at quarterback…"

She rolled her eyes then disappeared to the editor's office.

"Why do you invest so much energy in this town? I mean, recruiting companies, local government?" I asked.

As if to announce his presence, a phone began to ring the moment Phil entered the lobby. A couple of loose sheets escaped from the garbled stack crammed under Phil's arm. Of course, he was oblivious to it. "Great. Mister Boyd, you're here. Say, I'd liketa get an interview with Duane?"

"That's up to Coach Waddell, Phil."

Loosing more papers, Phil dropped the stack on his desk then retrieved his ringing phone. "Yeah," he barked. "Yessir! I got it right here." Phil scoured through his stack then realized that what he was searching for had been left on the office floor.

"Small-town Ohio." Boyd tapped the blunt end of a pen on the desk top. The gold custom-made pen spoke to his position in society, earned or otherwise. "When I recruited executives to come work for me at AGM, it was nearly impossible to get them to move here. But when it came time to transfer, not one wanted to leave."

Phil hung up his phone then blurted, "Prognosticator says South Heaven seventeen, Wheelersville ten."

Collecting a calculator and a notebook pad into a spotless black hardbound briefcase, Boyd pushed away from the desk and began moving toward the door. "By the way, have you heard the good news about Myra? She's returning to her old job in Philly."

First Basketball Game

An older gym, the home of the South Heaven cagers was no mecca for fans. By the time Miss Myra and I arrived, nearly six minutes into the first quarter of the junior varsity basketball game, the stands were probably eighty percent occupied. Most of the fans were not so much there to watch the basketball matchup, however. Most were present for the football pep rally that was to occur between the JV and varsity games.

Unfortunately for Coach Paul Burns of South Heaven, three of his returning starters would dress in the wrong uniform. His starting guard, Gary Redding, and two forwards, Hainesworth and Chris Meelee, would be donning football jerseys for the pep rally. From records in the previous two years, South Heaven had an average basketball team. Without three returning starters, including the top-scorer in Redding, Frederick was due to run the Rangers out of the gym.

At the end of the first quarter, the Ranger JV team trailed by two.

Like any aged gymnasium, the heat and noise were irritating.

"And when were you going to tell me?"

She applauded the team's re-entry onto the court for the start of the second.

Without much grace, two gentlemen, carrying an aroma of stale beer, stumbled by us in search of open seats.

The Frederick JV team had a tall center, with an awkward, almost flat-footed stride. Hhe was on fire with a jump hook shot.

"Well?"

Quite a few of the football players had filtered into the gym, lining the end boundaries of the court. The evening's attire was road-game white.

Miss Myra, claiming to be thirsty, climbed over knees and ankles in search of the concession area. In her absence, a man used to walking the sidelines, instead of sitting in the bleachers, pushed by me without offering any apology then sat in Miss Myra's open seat.

"Uhh, someone's sitting here."

"Do you know who I am?"

"It won't really matter who you are, when she gets back."

"My son's the quarterback and point guard of the basketball team." He tore at the sleeves of his expensive and snug brown-leather jacket to remove it from his person then gave a disingenuous head nod in response to a wave from the front row. Papa Redding was a large enough man that doffing his jacket, in the cramped bleacher space, created a disturbance. "And lemme tell you something, that freshman'll never be able to lead us to no championship on Thursday. My boy's the only one who can win the game. God help that Boyd kid, if he plays and we lose. You put that in your paper!"

In every organization, club, team, town, or city, there must always be at least one Papa Redding—a man who could not appreciate the game.

Of course, I could not resist adding my own jab. "Lamont's the one carrying this team. Quarterback or not. This team goes only as far as Lamont can take them."

With his insurance pedigree, Papa Redding believed too much in his spoken word, and it was often a few octaves above that of the normal man. "Listen here!" he blurted as Myra finally returned from her extensive trip. Face in crimson, he retrieved his pointed finger. "My boy's been wronged. Wronged by Waddell!" Without much chivalry, he acknowledged Miss Myra then slid as far as he could from the two of us.

As the JV game bled into the fourth quarter, the clown-foot center for Frederick began to dominate and pushed the Pirate lead into double-digits. The Frederick coach, who I also coincidentally recognized as the football coach who had berated me in the press box, refused to hold the ball and stall the clock. With each possession, he forced the ball to his center. As the score expounded to a twenty-point margin of difference, the coach refused to substitute for his starters, drawing displeasure from some in the stands. By the time the buzzer sounded to end the game, the margin of victory for the coach was twenty-five. I supposed it was an apparent form of retribution.

As quickly as Ted Foxx could, he rushed the two JV teams off the court. In the meantime, more and more fans continued to pile into the gymnasium. A mobile podium was hastened toward the middle of the court, directly in front of the Ranger logo painted on the hardwood. All of Coach Waddell's players had disappeared into the lobby that led to the locker rooms.

With many more horns than woodwinds, the pep band littered the stuffy gym further with "Across the Field." Foxx cued the bandmaster to cue his musicians to halt. "Good evening, South Heaven!" Resting on either side of the podium was The Rifle, the Zugellder Trophy, and the recently earned hardware for the Regional Championship. "I want to thank each of you for coming out to support your Rangers. We are two days away from concluding the greatest season in the history of South Heaven football!" His eruption stirred the crowd. "There's one trophy that is missing up here. And you know what I'm talkin' about! Come Thursday, we will have that trophy."

The pep band broke into the fight song.

"And now, let's bring out the coach of your Rangers: Coach Waddell!"

With the exception of those hundreds of fans who traveled from Frederick, the stands erupted in standing applause.

The pep rally was cased with irony. Frederick was steaming over South Heaven's entry into the playoffs through the back door. Frederick faithful wholeheartedly believed their team belonged in the playoffs. Looking around at the stone-cold faces who were seated during the standing ovation, I could not help but smile.

"We wouldn't be where we are without your support." Coach Waddell had yet to overcome his apparent fear of the microphone. "All of us, we owe you all thanks." Even if taking into consideration his lack of a rah-rah personality, Coach Waddell appeared abnormally subdued for a man on the verge of coaching in a championship game. Since the Fort Washington game, he had become nearly reclusive, unable to be reached for any story or interview.

A few obvious Frederick fans began to depart the stands, to the consternation of the South Heaven faithful.

Coach Waddell quickly yielded to his captains. The remainder of the squad joined their captains at center court. With the exception of a few, the team had a diffident disposition. It was, of course, Gary Redding who took control of the microphone. Through incoherent screams, he worked up the crowd, eventually getting most of them to spell out R-A-N-G-E-R-S before shouting the nickname three times. He snatched the regional trophy then lifted it into the air. "We will bring the state trophy home on Thursday!"

A few voices in the crowd could be heard chanting the last name of the Rangers' tailback.

"We wanna thank all of you," said the unassuming Lamont Dickies. "All of us play for you all, the people of South Heaven." His vocal presentation was taciturn. The awkwardness in his face was symbolic of the pep rally and the season, for that matter—impromptu and spur of the moment.

Wednesday at the Blue Moon Hotel

The nearest establishment of the modest hotel chain was fifteen minutes from Ohio Stadium. With a caravan of nearly fifty, we occupied two-thirds of the rooms in the three-story hotel.

On the northern edge of the city, the hotel of our choosing was one of two parked off exit 111, near the French Market: a themed collage of restaurants and shops that sold and represented fare from various countries. Advertising for the establishment was praise and recommendation from the hotel desk clerks, Kathy and her cohort Becky. Before cashing in on their dinner suggestion, however, Miss Myra and I drove onto the Ohio State Fairgrounds.

"Daddy used to bring us here every year. He loves the novelty of Ohio."

Devoid of activity, except for the naked branches of oaks, maples, and pears shivering in the cold wind, the fairgrounds resembled more of a Hugo scene of desolation than a representation of a celebration in Ohio.

"All those visits to Pittsburgh that your father is making aren't business-related, are they?"

Miss Myra directed the vehicle to another parking lot.

Adjacent to the fairgrounds was the complex of the Ohio Historical Society.

"The Alleghany Cancer Center called the paper before we left, looking for you, Myra."

Oblivious to my inquiry, Miss Myra insisted that we enter the museum, despite having less than thirty minutes before the doors were locked to observe closing time. A meager entrance fee provided us access to the dual exhibits on display for the month of November.

On the main bill was an artifact history of the Shawnee Indians, a brilliant collection from the early and mid-eighteenth century.

"How long does he have?" I continued, retrieving one of the scores of pamphlets held in a three-foot-wide by four-foot-tall free-standing stained wooden display case—an oversized spice rack. My pamphlet advertised the hiking trails around Ash Cave near the Hocking Hills area. It was but one of many that ballyhooed the various attractions the state of Ohio had to offer.

"Don't worry none, sport. Daddy's in good hands. Besides, he loves the Rangers and South Heaven too much to leave us." She then read verbatim, from a sample pamphlet, the daily schedule of Hughes' Ferry from Sandusky to the various islands on Lake Erie.

"How long have you known your dad was the mystery Prognosticator?"

Miss Myra commented that she possessed a weaker-than-normal stomach, one that would probably not be conducive to an enjoyable water voyage. She replaced the ferry pamphlet with one on the U.S. Air Force Museum.

"He wants me to take over the role next year, Myra. Why would he do that if he loved the Rangers so much?"

"So are you taking the job?" Miss Myra stared through the glass at a model and miniscule display of a characteristic Shawnee village.

Olive-drab coveralls devoured a troll-like frame. The mop bucket was no more than a heavy chain shackled to his ankle. Well past any suggested age of retirement, the museum's janitor hardly noticed the two of us before disappearing into a cleaning closet.

"And the paper? Who's going to run the paper, Myra, when you leave? Philly, right? Back to civilization?"

Filling a second floor of the society was an exhibit dedicated to the memory of Ohio's Medal of Honor recipients. Frustrated with her lack of responses to my questioning, I separated from Miss Myra and rode the narrow escalator to the pre-twentieth-century wars exhibit. I stopped to read about the exploits of the thirteen Medal of Honor winners. For every individual, there was some form of a biography.

During the opening stages of the Battle of Shiloh, Private Henry Cooper, a mere teenager from Ripley, fell on the battlefield, seriously wounded. Despite multiple wounds to his left leg, Cooper gathered his senses and began pulling fellow wounded men of the Eighty-First Ohio from the battlefield to a rear aid station. Under withering fire, from both frontline troops and snipers, Cooper carried some twenty-five wounded soldiers to the aid station. Eventually, he succumbed to blood loss and fell inconspicuously on the battlefield.

"Walk over to the Vietnam War display, would ya?" Old Man Schmidt was decked out in his best all-white double-breasted church suit.

"How the ... did you get in here?"

"Private First Class Burle Wallace Utley was a kid from Harper County," Old Man Schmidt continued, despite my insistence the museum was closing. "Joined the Corps right after school."

I stopped guessing how Old Man Schmidt found me in such odd places. "Utley? As in…"

Moving with me toward the elevator, he continued, "In the Fall of '67, he held off two companies of Vietcong with his squad of eight and two BARs."

"Wally? The same guy that struggles getting through a radio broadcast?"

As the elevator door crept to closure, he snuck his cane into the opening.

A little shocked, I quickly reacted by deploying the open-door button. "Whhat…"

He smiled. "There's magic in this game called high school football. This team's special, and they've allowed all of us to feel special. I guarantee you ain't never gonna forget these past few months."

Thursday

Combining the early-morning game time with the traffic of a holiday and the half a dozen roads needed to navigate to reach the stadium, the caravan departed the Blue Moon lot at six o'clock sharp.

Coach Waddell and his team were actually housed on campus in a dormitory less than five minutes from Ohio Stadium. Breakfast was served on campus and free of charge for both teams. Near half-past seven, the two buses hauling the Rangers pulled into the lot area where our caravan had established a tailgate party.

The forecasters for the Columbus area had predicted a cold and crisp Thanksgiving holiday. A bright sun welcomed us to the day, but even with no wind present, temperatures were hovering in the high twenties.

Several vans and a couple of RVs hauled a score of grills, a few portable griddles, and a couple of monstrous coffee urns. To no one's surprise, it was Aunt Jenny in the lead, grilling sausage and bacon, pancakes, and scrambled eggs. Her concoctions were nothing short of tasty, given the extreme cold and lack of resources.

The South Heaven fans were true amateurs in the art of tailgating. It was obvious that nerves were apparent in the faithful. Enjoyment and smiles were few in number. Confidence could not be found in eyes or faces. The cold only exacerbated the nervous tension.

Occupying two lawn chairs under the awning of the nearest RV, Miss Myra and I were hardly enjoying the cold either.

Miss Myra was absorbed in the steam from her coffee. "You … uhh … think you'll be okay with the camera today, sport?"

Rikki Sake had been called away on a family emergency. Without a suitable replacement, the paper had no ability to shoot photos, despite the most important game in the history of South Heaven. Therefore, I carried a 35mm camera in hopes that my shutter would be quick enough to capture even the lamest of action. "I took a class in photography, you know, to cover the journalism major. It was an early-morning start, and I missed more than my fair share of classes. But I think I could squeeze the trigger."

"On the sidelines, right?"

Aunt Jenny wandered the ranks, refilling coffee cups and mugs. "I got two kinds." She caressed two large silver-colored carafes and was covered from head to toe in knitwear and wool. "This'n here has a bit of back home." She winked.

Miss Myra gasped with the first sip of Irish coffee, prompting a mother's grin from Aunt Jenny.

As the team amassed directly outside the tandem of buses, they received numerous cheers from the tailgaters.

From my location, I snapped a few shots of Coach Waddell's crew being led into the caverns of Ohio Stadium.

For the elite and more successful Ohio teams, Ohio Stadium, the home of the mighty and beloved Buckeyes, was the promised land or mecca of the journey to a championship. A few years prior to South Heaven's trip, Ohio moved its football championship game to the state's ultimate university.

Wheelersville held up the rich tradition of football in southeast Ohio. Throughout the nascent establishment of the professional game, more than a handful of various semipro ball teams called the southeast corner of the state home. Hard-core blue-collar towns and cities like Wheelersville provided the newly founded professional leagues with a fan base that had an insatiable appetite for the game and a talent pool of toughened men to fill rosters.

A mainstay in the final four of the AA championship, the Wheelersville Whippets had played bridesmaid a couple of times, but never the bride. Like South Heaven, they rolled into the title game with an unbeaten record. Unlike the Rangers, however, Wheelersville had thoroughly beaten opponents by an average margin of thirty-two points. Until then, the toughest game on the schedule had been with a rival in the Southern Athletic Conference, Portsmouth East. In the last game of the regular season, with a playoff spot on the line, Wheelersville outlasted East by six points.

With a party of thirty or more, I walked through the main gate, eyes wide open, knowing my press pass would get me onto the field.

"Whereya goin,' partner?" The grizzled and shriveled older man, dressed in a yellow security jacket, stole some of my juvenile enthusiasm. He reminded me of the laconic and often unpleasant ushers who worked the lower sections of Major League ballparks.

"I work for the paper in South Heaven, here to take pictures." It was not difficult to see over the man's head, even with the scarlet beanie attached to his gray ski cap.

Over the top of his bifocal lenses, Mister Security read the credentials on my press pass, as if struggling through a job application. "Already let one of you guys in from that there South Heaven Sun." And I thought immediately of Phil.

I tucked my badge back into my coat pocket.

"Only s'posta let one in per paper, but I make an exception for ya."

"You're kidding, one per paper? There can't be more than twenty-thousand people combined in both cities that are playing today to fill this big bowl of a stadium." I suggested that certainly there would be room for one more representative of the paper.

"Don't make the rules."

Fortunately for me and the South Heaven faithful, the full sun was spreading whatever warmth available on the Rangers' sideline. Across the field, however, shadows still persisted. By the time I found the sideline, the Whippets were in full gear and warming up on one side of the field. As the Rangers began to filter onto the field, I wandered onto the actual playing surface and could then only imagine the great ones who once excelled for the Buckeyes. I bent at the knee just to run my hand across the carpet surface.

"Astroturf." Coach Waddell blew some warmth into his cupped hands. He hid his eyes with pitch-black sunglasses.

Stuck in the doldrums of embarrassment, I rose, accompanied by a couple of coughs.

"Sure is big." He glared up at the far reaches of the stadium.

I asked him if he had any worries.

He snapped the buttons on his maroon coaching jacket. The silk-screened letters over his left breast indicated it belonged to him. "We'll make sure you get a few good shots today."

Gathered around the large scarlet "O" at midfield, several Rangers, dressed only in game pants and heavy jackets, had become instant fans of the Wheelersville placekicker. While the majority of teammates tossed footballs, jogged, fidgeted with equipment, or simply chatted in pairs or groups, over a dozen stood motionless, staring at the Whippets' kicker boom kick after kick high and deep.

Number one for the Whippets had inched the ball backwards to the forty-five-yard line. In each of his five-yard segment stops, he was long, straight, and true. The ball seemed to rocket off his right foot. As he lined up for the fifty-five-yard attempt, more Ranger fans came to life. With ease, number one drilled the long field goal. After another two successful attempts at fifty-five yards, he moved the ball back another five. On his first attempt, the ball hit the crossbar and bounded over.

I focused in on the kicker, trying to nail down my timing. From foot touch to a distance of ten yards, I succeeded in tracking the flight of the ball. Beyond that, I was happy my profession was not in snapping pictures.

With three short blasts from his whistle, Coach Waddell retrieved all players and grouped them in a circle near the thirty. "Don't have time for worries now. I got me fifty-five kids in need of a little guidance."

As the Rangers broke into their individual drills, I snapped off a few shots of Duane Boyd receiving all snaps from center, then I climbed stair after concrete stair until reaching the Summit.

Again, WSHV assumed an open-air press box that took on the identity of the great outdoors: cold and cold.

"At least we get some shelter up here, boy."

Without solicitation, I helped myself to the thermos of coffee on the press counter. "Where's Wally?"

"Ya even know how to work that camera?"

Although focusing was sufficient, I didn't have the ability to zoom in at the field level. "Did he forget something?"

"Who, Wally?" Old Man Schmidt rubbed his hands together to generate some warmth. "Wally, he won't be joinin' us today."

"Won't be joining us? It's the championship game!" I laughed. "Only the biggest game in South Heaven, ever, and Wally's not on the air? Come on!"

Old Man Schmidt adjusted the size strap on his radio headset. "Wally ain't never been no fan of the cold."

"This is the championship. We need Wally here, for crying out loud!"

Old Man Schmidt assured me that the Rangers would not be affected, whether Wally was in the booth or not.

"Well, is he okay?"

"Apparently, we're in for a real treat with this Wheelersville quarterback. Garcia's his name." He read from the roster page of the program. "Sometimes, boy, we just don't realize why we're put on this earth."

"What? Listen, is Wally okay or not?"

He tossed me the magazine-like program. "Wally's in good hands."

For each of the three title games, A, AA, and AAA, a program had been compiled containing all six teams. For the price of three quarters, a fan received six rosters, previous playoff game summaries, and vital statistics that included individual leaders. Under the Whippets' bio, Rudy Garcia's numbers were impressive, mostly his number of attempted passes: 510, to be exact.

The other two contests listed in the program were the A and the big-school AAA matchup. In the game scheduled for 2 p.m., the unbeaten and number-one ranked Bristol Catholic Bishops invited a challenge from the Newton Braves out of Ashtabula County. The big-school game was the marquee event of the day and one of the most anticipated matchups in a decade. Out of Cincinnati was the parochial powerhouse St. Thomas. Sporting an unbeaten and top ranking, the Crusaders were due to battle Canton Howard, which started a prized Ohio State recruit at tailback.

From the press box, the crowd for both South Heaven and Wheelersville appeared to be paltry at best, when compared to the overall size of the stadium. Bunched between the thirty-yard lines, neither set of fans could make a valiant effort at filling the lower bowl of Ohio Stadium. Still, collectively, fans were able to generate definitive and audible noise, applauding their respective teams as they left the field.

With a mere twenty-five minutes before kick-off, I somewhat shamefully left Old Man Schmidt, weaseled my way past another Golden Buckeye security guard, and found the Rangers' locker room—the same one used by one of the nine other Big Ten teams that play year after year at Ohio Stadium. Large enough to conceal a truck or oversized prehistoric mammal, the locker room provided shelter for me while I honed in on Coach Waddell and his pregame speech.

"Men, this game ain't no more difficult than any other—if we execute. Execution's our one key to winnin.' Control what's within your own hands, and I guarantee ya, we'll walk outta here winners. One game, men. One game is what dis season comes down here to. But ain't about just one game. Today's about our season. Men, I guarantee ya that all of ya will look back on this season and remember it forever—if ya win here today. A loss, and all you worked for'll be gone. It's up to you whether we walk outta here champs."

The reserved Father Greist, the leader of the St. Anthony's flock and long-time Ranger fan, requested that the team grasp hands. Decked out in his best maroon sweater, he led the Lord's Prayer.

"This is your day, men," said Coach Waddell, after thanking Father Greist. "This is your day to represent your town. This is your day tuh do sumthin' great for your town." Coach Waddell was smooth with his tone, in huge contrast to the last instances when I saw him speak publicly. Excitement began to build in his team. "People make great things happen. It's your day, men, to play like champs—and don't let no one take that from ya. Not today. Not ever, 'cause you are champs. I'm proud of each of ya'll. There ain't no other men I'd wanna take intuh battle with me. You've had one amazin' season. Don't let it end today!"

In a meager jog, following an uproarious frenzy that Coach Waddell eventually instilled into his squad, I trailed behind the team toward the field—as excited as the players to assume a position.

Coach Waddell collected his team at the tunnel entrance but relented the stage to his opponent.

Bursting from the opposite tunnel, the red and gray of Wheelersville flooded the field, led by three male students accompanied by a half a dozen Whippet dogs, tongues and tails wagging with excitement.

As Wheelersville filtered from the celebratory pile and the Whippet dogs were led to the sidelines, Coach Waddell took control of the moment. With "Across the Field" barely audible in the stadium confines, the Rangers sprinted onto the field, careful not to collide with the captains' meeting at midfield.

I, too, wanted to sprint, but decided instead to zoom in on the coin flip. I was able to read the lips of the referee awarding the ball to Lamont Dickies and Gary Redding. With a negligible breeze and powerful offenses for both teams, possession of the ball would be paramount.

From a reporter who covered sports in southeastern Ohio, I learned all the vitals on the Whippets' kicker—of course, after he boomed the opening kick seven yards deep into the end zone. Gavin Carlyle, with two state records, was to be the next placekicker for the Mountaineers of West Virginia.

From the twenty, with the weight of the entire town upon his shoulders, Coach Waddell fell victim to predictability: Lamont Dickies off left tackle.

As expected by many, it was Boyd who grabbed the starting quarterback spot. On the sideline, his teammate and captain, Redding, held the position next to Coach Waddell. He had helmet and chinstrap secured, as if prepared to enter the game at a moment's notice. Plugging the Rangers, I bragged to the Wheelersville reporter about our freshman quarterback, embellishing ever so slightly. Boyd's second play from the line of scrimmage was his own number on a sprint option.

At my position, I was on the same latitude as the line of scrimmage and, therefore, held a perfect camera angle. I zoomed in on Boyd hustling down the line, with just a hint of Dickies in tow. "Pitch it! Pitch…"

The lengthy arm of a Whippet defensive end struck down the tardy pitch.

Both Boyd and Dickies hastened after the bounding ball, but it was too late: Ball recovered on the South Heaven fifteen.

On his first toss, Rudy Garcia, the Whippets' quarterback, threw into a welcoming corner end zone and brought his hometown fans to their feet. A perfect lob fell on the hands of his receiver, just in front of the orange pylon. Judging Garcia's reaction to the touchdown pass, he had grown accustomed to such a play.

The South Heaven fans had grown accustomed as well—to falling behind early in the game. Their hero Lamont Dickies took another handoff on the first play of the second possession and reassured those who made the two-hour trip by car that all was not lost. An open hole helped produce an eight-yard gain.

"I'd be puttin' Redding into the game." Inevitably, Phil found me. "We ain't gonna win with Boyd."

Both the second- and third-down plays supported Phil's theory. Boyd fumbled the snap from center on second down then proceeded to overthrow Durning on a curl route.

Phil's ruby-red stocking cap was nearly pulled over the rim of his eyeglasses.

"Where's your buddy from Marietta?"

Redding's punt was average at best.

"On the other side," Phil said, before grimacing at the sight of the Whippets' return-man gaining twenty yards.

Rudy Garcia possessed a delivery of the football that coveted the classic theory of quarterbacking: over the top and elbow to the sky. The ball was delivered crisply, without a flaw in the spiral. Labor-intensive, the stroke could lull others to sleep, however. His second pass was a bullet to a crossing receiver near the Ranger eighteen.

My camera focused on a frustrated group of South Heaven defenders.

The flow of the game halted slightly when Big Pete trotted onto the field for a time-out.

"We ain't never gonna come back on this Garcia, unless Redding's in the game." Phil had become adept at voice-recording the action of any given game, for eventual translation to print. It was all he could do, though, to get his four D batteries to operate his tape recorder. "Dang thing!"

By the time Big Pete left the field, Kyle Knause had a new member of his defense, and his formation was something out of a sandlot playbook. From his standard five-man front, Big Pete replaced one of his down linemen with, of all players, Gary Redding. To the left of Knause, on the wide side of the field, Redding assumed one of three linebacker positions.

"What's Waddell doing?" demanded Phil.

On first down, Big Pete's strategy and gamble paid dividends. Redding's task, apparently, was to dog and mimic Garcia, following him everywhere. The Ranger quarterback-turned-defender played a draw to perfection, hauling down his counterpart for a two-yard loss.

It appeared that either Redding had practiced with the first-team defense or had tackled in the past, and he blitzed on second down and tripped up Garcia for another two-yard loss.

The camera never snapped a single shot of two great plays. But on third down, I was poised and not about to fail the team, and I captured a moment in time that could have doomed the fate of South Heaven.

Under pressure from another blitz, Garcia lofted a toss into the end zone. His receiver athletically snagged the ball over the opposite shoulder from where he was looking. With such a difficult play, Garcia's receiver, number twenty-one, juggled the ball before dancing along the end zone line.

The back judge emphatically ruled the pass incomplete.

I had worked my way close to the goal line and had a perfect angle to see number twenty-one drag his foot inside for six points. "Oh boy, I think that may have been a bad call."

"No way! He was out! The call stands!" Phil waved his arms to mimic the referee, looking every bit the fool.

With the failed third down completion, Carlyle was sent into the game, and was automatic from such a meager distance, pushing the Whippets ahead by ten.

Remaining long enough to see Lamont Dickies actually return a kick, I had my fill of the elements and headed on a jog to the Summit. In the passageway, Rhonda found me as she broke away from the guy selling programs.

"Hey, College Boy." Beyond the effervescent shade of red lipstick, she glistened with genuine excitement. "Ain't seen ya down at the restaurant lately. No matter." She glanced into a pocket mirror, primping her eyebrows. "Me and Rick, we're leavin' town after this game. Sure woulda liked just ta miss the game, but Rick, he says it's a chance of a lifetime, whatever that means."

"Well, good luck!"

"Goin' away. Ain't never comin' back neither. Nosuh, you'll never see me again."

"Okay."

"Don't ya wanna know where I'm goin'?" She snuck her hand under my elbow. "Down to Virginia Beach. It's for lovers, ya know, Virginia."

I peeled her hand from my person. "I'm sure you'll like it there."

"Sure I'll like it anywhere better if you were takin' me there." Without quickness, she leaned into me and dropped a kiss on my lips.

To the roar and applause from the shaded side of the stadium, I ran from Rhonda, bidding her good fortune with Rick and hoping that no South Heaven resident saw that kiss. By the time I reached the Summit, two more sudden eruptions occurred on the Whippets' side.

Old Man Schmidt shook his head with disappointment. "We punted again, and they've done nuthin' but complete passes all the way down the field."

With a first-and-goal situation, Rudy Garcia had the ball at the Rangers' eight and the hopes of an anguished town in the palm of his hand. Garcia took a shotgun snap and rolled right.

"He looks and looks ... and fires."

The ball ricocheted off a Ranger helmet, sprung from an extended reach of a Whippet, and then fell softly into the waiting arms of number eighty.

When the first-quarter gun sounded, the sun had finally christened the entire bowl of the stadium's lower deck, and the Rangers trailed by 17.

Third and six and with the ball at the Rangers' own twenty-four, most of us from the western part of the state were wondering if Coach Waddell would send the play in with Boyd or Redding.

A loss in confidence was evident in the freshman's gait as he jogged back into his huddle. Unfortunately, the second quarter was not about to be kind to Duane Boyd: An overthrown screen pass forced another punt.

"Folks, the only thing I've got to report so far is Redding's punts. And there's another. It's short, and it hits a Wheelersville player! It hit someone, and now it's free."

South Heaven's best field position would come as a result of a botched attempt at fielding a punt. But a break is a break. From the Whippets' forty-nine, Duane Boyd handed to Lamont Dickies.

"A huge hole! Dickies to the outside," Old Man Schmidt called to those who remained in Western Ohio.

The Ranger tailback tore through the opening and netted his team thirty-one yards.

"From the twenty, folks. There's the snap. Pitch to Dickies. No! A reverse."

Churning his legs as fast as he could, Sammy Gwynn secured a precarious exchange from Dickies, found the corner on a confused defensive end, and made a beeline for the end zone.

"Touchdown Rangers! Touchdown Rangers! Good God Almighty, Sammy Gwynn scores!"

The roar from South Heaven's stands shamed that from the favorite Whippets. Despite the vastness of the Horseshoe, the crowd noise was heartening.

As a favor to all who climbed the obstacles to reach the pinnacle of life, I snapped several shots of Stu Ginnette, from set-up to approach to follow-through. Unfortunately, I failed to track the ball ... as it sailed wide right of the target. I halted the shutter with Stu standing over his tee box, head flagged. His miss kept the deficit at an odd eleven.

Ginnette allowed the previous mistake to carry over into his kick-off, a shank that traveled a mere twenty-five yards.

"Folks, definitely not a good idea to give Garcia the ball at his own forty." Old Man Schmidt reapplied duct tape to his microphone.

As if awakened into another dimension, Garcia's first call from the line of scrimmage was an off-tackle dive to his lone set back. Apparently satisfied with a gain of only three yards, Wheelersville crashed into the line twice more, which brought about their initial fourth-down situation.

"Folks, not quite sure what they're doin' here."

With only a half-yard to attain to continue the drive, Rudy Garcia aligned his offense in the shotgun formation. With his receivers spreading out the defense, Garcia called his own number, darting toward the line.

"No! He didn't make it. First down Rangers!"

On a sweep right, Lamont Dickies followed Ricky Green into the open field before being tripped up near the first-down marker.

For the next four clock minutes, South Heaven methodically marched the ball to within three yards of a score. Three yards off-tackle here, five yards on a sweep there, and three yards on a counter, Lamont Dickies pounded at his opponent. Coach Waddell mixed in a couple of dives to his fullback. Tradition had been excused the weeks previous. On Thanksgiving Day, though, it was to be Dickies who would, once again, carry the load for Coach Waddell.

"First and goal, folks. Three minutes to go here in the half."

Boyd reversed, pivoted, and took off down the line to make amends for previous mistakes. Fortunately, there was no defensive end to option. Durning had taken him completely out of the play. Boyd planted and cut toward the goal line.

"Touchdown Boyd! The Freshman goes in untouched!"

A rumble of erupted noise from the Ranger side injected the colossal stadium with excitement.

From their own thirty-six, Wheelersville assumed control of the ball, and Garcia wasted no time.

"He throws. Complete!"

Two quick passes across the middle did more to kill the clock than progress the ball down the field.

"Almost at a minute to play, and it's third down."

With his strong arm, Garcia threw a bullet on an out that netted eleven yards. After yet another short completion, Garcia stopped the clock with a time-out; thirty-one seconds to go.

Big Pete pulled his entire squad to the sidelines, sending them back onto the field just as Wheelersville broke their huddle.

"Garcia in the 'gun. There's the snap. Fades into the pocket. Throws over the middle. It's caught by number eighty. He fumbles. No!"

The fans of Wheelersville shot to their feet as Adams, number nineteen, picked up the bounding ball in full stride and bolted down the sideline.

Luke Post rallied himself and began his chase with a ten-yard deficit.

"He's to the twenty! Post's right behind him."

Sacrificing life and limb, Luke Post leaped after his pursuit, body flat and parallel to the turf. With the assistance from a divine spirit, the luck of the Rangers, or those in South Heaven who had refused to succumb to fate...

"Post trips him up! Post got him! Good God Almighty, Luke Post chased the boy down! Whatta play."

From the eight, with less than twenty seconds to play, Garcia lofted a toss into the end zone.

"Incomplete! Off the hands of the receiver down there."

At the thirteen-second mark, Garcia took the snap from center then shuttled a toss to his back.

"Time-out! Time-out Wheelersville. He got up to the six, but no further. Oh my!"

I had already conceded the touchdown to Garcia and, as a result, could barely stomach watching him bring his team back to line.

A three-man front combatted Rudy Garcia on the next play.

"He steps to his right. Now, he scrambles ... throoows ... Outta bounds!"

Garcia's pass just pulled his receiver out of play.

"That's gotta be halftime, folks. Gotta be the end."

The officials were perplexed with the ending of the half.

"Has to be the end of the half," insisted Old Man Schmidt. "No way did that play only take six seconds!"

Both Big Pete and Coach Waddell berated the head referee for at least three to four minutes. Their arms flailing and fingers pointing toward the scoreboard, neither were able to win the argument.

Before one second could be added to an empty time clock, Carlyle was on the field and readying himself for a chip shot of a field goal.

Coach Waddell tried to ice the kid with a time-out.

"Get right back into it, then it's just taken from us!"

All became mute when Carlyle drilled a kick to add three points to end the half.

Yet another transition, and every fan I recognized stopped me to argue the lame call that ended the half. The disgruntled crowd was hovered outside of the main concession area, sharing the same gripe and a cup of coffee, with the exception of Papa Redding.

"Our offense is dead," Redding insisted. "Dead, I tell you."

Accepting a cup of coffee from a beleaguered Hank Knause, who was frustrated more with his son's play than the official's call, I replied to Papa Redding's assertion, "We have two touchdowns on the board. What do you want?"

In front of a crowd, through the excessive large hole on his round face, Redding let loose several epithets, including a few of the personal nature. He was held in the same regard as Phil, though—ignored by many and tolerated by few. However, he was indeed a true native son and a die-hard South Heavener who, with his business influence, could claim a stake as town royalty. His cup of hot chocolate splattered on the cement floor when he tossed it against the trash can.

"I swear I don't know what he's gonna do when Gary leaves." Not only had Sweetie been given the time off to make the trip to Columbus, but she had also been given a pink slip. "Frankie's dun gonna close the shop. Plannin' on packin' up and leavin' next week."

"I thought he was planning on selling?"

"Saturday." She tied her stocking cap under her chin. "He's plannin' on havin' one last hoorah for the team and the town, I guess."

By the time the Rangers filtered through and out of the tunnel, I was somewhat parched for breath, making my way to the field turf. On the way, I neglected to offer assistance to Phil and Phil's buddy, who were both verbally abusing the security guard. Neither man was being permitted to haul his load of food and drink onto the field.

Paper-thin but grayish clouds began to find the range of the sun and close in. Light, nearly transparent flurries fell without damage or even annoyance. It was a Thanksgiving Day of old.

The Whippets were due to receive first. Two receivers were deep and separated, with cleats on the ten-yard line.

Stu Ginnette propped the ball on his orange tee then reversed and jogged back toward his huddle of ten.

"You believe that guy made us eat and drink everything before we could come out here?" Phil had both a mustard and ketchup stain on his upper-body clothing, a black trench coat stretching to his ankles.

Phil's buddy insisted Wheelersville would never relinquish the lead. In fact, he was willing to lay down twenty-five bucks on a three-touchdown spread.

Ginnette hung the ball in the air.

"Tell ya what. Ten bucks and you don't talk to me the rest of game?" I said.

Despite the halftime break, Rudy Garcia remained sharp and connected on his first two passes: a ten-yard out and a twelve-yard curl.

From the forty-four of South Heaven, I captured a series of photos of the Whippets' hurler as he took a shotgun snap then rolled to his right and delivered a strike to this tight end.

On three plays, Big Pete's defense had surrendered thirty-five yards.

As the flurry activity acquiesced into heavier actual snowflakes, the weather forecasters were, once again, proven incorrect when the sun completely disappeared behind a blanket of gray.

Almost perfect with his play for the afternoon, Garcia appeared fallible on a projected slant pass that sailed behind the intended target and into the arms of Luke Post.

The camera caught Post from the time the ball ricocheted off his shoulder pad to his shocked and frustrated reaction when he dropped the pass.

Although it was certain that Garcia had seen the solid white precipitation in the past, his next two plays suggested differently: a fumbled snap and wobbled forward pass that died short of the target. The camera lens found the Wheelersville quarterback tugging to doff his helmet before looking up at the sky and shaking his head.

For Carlyle, the fourth-down situation left him with a forty-eight-yard attempt.

"He's got this," insisted Phil's buddy. "Automatic."

The ball sailed high, long, and true.

"Twenty-three to thirteen," Phil's buddy said.

Against the wind and with the snow sprouting the turf, Duane Boyd brought his squad up the line. Nothing had changed from first to second half, despite Papa Redding's belief that the offense had been nonexistent. Boyd's first-down option run, however, supported the beliefs of the senior Redding: A misread on a keeper netted nothing.

"Our defense is too tough," laughed Phil's buddy.

I was able to keep Phil's buddy at bay when Dickies bounced an off-tackle run to the outside for a gain of seven.

"Go ahead, eat up the clock with all those runs."

Third and three brought no hesitation from Coach Waddell. He called for his freshman to hit Billy Hainesworth on a slant pass left, which kept the drive alive.

A rather large contingent of fans entered the stadium through the closed horseshoe end. They were dressed in blue and gold and numbering in the several hundreds.

"Saint Thomas," said Phil.

South Heaven's faithful welcomed the Cincinnati contingent with a roar following a Dickies run of eleven yards. No fan had time to regain their seat when Ricky Green tore up the middle for eight, banging off defenders like an oblong pinball.

A gust came up that irritated exposed skin and halted, momentarily, the South Heaven mojo.

"Third and ten. Does that coach of yours got anything in the playbook, other than giving it to your tailback?" asked Phil's buddy.

Then, Boyd took the snap and dropped five steps into the pocket. On his fifth step, he lofted a perfect spiral toward the sidelines and into the arms of his tight end, Durning.

Both Phil and I lauded the play.

Lamont Dickies gained a mere three on a first-down scamper.

With the emotion of the game and the ire for Phil's buddy's arrogance, the camera fell still, which was probably fortunate considering the second-down play.

Duane Boyd tossed the ball to his tailback on a swing pass left. Unfortunately, Boyd felt the pressure of an all-out blitz and threw the pass behind Dickies.

The lateral toss was recovered by Dickies only after losing eight yards, though.

Yet another third down faced the freshman. With fifteen yards to gain, he saw Green exit and another receiver enter.

"Kid doesn't have the experience," insisted Phil's buddy. "I've seen it before."

Experience, though, Boyd needed not, and he handed the ball to Dickies on a sprint draw.

Weaving in and out of traffic, Dickies ardently accumulated thirteen yards of the fifteen needed. With two defenders on him, he leaned to reach the twenty-three.

At the five-minute mark, with the wind against him, snow decorating the turf, and the play of the game and season impending, Coach Waddell used a time-out. He pulled his quarterback out of the huddle and toward the sideline.

I focused the camera on the duo but could not read any lips. Before I snapped any pictures of significance, Boyd was back in his huddle.

We heard nothing but garbage from Phil's buddy, until Boyd brought a tight formation to the line of scrimmage.

It was fourth down and a long two yards to gain. A long cadence pushed the play clock to its limit before Boyd took the snap and handed the ball to Dickies. The five unsung heroes on the front line had lived in obscurity throughout the year. However, the five were as much a part of the magic of the season as any other players. The five had been called upon game after game to move the pile forward that one crucial yard, and, in the biggest game of their lifetimes, they pushed the Whippets just enough, once more, for Dickies to earn the cherished first down.

With Phil's buddy adamant South Heaven had gained the spot by a favorable side judge, Lamont Dickies swept right, made a cut, and bolted against the defensive flow to gain seven tough yards.

Boyd, from the fourteen-yard line, called Ricky Green's number on a simple trap play that netted the team three yards.

"You guys are gonna suck the life out of the third quarter." Phil's buddy had lost some of his brashness.

On the next two plays, Coach Waddell held conservative with an off-tackle run and another dive to Green. By fourth down, his team was across the five-yard line and had only a few inches to gain in order to keep the drive going.

The ball hovered in the middle of the field, providing Stu Ginnette with a relatively simple kick of twenty-one yards. However, snow continued to coat the green Astroturf, making footing precarious, at best. As a result, South Heaven would go for the first down, potentially jeopardizing the entire season.

Neither the snow nor the cold upstaged the nerves coursing through my system. I uttered a prayer as Boyd brought up the offense. My body language was such that I had one leg crossed over the other and the fingers of my right hand balled together. The need for just a few inches was somewhat reassuring, though. A sneak by Boyd could pick up the first down. My heart raced to the point where I became ill when Duane Boyd faked a handoff to Dickies … and rolled on a bootleg.

Not one defender read the play correctly.

Despite having open receivers, Duane Boyd jogged into the end zone.

Controlling my celebration jig, I was able to shoot a few pictures of all ten Rangers surrounding their quarterback, displaying the joy of children. We spared little in ribbing Phil's buddy.

In the middle of Ginnette's kick, I headed back inside the stadium for the Summit.

"Boy, where've you been? We just held 'em to three plays."

Duane Boyd was back under center when I found my seat next to Old Man Schmidt, who still held serve on the microphone.

As the game bled into its last quarter of play, the snow had ceased, but a light frosting concealed most of the green surface. To the weatherman's dismay, the gray clouds continued to hover above the stadium.

On a second-and-five play, Dickies took a counter off right guard for a gain of seven.

"I know of a few places for sale back in town, boy. Seein' as how you've grown accustom to South Heaven and all."

Through the pain of a botched center-quarterback exchange, I managed a small but meaningful grin. "I'd then have to call myself a resident."

From the Rangers' forty, Boyd called his own number on a keeper around right end. Unfortunately, the freshman didn't have the foot speed to beat a pursuing linebacker.

"That'll bring up a third down, folks."

"Not sure if I should give up on transient, for now."

A gust of wind stole the nose of the ball on Boyd's attempted pass.

"Folks, he had Sammy Gwynn but just overshot him. That'll bring up another fourth down."

Redding's punt was a missile hardly rising above head and shoulder height, but it struck the turf on the round side of the ball and rocketed forward, well past the Whippets' return man. By the time the ball lost forward momentum, half of the South Heaven punt team surrounded and downed it, inside the Wheelersville ten-yard line.

Nine minutes remained when Rudy Garcia hit his flanker on a quick strike across the middle.

"You do realize, boy, whaty're watchin' here today will never happen again?"

"You do realize we are still trailing?"

A surprise draw play caught Knause and the boys completely off-guard, pushing the defense back twelve yards.

"Greatness only comes 'round once for teams like South Heaven." For such a moment of tension and stress, and with the clock falling below eight minutes, Old Man Schmidt was collected. "One quarter left to savor playin' in the Horseshoe, and playin' for the entire town."

Pressured from a blitz, Garcia threw the ball off his back foot but still completed a bullet for a gain of ten.

Buttoning up and collecting my belongings, I cupped my hand on Old Man Schmidt's shoulder to bid adieu. A warm tingling sensation that started in my fingertips gradually radiated up my right arm. "I'd better be getting' back down to the field."

I caught an incomplete pass on camera before darting for the exit. The crowd noise from the Wheelersville stands stirred my nerves and increased my pace. On my quest, though, I nearly bowled over the mighty Butch Boyd. "Holy…" I blurted apologetically.

Boyd helped me to my feet. "You okay?"

Fortunately, the camera remained on the strap and around my neck. "What are you doing down here? Your kid's three points away from tying this game."

For a person who carried such a stalwart persona and reputation, to see him in a condition of sheer nervousness was a little disheartening.

"Are you okay?" I asked.

"I'll be fine."

Conversations were always awkward between Boyd and me. So I took the nearest exit, with only a head nod as a farewell.

Rudy Garcia had his team within the Rangers' twenty when I found the field again.

At the five-minute mark, Garcia took a shotgun snap and rifled a slant pass to a flanker, who, in turn, broke his first tackle to reach the twelve.

I snapped half a dozen shots of the South Heaven defense hugging hips and gasping for breath. Another score, particularly a touchdown, would no doubt dagger and kill the heart.

Wheelersville ran a dive, but the back slipped on the turf and lost a yard.

Quickly, as time continued to melt away, I replaced film. Unfortunately, however, Garcia beat me to the action and rolled left, finding an open lane to run.

The Whippets' quarterback dashed for the first-down maker, darting right at me.

I leaped out of the way to avoid him and two Ranger defenders. By the time of recovery, I was arguing in an attempt to convince the side judge to mark Garcia short of the nine, and short of a first down.

My hoarseness in speech was worthwhile when the official marked Garcia short.

Wheelersville trotted Carlyle onto the field. With a breeze against him and wet turf, Carlyle didn't have the elements in his favor.

Coach Waddell decided to push ten men to the line, with only Kyle Knause behind the scrimmage line.

The snap was high but manageable. Wheelersville led by six, with three minutes to play.

The kick and the late lead for Wheelersville were enough for me to concede the game. I no longer had the stomach or motivation to take any other photos.

Carlyle pushed a boot in the breeze that Dickies retrieved on the twenty and returned to the twenty-eight.

South Heaven hustled onto the field and directly to the line of scrimmage. On a short cadence, Boyd took the snap and quick-pitched to Dickies. The South Heaven back took the corner and caught a seam. By the time he was tripped up, Dickies had crossed the forty. The Rangers lineman lumbered to the line just as the referee whistled the play clock to start.

Hope had one foot in the grave.

Green's number was called on a quick-hitter. The fullback broke through the initial line but was hauled down within five yards.

The crowd around me demanded that Coach Waddell call a time-out. But he refused and called Boyd's number on a keeper. The play gained only four yards.

The clock hovered just above one minute when Boyd ran a sneak to earn a new set of downs. Coach Waddell decided to stop play.

We were seven points shy of the lead and fifty-two seconds from leaving Columbus a bridesmaid, and the skeptics were actually calling for Gary Redding—only he had the arm to pass South Heaven to a win.

Before Coach Waddell broke his team's huddle, the play clock was whistled to start. The entire Ranger sideline had joined the makeshift huddle for one last hoorah, then Coach Waddell hastened his offensive unit straight to the line of scrimmage.

On a long cadence, Boyd took the snap and dropped five steps into the pocket. He saw a rush of three men coming at him unmolested. However, before a mitt could be laid on the quarterback, Boyd dumped a screen pass into the waiting arms of Lamont Dickies.

"He's got…" I was several inches off the ground on a leap of excitement when the Rangers tailback slipped on the damp turf. The screen pass was the best call of the game. Lamont Dickies had nothing but his own lineman in front of him. The lump in my throat grew exponentially, and I rose from my knees, having fallen like a limp rag doll.

Dumbfounded and dejected, not one South Heaven player noticed their sideline desperately attempting to get attention to call a time-out. Precious seconds disappeared before the play clock was halted at thirty-three seconds.

Hearts had to be overextended and strained among the faithful of South Heaven.

There was infinitely more motivation and energy in the strides of the Wheelersville defenders than Boyd and his mates as both squads broke from sideline huddles. In response to their appearance, both sections of fans rose and rumbled.

A few deep breaths failed to relax me.

Boyd brought the team to the line and peered out on the defense, then he barked cadence. He had one receiver, Sammy Gwynn, split to the far left.

From me, it was one last word to the Almighty.

Then, Boyd dropped deep into the pocket on seven steps. With the discipline of a German Shepherd, he looked off the safety then threw deep to Gwynn on a curl route.

Gimmick plays usually only work once in a season. On a dead sprint, trailing behind Gwynn, Lamont Dickies gathered in a lateral pitch and darted down the sideline. No snow, no elements, no fluke or bad luck was going to stop him. The hook and lateral worked to absolute perfection once more.

The roar from the Ranger faithful probably could have been heard back in Harper County.

Extreme joy overcame me to the point where I was hugging any fan within reach. The feeling was indescribable. To tie the score of the championship game on such a backyard play added to the exuberance.

With absolute madness littering the South Heaven stands, a stunned Wheelersville team called a time-out to regroup.

Shaking uncontrollably, I made a feeble attempt to focus the camera on an obviously nervous Stu Ginnette, who was but one simple kick away from winning the state championship.

Stu muddled about, a few yards to the rear of said huddle. On at least three occasions, he repositioned the black block kicking tee and the rubber strap connecting steel toe to ankle.

As the huddles broke and the referee set the play clock into motion, I nestled a spot near the end zone.

Ginnette gradually paced backwards three steps then, following a deep inhale, hunched his shoulders forward. He heaved in and out on two breaths, then one big step led to another.

The kick flew high and straight.

Amid the frenzy, I bolted back into the stadium confines to celebrate with Old Man Schmidt. In full sprint, dodging people left and right, I thought little about the remaining seconds in the game. A formality of a kick-off and maybe a hail-Mary by Garcia would end the game. My sprint dragged to a crawl. I heard the crowd erupt again and stopped to sneak a glance onto the field, from the tunnel entrance on the upper tier.

It was a good roar.

South Heaven fans flooded the field to join in the celebration with their team. The state championship was coming home.

The door to Old Man Schmidt was glued in the closed position, as if there were a grand piano crammed against the other side. Putting an impressive shoulder butt against it, I burst into the booth. Empty. I saw no chairs, no cigar butts, no thermos, no remnants of a broadcast.

Confused, I hastened a retreat back toward the field. Amazingly, in the crowd of hollers, cheers, smiles, embraces, and giddy fans, I found Miss Myra.

"Oh my God! Can you believe it, sport?"

I grabbed her by the shoulders to calm her down. "Have you seen the Old Man?"

"What?"

"Have you seen Old Man Schmidt?"

Her smile immediately evaporated as she began looking around, searching for help. "Ira Schmidt?"

"Yeah. He was just in the booth!"

"Sport, Ira died in car accident with his grandson. Two years ago."

"That's ... not possible!" Before responding to her question on my health, I was in a heightened pace and climbing stairs to the Summit.

The door was left ajar, in the same position I had left it minutes earlier. The booth had changed complexion—slightly. There was still no indication of a radio broadcast. There was, however, a single object resting on the writing counter, directly in front of the chair that Old Man Schmidt had occupied. It was a chrome lighter.

About the Author

Kevin is a life-long fan of football, in particular those games that are played under the lights on Friday nights. Raised in a tight community, Kevin lived and experienced the ups and downs of small-town life, similar to the folks of South Heaven. Kevin lives in southern Ohio with his wife and two dogs.